pregnancy

Once the elation of finding out you're pregnant dies down, a zillion questions and concerns flood in. If this section doesn't provide all the answers, it points you to someone who can: the best ante-natal classes, where to get private scans, advice and support on breastfeeding, a full list of hospitals both NHS and private, where to hire a pool for a water birth – plus a pregnancy calendar to help guide you smoothly through the next 40 weeks.

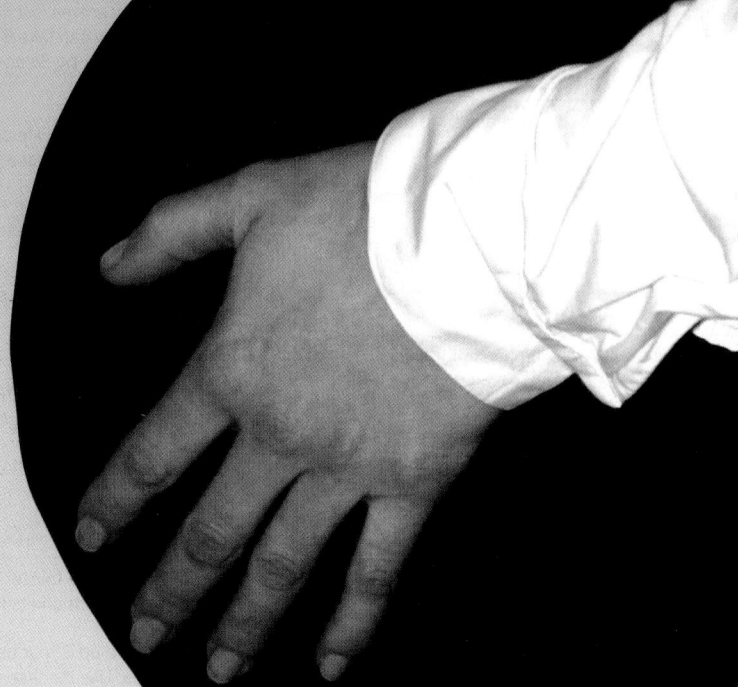

2 pregnancy and birth

Your pregnancy calendar

Follow the suggestions for each month and look up services in the directory where indicated.

Weeks 1-4

- Start taking a daily amount of folic acid (400mg).
- Avoid smoking and taking any drugs or medication.

Weeks 5-9

- Get in touch with local hospitals and see what facilities they have, or research home birth.
- Keep a note of everything you read in pregnancy books and magazines.
- Consider complementary therapies to keep morning sickness under control (see aromatherapy, pg 10 and reflexology, pg 17).
- Start looking for pregnancy exercise classes (see pg 12, yoga, pg 17).

Weeks 10-14

- You will be offered a 12-week scan - the first time you see your baby.
- Consider booking a maternity nurse or doula - popular ones get booked very quickly so contact agencies now for a list of candidates (see pg 49).

Weeks 15-19

- If your clothes are feeling uncomfortable, start ordering the maternity wear catalogues and visiting the stores (see pg 34).
- Book ante-natal/parenting classes as they get booked up (see pg 4).

Weeks 20-24

- Following your 20 week fetal anomaly scan book yourself a personalised baby shopping service
- Think about decorating the nursery (see murals, pg 35 and nursery furniture/interiors, pg 37).

Weeks 25-29

- If you would like one last trip abroad, now's the time to go. Some airlines won't let you fly after 28 weeks. Also check that your travel insurance covers pregnancy. Most will provide cover if you return by week 32.
- Think about whether you'll be returning to work, and make arrangements with your employer. You can take maternity leave from week 29.
- If you are thinking of returning to work, visit and register with your local nurseries - popular ones can have up to 1-year waiting lists (see pg 53-110).

Weeks 30-34

- Order some of the larger items you will need when your baby arrives (such as prams, cots and car seats), as they can take 6 weeks to order (see cribs and cots, pg 28 and prams and pushchairs, pg 51).
- Consider body painting, life casting and pregnancy photography (see pg 5).

Weeks 35-39

- Sort out all the things you need if you are having a home birth (see waterbirth pool hire, pg 8).
- Organise TENS hire (pg 7).
- Prepare your list of friends and family for sending birth announcement cards (see pg 21).
- Order your stem cell collection kit (see pg 7).

Weeks 40-42

- Stock your larder and freezer and get online with home delivery supermarkets (see pg 30).
- Don't get too fed up if your baby arrives after the estimated date. Use the time to relax, see friends and generally organise yourself.

introduction

Welcome to The South West Baby Directory: 1st edition

I grew up in Wiltshire (just outside Mere) and went to school in Dorset so it has been a real treat finding out about all the little things going on for young families in this area. And although I now live in London, I return frequently with my children to enjoy the fresh country air, making sandcastles on those beautiful south coast beaches and that down-to-earth way of life.

This Directory is an expansion of the Bath, Bristol and Somerset Baby Directory, published in 2002, but due to popular demand we have expanded the book to include all the South West counties. A year of research and the fruits of a highly active bush telegraph have gone into producing this little bible of information. Do let me know if you think someone deserves a slot in the next edition.

photograph: carolyn cowan

Clare, Georgia 4yrs and Max 2yrs

You can find the latest information, listings, news and reviews at our mightily useful website **www.babydirectory.com**, which also includes the Encyclopedia of Pregnancy and our guide to **Children's Health**. We also have a e-newsletter which keeps you informed about new product launches, special offers and giveaways - so don't forget to register.

There is no doubt that the South West is a great place to raise a young family. There is plenty to see and do, great baby and toddler activities, good-quality shopping, and loving nursery schools catering for even the busiest of mums. If we have left anything out, which you think deserves a slot, then please don't hesitate to complete the form at the back of the book - or just email me at editor@babydirectory.com.

Whether you are pregnant, a very new parent or planning your life with a toddler - we hope you will use this guide to make life that much easier! And remember if you are moving to another part of the UK, we have five regional publications and another 5 in the pipeline.

Clare Flawn-Thomas

Clare Flawn-Thomas
editor@babydirectory.com

Edited, designed and published by
The Baby Directory Limited

Tel **+44 (0)20 8678 9000**

Fax **+44 (0)20 8671 1919**

Editor	Clare Flawn-Thomas
Deputy Editor	Sue Carpenter
Researchers	Susie de Labillière
	Johanna Loubser
Sales Manager	Patricia Bellotti
Design, Photogrphy & Production	
	Christopher Burke
Printers	Polestar Wheatons Ltd

All Images © The Baby Directory except: page 165 © Eden Project; page 1, page 9, page 117, page 143, page 157, page 173, page 179 © Chris Burke

Disclaimer
While every effort and care has been made to ensure the accuracy of the information contained in this publication, the publisher cannot accept responsibility for any errors, inaccuracies or omissions it may contain. Inclusion in the Directory does not imply an endorsement of the service or product.

All rights reserved throughout the world. No part of this publication may be reproduced or transmitted in any form, or by any means, electronic, mechanical, photocopying, recording or otherwise, or stored in any retrieval system, without prior written permission of the publisher.

The Data Protection Act requires that we inform you that if your company or service is listed in the Directory, it is on our computer. Data Protection Register No: PX 4379316

Copright © The Baby Directory Limited. All rights reserved.

ISBN: 1-903288-16-9
1st Edition published March 2006

contents

pregnancy & birth 1
antenatal classes
antenatal 3D/4D scans
body painters
breastfeeding
home births
hospitals: NHS
hospitals: private
independent midwives
sex choice
stem cells
TENS machines
waterbirth pool hire

health 9
acupuncture
aromatherapy
complementary health
exercise: pre & post-natal
first aid & safety
homeopathy
hypnotherapy
immunisations
infertility
lice
massage
nutrition
osteopathy & cranial osteopathy
reflexology
yoga

shopping 17
baby accessories
birth announcements
bottles
breast pumps
car safety
carriers, slings & backpacks
castings: hands & feet
christening gifts
christening gowns
clothing shops: fashion
clothing shops: outdoor
clothing: online/mail order
cribs, cots & first beds
department stores
dressing up
food (organic)
garden toys
gifts
linens & sleeping bags
lotions & potions (natural)
magazines
maternity wear
maternity bra specialists
murals
name tapes
nappies, cloth
nappies, disposable
nursery furniture
nursery goods
nursery goods: online
photographers & portraits
rocking horses
shoes & shoe shops
swimwear & sun stuff
toy shops
toys: online
toys: early development
travel and changing bags
travel cots
twins

childcare 55
au pair agencies
babysitters
childminders
doulas
maternity nannies & nurses
nanny agencies
nanny payroll services

education 59
nurseries, playgroups, pre-schools
and pre-prep schools
• cornwall: pg 60-70
• devon: pg 70-87
• dorset: pg 87-100
• gloucestershire: pg 100-115
  somerset, bristol, bath: pg 115-132
  wiltshire: pg132-142

toddler activities 143
art and crafts
ceramic cafes
dance
drama
football
gyms – mini
indoor playcentres
leisure centres
model agencies
music groups
riding
swimming classes

parties 157
cakes
party entertainers
party equipment
party shops
party suppliers: online

days out 137
aquariums
beaches
castles
farms
houses, parks & gardens
theme parks
trains
zoos

travel 173
uk hotels
overseas travel agents
camping
home swaps
family villages & resorts
family skiing

good advice 179
adoption
councils
fatherhood
naming ceremonies
paternity testing
parenting classes
money matters
helplines

pregnancy and birth   3

Congratulations! You're pregnant. So what do you do first? Most women do a home pregnancy test to confirm that they are pregnant, and then book an appointment with their GP or local health centre. This confirms your pregnancy 'officially', giving you an idea of your due date and setting up an appointment with a midwife at your local ante-natal clinic for the first consultation and scans. You do, however, have the option to choose the style of your ante-natal care as well as where to have the baby:

1. **Hospital:** private or NHS
2. **Home Birth**
3. **Birth Unit:** care led by either midwives or obstetrician.

You can also visit www.drfoster.co.uk to find out whether tthe hospital you have chosen offers epidurals, waterbirth pools, the number of home births they support and the percentage of women who knew their midwife in labour.

ante-natal classes

National Health Service (NHS) Classes
If you have chosen a hospital birth you will be offered NHS ante-natal classes at the hospital or at a midwife-led clinic. The ante-natal teachers are midwives who will cover waterbirth (if available at the hospital), breastfeeding, labour and pain relief available, complications in labour and Caesareans. The classes are not very flexible in terms of when they are held, and classes are large so it may be difficult to get to know other mums-to-be at the classes. You can also just go on a hospital tour to see where you need to come when in labour.

National Childbirth Trust   0870 444 8707
www.nctpregnancyandbabycare.com
The NCT has over 40 years' experience of providing ante-natal and post-natal courses across the UK. The teachers have been trained by the NCT and the classes tend to be informal and are generally held in the teacher's home. There are couples courses, women-only courses, 8-week courses and weekend courses. The courses include relaxation and practising different positions for labour as well as information on pain relief, life with a new baby and postnatal care. There are often only 5-7 couples per course so you have a chance to get to know other people with a similar due date. NCT classes cost about £70+ per course depending on where you live. If you would like to attend but cannot afford it then the NCT will happily accept a contribution. They are popular so we recommend that you book early.

Choices Antenatal Classes   0800 977 4225
www.choicesantenatal.co.uk
This is a residential ante-natal classes held at a luxury hotel in the Cotswolds over a weekend.

www.babydirectory.com

Active Birth Centre   020 7281 6760
25 Bickerton Road, London, N19 5JT
www.activebirthcentre.com
Active Birth classes are centred around gentle yoga from your 12th week of pregnancy to help strengthen your body for birth and life with a new baby.

Jeyarani Gentle Birth   020 8530 1146
www.jeyarani.com
Founded by Dr Gowri Motha in 1987, the Gentle Birth Programme prepares you for a natural delivery by teaching you how to be "birth fit". The emphasis of the programme is to make you physically fit and supple, and have a positive and confident frame of mind to manage your own labour. Fortunately, due to Dr Motha's classes being so over-subscribed, you can purchase her month-by-month guide as well as other complementary products from her website.

The Having A Baby Company   01793 731 046
www.thehavingababycompany.co.uk
Sandy Bridges and Sian Beautyman have teamed their ante-natal expertise to bring a multitude of services to young mums in Wiltshire, North Somerset and Avon. Ante-natal classes and workshops are held in and around Swindon, Marlborough and Wroughton. Massage groups can be held in the home. They are both homebirth doulas and can hire out waterbirth pools and TENS machines. They also hold pre and post natal exercise classes to help recovery at Canons Health and Fitness in Swindon.

ante-natal 3D and 4D scans

The following are private ante-natal testing services which offer a range of scans and blood tests not necessarily available to you on the NHS without referral. Alternatively you may want to take advantage of the new 3D and 4D.

Baby Premier   0845 345 7262
www.babypremier.co.uk
For 4D ultrasound. A 4D DVD recording of the bonding scan. A CD of all colour and black and white images to enable printing of the pictures. Clinics accredited by BUPA, AXA, PPA and other private medical insurers.

Preview Ultrasound   01536 790 389
www.previewultrasound.co.uk
Mobile video and picture scanning service covering the UK.

body painters and castings

Everlasting Castings   0870 020 3593
www.everlastingcastings.co.uk
An easy-to-use deluxe belly casting kit to enable pregnant mums to capture their unique shape in plaster.

Body Painter for Pregnant Women   07803 121 923
www.embody.org.uk
Check out Julia Laderman's website for some fantastic bump painting and photography. A wonderful celebration of your pregnancy shape.

4 pregnancy and birth

breastfeeding

If you are trying to breastfeed and find it difficult (or your baby finds it difficult), then it is best to turn to people who really know how to help. The following breastfeeding counsellors can either come to your home or help you over the telephone and have considerable experience in sorting out problems or alleviating anxieties. The organisations also offer support and advice. For recommended breast pumps see the Shopping section (see pg 19)

Assoc. of Breastfeeding Mothers 0870 401 7711
www.abm.me.uk
A charity offering a network of local breastfeeding counsellors around the country.

Jane's Breastfeeding Resources
www.breastfeeding.co.uk
Website with many useful articles, FAQs, help and support for breastfeeding mothers.

La Leche League 020 7242 1278
www.laleche.org.uk
Aims to help mothers to breastfeed through mother-to-mother support, information and education, including for those in special situations, eg multiple births, premature babies, cleft or soft palate.

Lansinoh 0113 269 1000
www.lansinoh.co.uk
An ointment that soothes and protects dry, cracked nipples. It contains hypoallergenic lanolin which doesn't need to be removed prior to breastfeeding. Available from Lloyds Pharmacies, Mothercare and Waitrose.

Mums Essentials 0800 085 4320
www.mumsessentials.com
Pre- and post-birth nutritional supplements.

National Childbirth Trust 0870 444 8707
www.nctpregnancyandbabycare.com
The NCT provides trained consultants who are available via their breastfeeding helpline (8am-10pm). There is also a register for mothers and babies with special challenges, eg multiple births, feeding a toddler and a newborn at the same time or feeding after breast surgery.

UNICEF UK Baby Friendly Initiative
www.babyfriendly.org.uk
The UNICEF UK Baby Friendly Initiative provides a framework for the implementation of best practice by NHS Trusts and other health care facilities, with the aim of ensuring that all parents are helped to make informed decisions about feeding their babies and that they are then supported in their chosen feeding method.

Please say you saw the listing in the
South West Baby Directory

home births

For a home birth combined with continuity of midwifery care, we recommend looking into an independent midwife (see below). Their big strength is that they are very positive about the whole birth experience, and can reassure mothers who want to give birth at home rather than in a hospital. During your ante-natal care you will be visited by your midwife, who in some cases can recommend complementary therapists throughout your pregnancy and birth. They will also continue to provide support and visits post-natally to ensure that you are getting on well with your new baby. For further information visit www.homebirth.org.uk or www.independentmidwives.org.uk.

Sue Learner: 0117 927 6131
Sue's well-established midwifery practice of 17 years standing, based on 30 years midwifery experience, offers continuity of care at home for women throughout Bristol and outside the city. She has good links with obstetrician, health visitors, acupuncturists, homeopaths etc and will refer if necessary. Call her for a chat or to arrange a free informal meeting.

hospitals: NHS

CORNWALL
Derriford Hospital 01752 777 111
Derriford Road, Plymouth, PL6 8DH

Royal Cornwall Hospital 01872 250 000
Truro, Cornwall, TR1 3LJ

St Austell Community Hospital 01726 291100
Porthpean Road, St Austell, PL26 6AA

DEVON
Honiton Hospital 01404 540 540
Marlpits Road, Honiton, EX14 2DE

North Devon District 01271 322 577
Raleigh Park, Barnstaple, EX31 4JB

Okehampton Maternity Unit 01837 658 013
East Street, Okehampton, EX20 1AX

Royal Devon & Exeter 01392 411 611
Barrack Road, Wonford, Exeter, EX2 5DW

South Hams Hospital 01548 852 349
Plymouth Road, Kingsbridge, TQ7 1AT

Tiverton and District 01884 235 400
Bampton Road, Tiverton, EX16 6AN

Torbay Hospital 01803 614 567
Lawes Bridge, Torquay, TQ2 7AA

pregnancy and birth 5

DORSET
Dorset County Hospital 01306 251 150
Williams Avenue, Dorchester, DT1 2JY

Poole Hospital 01202 665 511
Longfleet Road, Poole, BH15 2JB

Royal Bournemouth 01202 303 626
Castle Lane East, Bournemouth, BH7 7DW

GLOUCESTERSHIRE
Cheltenham General 01242 222 222
Sandford Road, Cheltenham, GL53 7AN

Gloucestershire Royal 01452 528 555
Great Western Road, Gloucester, GL1 3NN

Stroud Maternity Hospital 01453 562 140
Field Road, Stroud, GL5 2JB

BRISTOL, BATH & SOMERSET
St Peter's Maternity Unit 01749 342 378
Old Wells Road, Shepton Mallet, BA4 4PG

Taunton Hospital 01823 333 444
Musgrove Park, Taunton, TA1 5DA

Southmead Hospital 01179 505 050
Southmead Road, Southmead, BS10 5NB

Ashcombe Maternity Unit 01934 636 363
Weston General Hospital, Grange Road, , Weston Super Mare, BS23 4TQ

St Michael's Hospital 01179 235 050
Southwell Street, Bristol, BS2 8EG

Wellington Cottage 01823 662 663
South Street, Wellington, TA21 8QQ
Ante-natal appointments only

Chard Hospital 01460 63175
Crewkerne Road, Chard, TA20 1NF

Crewkerne Hospital 01460 72491
Middle Path, Crewkerne, TA18 8BG

Mary Stanley Wing 01278 444 517
Bridgwater Community Hospital, Salmon Parade, Bridgwater, TA6 5AH

Frome Victoria Hospital 01373 463 591
Park Road, Frome, BA11 1EY

Minehead Hospital 01643 707 251
The Avenue, Minehead, TA24 5LY

Paulton Maternity Unit 01761 412 107
Salisbury Road, Paulton, Bristol, BS39 7SB

Royal United Hospital Bath 01225 428 331
Combe Park, Bath, BA1 3NG

Yeovil District Hospital 01935 475 122
Higher Kingston, Yeovil, BA21 4AT

WILTSHIRE
Chippenham Community 01249 447 100
Rawden Hill, Chippenham, SN15 2AJ

Devizes Community Hospital 01380 723 511
Commercial Road, Devizes, SN10 1EF

Great Western Hospital 01793 604 020
Marlborough Road, Swindon, SN3 6BB

Salisbury District Hospital 01722 336 262
Salisbury, SP2 8BJ

Trowbridge Community Hospital 01225 752 558
Adcroft Street, Trowbridge, BA14 8PH

hospitals: private

These hospitals offer birth and post-natal facilities which far outweigh those provided by the NHS. Some NHS hospitals do offer private post-natal care at around £300 per day

Hospital of St John & St Elizabeth 020 7286 5126
Grove End Road, London

Sir Stanley Clayton Ward 020 8383 3569
Queen Charlotte's Hospital, Du Cane Road, London, W6 0HS

St Mary's Lindo Wing 020 7886 1465
St Mary's Hospital, South Wharf Road

The Birth Centre 020 7498 2322
37 Coverton Road, Tooting, London SW17
www.birthcentre.com
Give birth at home, in hospital or in their purpose-designed Birth Centre.

The Kensington Wing 020 8746 8616
Chelsea & Westminster Hospital

The Lansdell Maternity Suite 020 7188 3457
St Thomas's Hospital, 6th Floor, North Wing, SE1
The Lansdell Suite offers access to consultant obstetrician and private ante-natal scans alongside private midwife led care for pregnancy, labour and birth, using the facilities of one of the UK's top teaching hospitals. There is breastfeeding support given as and when necessary and continuous post-natal care.

The Portland Hospital 020 7580 4400
205-209 Great Portland Street, W1
www.theportlandhospital.com
Consultant and midwife led maternity care. They also have a specialist, private children's hospital with in-patient and out-patient care.

6   pregnancy and birth

MIDWIVESONLINE.COM

Ask A Midwife

about

your pregnancy, birth and newborn baby

pregnancy and birth 7

The BabyShow

The UK's biggest event for pregnancy, birth and beyond

- Huge savings on 1000s of nursery essentials
- Expert advice on pregnancy and early parenting
- Maternity and toddler fashion

For a full list of companies, dates and venue visit
www.thebabyshow.co.uk/bd

midwives

Midwivesonline.com   **01274 427 132**
This is a website service providing advice and support to new parents and families in every aspect of pregnancy and parenting (see ad pg 3).

Sue Learner: **0117 927 6131**
Sue's well-established midwifery practice of 17 years standing, based on 30 years midwifery experience, offers continuity of care at home for women throughout Bristol and outside the city. She has good links with obstetrician, health visitors, acupuncturists, homeopaths etc and will refer if necessary. Call her for a chat or to arrange a free informal meeting.

stem cells

For the treatment of many terminal childhood illnesses you can have your baby's stem cells collected at birth and stored for any necessary medical treatments in the future. With a monthly payment schedule to cover the costs, what price would you put on a potentially life-saving opportunity? The collection of stem cells is from the placenta and umbilical cord and is totally painless. Your midwife or consultant can perform the collection immediately after the birth of your baby. Double check with the hospital policy on this issue. If they refuse you can contact an independent midwife (see pg 5).

The Portland Hospital for Women and Children
Specialists in maternity services

The Portland Hospital
for Women and Children

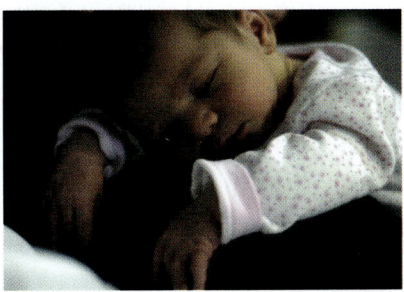

- Midwife and Consultant led care plans
- 24 hour support and advice
- Individual, flexible service
- Specialist emergency facilities
- On-site antenatal appointments for scans and classes
- Luxurious accommodation and hotel services
- All-inclusive packages available

For further information and hospital tour contact:

The Portland Hospital, London W1
T 020 7390 8269
F 020 7390 8198
E info@portland.hcahealthcare.co.uk

www.theportlandhospital.co.uk

8 pregnancy and birth

Cells 4 Life 0870 049 3360
www.cells4life.co.uk
Stem cell collection and umbilical cord blood storage to use in potentially lifesaving cases of serious childhood illnesses

sex choice

Materna S.A. 020 7225 3234
www.babychoice.com
Choose the sex of your baby.

tens hire

Pain relief without drugs. An effective form of pain relief in labour, the TENS machine (Transcutaneous Electrical Nerve Stimulation) consists of four electrodes taped to your back which give a tingling sensation as a current passes through

Mama Tens 020 8547 1999
PO Box 43537, London, SW15 3XF
www.mama-tens.info
Mama TENS is a digital unit that has proved far more effective at relieving the pains of labour than other machines on the market. No more fiddling with dials, Mama TENS gives pain relief at a touch of a button, and is so easy to use. Recommended by midwives and doctors nationally, and delivered mail-order to your door.

ObTENS Obstetric TENS Hire 0117 924 1982
www.obtens.co.uk
Reliable mail order hire service based in Bristol offering next day delivery.

BabiTENS 01491 578 446
www.babitens.com
Drug free, safe and effective pain relief during pregnancy and labour. 4 week Tens hire £27.50 inc pandp plus free extension period with notification.

waterbirth pool hire

Birthworks (Cornwall) 01822 834 452
Waterbirth pool hire.

Babymoon 01425 655 833
www.babymoon.co.uk
Based in the New Forest, Babymoon supply quality water birth pools throughout the UK, with special local delivery rates (Hampshire, Dorset and Wiltshire). Their website provides a wealth of information about choosing a water birth, with local resources for pregnancy and after. An online shop includes Bravado maternity underwear, My Brest Friend breastfeeding pillows, and birth balls.

Splashdown Water Birth Services 0845 612 3405
www.waterbirth.co.uk
All shapes supplied as well as inflatables. Waterbirth workshops also run for Mums-to-be and couples.

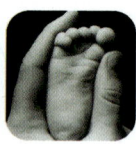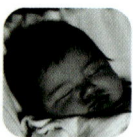

Today's Science - Tomorrow's Possibilities

The Experts in Stem Cell Storage

✓ Whole umbilical cord blood storage at the first private UK storage facility
✓ All samples banked within 12-24hrs via our same day medical courier service
✓ Confidential advice and support from specialist doctors

For all general enquiries please call our Customer Support Team on: **0870 049 3360**
enquiry@cells4life.co.uk   www.cells4life.co.uk

health and wellbeing

Good health is not just about a lack of illness, but a sense of positive wellness – something overworked and stressed mums and mums-to-be can find elusive. Here we list practitioners of a variety of therapies to help you relax before, during and after labour, to deal with common ailments in both mothers and babies, and to help you regain your shape and vitality after the birth. You'll find everything from acupuncture to yoga, as well as complementary health centres, health clubs and details of professional bodies such as the International Federation of Aromatherapists, which can provide a list of therapists in your area. And if you're worried about immunisations or need tips on first aid, read on.

10 health and wellbeing

acupuncture

(see also complementary health)

Acupuncture has been used since ancient times to support women through pregnancy. Treatment involves the insertion of fine needles into the skin. The majority of pregnancy ailments can be treated successfully and safely with acupuncture. These include: morning sickness, backache, sciatica, oedema, anaemia, headaches, spotting, abdominal pains, urinary problems, haemorrhoids, insomnia, fatigue, muscle cramps, carpal tunnel syndrome, slow growth of the baby, breech position, delayed labour. Emotional problems such as worry, depression, fear, and anxiety can be addressed and treated. Acupuncture can be used to increase both female and male fertility and to support a woman through IVF treatment. Young mothers appreciate the support through acupuncture with fatigue, weakness, pains and emotional problems.

British Acupuncture Council   020 8735 0400
63 Jeddo Road, W12
www.acupuncture.org.uk
Members (MBAcC) have all completed a 3yr training course and are bound by the BAcC code of conduct. The website lists practitioners by postcode.

British Medical   01606 786 782
Acupuncture Society
www.medical-acupuncture.org.uk
You can find a local practitioner, specialising in pregnancy and post-natal conditions via this excellent website, or ring for a list to be sent to you.

aromatherapy

(see also complementary health and massage)

Aromatherapy is an easy and portable way of helping to look after yourself throughout your pregnancy. Often used to relieve tiredness, nausea, fluid retention as well as pain and anxiety during labour. For baby the oils can be used for gentle massage or in the bath

Natalia
helps you through the
ups and downs of pregnancy
aromatherapy products for pregnancy,
birth and new parenthood

products for life naturally

for a free brochure and mail order enquires
contact Vital Touch on **01803 840670**
shop online at **www.vitaltouch.com**

by vital touch

ISPA   01455 637 987
www.the-ispa.org
International Society of Professional Aromatherapists. List of local practitioners available online or by request.

MAIL ORDER
Absolute Aromas   01420 549 991
www.absolute-aromas.co.uk

A. Nelson & Co   020 7495 2404
www.nelsonbach.com

Jurlique   0870 770 0980
www.jurlique.co.uk
Organic essential oils also available as water sprays, massage and bath oils.

Mama Mio   020 7287 3028
www.mamamio.com
This is pregnancy skincare at its best - a range of luxurious and safe creams that help skin cope with the nine month s-t-r-e-t-c-h! Developed by three mums, with thirteen children between them, their Tummy Rub, Boob Tube and Massage Oil are already favourites among the likes of Christy Turlington and Gwyneth Paltrow. They worked with their favourite chemists and aromatherapists to create perfect pregnancy salvation products for the supermama under construction.

Tisserand   01273 325 666
www.tisserand.com

Verde   0870 603 9186
www.verde.co.uk
Mother and baby range. 16 products including Extra Rich Stretch Mark Oil, Chamomile Baby Body Balm, Bizzy Kids Bathtime Soother, Lice Repel Lotion. Organic and pure plant preparations.

Vital Touch   01803 840 670
www.vitaltouch.com
Organic aromatherapy products for pregnancy, labour and new parenthood.

complementary health

Treatments include acupuncture, hypnotherapy, osteopathy, cranial osteopathy, reflexology, massage, homeopathy, reiki and counselling. To find your nearest centre visit the website of the ICM (see below)

Institute for   020 7237 5165
Complementary Medicine
www.i-c-m.org.uk
The Institute for Complementary Medicine is a registered charity providing the public with information on complementary medicine. You can obtain lists of practitioners of all types of complementary medicine who have proved to be qualified and safe to practise.

Please say you saw the listings in
The South West Baby Directory

health and wellbeing 11

Little Miracles   020 7431 6153
PO Box 3896, London, NW3 7DS
www.littlemiracles.co.uk
These are a special range of flower remedies to treat children's behavioural problems; such as anxiety, lack of concentration or for the "terrible twos" tantrums. With names such as Braveheart (for anxiety), Short Fuse (toddler tantrums) - and customer's testimonials - they are worth a closer look.

exercise

Exercise during pregnancy can help you improve posture, maintain circulation to prevent varicose veins, control your weight gain and improve your stamina and energy levels. Most private memebership clubs offer a one-to-one personal training programme to suit you ante- and post-natally. Or you can go for the personal trainer at home.

Nurturer   0141 337 3328
www.nurturer.co.uk
Khutso Dunbar has outlets and groups of therapists nationwide who offer a range of services including; ante-natal massage, baby massage, ante- and post-natal yoga, pedicure, manicure, facials and personal trainers.

Esporta
www.esporta.co.uk
Bridgend	01656 644 160
Bristol	01179 749 740
Plymouth	01752 237 000
Poole	01202 642 600
Taunton	01823 447 000
Weston-Super-Mare	01934 410 250

The Esporta clubs offer a good range of sporting facilities, including gyms, swimming pools, spas and tennis facilities. They also have creches for babies and playzones for toddlers. During half-term and holidays they offer activity clubs for 3yrs+ children.

Virgin Spas
www.virginactive.co.uk
Gloucester   0845 260 0072
This gym has a 25m Pool and a separatekids pool, sauna and steam room, Teddies nursery, hair and beauty salon as well as a cafe/bar.

David Lloyd Leisure
www.davidlloydleisure.co.uk
Bournemouth	01202 394 333
Bristol	01179 531 010

This is the UK's largest provider of specialist junior tennis camps. In addition they offer swimming prgrammes, and ACE club facilities such as music groups, mini-gym, and dance classes.

Holmes Place
www.holmesplace.co.uk
Bristol	01275 395 888
Poole	01202 658 188

These Holmes Place clubs offer creche facilities whilst you exercise or enjoy a spa treatment.

first aid and safety

These companies offer practical tuition and peace of mind for parents and carers wanting to know the principal causes of accidents and how to prevent and treat them, including resuscitation and general first aid (burns, breaks and poisoning) and how to look at your home and assess it for potential hazards

Childalert   020 7384 1311
www.childalert.co.uk
Childproofing, home safety products and product fitting service supported by childalert for shopping info and advice.

First Aid for Kids   020 7854 2861
www.firstaidforkids.com
First Aid for Kids is a complete CD-ROM that gives comprehensive first aid advice, tuition, reference and guidance to any parent or child carer, so that you can deal quickly, confidently and effectively with many childhood emergencies. A percentage of sales goes to Great Ormond Street and the King's College Hospital Silver Lining Appeal.

St John Ambulance   020 7258 7044
www.sja.org.uk
The Lifesaver Babies and Children's course takes place over a two week evening course from £35 and covers baby and child resuscitation, choking, unconsciousness, meningitis and croup.

Would you know what to do if your child is choking?

first aid for kids

The Complete Interactive CD ROM
Guide to First Aid Emergencies

- *A comprehensive multimedia first aid guide for dealing with childhood first aid emergencies*
- *Content approved by paediatric specialists from Great Ormond Street Hospital for Children & King's College Hospital London*
- *Course clearly presented using video, voice, text and state of the art 3D animation*
- *Easy to use requiring minimum computer skills*

For further information please visit
www.firstaidforkids.com

12 health and wellbeing

homeopathy

Homeopathy is a very safe, gentle and effective form of treatment. Because homeopathic remedies gently stimulate the body's natural tendency to heal itself, and are natural, non-addictive and do not have side effects, they are ideal for use during pregnancy, labour and for any problems that may arise for mum or baby after the birth. Used during pregnancy to treat conditions such as nausea, heartburn, thrush, cramps and emotional distress during labour. In children used for building up overall health and immunity to common colds.

British Homeopathic Association   0870 444 3950
15 Clerkenwell Close, EC1R 0AA
www.trusthomeopathy.org
On this website you can read about how homeopathic treatment works as well as access a directory of homeopathically qualified doctors, nurses, dentists and pharmacists.

Society of Homeopaths   0845 450 6611
www.homeopathy-soh.org
This association has a register of licensed members who have completed at least 3 years training. They can provide this as a hard copy or if you visit their website there is a link to "find a homeopath" by county. They also provide a number of useful booklets, including one on pregnancy and childcare.

Weleda   0115 944 8200
www.weleda.co.uk
Homeopathic remedies can be purchased mail order or online via the Weleda website. There is also a remedy finder for a variety of conditions. For children ask for the "soft tablets" which dissolve very quickly on the tongue.

hypnotherapy

Hypnotherapy is a safe, gentle process that relaxes mind and body. It can be particularly helpful in pregnancy by helping you approach the birth in a positive, calm frame of mind. It can help you maintain a healthy lifestyle and modify behaviours to ensure that you exercise, eat healthily and, if applicable, stop smoking. Below you will find hypnotherapy associations and therapists who offer hypnotherapy and self-hypnosis for birth.

Natal Hypnotherapy   01428 712 615
www.natalhypnotherapy.co.uk
The UK's leading provider of Hypnosis CDs for pregnancy and birth. The CDs teach safe, easy-to-use techniques, including effective breathing, relaxation and pain management.

NRHP   01282 699 378
www.nrhp.co.uk
The National Register of Hypnotherapists & Psychotherapists is a leading, non-profit making register of qualified hypnotherapists and psychotherapists.

Immunisation checklist   Source: NHS

Age	Protects against	How it is given
2 mths	polio	by mouth
	meningitis C	1 injection
	Hib haemophilus influenza B DPT - diphtheria, pertussis (whooping cough) and tetanus	1 injection
3 mths	same as for 2 months	
4 mths	same as for 2 months	
12-15 mths	MMR	1 injection
3-5yrs	polio	by mouth
	DTaP - diphtheria, tetanus & accellular pertussis	1 injection
	MMR	1 injection
10-14yrs	BCG - tuberculosis	skin test then injection if needed
13-18yrs	Tb-tetanus and diphtheria	1 injection
	polio	by mouth

immunisation

Halcyon Health   01225 448 348
2-4 Henry Street, Bath, Somerset, BA1 1JT
www.halcyonhealthclinic.co.uk
A private clinic offering single measles, mumps and rubella vaccinations.

JABS   020 8442 0105
www.jabs.org.uk
This is the support group for "vaccine-damaged" children. Also provides details of local doctors who give single vaccinations for measles, mumps and rubella.

NHS Immunisation Information
www.immunisation.org.uk
Free government information for parents who have concerns about childhood vaccinations.

Vaccinations - Yes or No?   0870 720 0067
www.vaccinations-yesorno.co.uk
A must-have, unbiased book for parents facing the dilemma of MMR and the other childhood vaccinations.

Please say you saw the listings in
The South West Baby Directory

health and wellbeing 13

infertility

CHILD - National Infertility   **01424 732 361**
Support Network
Charterhouse, 43 St Leonards Road, Bexhill on Sea
www.infertilitynetworkuk.com

Human Fertilisation and   **020 7291 8200**
Embryology Authority
www.hfea.gov.uk
This authority is a government body which regulates and inspects all UK clinics providing IVF treatment. They send out information packs along with a list of local clinics. You can also visit www.fertilityfriends.co.uk or www.bica.net for counselling and local support groups.

The Zita West Clinic   **020 7580 2169**
43 Devonshire Street, London, W1G 7AL
www.zitawest.com
Complementary therapies, advice and support for fertility and pregnancy, plus IVF support programme.

head lice and nits

It is almost impossible to avoid getting nits if your child is at a nursery or playgroup and has close friends. The eggs take 7 days to hatch and mature in 2 weeks. So an application of nit lotion is highly recommended

Lockcomb   **01761 413 766**
www.headlice-cure.com

Natural Science   **01597 823 964**
www.lice.co.uk
Nice'n' Clear Head Lice lotion - safe, effective, 10 minutes per application.

Nitty Gritty   **020 7460 0166**
www.nittygritty.co.uk
The Nitty Gritty lotion and comb when used together are remarkably effective.

Verde   **020 7720 1100**
www.verde.co.uk
Verde Lice Repel Lotion and Conditioner for children contains essential oils of tea tree, lavender, rosemary and eucalyptus.

massage

Massage during pregnancy is a luxury everyone should treat themselves to. Easing tension and boosting energy levels are some of the benefits. Newborns and babies, who are too young to play, benefit mentally and physically from regular massage. It is both a communicative experience for parents and can settle a baby prior to sleep. With some tuition you can learn to use more complex strokes as your baby grows. These practitioners hold local classes or come to your home

Nurturer   **0141 337 3328**
www.nurturer.co.uk
Khutso Dunbar has outlets and groups of therapists nationwide who offer a range of services including; ante-natal massage, baby massage, ante- and post-natal yoga, pedicure, manicure, facials and personal trainers.

A-Z of Baby Massage   **020 7639 2397**
www.blissfulbaby.co.uk
A great guide for new mothers who naturally want to touch and cosset their newborn, but need some guidance as to how to direct their efforts.

International Association   **01279 319 896**
of Infant Massage
www.iaim.org.uk
The IAIM offers courses for people wanting to become a certified infant massage instructor.

Clare Lowing Baby Massage   **01404 814 405**
Certified Infant Massage Instructor based in Sidmouth, Devon. She offers baby massage from birth to pre-crawling. Intimate group of parent and baby, one session per week (structured five week course). Relaxation techniques, help with colic etc. Also will do home visits.

nutrition

British Dietetic Association   **0121 200 8080**
www.bda.org.uk

The Zita West Clinic   **020 7580 2169**
43 Devonshire Street, London, W1G 7AL
www.zitawest.com
Complementary therapies, advice and support for fertility and pregnancy, plus IVF support programme.

The Centre for Nutritional   **020 7907 1660**
Medicine
www.nutritionalmedicine.co.uk
A medically supported nutrition service with expertise in pregnancy.

www.babydirectory.com

14 health and wellbeing

ZITA WEST

Good nutrition for fertility, pregnancy, birth and recovery

A superb range of multi-vitamins and minerals formulated by the Harley Street fertility and pregnancy consultant

www.zitawest.com
Tel 0870 166 8899

osteopathy & cranial osteopathy

Osteopathy is a hands-on therapy that combines soft-tissue massage and manipulation and spine-cracking. Osteopathic treatment may relieve back pain in pregnancy and aid recovery post-natally. In babies, cranial osteopathy has been used to treat sleeplessness, colic, sticky eye, teething and earache

CORNWALL

Adrian Banbury   01579 342 273
3 Manley Terrace, Liskeard, PL14 4DW

PA Keilbart BSc DO   01726 677 88
The Beeches, 60 Charlestown Rd, St Austell, PL25

Ryde House Clinic   01736 364 603
15 Morrab Road, Penzance, TR18 4EZ
Specialising in babies & young children

The Devery Practice   01326 371 347
St Marys House, Commercial Rd, Penryn, TR10

The Walsingham Clinic   01872 263 163
2 Walsingham Place, Truro, TR1 2RP

Wadebridge Osteopathy   01208 812 048
48 Molesworth St, Wadebridge, PL27 7DP

DEVON

Abbey Mead Nat. Health Centre   01822 614814
7 Plymouth Road, Tavistock, PL19 8AU

Blackfriars Court   01752 206018
South Side Street, The Barbican, Plymouth, PL1

Clinic of Natural Medicine   01626 835068
19-21 Fore Street, Bovey Tracey, TQ13

The Surgery   01803 762772
1 Eastern Road, Ashburton

Cranial Osteopath   01364 652585
Iona, Old Totnes Road, , Ashburton, TQ13 7EE

Bedwell Osteopaths   01803 865356
Dartington, Totnes, TQ9 6NR

Crediton Comp. Health Centreh   01363 774175
Tanner's Yard, 100 High Street, Crediton, EX17 3LF

Argyle House   01392 213899
New Buildings Lane, Gandy Street, Exeter, EX4

Riviera Osteopathic Clinic   01803 550539
21-23 Dendy Road, Paignton, TQ4 5DB

St Davids Osteopathic Clinich   01392 221321
1 Walnut Gardens, St Davids Hill, Exeter, EX4 4DH

Plymouth Chiropractic Clinic   01752 770131
152 Manamead Road, Hartley, Plymouth,

Honiton Osteopathic Centre   01404 416 78
The Manor House, 143 High St, Honiton, EX14 1LJ
Cranial Osteopaths specialising in babies and children.

Penny Price   01395 578 082
1 Kingsleigh Barns, Weston, Sidmouth, EX10 0PH

Tarka Clinic   01271 345 546
Paiges Lane, Barnstaple, EX31 1EF

DORSET

Barton Brooks Ost. Practice   01202 511 306
164 Kingswell Road, Bournemouth, BH10 5DW

Bournemouth Clinic   01202 554 098
51a Christchurch Road, Eastcliff, Bournemouth

Highcliffe Osteopathic Clinic   01425 270 222
287 Lymington Road, Highcliffe, BH25 5EB

Twin Oaks Medical Centre   01425 672741
Ringwood Road, Bransgore, Christchurch

Richmond House   01308 427033
69 South Street, Bridport, DT9 3NZ

Chimes Therpay Centre   01202 661966
21 Parkstone Road, Poole, BH15 2NN

Lyme Community Care Centre   01297 445242
Uplyme Road, Lyme Regis, DT7 3LS

health and wellbeing 15

Poole Bay Osteopaths   07814 982 060
9 Mitchell Road, Canford Heath, Poole, BH17 8UE

The Osteopathic Clinic   01305 267 052
46 Prospect Road, Dorchester, DT1 2PF

Trinity Osteopathic Practice   01747 851 726
Trinity Centre, Bimport, Shaftesbury, SP7 8BW

Twist & Shout Ost. Centre   01308 459 996
32 South St, Bridport, DT6 3NQ

GLOUCESTERSHIRE
The Ashcroft Practice   01285 643 958
42 Ashcroft Road, Cirencester, GL7 1QX

Bishop's Cleeve Osteopaths   01242 676 762
10 Oakfield Rd, Bishops Cleeve, Cheltenham, GL52

Body Craft Natural Health   01285 740 892
2 The Stables, Barnsley Par, Cirencester, GL7 5EG

Chruchdown Osteopaths   01452 714 511
102 Chosen Drive, Churchdown, GL3 2QU

SOMERSET, BRISTOL & BATH
Alma Vale Centre   0117 377 1186
30 Alma Vale Road, Clifton, Bristol, BS8 2HY

Bath Natural Health Clinic   01225 313153
James Street West, Bath, BA1 2BT

The Pulteney Practice   01225 464567
Holombe Lane, Bathampton, BA2 6UL

The Chandos Clinic,   0117 974 5084
21 Chandos Road, Redland, Bristol, BS6 6PG

Natural Health Clinic   0117 974 1199
39 Cotham Hill, Cotham, Bristol, BS6 6JY

Stephen Plumb DO   01373 463 548
18 Christchurch St West, Frome, BA11 1EG

The Albury House   01823 332 871
134 Wellington Road, Taunton, TA1 5LA

WILTSHIRE
Box Osteopathic Clinic   01225 742 923
2 Kingston Villas, London Rd, Box, Corsham, SN13

Colyn Blundell DO   01225 791 256
11 Spa Road, Melksham, SN12 7NP

Pauline Mather   01793 465 629
The Health Hydro, Milton Rd, Swindon, SN1 5JA

The Old Orchard Surgery   01747 820 021
South Street, Wilton, Salisbury, SP2 0JU

Warminster Osteopathics   01985 213 927
4 Station Road, Warminster, BA12 9BR

reflexology

Reflexology has been around for thousands of years, but the modern form was established in the early 20th century when a system of massage through reflex points on the feet, hands and head was developed and used to relieve tension and treat illness in the corresponding zones of the body. In pregnancy reflexology can alleviate morning sickness, constipation and rid the body of excess catarrh and stubborn colds. Post-natally, the therapy is said to boost energy levels and increase breastmilk supplies

Association of Reflexologists   0870 567 3320
www.aor.org.uk
Largest association of reflexologists in the UK. The website offers listings of members county by county.

British Reflexology Association   01886 821 207
www.britreflex.co.uk
The British Reflexology Association was founded in 1985 to act as a representative body for students practising the method of reflexology as a profession. An up-to-date list of registered members is available via their website or by telephone.

yoga

Yoga classes are particularly recommended during pregnancy as they are not too strenuous, but build and maintain strength as your body changes shape. Recommended from 12 weeks (see also ante-natal teachers for ante-natal and yoga classes pg 4)

British Wheel of Yoga   01529 306 851
www.bwy.org.uk
The main organisation in the UK for yoga. Visit their website or send an SAE for a list of relevant practitioners in your area for teachers and classes.

Nurturer   **0141 337 3328**
www.nurturer.co.uk
Khutso Dunbar has outlets and groups of therapists nationwide who offer a range of services including; ante-natal massage, baby massage, ante- and post-natal yoga, pedicure, manicure, facials and personal trainers.

Birthlight   01223 362 288
www.birthlight.com
The principal approach behind Birthlight is to ensure a holistic approach to pregnancy, birth and babyhood using yoga and breathing methods to enhance you and your baby's well-being. Their website lists ante-natal and post-natal yoga classes, aquayoga classes, baby yoga teachers and a whole range of top yoga books relevant to pregnancy, childbirth and children.

Please say you saw these listings in
The South West Baby Directory

16 health and wellbeing

Yogabugs   020 8772 1800
www.yogabugs.com
Classes developed by yoga teacher Nell Lindsell for children aged 2½ to 7yrs, available at locations in the South West: Bath, Bristol, Cattistock, Cheltenham, Christchurch, Corsham, Exeter, Frome, Glastonbury, Poole, Plymouth, St Austell, Salisbury, Swindon, Torquay, Weston Super Mare, Wimborne, Woodcombe For those who don't have a local class you could consider the Yogabugs video. We all know the benefits of yoga for flexibility, strength, concentration and relaxation, but Yogabugs transforms the postures into mime adventures and creative stories, which further benefit children's confidence and imagination.
For example, swimming through the ocean and meeting a crab, fish, shark and a mermaid and finding a pearl from an oyster. There is a similarly imaginative romp through the jungle, where you seamlessly evolve from monkey to snake to lion. It's a great way to get yourself exercising, too, as well as an opportunity to do something with your child, without taking on the alienating role of teacher.

The Baby Yoga Company   01371 873 138
www.thebabyyogacompany.com
Baby yoga and toddler yoga videos and DVDs. The lessons on the DVD are given by Dr Françoise Barbira Freedman, a medical anthropologist at the University of Cambridge and a highly acclaimed yoga teacher.

CORNWALL
Kath Field   01503 230 795
Classes held in Liskeard and Saltash.

Kassandra Clemens   01752 880 031
Classes in Liskeard and Saltash, Cornwall as well as Plymouth and Exeter in Devon.

Leif Olsen   01736 367 248
Classes held in Penzance.

DEVON
Leila Seel   01548 854774
Pre and Postnatal Yoga and Baby Yoga run in conjunction with Sarah Wood (see over) in Totnes. Alternate weekly classes between Kingsbridge and Totnes from birth to crawling.

Jane Snedeker-Cohen   01803 865 657
Pre and post-natal yoga classes in Totnes, Devon.

Sarah Wood   01803 762600
Pre and Postnatal Yoga and Baby Yoga run in conjunction with Leila Seel in Kingsbridge. Alternate weekly classes between Kingsbridge and Totnes from birth to crawling. Please telephone to find out dates and times.

DORSET
Lisa Bartlett   01935 863169
A Birthlight Tutor, Lisa teaches baby yoga from 3mths+ upwards. These are held weekly in Yeovil and the surrounding area. Lisa is also available for private sessions as well.

Marion Symes   01962 864823
Pregnancy yoga, active birth and post natal yoga for mums and babies from 6 weeks to 6 months in Wiltshire. Run in group classes for six week sessions tailored specifically to the individuals within the class. Marion is Birthlight trained and is a qualified Yoga Biomedical Trust Yoga Therapist.

GLOUCESTERSHIRE
Gill Milsom   01454 850033
Gill is a Senior Birthlight Trainer teaching potential tutors all about baby massage and yoga. She also teaches a few select classes about Nurture for Babies through Massage and Movement in Gloucestershire.

Fiona Wells   01256 761353
52 Wedman's Lane, Rotherwick, Hook, Hampshire
Fiona teaches pre and post natal yoga for mums as well as Mother with Baby Yoga and Infant Massage, when she teams up with a fully-trained massage therapist. These courses for babies are weekly over eight weeks in total, from a starting age of 8 weeks to 6 months, up until 10 months when the courses finish.

SOMERSET, BATH AND BRISTOL
Leonie de Mearns   0117 966 3145
Leonie is a Birthlight Tutor in Baby Yoga and Massage, running 6 week block courses in Bristol for babies aged 0 - 7 months approximately.

Frankie Duggan   01179 429598
As a Birthlight Tutor, Frankie teaches Pre and Post Natal Yoga, plus Birth Preparation classes which are weekly in Bristol. Private sessions also available, please telephone for further information.

Wendy Teasdill   01458 833 967
www.teasdill.com
Wendy is a British Wheel of Yoga teacher, as well as training yoga teachers who specialise in pregnancy. She hold ante-natal yoga classes on Wed afternoons at Wells Leisure Centre. Post-natal yoga classes are held monthly. She has also published a book "Yoga for Pregnancy" published by Gaia Books and a Yoga for Pregnancy and Childbirth DVD, both available on Amazon.

WILTSHIRE
Afron Munro   01249 701552
Pre and post pregnancy yoga, and yoga for babies run for individuals or classes in a 15 mile radius of Chippenham .

Eryl Holt   01962 760778
Pregnancy yoga, active birth and post natal yoga for mums and babies from 6 weeks to 6 months in Shawford Parish Hall. Run in group classes for six week sessions tailored specifically to the individuals within the class. Eryl is Birthlight trained and is a qualified Yoga Biomedical Trust Yoga Therapist.

Did you know that the Baby Directory has a comprehensive online Encyclopedia of Pregnancy? (it is one of our most popular sections of our website). Visit
www.babydirectory.co.uk/encyclopedia

shopping

Your favourite pastime is about to skyrocket to new levels. That burgeoning bump will require a new wardrobe for a start. Next, you'll be stockpiling bottles, breast pumps, nappies and not to mention the baby carrier, the buggy, the car seat, the cot and the new linen. Then comes the fun bit – dear little outfits for babies, toddlers and tweenies, as well as dressing-up gear, swimwear and toys. Not sure where to find all this? Here we guide you to the best shops, mail-order catalogues and websites in the country.

18 shopping: essential items

✓ Items	Buy from…	Borrow from…	Gift from…

For the nursery
- [ ] cot and mattress
- [ ] moses basket/crib
- [ ] **linen (sheets, blankets, etc)**
- [ ] changing mat/table
- [ ] wardrobe
- [ ] chest of drawers
- [ ] playmat

Clothing
- [ ] 6 cotton sleepsuits
- [ ] 3 sleeping bags
- [ ] 4 cotton vests
- [ ] 1-2 two-piece outfits
- [ ] 2-4 cardigans
- [ ] 4-6 pairs socks/bootees
- [ ] 1 pair gloves/mittens (for winter)
- [ ] 1 snowsuit (for winter)
- [ ] muslin cloths/ bibs
- [ ] 1 hat

Essential supplies
- [ ] disposable or washable nappies
- [ ] baby wipes, cotton wool
- [ ] nappy bags
- [ ] barrier cream, Vaseline
- [ ] breast pump
- [ ] bottles
- [ ] sterilizer

For travelling
- [ ] pram/pushchair
- [ ] rain cover and Buggysnuggle
- [ ] car seat
- [ ] baby carrier/sling
- [ ] travel and changing bag
- [ ] travel cot

shopping 19

baby accessories

These suppliers provide unique products that offer practicality with a great sense of style

Babylist 020 7371 5145
The Broomhouse, 50 Sulivan Road, SW6 3DX
www.babylist.com
You might be wondering how much baby stuff is really necessary. If so, then book an appointment with Babylist, the longest-running nursery advisory service in London's SW6. They will take you through their lists of essentials, as well as the nice-to-haves, in the comfort of their showroom. This is not just an exclusive, A-list celebrities-only service (although they have had quite a few), but a thoroughly sensible way of shopping.

Babyworld 01491 821 477
babyworld.co.uk
Online store with a unique range of high-quality, innovative accessories, delivered within 2 working days (see ad pg 37).

BitsnStuff 020 8289 7860
www.bitsnstuff.co.uk
On-line shop that has over 1800 unique products to choose from not available on the high street. Sections include baby equipment, childrens home décor, maternity wear, gifts, toys and games.

Bonne Nuit 020 8871 1472
www.bonne-nuit.co.uk
Beautiful French baby sleeping bags, pyjamas and bed linen.

Groovy Mummy 020 8650 1286
www.groovymummy.co.uk
Refreshingly stylish accessories for you and your baby. Luxurious changing bags and exquisite blankets.

Hippychick art/eater suit 01278 434 440
www.hippychick.com
All-in-one protective bib for painting and eating sessions. Less mess, less stress.

ZPM 020 8288 1091
www.zpm.com
Funky range of bibs, bags, aprons, sponge bags and changing mats.

happyhands™

The ulltimate birth announcement or thank you cards

"Ingenious idea" *Pregnancy & Birth*
"Simply Irresistible" *Prima Baby*

Your own baby's foot prints on personalised cards

An easy to use inkless footprint kit is provided

Call us on **020 8671 2020**
www.happyhands.ws

birth announcements

Happyhands 020 8671 2020
www.happyhands.ws
Your baby's hand and foot prints on cards. Ingenious ink-free kit provided. Cards delivered within 5 days.

Heritage Personalised Stationery 01256 861 738
www.heritage-stationery.com
Top-quality, traditional hand-finished birth announcement and christening stationery, delivered in days.

Kittysash 07764 588 562
www.kittysash.com
Adorable personalised birth announcements and matching thank you cards. Beautiful invitations including baby shower invites. Charming and unique designs, high quality and fast turnaround.

Stork Post 07092 347 074
www.storkpost.co.uk
A wonderful range of birth announcement cards hand-selected from The Netherlands, Germany and France (including the Anne Geddes footprint cards) which can be customised with your own message and photographs.

Please say you saw the listings in
The South West Baby Directory

20 shopping

bottles

The following companies manufacture a wide range of bottles and feeding accessories. They are widely available through supermarkets, chemists and nursery goods stores

Steri-bottle 0500 979 899
www.steribottle.com
The only pre-sterilised, ready-to-use, disposable bottle. Perfect for holidays, days out or when you're extra busy. Ideal for breast or formula milk.

Avent 0800 289 064
www.avent.com
This bottle has a silicone teat and a broad design which encourages baby to latch on with a wide open mouth.

Baby B Free 020 8731 7776
www.babybfree.com
This bottle has been voted the best anti-colic bottle on the market as the air vent stops the build up of air taken in with the milk. The bottle is made from safe BFree® plastic which does not contain the hormone Bisphenol A which is considered unhealthy for newborns.

MAM 020 8943 8880
www.mamuk.com
The wide-necked ULTIvent bottle that has a base which can be unscrewed for easier cleaning.

breast pumps

Breast pumps allow you to express and store milk, which can then be bottle-fed to your baby. You can either select a hand-operated model or an electric/battery model. The manual models are quieter, lighter and easier to travel with – but can be slow and tiring on the hand. Electronic pumps are faster and generally more effective

Ameda Lactaline 01823 336 362
www.ameda.demon.co.uk
The Lactaline breast pump can be operated on mains, batteries or with a car adaptor yet offers all of the features of a heavy duty hospital dual electric breast pump. It weighs less than 0.5 kg, but allows you to either dual or single pump with variable suction levels to accommodate your needs. The pump is supplied with 2 milk collection systems which have a unique protective barrier against bacteria and viruses, and at £79.85 plus p&p, it is undoubtedly one of the best available. Amber Medical also run a direct hire programme of the Ameda Elite and SMB dual electric hospital-grade breastpumps delivered straight to you door. For further information call or visit their website.

Chicco UK 01623 750 870
www.chicco.com
The Chicco adjustable breast pump is an uncomplicated manual pump with silicone breast shield and lever action. They also have a battery-operated model and a syringe breast pump, which ensures a gentle, adjustable suction of excess milk.

Medela 0161 776 0400
www.medela.co.uk
Medela manufactures a range of manual, battery and electric breast pumps. They also have a small travel set which can be used effectively for mums who go back to work but want to continue feeding breast milk full time; and a set of pumps if you are breastfeeding twins. Pumps can also be hired.

NUK 0845 300 2467
www.nuk.de
NUK make a manual and battery-operated model. The manual model has adjustable strength, swivel handle for left- or right-handed mothers, plus a soft silicone cushion which massages as you express.

The First Years 0800 526 829
www.thefirstyears.com
This pump offers adjustable hand-positioning options to maximize comfort while pumping. Available from many leading nursery retailers.

Whittlestone Expresser 01538 386 650
www.whittlestone.co.uk
The Whittlestone Expresser uses gentle pulsation to stimulate the let-down of your breast milk, and then expresses your breast milk.

car safety

Autosafe 020 7372 3141
www.auto-safe.co.uk
Seat belt fitting specialist and makers of the new seat belt height adjuster for children aged 4-12yrs combining comfort and safety.

Halfords 0845 7626 625
www.halfords.com
If you purchase a car seat from Halfords their specially trained staff will ensure that it is correctly fitted in your car. Take your receipt or they'll charge you an extra £9.99.

carriers and slings

In the early days a comfortable baby sling is an essential. There are two types to look into: the fabric slings which have become very fashionable and can be used to carry both babies and toddlers; or the more structured carriers which are more comfortable for long periods. Best thing is to try them on to see which suits your own physique and weight of your baby

Babyhut 01273 245 864
www.babyhut.net
Experts in cotton baby slings and baby hammocks.

Baby Bjorn 0870 120 0543
www.babybjorn.com
The Baby Carrier Active, suitable from 0-18mths has a unique lumbar support panel sewn into the back to give a good fitting and more comfortable weight distribution.

shopping 21

Babybackpacs   01872 270 213
www.babybackpacs.co.uk
Online retailer of carriers and accessories including Bushbaby, Hippychick, Kelty Kids and Karrimor.

Babypouch   0845 009 6644
www.babypouch.co.uk
Stockists of the world's best baby carriers, including Maya Wrap, Ergo, New Native and Hug-a-bub. Organic & fair trade.

Babyworld   01491 821 877
www.babyworld.co.uk
Online retailer of carriers and accessories including Bushbaby, Wilkinet, Hippychick and Tomy. Orders delivered within 2 working days (see ad pg 27).

Better Baby Sling   01923 444 442
www.betterbabysling.co.uk
'Wonderfully easy to put on and very comfortable' *The Independent*

Bill Amberg   020 7727 3560
www.billamberg.com
Leather and sheepskin baby carrier. Very luxurious.

Hippychick Child Hip Seat   01278 434 440
www.hippychick.com
If you carry your child around on your hip you may end up with a twisted spine. Enter the Hipseat, a back-supporting belt with a shelf for the child to sit on, which supports its weight and allows your back to stay straight. From 6mths-3yrs.

Huggababy   01874 711 629
www.huggababy.co.uk
Designed by a mother, this double-thickness cotton twill sling is favoured by many other mums, and tough enough to last baby from birth to 2 or 3 yrs.

Wilkinet   0800 138 3400
www.wilkinet.co.uk
The Wilkinet Baby Carrier is lauded for its comfort, strength and unique wrap-around method that doesn't strain or ride up the back. Comes in soft cotton or cord.

castings: hands and feet

Most mothers regret that they never got round to taking their baby's hand or foot prints, or struggled with a tube of paint. The companies below offer a range of styles (casts, prints and imprints) to suit all budgets

Happyhands   020 8671 2020
www.happyhands.ws
Your baby's hand and footprints on ceramics. Ink-free kit provided for taking prints at home.

Lowestoft Porcelain   01502 572 940
www.lowestoftporcelain.com
Unique gift from you at the time of the birth, christening or confirmation. Few will source such a cherished family heirloom personalised to the child. Easily commissioned and sent direct to you.

Wrightson & Platt   0845 226 5775
www.wrightsonandplatt.com
Perfect castings in gold, silver, bronze, glass and resin. Baby hands and feet, portraits, wedding pieces - call for brochure.

christening gifts

There is now such a plethora of items suitable for godchildren, we have selected those companies which we think offer the highest quality, originality and personalised service at the right price. See also gifts page 28.

Asprey & Garrard   020 7493 6767
www.asprey-garrard.com
Cups, spoons, plates and yo-yos - engraved with initials/name.

Heirlooms UK   020 7738 1868
Personalised cushions, ring cushions, shawls and decorative pictures using words and images you provide.

Babylist   020 7371 5145
www.babylist.com
The Babylist team have hand-selected a range of traditional and contemporary christening gifts, which include luxuries such as a Daniella Besso cashmere blanket or the Catherine Everest range of organic mother and baby bath and massage oils. They can also organise for gifts to be personalised or engraved as necessary.

shopping

happyhands™
Your own baby's hand or foot prints on framed ceramic tiles

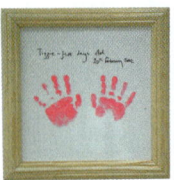 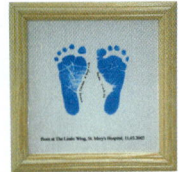

An easy to use inkless footprint kit is provided

"Simply irresistible – here's a lasting memory that makes a perfect present for friends and relatives."
Prima Baby Magazine

Call us on **020 8671 2020**
www.happyhands.ws

Braybrook & Britten — 020 8993 7334
www.braybrook.com
A large range of silver gifts for children from £30 upwards - most can be personalised. 'Silversmiths by Post', they can receive orders from anywhere in the UK.

Christening Stuff — 0870 777 0285
www.christeningstuff.co.uk
Fabulous christening gifts. Including pewter, silver plated and sterling silver gifts. Gift wrapping available.

Happyhands — 020 8671 2020
www.happyhands.ws
Gift box for hand and foot imprints on ceramic, packaged in a red box with white ribbon. Price £35.

Junior Traditions — 01884 860 063
www.juniortraditions.co.uk
Chairs and chests for children 1-6yrs made from oak and walnut for exceptional christening gifts.

The Little Picture Gallery — 020 8998 9880
www.thelittlepicturegallery.co.uk
Delightful range of watercolour prints for children featuring a range of farm animals, trains & boats etc.

christening gowns

If you are starting from scratch and don't have a family heirloom christening gown, then a trip to Christening Gowns is well worth a visit

Christening Gowns — 01536 515 401
www.christeningoutfits.co.uk
Over 500 gowns, dresses and romper suits in stock. Accessories including personalised bibs. Mail order throughout the UK.

Heirs Wears — 020 8809 7160
Mail order traditional and contemporary christening gowns, bonnets, shoes and bootees.

Little Darlings — 01604 846 655
www.littledarlings.co.uk
Visit the website to view their full christening and fashion ranges.

Patrizia Wigan Designs — 020 7823 7080
www.patriziawigan.com
Refined gifts, babywear, christening, bridesmaid and pageboy outfits.

clothing shops: fashion

We have covered this category comprehensively. But if your once-favourite pastime has diminished now that you can't browse the shops at leisure, many brands have good catalogue and online purchasing routes

CORNWALL
Adams Childrenswear
- 24 Victoria Square, Truro, TR1 — 01872 275 277
- 97 Market Jew St, Penzance, TR18 — 01736 350 944

Boys & Girls — 01208 763 28
3 Town Arms Passage, Bodmin, PL31 2JQ

Boys & Girls — 01208 812 992
Hamilton House, The Platt, Wadebridge, PL27 7AD
Clothing from 0-12yrs (premature babies clothing incl).

Bumble Bees — 01326 573 980
8 Church St, Helston, TR13 8TG
Baby & children's wear from 0-5yrs, plus soft shoes. Also have Christening robes & outfits. Nursery linen, bedding, high chairs and cots (don't stock but can order). Full range of Maternity wear, mainly casual clothing and some evening wear.

Cobweb Childrens Clothes — 01637 872 106
5 Fore St, Newquay, TR7 1HB
Clothing from 0-12yrs & soft shoes - mainly casual but some Christening outfits. Collection tends to be different from what you would find in high street stores, but prices are middle of the road.

Please say you saw the listings in The South West Baby Directory

shopping 23

Fabulous Kids 01736 791 900
40 Fore St, St Ives, TR26 1HE
Just started up by two local mums, stocks baby & children's clothing 0-10yrs, shoes, bedlinen, tableware, craft kits, feeding accessories, money boxes etc

Feeline Clothing 01326 565 707
Salt Cellar Workshops, Salt Cellar Hill, Porthleven, Helston, TR13 9DP
Clothing shop - handmade items. Clothing for 3mths plus, will make anything to order so flexible.

JoJo Maman Bebe 01752 221 960
www.jojomamanbebe.co.uk
Dingles of Plymouth, Children's Wear Department, 40 - 46 Royal Parade, Plymouth, PL1 1DY
In this concession you will find maternity wear including breastfeeding tops, maternity jeans, occasion and evening wear. You will also find the 0-5yrs clothing range which has a wonderful French inspired Breton range.

Moonbeam 01872 223 149
6 Nalders Court, Truro, TR1 2XH
Clothes from 0-10yrs & shoes. Real mixture of classic & contemporary styles.

Piglets 01752 844 326
120 Fore St, Saltash, PL12 6JW
Baby clothes up to 2yrs - stocking quality brands. Also sell baby sleeping bags, blankets, hats, gloves etc.

South Shore Kids 01736 361 615
Market House, Market Jew St, Penzance, TR18 2JE
Childrens & baby's clothing from 0-16 plus shoes. All surf brands - Quiksilver from 2yrs.

Wild Waves 01736 795 333
Tregenna Hill, St Ives, TR26 1SE
Clothing from 0 upwards, not high street brands. Also sell flip flops in the summer and soft shoes (Daisy Roots)

DEVON

Adams Childrenswear
• 64 High St, Barnstaple, EX31 01271 372 810
• 5-6 Market Walk, Newton Abbot 01626 360 423
• 17 Cornwall St, Plymouth 01752 265 548
• 34-36 Chapel St, Exmouth 01395 264 732
• 32 Victoria St, Paignton, TQ4 01803 528 902

Buttons & Bows 01409 259 345
3 The Market Square, The Square, Holsworthy, EX22 6AN
Clothing range from 0-5yrs plus soft shoes.

Friday's Child 01392 273 254
11 Martins Lane, Exeter, EX1 1EY
Boutique clothing for 0-8yrs, incl. Christening & occasion wear. Shoe department. Toys & gifts.

Friendly local boutiques with clothing for new born to 8 years. Exquisite layette, christening and occasionwear collections & unusual new baby & birthday gifts. Taggies, voted best baby gift, Moulin Roty, Takinou & Toys Made from Wood are some of the toy ranges stocked.

49 North Street, Exeter, Devon, EX4 3QR Tel: 01392 671655
2 Riverside Pl, Taunton, Somerset, TA1 1JH Tel: 01823 254484
Website: www.kaboodle-uk.com Email: kaboodle@onetel.com

Graffiti 01822 616 191
Unit 2 The Market, Tavistock, PL19 0AL
Clothing and shoes from 2-12yrs.

Kaboodle 01392 671 655
49 North Street, Exeter, EX4 3QR
Clothing from 0-6yrs mainly from European designers. Also stock shoes and some toys. Christening wear for boys & girls, including full length robes.

Kidzone 01297 234 44
23 Fore St, Seaton, EX12 2LE
Clothing from 0-13yrs, and shoes, both soft and walkers

Kindercare 01392 435 888
10 Honeylands Way, Exeter, EX4 8QR
Clothing for premature babies up to 7yrs. Also provide a hire service on equipment - cots, high chairs, buggies etc.

Little Angels 01752 480 111
12 Sugar Mill Business Park, Billacombe Road, Plymouth, PL9 7HT
Ex-chain store stock clothing from birth to 14 yrs. All new and tagged - Gap, Next, Disney, Ralph Lauren etc, about half price.

Little Cherubs 01803 325 715
1 Foxlands Walk, St Marychurch, Torquay, TQ1
Individual boutique clothing from premature babies to 8 yrs. Stocking both traditional, classic wear (smock dresses, sailor suits etc) through to modern, funky clothing eg Quiksilver.

Mini-Me 01822 611 322
14-14b Market St, Tavistock, PL19 0DB
Clothing and shoes from 0-2yrs.

M's Childrens Wear 01752 254 702
1, 11, 21 The Pannier Market, Plymouth, PL1 1PW
Large range of clothing and shoes, from premature to 2-3yrs, also stock suits for little boys & Sarah Louise smock dresses.

Nonsuch 01548 852 892
13 Fore Street, Kingsbridge, TQ7 1PG
Children's wear 0-8 yrs, including accessories, swimwear, rainwear, dressing up clothes and baby sleeping bags.

24 shopping

Up-See-Daisy   01803 840 303
1 Rotherfold, Totnes, TQ9 5ST
Quality clothing from 0-8yrs, wellies, macs, umbrellas. Scandinavian nursery furniture - cots, tables & chairs, wardrobes. Nursery interiors, bedding etc. Also have play tents.

Wee Willie Winkies   01392 410 330
5-7 West Street, Exeter, EX1 1BB
Designer childrenswear, shoes and accessories.

Whizkidz   01822 612 700
23 Market St, Tavistock, Pl19 0DD
Clothing from 2yrs upwards

DORSET

Adams Childrenswear
- 5 Falklands Square,   01202 668 766
  Towngate Place, Poole, 1ER BH15
- 198-206 High St, Poole, BH15   01202 683 459
- 15 The Sovereign Centre,   01202 399 956
  Christchurch Road, Bournemouth, BH1 4SX
- 62 St Mary St, Weymouth, DT4   01305 789 715
- Unit L, The Ferndown Centre,   01202 861 217
  Ferndown, BH22 9TH
- 1b South St, Dorchester, DT1   01305 269 206

Ginger & Pickle   01935 816 111
37 Cheap St, Sherborne, DT9 3PU
Upmarket clothing from 0-16yrs, also soft toys, rattles, soft shoes and accessories

Heybaby Shop   01305 259 929
24 Middlemarsh Street, Pummery Square,
Poundbury, Dorchester, DT1 3FD
Quality clothing from 0-5, soft shoes, washable nappies and a selection of wooden toys

Jack & Jill   01747 858 719
Sun & Moon Cottage, 1 Gold Hill, Shaftesbury, SP7
Boutique clothing shop for 0-4yrs including some toys, books and soft shoes

Les Enfants   01202 763 526
24 Westbourne Arcade, Bournemouth, BH4 9AY
Quality clothing and shoes for 0-16yrs

Little Monsters   01935 812 282
Half Moon St, Sherborne, DT9 3LN
Clothing, shoes and accessories for 0-16yrs.

Look Mum   01202 760 163
128 Poole Road, Bournemouth, BH4 9EF
Quality clothing for 0-16yrs, soft toys, gifts and shoes

The Giant Peach   01202 880 330
3 Kings Court, Wimborne, BH21 1HS
Boutique clothing for babies and children

Please say you saw the listings in
The South West Baby Directory

GLOUCESTERSHIRE

Allsorts   01594 810 505
Unicorn House, Market Place, Coleford, GL16 8AA

Cherubs   01453 842 985
17, Long St, Wotton-Under-Edge, GL12 7ES

Clothes Plus   01594 824 478
2, Commercial St, Cinderford, GL14 2RR

Cute   01453 835 096
The Old George, Fountain St, Nailsworth, Stroud

Jack In The Box   01285 655 875
Foxleaze Court, Preston, Cirencester, GL7 5PS

JoJo Maman Bébé   **01242 581 505**
2c Regent Street, Cheltenham, GL50 1HQ
www.jojomamanbebe.co.uk
This trusted brand brings everything together for mums and mums-to-be including maternity wear, baby and children's clothing, nursery furniture with co-ordinating bed linen and organic baby sleeping bags; toys and gifts; outdoor clothes, you name it they've got it covered.

Mini-Me   01242 577 441
Regent Arcade, Regent St, Cheltenham, GL50 1JZ

Petit Patapon   01242 285 678
Beechwood Shopping Centre, High St, Cheltenham

Polka Dot Blue   01666 500 008
21, Market Place, Tetbury, GL8 8DD

Tangerine   01285 657 865
57, Cricklade St, Cirencester, GL7 1JE

The Little People Co   01453 839 010
Wilton House, Bridge St, Stroud, GL5 3EP

The Orange Pig   01684 297 935
122, High St, Tewkesbury, GL20 5JU

Tots & Tearaways   01451 822 200
Moore Rd, Cheltenham, GL54 2AZ

Wonder Years   01608 652 882
5, Old Market Way, Moreton-In-Marsh, GL56 0AJ

Ziggy's   01242 228 892
First Floor, Beechwood Shopping Centre,
Cheltenham, GL50 1DQ
Funky children's clothing, soft shoes and accessories. Quality/individual labels, some designer wear, wooden toys and wellington boots.

Zip   01285 643 377
3-5 Ashcroft Road, Cirencester, GL7 1RA
Zip is a new and exiting childrenswear shop offering a wide selection of top designer labels for both boys and girls from birth to 14 years. Collections include Burberry, Elle, O'Neill, Timberland, Nike, DKNY and Kenzo.

shopping

SOMERSET, BRISTOL & BATH

Blooming Marvellous 0845 458 7401
5 Saracen Street, Bath, BS8 4JG
www.bloomingmarvellous.co.uk
This favourite brand puts almost everything on show from it's excellent website and catalogue in this Bath shop. Maternity wear, baby clothes, nursery goods and essential equipment. And now upstairs the brand new Mini-Marvellous range of toys and gifts.

Baby Care 01934 742 185
Magnolia House, Union St, Cheddar, BS27 3NA
Clothing from 0-2yrs plus designer range up to 3yrs, soft shoes, cots, cribs, moses baskets, feeding and safety equipment. Also sell natural baby bath & skin products.

babyGap 0117 950 9698
Upper Mall, Cribb's Causeway, Bristol, BS34 5UR

Bon Bleu 01458 441 888
Unit 48 Clarks Village, Street, BA16 0BB
Baby and children's clothing from 0-14yrs. Designer items at high street prices. Also stock some soft toys & bags etc.

JoJo Maman Bébé 01225 335 870
5 Cheap Street, Bath, BA1 1NE
www.jojomamanbebe.co.uk
This is the ever popular range of materntiy clothings, baby and children's clothing, nursery furniture and practical baby equipment; toys and gifts as well as things for pampering mums.

Kaboodle 01823 254 484
2 Riverside Place, St James St, Taunton, TA1 1JH
Friendly local boutique with clothing for newborn to 8yrs. Beautiful layettes, christening and occasionwear. Also sells a range of wooden toys, taggies and baby gifts (see ad pg 23).

Little Shrimp 01373 455 527
3 Bath St, Frome, BA11 1DH
Own label 100% cotton stripy clothing from 3mths -10yrs, all made in the UK (also available through their mail order catalogue). Also stock Ecco shoes, baby birkenstocks, leather shoes, slippers. The Organic Pharmacy has a mother and child range of bath and skin products such as baby massage oil, baby balm and nappy balm.

Oranges & Lemons 0117 973 7370
20 Princess Victoria Street, Clifton, BS8 4BP
Designer childrenswear from newborn to 14yrs. Diesel, Dior, IKKS and French Connection to name a few of the brands. They also stock shoes and accessories.

Ruff & Tumble Babywear 01373 452 991
9 Cheap Street, Frome, BA11 1BN
Children's clothes from 0-6yrs including both affordable and individual labels. They also have a small selection of toys (soft and wooden)

Please say you saw the listings in
The South West Baby Directory

Simply Kidz 01934 419 550
10 High Street, Weston-Super-Mare, BS23 1JF
Designer label clothing for 0-16yrs.

The Rocking Horse 01458 274 393
The Market Place, Somerton, TA11 7NB
Designer label clothing for 0-16yrs.

Trendy Kids 0117 9227 337
6 Broadmead, Bristol, BS1 3HH
Designer label clothing, shoes and accessories for 0-16yrs.

WILTSHIRE

Adams Childrenswear 01722 411 196
45 New Canal, Salisbury, Wiltshire, SP1 2AA

Cucci Coo 01793 694 499
Unit 34 The Arcade, Brunel Centre, Swindon
Designer baby and chidrenswear from 0-14yrs and accessories

JoJo Maman Bébé 01722 421 227
42 Silver Street, Salisbury, SP1 2NE
www.jojomamanbebe.co.uk
Another great store for maternity wear, including 4 styles of maternity jeans, nursery furniture and practical and essential nursery goods; a great range of French inspired baby clothing and toys/gifts.

26 shopping

Mini Expressions 4 Kidz 01373 822 225
15 High St, Westbury, Wiltshire, BA13 3BN
Wide range of good value baby and childrens clothing and accessories, from 0-15yrs, soft toys, christening wear and accessories, safety goods and a huge range of footwear.

Peapod Childrens Wear 01225 863 733
The Old Post Office, 10 The Shambles, Bradford-on-Avon, Wiltshire, BA15 1JR
Mid-range priced clothing and toys for 0-10yrs. Also a new branch recently opened in Wiltshire: 73 New Street, Salisbury, SP1 2PH. Tel: 01722 411148

Peapod Childrens Wear 01722 411 148
73 New Street, Salisbury, Wiltshire, SP1 2PH
Quality clothing for 0-10yrs & wooden and soft toys, also wellies, slippers and soft shoes

Tangerine 01380 722 388
28 Maryport Street, Devizes, Wiltshire, SN10 1AG
Clothing & accessories for 0-8yrs, shoes and toys

Wear It 01373 823 098
12 Maristow Street, Westbury, Wiltshire, BA13 3DN
Good value clothing and accessories from Premature Babies - 16 yrs. Plus a small range of maternity wear.

Whirlybobs 01666 822 600
6 Oxford Street, Malmesbury, Wiltshire, SN16 9AX
Quality clothing and accessories from 0-8yrs at a wide range of prices (designer to affordable).

clothing: outdoor

Hippychick Togz 01278 434 440
www.hippychick.com
The Togz range of outdoor clothing is 100% waterproof and made from Teflon-coated, breathable nylon fabric. A choice of dungarees, trousers, jackets and bootees, all in great colours. Machine-washable with velcro leg and arm fastenings.

Little Trekkers 01484 868 321
www.littletrekkers.co.uk

Muddy Puddles 0870 420 4943
www.muddypuddles.com

Welligogs 01785 662 277
www.welligogs.com

clothing: online/mail order

37° 020 7603 8666
www.37degreesltd.com
These clothes are made from 'smart' textiles that keep a constant 37 degrees temperature despite external conditions.

Boden - Mini 0845 677 5000
www.boden.co.uk
Great range of everyday, practical clothing for babies and children - especially their 'pull-ups', which make getting dressed such a simple task.

GROE Baby!
Baby Stimulation T-Shirts

High contrast images and simple designs are known to help visually stimulate young babies and help them develop
T-Shirts for grown-ups to wear make it easy to include stimulatory images in your everyday lives!

www.groebaby.co.uk

Smarter babies by design.

Clothes 4 Boys 01420 520 677
www.clothes4boys.co.uk
Online store that specialises in boys' clothing.

Cut 4 Cloth 01326 340 956
www.cut4cloth.co.uk
Cut4Cloth specialises in 100% organic cotton clothing, cut for the bulkier cloth nappy bottom.

Cyrillus 020 7734 6660
www.cyrillus.com
Classic French catalogue for babies and children.

Eat Yer Greens 020 8744 0330
www.eatyergreens.com
Fashionable, practical clothing for 0-4 year olds, combining fresh and imaginative design with a sense of humour.

Groe Baby 01258 452 175
www.groebaby.co.uk
Stimulate your baby's eyesight and brain development by wearing the right kind of T-shirt - that is, one of Groe Baby's new designs with geometric swirls and stripes in eye-smarting black on white.

Iriss 01736 366 568
www.iriss.co.uk
Collection of baby and children's hand-knitted cardigans, jumpers, hats and bootees in pure wool, with embroidered details and mother of pearl buttons.

JoJo Maman Bébé 01225 335 870
www.jojomamanbebe.co.uk
Great range of baby basics including babygros, t-shirts, in the French inspired Breton design.

Mitty James 020 8693 5018
www.mittyjames.com
Luxuriously soft towelling beach and holiday wear.

Schmidt Natural Clothing 0845 345 0498
www.naturalclothing.co.uk
Organic fairtrade clothing, washable nappies and bedliners. Babies', children's and adults' underwear, slippers and nightwear in soft cotton, merino wool and silk. Biodynamic lambskins and soft toys. Sensitive skin specialists.

shopping 27

So Pretty 020 7224 1166
www.sopretty.co.uk
Contemporary fabrics combined with traditional English designs - smocked dresses, Harris tweed coats and bonnets, silk tartan party dresses and cosy cashmere cardigans.

The Baby Closet 020 7924 4457
www.thebabycloset.co.uk
Selection of quality, original items which are hand-wrapped and despatched within 24 hrs of placing the order.

White Rabbit Clothing 020 8440 3227
www.whiterabbitclothing.com
Long-sleeved baby suits with an attached t-shirt overlay, giving twice the layers with half the hassle - and no ride up.

Young England 020 7259 9003
www.youngengland.com
Traditional clothing for children from birth to eight years.

cribs, cots & first beds

All the following offer high-quality cots, cot-bed and first beds. For standard cots with adjustable bases we recommend visiting nursery goods stores (pg 37) to see standard models on display

Aspace 01985 301 222
www.aspaceuk.com
Range of classic and contemporary beds, sleepover truckles and bedside cabinets. Good quality and affordable.

Babylist 020 7371 5145
The Broomhouse, 50 Sullivan Road, SW6 3DX
www.babylist.com
Babylist offers one of the largest range of cribs and cots, including many unique brands from Europe and the Far East. They come in all sorts of designs, hand-painted or in solid beech, oak or cherry. And you have the luxury of looking at them all from the comfort of their SW6 showroom.

Babyworld 01491 821 877
babyworld.co.uk
Huge range of quality cribs, cots, cradles, hammocks and mattresses from Global, Amby, Leander, Lindam, BabyDan and Kaloo. Order online for fast delivery (see ad pg 41).

European Nursery Furniture 01270 767 070
www.enfltd.co.uk
This is an exceptional range of good quality and well priced nursery furniture. It is offered in a range of woods and can be seen on their website or in retailers such as Daisy & Toms. You can order online or via telephone and the order is delivered to your home by their staff and assembled in your nursery or chosen room.

Simon Horn 020 7731 1279
www.simonhorn.com
Hand-made wooden cots which transform into a bed then a sofa.

www.babydirectory.com

The Children's Furniture Company 020 7737 7303
www.thechildrensfurniturecompany.com
Beautiful hardwood and painted furniture - beds and bunks.

MATTRESSES
Greenfibres 0845 330 3440
www.greenfibres.com

Natural Mat Company 020 7985 0474
www.naturalmat.com
The best range of baby mattresses on offer in 100% natural materials and 100% safe. Standard sizes available as well as made-to-measure.

Hippychick Bed Protector 01278 434 440
www.hippychick.com
Two layers of brushed cotton, sandwiching a waterproof polyurethane

dressing up

No nursery toybox would be complete without a few dressing-up clothes to extend the imagination and explore role play. Many of these suppliers manufacture in the UK and therefore you can be assured of good-quality fabrics and well made accessories. Kits are also provided so when you are required to make something for the school play you won't be letting the side down

MAIL ORDER
Charlie Crow 01782 417 133
www.charliecrow.co.uk

Frilly Lily 01666 510 055
www.frillylily.co.uk

Hopscotch Dressing Up Clothes 01483 813 728
www.hopscotchdressingup.co.uk
Shop online for high quality children's fancy dress costumes and hats - delivered to your door.

food: organic

By feeding your baby on organic baby food whether pre-prepared or by organising organic home delivery, you can be assured that the residual level of pesticides is minimised. Below are the UK's top organic producers and suppliers

The Soil Association 0117 929 0661
www.soilassociation.org
The main UK body which supervises the standard for UK organic produce and promotes organic farming.

Links Organic 020 7590 9272
www.linksorganic.com
An online directory of organic businesses, including home delivery services, retailers and organic farmers.

shopping

ORGANIC BABY FOOD BRANDS

Baby Organix 0800 393 511
www.babyorganix.co.uk

Babylicious 020 8998 4189
www.babylicious.co.uk

Babynat 0118 951 0518
www.organico.co.uk

Easy Freezy 01403 710 935
Organic frozen baby food and toddler meals.

Fresh Daisy Organic Babyfood 0870 240 7028
www.daisyfoods.com

HIPP 01635 528 250
www.hipp.co.uk

MiniScoff 07798 526 090
www.miniscoff.co.uk

Pots for Tots 0845 450 0875
www.potsfortots.co.uk
Fresh organic home-cooked baby and toddler meals. National delivery. Non-dairy, non-gluten menus available.

Truuuly Scrumptious Organic 01761 239 300
www.bathorganicbabyfood.co.uk
Frozen organic baby and toddler food, home deliveries.

HOME SHOPPING

Pure Meat Direct 01409 211 127
www.puremeatdirectonline.co.uk

Organic Delivery Co 020 7739 8181
www.organicdelivery.co.uk

The Real Meat Company 01985 840 562
www.realmeat.co.uk

Swaddles Green Farm 01460 234 387
www.swaddles.co.uk

West Country Organics 01647 270 056
www.westcountryorganics.co.uk

garden toys

With childhood being lost to hand-held gameboys and television, these companies encourage a return to good old-fashioned unsupervised fun. So if you're redeveloping your garden or house this year, why not allocate some of your budget towards imaginative and physical play

Advanced Play Systems 01367 850 423
www.advancedplay.co.uk
Ready built and DIY garden toys such as Wendy houses. Built to order and designed with finger-friendly doors.

Dunster House 01234 272 445
www.dhleisureandgarden.com
Outdoor playframes, playhouses, electric wheeled toys and toy boxes.

Great Little Trading Co 0870 860 6000
www.gltc.co.uk
Impressive range of activity toys and furniture for babies and children. Excellent catalogue of 100s of items, many exclusive.

Insect Lore 01908 563 338
www.insectlore-europe.com
Take five caterpillars and watch them hatch into beautiful Painted Lady butterflies. They also sell ladybird eggs, giant land snails, or how about a giant hissing cockroach?

Lodden Valley Garden Toys 0845 644 1546
www.lvgt.co.uk
Leading brands of outdoor play equipment for all your family, including swings, slides, climbing frames, wooden playsets, sandpits, trampolines and more.

The Active Toy Company 01635 248 683
www.activetoy.co.uk
TP and Little Tikes outdoor equipment all on show for trial and display. Wooden/steel climbing frames, swings and slides, trampolines and paddling pools.

PLAYHOUSES & TENTS

Just Playhouses 07768 727 016
www.justplayhouses.co.uk
Timber Wendy houses.

Little Red House 01544 319 238
www.littleredhouse.co.uk
Contemporary wooden playhouse designs.

The Children's Cottage Company 01363 772 061
www.play-houses.com

The Win Green Company 01622 746 516
Reason Hill, Westerhill Road, Coxheath, Kent
www.wingreen.co.uk
Wonderful fabric playtents such as Sheriff's tent or Gingerbread house for use inside or outside.

Honeypot Playhouses 0870 164 4002
www.waltons.co.uk
Choose from five different cottage-style timber playhouses.

gifts

Babylist 020 7371 5145
www.babylist.com
Wonderful hand-embroidered range of clothing from Dimples, or hand-painted lamps from Daisy Kelly. Babylist also offers a wish list service, where clients can choose a few things which are made available to friends and family via their website or on email.

shopping

BitsnStuff 020 8289 7860
www.bitsnstuff.co.uk
On-line shop that has over 1800 unique products to choose from not available on the high street. Sections include baby equipment, childrens home décor, maternity wear, gifts, toys and games (see ad pg 19).

Happyhands 020 8671 2020
7 Brockwell Park Row, SW2 2YH
www.happyhands.ws
Hand and foot prints on personalised ceramic mugs.

Hippins 01531 650 843
www.hippins.co.uk
On line - wide range of nursery goods including furniture, blankets & bedding, playhouses, toys, shoes and clothing, nursery Accessories, gifts including Christening gift ideas (see ad page 41).

My Day Diary 0870 432 4664
www.mydaydiaries.com
A diary for babies and young children, where those people who care for them can record day-to-day events, special moments, favourite games and foods. A great idea for communication between parents and their nanny, childminder or nursery.

Noonoo Design Company
www.noonoodesign.com
Patented craft-based textile products. The first range is the NooNoo Comfort Blanket. Individually felted to produce a practical, soft, tactile and sturdy infant-sized mini-blanket, hand embroidered and applied with child art imagery.

Stork Gifts 0845 644 3877
www.storkgifts.co.uk
We were really impressed by the fantastic quality and selection of unusual baby goods on this website. Very well laid out and easy to use.

hairdressers

Nippers 01392 490 410
33 South Street, Exeter, Devon, EX1 1ED
This is the first exclusively kids-only salon in the UK - at last! The children sit on "merry-go-round" horses or motorbikes and watch their own choice of DVD on a personal flat-screen DVD while a specially trained, child-friendly stylist snips away. Parents are flocking as far away at Manchester and London. This is more than just a haircut - it's a proper day out.

linens and sleeping bags

Bonne Nuit 020 8871 1472
www.bonne-nuit.co.uk
Beautiful French baby sleeping bags, pyjamas and linen.

Comfort Blankets 020 8302 6510
www.comfortblankets.co.uk
Comfort blankets made from fleece and edged in satin, in a range of funky designs.

NOONOO© COMFORT BLANKETS
ADORABLE, STIMULATING AND ERGONOMIC
SOFTEST FELTED LAMBSWOOL WITH EMBROIDERED CHILD ART
FUN-SIZE INTERACTIVE FELTED ADD-ONS FOR LITTLE FINGERS
A GREAT ALTERNATIVE GIFT IDEA!
WWW.NOONOODESIGN.COM

happyhands™
The Perfect Christening Gift

The gift box entitles the recipient to either one framed Happyhands tile or 25 cards
An easy to use inkless footprint kit is provided

Their own baby's hand & foot prints
Call us on **020 8671 2020**
www.happyhands.ws

Bonne Nuit™
Baby Sleeping Bags & Nursery Classics

For stockists or a brochure call
020 8871 1472 or order online at
www.bonne-nuit.co.uk

shopping

Hippychick   01278 434 440
www.hippychick.com
100% natural cotton fleece baby blankets in a wonderful array of colours.

Fig   020 7884 1312
www.figchildrensnightwear.co.uk
Children's classic nightwear from 12mths to teenagers.

Grobag   0870 420 4920
www.gro-group.com
The UK's bestselling baby sleeping bags. For your nearest stockist and details on their full range visit their website.

lotions and potions (natural)

If you are looking for something a little more special than the supermarket standards, all these suppliers offer an organic, additive- and SLS- free alternative

Barefoot Botanicals   0870 220 2273
www.barefootuk.com
Good-quality natural skincare including an SOS Skin Rescue Bath Oil with lavender, neroli and chamomile.

E45 Junior
www.e45.com
Dermatologist- and paediatrician-approved. Developed for children with dry, sensitive skin or eczema.

Earth Friendly Baby   020 8424 8844
www.earthfriendlybaby.co.uk
A range of high-quality, natural products that use natural plant-based products with no artificial colouring or synthetic fragrances. Their range includes Lavender cleansing bar, Chamomile Shampoo, Calendula Daily Cream and Red Clover Nappy Cream. Available from Sainsburys, Green Baby and other health shops across the UK.

Green Baby   020 7359 7037
www.greenbabyco.com
Natural baby toiletries and baby massage oils.

Little Miracles   020 7435 5555
A special range of flower remedies, developed by Serena Helene Smith, to treat children's behavioural problems such as anxiety, lack of concentration or for the terrible twos tantrums. With names such as Braveheart (for anxiety), Short Fuse (toddler tantrums) they are worth a closer look.

Smilechild   01242 269 635
www.smilechild.co.uk
Earth Friendly Baby, Badger, Faith in Nature brands offered as well as natural toothbrushes and sponges (includes natural lice products).

Neal's Yard Therapy Rooms
www.nealsyardremedies.com
Neal's Yard Remedies shops are staffed by trained personnel and stock an extensive range of complementary medicines, including homoeopathic remedies, essential oils and herbs, in addition to the complete 'blue bottle' hair and skin care range.

- 126 Whiteladies Road, Clifton,   0117 946 6034
  Bristol, BS8 2RP
- 9 Rotunda Terrace,   01242 522 136
  Montpellier Street, Cheltenham, GL50 1SX
- 7 Northumberland Place, Bath,   01225 466 944
  BA1 5AR
- 27 Market Place, Salisbury,   01722 340 736

Verde   020 7720 1100
www.verde.co.uk
Mother and baby range. 16 products including Extra Rich Stretch Mark Oil, Chamomile Baby Body Balm, Bizzy Kids Bathtime Soother, Lice Repel Lotion.

magazines

Baby & Toddler Gear   0870 262 6900
www.babyandtoddlergear.co.uk
Biannual specialising in in-depth product reviews, price comparisons and detailed fabric swatches.

Babyworld   01391 821 870
www.babyworld.co.uk
The UK's best online parenting magazine for parents and new mums, including a comprehensive online nursery goods store and 100s of informative articles.

Bumps & Babies   0870 444 8707
www.nctpregnancyandbabycare.com
A free publication given out to new members of the NCT and at some ante-natal checks at 20 weeks.

Flying Start   01772 499 014
www.flyingstartmagazine.co.uk

Junior Pregnancy & Baby   01858 438 874
www.juniormagazine.co.uk

Mother & Baby   01733 555 161
Bestselling monthly magazine with good advice, product reviews and reader experiences.

Practical Parenting   01444 475 675
From pregnancy to early childhood.

Pregnancy & Birth   020 7347 1800
www.pregnancyandbirth.co.uk

Prima Baby   01858 438 838
www.primababy.co.uk

Right Start   020 7878 2336
Produced in association with Tumble Tots for parents with children aged 6mths-7yrs. Comes out 6 times a year.

The Lady   020 7379 4717
www.lady.co.uk
Weekly magazine which advertises jobs for nannies, aupairs, mothers' helps - highly recommended if you are looking for quality childcare.

ISABELLA OLIVER
for pregnant women who love clothes
www.IsabellaOliver.com
0870 2407612

cravematernity.co.uk
0870 240 5476
crave
with child. in style.

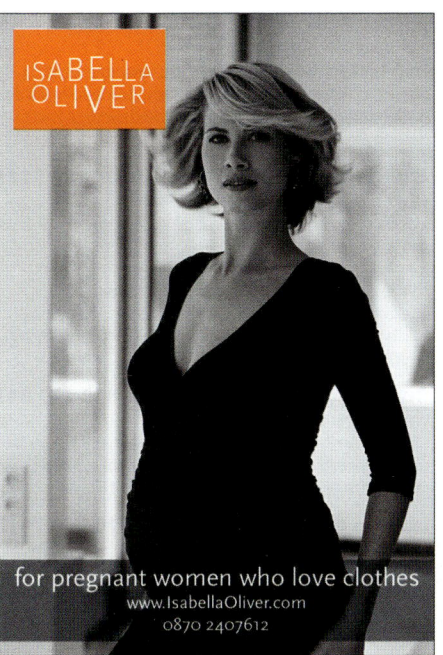

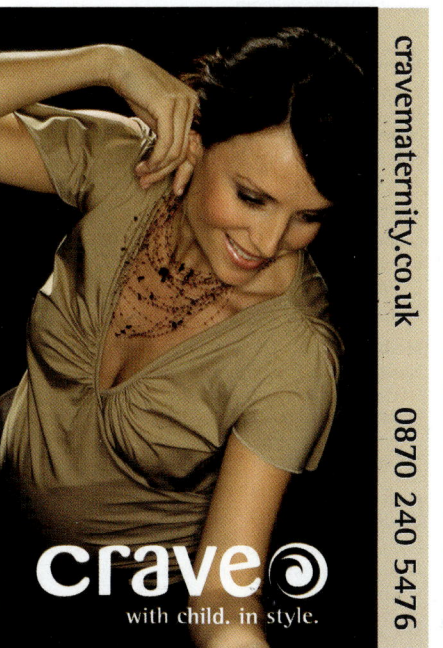

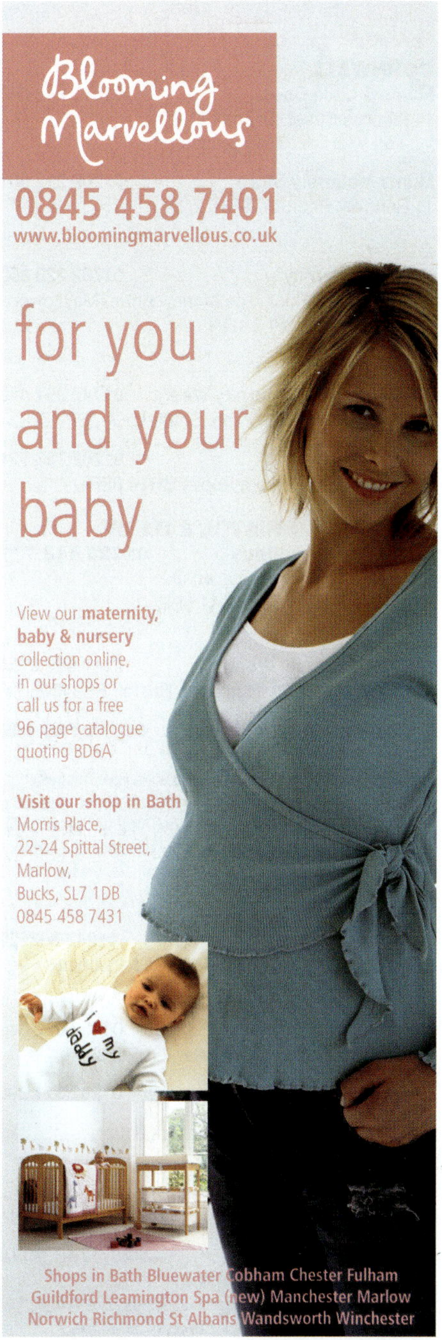
Blooming Marvellous
0845 458 7401
www.bloomingmarvellous.co.uk
for you and your baby
View our maternity, baby & nursery collection online, in our shops or call us for a free 96 page catalogue quoting BD6A
Visit our shop in Bath
Morris Place,
22-24 Spittal Street,
Marlow,
Bucks, SL7 1DB
0845 458 7431
I love my daddy
Shops in Bath Bluewater Cobham Chester Fulham Guildford Leamington Spa (new) Manchester Marlow Norwich Richmond St Albans Wandsworth Winchester

32 shopping

maternity wear: retail

CORNWALL
Mums & Little Ones   01872 242 446
14 Frances Street, Truro, TR1 3DN
Maternity wear and nursery goods shop

Mums Maternity Store   01209 212 001
11 Bond St, Redruth, TR15 2QA

DEVON
Unique Maternity   01752 229 806
Lower Ground Floor, The Moneycentre, Mayflower Street, Plymouth, PL1 1QH

DORSET
Blooming Gals Maternity Wear   01747 854 443
Hill House, Cann Common, Shaftesbury, SP7 0DL

Bumps To Ten   01202 736 521
23 Bournemouth Road, Poole, BH14 0EF

SOMERSET, BRISTOL & BATH
Blooming Marvellous   01225 442 777
www.bloomingmarvellous.co.uk
5 Saracen Street, Bath, BA1 5BR
Open Mon-Sat: 9.30am-5.30pm, Sun 10.30am-4.30pm.

Mamas Maternity Wear   0117 962 8704
184 Henleaze Road, Henleaze, Bristol, BS9 4NE

Venus Maternity Wear   01179 736 400
56 The Mall, Bristol, BS8 4JG
International collection of maternity clothes from Australia, Paris, Italy and Canada including smart casuals, business and evening wear plus a great denim range. Also stocks maternity underwear (with a comprehensive fitting service), plus some baby clothes and shoes, gifts and aromatherapy essentials.

GLOUCESTERSHIRE
Beached Whale Maternity wear   01242 863222
8 Mimosa Avenue, Up Hatherley, Cheltenham, GL51 3WB

H&M Mama   01452 872 040
26 Eastgate Street, Gloucester, GL1 1PA

Aphrodite Maternity Swimwear   01202 311 289
www.aphrodite-designs.com
Aphrodite specialises in producing comfortable swimwear using innovative designs specially for pregnant women.

maternity wear: mail order

Blooming Marvellous   020 8748 0025
www.bloomingmarvellous.co.uk
A great range of maternity wear, nursery goods and toys available from this well known mail-order catalogue.

Brides n Bumps   01252 377 725
www.bridesnbumps.com
This website is not to be missed if you have your wedding planned in the middle of your pregnancy. Made-to-measure wedding dresses, bridesmaid dresses and evening gowns. Based in Farnborough they take private appointments only.

Bravado Designs Maternity Bras   020 7738 9121
www.bravadodesigns.co.uk
Makers of the "Original Nursing Bra" which comes in 12 sizes and 6 fabulous colours, and a "Supreme Nursing Bra" for fuller-breasted women. They are made from a new super-soft cotton/spandex blend fabric and are extremely comfortable. They also produce a revolutionary breast pad, which has 4 layers of very absorbent material combined with a cool mesh which keeps nipples dry.

Crave Maternity   0870 240 547
www.cravematernity.co.uk
Crave Maternity offers a stylish range of nearly 50 high-quality complementary separates, from chic day wear to funky or formal office styles and glamorous evening options.

Isabella Oliver   0870 240 7612
www.IsabellaOliver.com
A stylish collection of maternity essentials, loungewear and sleepwear made from stretchy, soft, easy-care jersey fabric. With Ulrika Jonsson and Trinny Woodall buying the whole collection, need we say more?

Long Tall Sally   020 8649 9009
www.longtallsally.com
Maternity jeans for the long-legged.

Mama & More   01869 357 735
www.mama-and-more.com
Mama & More have a fantastic range of trendy, affordable maternity wear for every occasion. They also have a brilliant range of gorgeous baby wear as well as great quality nursery essentials. In fact, they have everything for the mum-to-be and a new baby.

Mamas & Papas   0870 830 7700
www.mamasandpapas.co.uk
Stylish collection of maternity clothes and maternity underwear (white, black and grey marl) as well as black hosiery.

Melba Clothing   020 8347 8811
www.melbaclothing.com
Fabulous, functional maternity wear for stylish mums to be. Using gorgeous fabrics and clever design detail, Melba's essential maternity active and leisure wear collection will take you from month 1 to 9 in both comfort and style.

Next Maternity   0845 6100 500
www.next.co.uk
Good quality baby and childrenswear from this high-street favourite. Buy from their big catalogue or online.

Please say you saw the listings in The South West Baby Directory

shopping 33

maternity bra specialists

Bravado Designs 020 7738 9121
www.bravadodesigns.com
Makers of the "Original Nursing Bra" which comes in 12 sizes and 6 fabulous colours, and a "Supreme Nursing Bra" for fuller-breasted women. They are made from a new super-soft cotton/spandex blend fabric and are extremely comfortable. They also produce a revolutionary breast pad, which has 4 layers of very absorbent material combined with a cool mesh which keeps nipples dry.

Figleaves 0800 279 2557
www.figleaves.com
Possibly the best online and mail-order catalogue for lingerie shopping. All brands, all sizes stocked and delivered.

Mothernature 0161 485 7359
www.mothernaturebras.co.uk
Comfortable pregnancy and breastfeeding bras.

murals

Walls of the Wild 020 8912 2912
www.wallsofthewild.co.uk
You can create an impressive design in minutes using these giant stickers. No glue needed and if you decide to move you simply take the stickers with you.

name tapes

Iron on, stick on and peel & press are all the rage. These suppliers still do the traditional embroidered name tapes as well as shoe stickers, bag tags and tapes that go on plastic (and in the dishwasher)

Easy 2 Name 01635 298 326
www.easy2name.com
Suppliers of dishwasher-proof stickers and iron-on tapes. We like the white transfer name tapes which are perfect for dark-coloured socks.

Name-It Labels 01823 451 281
www.nameitlabels.co.uk

shopping

nappies, cloth

There is now a huge range of cotton nappies available and many websites helping you select the most suitable design for your baby and lifestyle

MANUFACTURERS

Bambino Mio 01604 883 777
www.bambino.co.uk
Cotton nappies which come in 3 different sizes, with a range of nappy covers, biodegradable liners and wipes, and swim nappies. Birth to potty pack £197.

Cotton Bottoms 0500 979 899
www.cottonbottoms.co.uk
Easy-to-use, two-piece cotton nappy system.

Kushies 0870 120 2018
www.thebabycatalogue.com
All-in-one washable nappy made with 7 layers of cotton flannelette. It has an integrated waterproof layer so no need for wraps. Infant and toddler sizes with great outer wrap designs.

OneLife 01736 799 512
www.teamlollipop.co.uk
This OneLife cotton nappy is stylishly packaged and very similar to the Motherease brand.

Tots Bots 0141 550 1514
www.totsbots.com
Highly rated and award-winning shaped cotton nappies made from fluffy towelling with velcro fastenings and elasticated legs.

Yummies 01273 672 632
www.yummiesnappies.co.uk
Yummies makes cotton nappies and accessories. 'An easy to put on pre-fold,' is one mum's comment.

RETAILERS
Born
- 64 Gloucester Road, **0117 924 5080**
  Bishopston, Bristol, BS7 8BH
- 134 Walcot Street, **01225 334 434**
  St Swithins Yard, Bath, BA1 5BG

www.borndirect.com
Born offer a comprehensive range of natural and practical product for parents via their two shops in Bath and Bristol, as well as online.

Nappies Online 01202 768 070
www.nappiesonline.co.uk
This site sells leading brands of washable nappies, plus offers lots of advice.

Naturally Nappies 0845 1664716
www.naturallynappies.com
They stock all major brands except those they don't consider up to scratch. You can try before you buy which is the key to getting the right fit for your baby.

Naturebotts 0845 226 2186
www.naturebotts.co.uk
An eco-friendly disposable nappy (Moltex Oko) that's kinder to baby and the environment. Via mail order; call for a free sample.

The Nappy Lady 0845 456 2441
www.thenappylady.co.uk
If you need advice before choosing your cotton nappy then the Nappy Lady has lots on offer including eco-disposables.

nappies: disposable

Huggies Newborn
Price 12p per nappy. The most absorbent nappy on the market, and with its stretchy waistband and curved leg elastic there are simply no leaks. The sizes cover Newborns, Active Babies 3mths+ and Toddlers 10mths+. They also do Little Swimmers swim nappies (essential).

Moltex OKO
Price 21p per nappy. Although more expensive than some other brands, if you buy them in bulk from suppliers such as Smilechild, you can significantly save on the pack cost.

Pampers Active Fit
www.pampers.com
Price 21p per nappy. Good shaped nappy with sticky fastenings. The range includes New Baby, Active Fit and Baby Dry. Good Easy Up Pants which have clever tear-away sides for toddlers who won't lie down.

Safeway Baby Wriggler
www.safeway.co.uk
Price 9p per nappy (the cheapest on the market currently). Not brilliant on absorbancy through the night – but great through the day with active babies.

Tesco Unisex
Price 13p per nappy. Winning top marks for absoption from Mumsnet reviewers - and particularly good for skinny babies as they have a stretchy waistband.

Tushies
www.tushies.co.uk
Price 25p per nappy. An American range of gel-free disposable nappies and alcohol-free wipes. They use a cotton and non-chlorine bleached wood pulp so are highly absorbant - but very expensive and shipped from the US - so we're not totally convinced of their eco-friendly status.

nursery furniture

Aspace 01985 301 222
The Old Silk Works, Beech Avenue, Warminster
www.aspaceuk.com
A full range of beautiful beds, wardrobes, chests of drawers, etc, with bedding to match.

Baby Flair 0870 246 1875
www.babyflair.co.uk
Unique furniture and linens including cots, bumpers, rockers and fleece sleeping bags in natural colours.

shopping 35

Babyworld 01491 821 877
www.babyworld.co.uk
See the beautiful, exclusive range of Kaloo matching cots, changing units, wardrobes and cupboards online or arrange to visit Babyworld at their premises near Wallingford (see ad pg 37).

Billie Bond Designs 01245 360 164
www.billiebond.com
Specialists in children's hand-painted beds, cots, toy boxes. They also offer personalised gifts such as hairbrushes, stools and door plaques.

European Nursery Furniture 01270 767 070
www.enfltd.co.uk
This is an exceptional range of good quality and well priced nursery furniture. It is offered in a range of woods and can be seen on their website or in retailers such as Daisy & Toms. You can order online or via telephone and the order is delivered to your home by their staff and assembled in your nursery or chosen room.

Lionwitchwardrobe 020 8318 2070
www.lionwitchwardrobe.co.uk
Hand-crafted contemporary furniture for style-conscious parents, including a bespoke design service.

The Children's Furniture Co 020 7737 7303
www.thechildrensfurniturecompany.com
Exclusive range of children's furniture in hardwoods or painted finishes.

Dutailier 020 8810 8818
www.dutailier.co.uk
Manufactuers of the Glider rocking chair and foot rest. In four wood finishes and a good range of different fabrics.

Sandman Beds 01923 283 598
www.sandmanbeds.com
Wonderful fantasy beds all hand-made and painted to look like boats, trains, fairy castles etc - as well as underbed truckles, fairy nets and tent canopies.

Tots to Teens Furniture 01438 815 355
www.totstoteensfurniture.co.uk

nursery goods

You may feel bombarded by the vast array of nursery products when you start shopping for your first baby. Your options are independent high street stores, department stores, supermarkets, mail order catalogues, nearly new shops and online stores.

Babylist 020 7371 5145
The Broomhouse, 50 Sullivan Road, SW6 3DX
www.babylist.com
Established over 10 yrs ago, you can purchase all your nursery goods from Babylist whether that's a simple muslin or a china night light. And it's delivered directly to your home at a time convenient to you. You can try out many of the brands in their SW6 showroom and visit again when the baby is 6mths old to stock up on the next range of items required.

europeannurseryfurniture
quality & design for your baby
www.enfltd.co.uk
Telephone: 01270 767070

RETAIL
Mothercare
www.mothercare.com
Mothercare is the largest and best known nursery chain in the UK. There are a good number of stores across the UK, and the out of town locations provide parents with ample space to try out a huge range of products. The range in some items can be limited to the Mothercare brand – but they are generally good value for money. Buying online and via their mail order catalogue is also easy. For stores, see under each county

Babies R Us
www.toysrus.co.uk
The Babies R Us chain offers just about everything you need from a complete set of nursery furniture to a packet of disposables. It's a similar range to that of Mothercare, but the products are generally less expensive. However, there are fewer stores and they are situated further apart. They have a catalogue and website which offer a greater range than can be found in-store.

CORNWALL
Adeba Nurseryworld 01726 731 25
13 Truro Road, St Austell, PL25 5JE

Baby Days 01209 718 181
44 Trelowarren St, Cambourne, TR14 8AF

Mothercare 01872 222 491
Pydar Street, Truro, TR1 2BD

shopping

Visit our showroom and see a large range of goods for your happy event.

Stockists of Jane, Britax, Maxi-Cosi, Bambino Mio, Maclaren, Bugaboo & much more.

Our trained staff will help with all your queries.

We give a Car Seat Safety Fitting Service.

48 North Street, Exeter EX4 3QR   **01392 218088**   www.bambino-online.co.uk

Competitive prices, friendly service by mums who care

26-27, Market Place, Bideford, Devon EX39 2DR
Tel: **01237 473451**

Nurseryworld   01736 364 400
5 Parade St, Penzance, TR18 4BU
Broad range of nursery goods (high chairs, prams, cots, car seats, rocking horses, soft toys, educational toys, clothes (from prem - 2yrs), wellies, coats and soft shoes.

Peter Pan   01326 373 347
11 Commercial Road, Penryn, TR10 8AQ
Large range of nursery goods including pushchairs and car seats by Mamas & Papas, Maclaren, Britax and Maxi-Cosi; they also stock nursery furniture, cloth nappies (OneLife and Bambino Mio), as well as toys, gifts, monitors and baby carriers. Clothing ranges come from M&P, Grobags and carriers from Tomy, Bjorn and M&Ps.

The Baby Store   01579 347 722
23 Fore Street, Liskeard, PL14 3JA

DEVON
Allsorts   01395 225 220
99 Exeter Road, Exmouth, EX8 1QE
Second hand nursery goods and equipment.

Babe-Equip   01884 257 938
9 Leat St, Tiverton, EX16 5LG

Babies R Us   01752 226 161
Flora Street, Western Approach, Plymouth, PL1

Babytots South West   01626 333 633
15 Rydons Ind Est, Canal Way, Kingsteignton, Newton Abbot, TQ12 3SJ
Huge range of equipment, cots, prams, high chairs - everthing you need. Car seat fitting service. Also possible to hire any equipment. Ex-hire equipment for sale.

Bambino   01392 218 088
Childs House, 48 North Street, Exeter, EX4 3QR
Bambino's is a highly specialised nursery goods and furniture store run by Hazel Slack. They pride themselves on offering very good advice and deep knowledge of the products they stock. They stock an excellent range of prams and pushchairs including Jane, Bugaboo, Quinny, Maclaren and Silver Cross to mention a few. High chairs; East Coast and Tripp Trapp. Cots and car seats plus clothing from 0-1yrs and some wooden toys. They also offer a car seat fitting service.

Cyril Webber Cycles & Prams   01271 321 988
50-51 Bear St, Barnstaple, EX32 7DB
Complete range of baby goods specialising in buggies & prams, small range of clothing, baby sleeping bags, feeding equipement etc.

Happitot   01392 216 227
Unit 3a Exeter Central Station, Queen St, Exeter
Stockists of Mamas & Papas range (incl. Toys). Cots, car seats, high chairs, buggies etc. Rocking horses and larger toys.

Jackanory   01392 221 290
57 Buller Road, Exeter, EX4 1BJ
Second hand range of everything you would need for a baby/young child - equipment, toys, clothing, shoes etc

Little Acorns (Devon)   01237 473 451
26-27 Market Place, Bideford, EX39 2DR
Complete range of baby goods and equipment. Small range of clothing, natural & biodegradable disposable nappies. Also possible to hire baby equipment.

Mothercare
- Wren Retail Park, New Newton Rd, Scotsbridge, Torquay, TQ2 7AJ   01803 613 143
- Unit 6 Green Lanes Shopping Centre, Barnstaple, EX31 1DD   01271 327 171
- 20-24 Old Town St, Plymouth   01752 661 423
- Green Lanes Shopping Centre, Barnstaple, EX31 1DD   01271 327 171
- Wren Retail Park, Scottsbridge, New Newton, Torquay, TQ2 7HZ   01803 613 143
- Guildhall Shopping Centre, Exeter, EX4 3HJ   01392 259 483
- 20 Old Town Street, Plymouth   01752 661 423
- Unit 10-12 Guildhall Shopping Centre, Exeter, EX4 3HJ   01392 259 483

Nonsuch   01803 835 494
11 Duke Street, Dartmouth, TQ6 0PY

38 shopping

Exmouth Nursery Supplies
at

(now including NEW toy shop)

Car seats, cot beds, highchairs, christening premwear etc.

Hire service on all products - over 50 buggies on display!

11 Exeter Road, Exmouth T: **01395 225 660**
www.baby-equipment-devon.co.uk

Paignton Nursery Furniture 01803 551 889
321c Torquay Road, Paignton, TQ3 2EY
Stock new & second hand nursery goods - cots, highchairs, travel cots, bedding, buggies plus dolls prams & toys, children's chairs. Also have a hire service for most of the equipment.

Scooters (Nursery Goods) 01395 225 660
11 Exeter Rd, Exmouth, EX8 1PN
Huge range of baby goods, both new and to hire. Clothing from 0-6mths, soft shoes. Hire monitors, cots, highchairs, christening gowns & outfits, buggies etc. Also have reconditioned equipment, lots of special offers on old stock and will order in from catalogues.

Second Childhood 01626 202 722
40 Devon Square, Newton Abbot, TQ12 2HH
Nursery goods, backpacks, cots, highchairs, baby sleeping bags and clothes from premature babies to 2yrs.

Tiddleys Treasures 01803 293 111
2 Ellacombe Road, Torquay, TQ1 3AT
Second hand nursery goods & furniture. Also possible to hire equipment.

Tiddleys Treasures 01803 296 000
61 Market St, Torquay, TQ1 3AW
Wide range of nursery goods, if it isn't in store they can order it in. Also stock premature baby clothing.

Tots N Cots 01271 378 840
48a Bear St, Barnstaple, EX32 7DB
Clothing for premature babies up to 9mnths. Cots, bedding and other nursery goods. Also have Christening gowns and outfits, romper suits.

DORSET

A Snow 01305 782 526
12 Frederick Place, Weymouth, DT4 8HQ
Wide range of baby goods and equipment including clothing from 0-2yrs and christening wear (robes, outfits, bibs, tights etc).

Babies R Us 01202 660 406
5-9 Nuffield Road, Nuffield Industrial Estate, Poole, Dorset, BH17 0SS

Baby Birds 01305 853 799
24 St Albans Street, Weymouth, DT4 8BZ

Babygear 01308 422 552
The Old School, Gundry Lane, Bridport, DT6 3RL
Wide range of baby equipment for sale new or to hire.

Discount Baby Equipment 01202 730 630
15 Mansfield Road, Poole, BH14 0DD
Large range of baby equipment at discounted prices. Car seat fitting service.

Just Kidding UK 01202 528 008
317 Wimborne Road, Bournemouth, BH9 2AD
One stop shop for all baby goods and equipment, furniture, bedding, soft toys, clothing from 0-2yrs, natural nappies etc. Also provide a hire service for travel cots, highchairs and pushchairs.

Les Enfants 01202 763 523
11 Seamoor Road, Bournemouth, BH4 9AA
Nursery goods & interiors, bedding, feeding accessories, gro-bags and wide selection of traditional toys, wooden & tin and rocking horses.

Little People
- 219 Seabourne Road, **01202 430 635**
  Bournemouth, BH5 2HL
- 205 Seabourne Road, **01202 425 142**
  Bournemouth, BH5 2HL

New and secondhand baby equipment plus car seat fitting service. Clothing 0-14. Also possible to hire cots, buggies, highchairs etc. Mail order on web site as well as store.

Mothercare
- 9-9a Tudor Arcade, South Street, 01305 251 226
  Dorchester, DT1 1BN
- High Street, Poole, BH15 1ER 01202 680 707
- 104 St Mary's Street, Weymouth 01305 789 266
- 9-9a Tudor Arcade, South St, 01305 251 226
  Dorchester, DT1 1BN
- 17 Falkland Square, Poole 01202 680 707
- 1 Clinton Arcade, Coburg Place, 01305 789 266
  Weymouth, DT4 8HP
- BHS, 48-54 Commercial Road, 01202 555 308
  Bournemouth, BH2 5RL
- 351 Chickerell Rd, Weymouth 01305 779 678

Wide selection of baby goods and equipment also sell factory seconds. Hiring service on travel cots, buggies, highchairs etc. Car seat fitting service

Ragtags **01258 455 707**
29 West Street, Blandford Forum, DT11 7AW
Wide range of baby goods & equipment, available new, second hand or to hire. Also stock baby clothes and gifts.

Please say you saw the listings in
The South West Baby Directory

shopping 39

GLOUCESTERSHIRE
Babies R Us   01452 311 315
Stann Road, Gloucester, GL1 5SF

Mothercare
36 Regent Arcade, Regent Street,   01242 571411
Cheltenham, GL50 1JZ

BHS, 27 - 39 Eastgate Street,   01452 525713
Gloucester, GL1 1YU

New Beginings   01684 274 448
112 High Street, Tewkesbury, GR20 8JA

SOMERSET, BRISTOL & BATH
Babies R Us   0117 959 1430
Cantaurus Road, Patchway, Bristol, BS12 5TQ

Baby Fayre   01934 418746
10-12 Orchard Street, Weston Super Mare, BS23 1RQ

Bibs & Bobs   01373 452 471
3 Catherine Hill, Frome, BA11 1BY
Complete range of baby & nursery equipment including clothing from 0-3yrs and toys.

Born
- 64 Gloucester Road,   **0117 924 5080**
  Bishopston, Bristol, BS7 8BH
- 134 Walcot Street,   **01225 334 434**
  St Swithins Yard, Bath, BA1 5BG

www.borndirect.com
Born offer a comprehensive range of natural and practical product for parents via their two shops in Bath and Bristol, as well as online.

Humpty Dumpty   01275 340671
28 Old Church Road, Clevedon, BS21 6LY

Hurwoods Nursery World   0117 926 2690
32 Old Market Street, Bristol, BS2 0HB
www.hurwoods.co.uk
Established for over 100 years and stockists of all major brands. Fully trained staff and car seat fitting service offered.

Kids Stuff of Wells   01749 676 217
20 Queen St, Wells, BA5 2DP
One stop shop for all baby goods and equipment including car seat fitting service, premature baby clothing up to 9mths, Gro-bags and Inch Blue soft shoes.

Mama Mia   01278 433 255
Unit 2 Fishermans Wharf, West Quay, Bridgwater
Wide selection of quality baby goods and equipment - many European makes and designs of furniture, bedding etc. Silvercross, Maclaren buggies, plus traditional clothing from 0-2yrs (can order in for older children) and toys. They have a Christening Centre, with a complete range of gowns, outfits and gifts.

Mothercare
- Avon Meads Retail Park, St Phillips   **0117 971 9815**
  Causeway, St Phillips Marsh, Bristol, BS2 0SP
- 3 Vicarage Walk,   **01935 478823**
  Quedam Centre, Yeovil, BA20 1EU
- 44 Southgate, Bath, BA1 1TG   **01225 466 245**
- Hankridge Rarm Retail Pk, Taunton   **01823 443 862**
- The Mall, Cribbs Causeway   **0117 950 9760**
  Shopping Centre, Pegasus Road, Bristol, BS12 5DG
- Lower Level, The Mall, Cribb's   **0117 950 9760**
  Causeway, BS34 5DG
- 40-48 Southgate Street, Bath   **01225 466 245**
- 3 Vicarage Walk, Quedam Centre,   **01935 478 823**
  Yeovil, BA20 1EU
- Unit 1, Hankridge Farm Retail Park,   **01823 443 862**
  Taunton, TA1 2YQ
- Units 24-25 Sovereign Centre,   **01934 626 977**
  Weston Super Mare, BS23 1HL
- The Eastgate Centre, Eastville,   **0117 951 8200**
  Bristol, BS5 6XZ

WILTSHIRE
Babies R Us   01793 826 880
Oxford Road, Swindon, SN3 3DG

Eric Snooks - The Golden Cot   01225 463 739
2 Abbey Gate Street, Bath, BA1 1NP

Mothercare
- 41 New Canal, Salisbury, SP1   **01722 333196**
- Unit 9 Greenbridge Retail Park,   **01793 423 595**
  Drakes Way, Swindon, SN3 3SG

Nursery Rhymes   01722 412 872
15 Cross Keys Mall, Salisbury, SP1 1EL

Nursery Thyme   01380 721 747
Wharfside, Couch Lane, Devizes, SN10 1EB
Wide range of baby goods and equipment (Mamas and Papas platinum stockist), clothing, feeding equipment, toys, rocking horses. Also provide a car seat fitting service.

That's My Baby   01793 432 111
14-15 Orbit Centre, Ashworth Road, Swindon
www.thatsmybaby.biz
Wide range of baby goods and equipment including a car seat fitting service (see ad pg 40).

The Baby Carriage   01225 765 279
Castle St, Trowbridge, BA14 8AS
Wide range of baby goods - prams, buggies, highchairs, cots, natural nappies, small range of clothing for 0-12mths (incl. Premature babies), car seats (incl. Fitting service) etc

Please say you saw the listings in
The South West Baby Directory

shopping

New Arrival!
That's My Baby
"because they're only little once"

Everybody knows the excitement a baby brings and we know that like you, your baby is unique, so expect the best.

For a truly individual experience, visit Wiltshire's largest independent specialist nursery store now in Swindon, because we're not tied to a large chain, we stock what's best for you, and not what's best for us!

Come and view our inspirational and extensive range of new born, baby and nursery equipment in a relaxing and comfortable environment.

Our mini department store offers
- Most leading designer names available from stock
- Premature & newborn clothing, toys and gifts
- 7 enchanting nursery room settings including wall papers and co-ordinated bedding & accessories
- Over 100 prams and pushchairs on view
- Over 40 car seats on display
- Exclusive brands
- Christening ware
- 6 days a week, Wed - Mon 9.30-5.00 and Sun 11.00-4.00
- **FREE** convenient parking
- Car seat advice and fitting by trained professionals

We aim to exceed our customers expectations for choice, service and quality.

The alternative world for mother care.

bugaboo

JANE

Silver Cross
SINCE 1877

MOUNTAIN BUGGY

Phil & Teds

out n about
all terrain baby gear

Quinny

Mamas & Papas

STOKKE

That's My Baby,
Unit 14-15 Orbit Centre
Ashworth Road, Bridgemead
Swindon, Wiltshire SN5 7YG
Tel: 01793 432111
Email: info@thatsmybaby.biz
www.thatsmybaby.biz

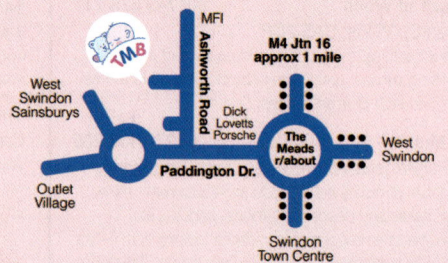

Image courtesy of Brian Shaw Photography.

shopping 41

nursery goods: mail order

Babyworld   01491 821 877
www.babyworld.co.uk
The UK's most efficient and well set-out online store, with customer reviews and articles to help you choose which are the most relevant products for your needs. Good delivery and stock levels. Full range of nursery furniture, prams, pushchairs and accessories.

Blooming Marvellous   0845 458 7408
www.bloomingmarvellous.co.uk
A well-established mail order and internet service providing a large range of everyday maternity basics, baby and children's clothing, as well as nursery goods, furniture, lots of really useful everyday items as well as toys, gifts and some exclusives.

Born   0845 130 2676
www.borndirect.com
One of the leading online sites for natural parenting and organic baby products. Babygowns, blankets, sheets, Nursing bras. Furniture such as Stokke and Trip Trapp. Aromatherapy and homeopathic products.

Great Little Trading Company   0870 850 6000
www.gltc.co.uk
Hundreds of practical products designed to make your life as a parent a great deal easier- catalogue and online.

Hippins   01531 650 843
www.hippins.co.uk
On line - wide range of nursery goods including furniture, blankets & bedding, playhouses, toys, shoes and clothing, nursery Accessories, gifts including Christening gift ideas.

Hippychick   01278 434 440
www.hippychick.com
Innovative range of baby goods and accessories from this much loved brand of children's products.

JoJo Maman Bebe   0870 241 0560
www.jojomamanbebe.co.uk
JoJo's have a great website and mail order catalogue stocking both maternity and childrenswear, as well as a number of practical products for the nursery including linen and other nursery bedroom accessories, bottle and breastfeeding equipment, moving on to many practical toddler items as your baby grows up. They also have a toy and gift section with many exclusives. Highly recommended catalogue and easy-to-use website.

Urchin   0870 112 6006
www.urchin.co.uk
Furniture, nursery goods, travel items, toys, kitchen and bathroom products - all delivered hassle-free. Free catalogue by phone or online.

www.babydirectory.com

---

www.hippins.co.uk

Visit our website for
* personalised gifts
* nursery furniture
* children's bedding
* traditional toys
* Christening gifts

and much more...
come and browse

(01531) 650843
www.hippins.co.uk

Aromakids   Art suits
Bed protectors   Eater suits
Hipseats   Natural blankets   Togz
Shoo Shoos   Wheelybugs

Hippychick

Mail order/Stockists: 01278 434440
www.hippychick.com

shopping

Helen Barnecutt Photography

Capture your baby's first year, absolutely free

Truro: 01872 260422
helenbarnecutt.photography@virgin.net

David McGirr Photography

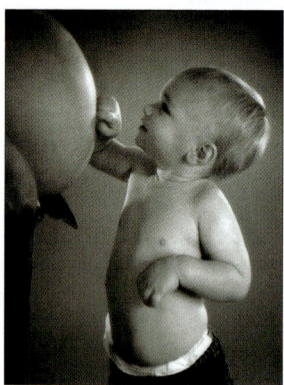

Please call the studio or visit our website for further information.

Chinns Court   Warminster
01985 218625
www.davidmcgirr.com

Sarah North Photography
07970 863154
www.theflyingstudio.com

Unobtrusive photographer capturing delightful and informal moments for you to treasure forever

Kernow Natural Light Photography

T: 01637 873847
27 Rialton Heights, Newquay TR7 3HU
www.kernownaturallightphotography.co.uk

shopping 43

photographers

Images 0845 257 2418
Trowbridge, BA14 7TS

Cameracraft 01872 272480
Truro, Cornwall, TR1 2JB

Kernow Natural Light Photography 01637 873847
Newquay, Cornwall, TR7 3HU

Little Angels / Helen Barnecutt 01872 260422
Trispin, Truro, Cornwall, TR4 9AH

Sarah North Photography 01285 640659
Cirencester, Gloucestershire, GL7 1UR

David McGirr Photography 01985 218465
Warminster, Wiltshire

rocking horses

Quality Rocking Horses 01326 231 053
www.qualityrockinghorses.co.uk
We like their Western saddle and removable tack with coloured numnah. Prices from £825.

Robert Mullis 01793 813 583
www.rockinghorsesmaker.com
Robert Mullis is a craftsman producing traditional rocking horses. In addition to the dappled greys made from hardwoods you can also choose Muffin the Mule, a duck, tortoise or The Loch Ness Monster.

Stevenson Brothers 0808 108 6120
www.stevensonbros.com
Take your pick from the Golden Jubilee dappled grey complete with the Queen's racing colours, or a limited edition of the Serengeti Zebra. Prices start from £700. Website also includes antique rocking horse sales.

shoes: online

Babyworld 01491 821 877
www.babyworld.co.uk
Babyworld stocks lovely Starchild baby shoes, Kaloo boots and TOGZ overboots for when you're out and about. Order online for delivery within 2 working days.

Hippychick 01278 434 440
www.hippychick.com
Their Shoo Shoos are imaginative and refreshingly different, soft leather baby shoes 0-24 months.

Papillon Shoes 020 7834 1504
www.papillon4children.com
Ballerinas, moccasins, Jack Rogers flip flops and canvas mules also available from Semmalina in London's SW3.

Starchild Shoes 01509 817 600
www.starchildshoes.co.uk
Handmade soft leather shoes that stay on. Wonderful designs for boys and girls (0-4yrs).

shoe shops

CORNWALL

Brantano 01872 241 167
Unit 3 The Liskeard Ret Park, Truro, TR1 1LN

John Farmer 01872 272 315
1 Pydar St, Truro, TR1 2AR

John Farmer 01326 572 149
25 Meneage St, Helston, TR13 8AA

Jones Bootmaker 01872 222 576
4-5 Duke Street, Truro, TR1 2QE

Kulfi Kids 01840 211 144
7 Market Place, Camelford, PL32 9PB

The Clarks Shop
- 40 Bank St, Newquay, TR7 1AX 01637 879 290
- 22 Market St, Falmouth, TR11 01326 313 289
- Unit 2 19-21 Fore St, St Austell, PL25 01726 733 30
- 19-20 King St, Truro, TR1 2RQ 01872 277 566

DEVON

Clarks (within Mothercare) 01803 615 404
Wren Ret. Park, New Newton Road, Torquay, TQ2

Derrys Store 01752 303 095
Derrys Cross, Plymouth, PL1 1HA

E. Ridgway 01626 353 156
11-15 Bank St, Newton Abbot, TQ12 2JL

Fields (Clarks) 01395 515 665
The Market Place, Sidmouth, EX10 8AR

Ivor Coram 01363 772 929
25 High Street, Crediton, EX17 3AH

Ivor Coram 01271 342 557
73 Boutport St, Barnstaple, EX31 1SR

Mini-Me (Encore) 01822 611 322
14 Market Street, Tavistock, PL19 0DB

Peter Briggs 01752 662 739
34 Royal Parade, Plymouth, PL1 1DU

Robins Shoes 01769 572 664
79 South Street, South Molton, EX36 4AG

Russell & Bromley 01392 215 614
26 High Street, Exeter, EX4 3LN

Start-rite at Instep 01752 668 940
Debenhams Ltd, Royal Parade, Plymouth, PL1 1SA

shopping

The Clarks Shop
- 14-16 Bampton St, Tiverton, EX16　01884 252 575
- 233 High St, Exeter, EX4 3NE　01392 271 070
- 11 Market Walk, Newton Abbot,　01626 351 460
- 6 Fore Street, Bodmin, PL31 2HQ　01208 756 72
- 3 High St, Sidmouth, EX10 8NL　01395 578 190
- 63-68 High St, Barnstaple, EX31　01271 322 165
- 42 The Parade, Magnolia Court,　01395 277 298
  Exmouth, EX8 1RH
- 42 Cornwall St, Plymouth, PL1　01752 266 447
- 10-12 Crossways Centre, Paignton　01803 551 855
- 89 Union St, Torquay, TQ1 3YA　01803 212 038

DORSET
A Jones & Sons Plc　01202 290 944
9-11 Gervais Place, Bournemouth, BH1 2AN

Cemes Davies　01935 812 283
85 Cheap Street, Sherborne, DT9 3BA

County Shoes　01305 251 555
10 Antelope Walk, Dorchester, DT1 1BE

Douglas Read Ltd　01308 422 744
34 South Street, Bridport, DT6 3NQ

Jones Bootmaker　01202 290 944
9-11 Gervis Place, Bournemouth, BH1 2AN

Little Monsters　01935 812 282
Half Moon Street, Sherborne, DT9 3LN

Matthews Shoe Centre　01202 482 231
25 High Street, Christchurch, BH23 1AB

Parfitt Shoes　01747 852 559
6 Salisbury Street, Shaftesbury, SP7 8EJ

Shoe Tree　01202 887 373
3 Crown Court, Wimborne, BH21 1LP

Simpkin & Son　01202 426 017
193 Seabourne Road, Southbourne, BH5 2HJ

Solemates Shoes　01225 445 345
29 North Street, Wareham, BH20 4AD

The Clarks Shop
- 31-33 High St, Wimborne Minster,　01202 842 148
- 29-30 The Dolphin Centre, Poole,　01202 676 338
- West Mall, Castlepoint,　01202 547 120
  Bournemouth, BH8 9UY
- 16 Commercial Road,　01202 290 109
  Bournemouth, BH2 5LP

Threads & Treads　01202 826 467
5 Station Road, Verwood, BH31 7PY

GLOUCESTERSHIRE
A Jones & Sons　01242 232 432
30-32 The Promenade, Cheltenham, GL50 1LY

Adcock Shoes　01242 515 862
218 Bath Road, Cheltenham, GL53 7ND

AG Meek　01452 525 658
14 Westgate Street, Gloucester, GL1 2NL

Brantano　01452 729 559
Unit 1, Quedgeley Centre, Gloucester, GL2 4RN

George Lewis Footwear　01242 672 040
Church Road, Bishops Cleeve, GL52 8LP

Russell & Bromley　01242 232 762
100 The Promenade, Cheltenham, GL50 1NB

Russell & Bromley　01242 232 762
100 Promenade, Cheltenham, GL50 1NB

Shop 4 Shoes　01452 310 115
3b Peel Centre, St Ann Way, Gloucester, GL1 5SF

Sole Trader　01242 260 044
48a Regent Arcade, Cheltenham, GL50 1JZ

The Clarks Shop
- 110 High Street, Tewkesbury,　01684 292 251
- 4a High St, Stroud, GL5 1AU　01453 764 453
- 9-11 Eastgate St, Gloucester,　01452 521 078
- 9 Castle Street, Cirencester, GL7　01285 653 281
- 191 High St, Cheltenham, GL50　01242 516 050

SOMERSET, BRISTOL & BATH
Brantano　01935 431 888
Unit 3, Sherborne Road, Yeovil, BA21 5BT

Charles Clinkard　0117 959 2484
Lower Level, The Mall at Cribbs Causeway, Bristol, BS34 5GG

Clarks (within Mothercare)　01179 719 860
2 Avonmead Ret Park, Bristol, BS2 0SP

Clarks (within Mothercare)　01823 444 519
1 Hankridge Farm Retail Park, Taunton, TA1 2LR

Clarks Factory Shop　01278 794 668
10a High Street, Burnham on Sea, TA8 1NX

Clarks Factory Shop　01458 842 395
112-114 High St, Street, BA16 0EW

Clarks Factory Shop　01458 843 156
Clarks Village, Street, BA16 0BB

Holbrooks Shoes　0117 962 2478
190 Henleaze Road, Bristol, BS9 4NE

Jones Bootmaker　01823 350 125
12 North Street, Taunton, TA1 1LH

shopping   45

Jones Bootmaker   01225 334 329
19 Cheap Street, Bath, BA1 1NA

Jones Bootmaker   01823 350 125
12 North St, Taunton, TA1 1LH

NSC Wells   01749 670 000
23 Broad Street, Wells, BA5 2DJ

One Small Step One Giant Leap   01929 553 555
5-6 Cheap Street, Bath, BA1 1NE

Russell & Bromley   01225 460 951
16-17 Old Bond Street, Bath, BA1 1BP

Sole Trader   01225 333 998
9 Stall St, Bath, BA1 1QE

Stuart Marsh   01460 720 45
14 Market Street, Crewkerne, TA18 7LB

The Clarks Baggage Factory   01458 843 163
Clarks Village, Street,

The Clarks Shop
- 1 Silver St, Yeovil, BA20 1HN   01935 476 661
- 35 Broadmead, Bristol, BS1 3EU   01179 290 992
- 2 The Parade, Minehead, TA24   01643 705 624
- 118 Upper Level,   01179 592 290
  The Mall Cribbs Causeway, Bristol, BS34 5UP
- 1 High St, Taunton, TA1 3PG   01823 331 998
- 48-54 High St, Keynsham, BS31   01179 864 330
- 10 Union St, Bath, BA1 1RP   01225 462 632

Thomas Ford
- Kingschase Centre, Kingswood,   0117 961 3807
  Bristol, BS15 8LP
- 17 Old Church Road, Clevedon   01275 879512

Trevor Ward   01275 852 406
4 Somerset Square, Nailsea, BS48 1RP

Walking Small, Walking Tall   01373 455 638
10 Palmer Street, Frome, BA11 1DS

WILTSHIRE
Clarks (within Mothercare   01793 536 987
3 Greenbridge Park, Drakes Way, Swindon, SN3

Clarks Factory Shop   01793 523 723
32-36 Kemble Drive, Great Western Outlet Centre,
Swindon, SN2 7AA

Little Big Feet   01380 816 161
79 High Street, Littleton Pannell, Devizes, SN10

R Blaylock   01793 534 271
1-3 Bath Road, Swindon, SN1 4AS

Splosh   01225 700 711
17 Church Street, Melksham, SN12 6LS

The Clarks Shop
- 31 High St, Malmesbury, SN16   01666 825 142
- 133 High St, Marlborough, SN8   01672 514 362
- 22-23 The Brittox, Devizes, SN10   01380 722 976
- 48 Fore St, Trowbridge, BA14 8EJ   01225 752 416
- 9-10 The Brunel Plaza,   01793 521 241
  Swindon, SN1 1LF

swimwear and sun stuff

Baby Banz   01460 281 229
www.babybanz.co.uk
UV protective clothing and sunglasses.

Babyworld   01491 821 877
www.babyworld.co.uk
Arm bands, buoyancy aids, sun protection suits and caps,
wraps and snugs, Happy Nappy, Shade a Babe and Auto
Shade brands. Order online, fast delivery.

Incy Wincy   0118 377 3581
www.incywincy.org
Comprehensive catalogue and website selling buoyancy aids
and swimming accessories.

Kool Sun   01483 417 753
www.koolsun.com
Sun-protective clothing and accessories for children
6mths-12yrs.

P20
www.p20.co.uk
The once-a-day application sun cream for children who are
constantly in and out of water – recommended by many mums.

The Beach Factory   020 8332 7467
www.beachfactory.com
The Beach Factory leads the way with a wide choice of UV
swimwear and sunsuits to protect babies, children and adults
from the sun. Select from a range of styles and fabrics
offering UVF50+ protection by Lion in the Sun, Sposh or Gul.
They also have fun beach bags, pool toys, aqua shoes, wet
suits and a variety of swimming aids.

toy shops

CORNWALL
Adeba Toys & Adeba Nurseryworld   01726 731 99
13 Truro Road, St Austell, PL25 5JE
Two separate stores on the same street, one for Toys and
the other Nursery goods

Blewett's of Hayle   01736 753 012
19 Penpol Terrace, Hayle, TR27 4BQ

Bricknells   01208 770 88
35 Fore Street, Bodmin, PL31 2JD
Wide range of baby goods from toys, cots, prams & books.
Also has a branch in Liskeard

shopping

Early Learning Centre   01872 222 582
23 Victoria Square, Truro, TR1 2SD

Just Toys   01736 799 988
Lifeboat Hill, St Ives, TR26 1LE

Kernow Model Rail Centre   01209 714 099
98 Trelowarren St, Cambourne, TR14 8AN
Complete range of model railways, trainsets. Slot cars, Scalextric etc

More Value   01288 359 061
40-44 Queen St, Bude, EX23 8BB

Toymaster (Millers)   01872 272 452
4 Calenick St, Truro, TR1 5JE
Large store with huge range of toys and models.

Toys in the Wood   01579 350 045
Bartletts, Harrowbarrow, Callington, Pl17 8BP
Open Tues, Thurs, Sat 10-5pm

Wonderland Toys   01326 312 571
18 Arwenack St, Falmouth, TR11 3JD

DEVON

Baby Talk   01837 535 42
20-22 Red Lion Yard, Fore St, Okehampton, EX20
Nursery goods, Toys etc. Wide range of car seats, cots, highchairs, travel cots, toys & clothes.

Bambino's   01271 375 300
12a High St, Barnstaple, EX31 1BG
One stop shop for all baby goods (prams, cots, furnishings, toys etc).

Beach Buoys   01271 870 736
4 West Rd, Woolacombe, EX34 7BW
Broad range of beach goods, inflatables, toys, buckets & spades, armbands. Everything you would need for a day at the beach.

Bears & Beanies   01803 200 052
1 Victoria Parade, Torquay, TQ1 2BB

Coral Reef   01626 778 904
7-8 Hollands Rd, Teignmouth, TQ14 8SR

Davidson's   01626 866 226
12 The Strand, Dawlish, EX7 9PS

Early Learning Centre
- 65 Hign St, Barnstaple, EX31   01271 323 031
- 60 Union St, Torquay, TQ2 5PS   01803 297 364
- 192 High St, Exeter, EX4 3DU   01392 216 154

Henry & Mae   01803 663 634
Unit 16, The Crossways Shopping Centre, Hyde Road, Paignton, TQ4 5BL
Very traditional wooden and more unusual toys, wooden name plaques, personalised height charts, soft toys, childrens books, plus Robeez shoes (0-4), and washable nappies.

Honiton Toy Shop   01404 437 41
85-87 Hign St, Honiton, EX14 1PG
Vast range of toys plus a large arts & crafts section

House of Hardings   01271 373 100
11 Holland Walk, Barnstaple, EX31 1DW
Cuddly toys, Beany Babies & wooden toys

Jackmans Toy Box   01626 778 755
9A Teign St, Teignmouth, TQ14 8EA
Wide range of toys and fancy dress costumes. Anything they don't stock they can order in.

Kingswear Bears & Friends   01803 752 632
2a The Square, Kingswear, Dartmouth, TQ6 0AA

Magical Planet   01392 879 297
79 Fore St, Topsham, EX3 0HQ
Small shop stocking toys, puppets, books, kites etc all with a Wildlife theme.

North Devon Activity Toys   01271 345 888
Combrew Farm, Combrew, Bickington, Barnstaple,

Puddleducks   01395 515 999
Baskerville House, Old Fore St, Sidmouth, EX10

Rainbow Toys   01392 412 969
Unit 6 & 9, The Harlequin Centre, Paul St, Exeter,
Two stores within the Harlequin Centre, one stocking traditional toys and the other childrens clothing from 0-10, also fancy dress - Lucy Lockett, Angelina Ballerina, fairy costumes, mermaids etc

Rainbow Trading   01395 275 666
20 High St, Exmouth, EX8 1NP
Traditional Toys & Wooden Toys. Clothing from 0-10, boutique range but affordable prices.

Swings & Roundabouts   01822 852 053
Stroll, Yeoland Lane, Yelverton, PL20 6BX
Swings, Trampolines etc

Taylors Super Toys   01395 277 879
6 & 7 Magnolia House, Church St, Exmouth, EX8

The Model Shop   01392 421 906
4 St Davids Hill, Exeter, EX4 3RG
Stockists of Thomas the Tank Engine

The Toy Cupboard   01271 863 598
128 High St, Ifracombe, EX34 9EY

The Toy Shop   01363 773 444
32 East St, Crediton, EX17 3AX
Wide range of toys, Mamas & Papas, Little Tikes, wooden toys, musical toys, Disney etc.

The Tree House   01548 844 133
61b Fore St, Salcombe, TQ8 8ET
Range of traditional toys, soft toys, Zapf dolls, Lego, Jellycat range etc.

shopping 47

The Wood Shop 01803 200 157
Unit 4H, The Winter Gardens, Fleet Walk, Torquay

Toy Town 01803 292 029
34 Lucius Street, Torquay, TQ2 5UN

Toys Plus 01803 212 140
Unit 6 Torquay Market, Market St, Torquay, TQ1
Wide range of toys - lower price bracket (Thomas the Tank Engine, Postman Pat, Bob the Builder + baby toys, model kits etc)

Toys 'R' Us 01752 226 161
Western Approach, Flora St, Plymouth, PL1 1TQ

Toysale 01803 200 958
80 Fleet St, Torquay, TQ2 5EB

Toyzone 01805 624 790
3 Fore St, Torrington, EX38 8HQ

Tridias Toys 0870 420 8631
The Cider Press Centre, Shinners Bridge, Dartington, TQ9 6JB
Traditional, independently-run toy shop (wooden & educational toys) plus childrens books

Whoopee 01752 225 030
74 Royal Parade, Plymouth, PL1 1EW

Youings Toy Box 01271 377 386
72 Boutport St, Barnstaple, EX31 1SR
Also do fancy dress for children & adults

DORSET
The Toy Box 01258 475 100
Market Place, Sturminster Newton, DT10 1AS
Small shop stocking wide range of toys and also x-branded high street children's clothing

Early Learning Centre 01202 668 737
Unit 28 The Dolphin Centre, Poole, BH15 1SS

Early Learning Centre 01202 249 200
75 Old Christchurch Road, Bournemouth, BH1 1EW

Early Learning Centre 01305 761 348
34 St Mary St, Weymouth, DT4 8PN

Formative Fun 01308 868 999
Education House, Horn Park Business Centre, Broadwindsor Road, Beaminster, DT8 3TT

Jammy Joes Toy Shop 01202 745 723
93 Commercial Road, Poole, BH14 0JD
Creative, Discovery & Thinking toys. Arts & Crafts, Ride-on toys, wooden toys, musical & Angelina Ballerina dressing up costumes

Myriad Natural Toys 01725 517 085
The Buckman Building, 43 Southampton Road, Ringwood, BH24 1HE
Handcrafted wooden toys, unique collection of natural toys and arts/crafts materials

Tails from the Woods 01202 841 676
9 West St, Wimborne, BH21 1JP
Traditional wooden toys, baby range including rattles & soft toys. Also stock small wooden nursery goods (height charts, mobiles etc)

The Toy Barn 01935 815 040
Blackmarsh Farm, Dodds Cross, Sherborne, DT9 4JX
Full range of toys from 0-8yrs. Soft toys, Mecano, Lego, wooden toys. Outdoor play equipment - castles, swings, slides & trampolines. Also have a paddock where you can try things out.

Toys Games Models 01202 531 919
336 Wimborne Road, Winton, Bournemouth, BH9
Small supply of pre-school educational toys and wooden toys

Toys 'R' Us 01202 660 406
5-9 Nuffield Rd, Nuffield Industrial Estate, Poole

GLOUCESTERSHIRE
Cheltenham Activity Toys 01242 621 223
April Cottage, 39 Newtown, Toddington, Cheltenham, GL54 5DU
Open all year 10am to 5pm for wonderful range of outdoor activity toys, including TP Activity Toys, Hout-Land. Swings, slides, sandpits etc sold from home with large garden to try out and see all the products. NB Oct to Feb open by appointment only.

Crocodile Toy Shop 01285 656 050
4 The Woolmarket, Cirencester, GL7 2PR
Traditional toy shop owned by an ex-teacher with emphasis on good "play value". Caters for all ages but specialises in 0-5 yr olds. Wooden toys, beautiful dolls, dolls houses, Sylvanian Families, Playmobile, Lego etc. Super quality products covering two floors of large shop.

Early Learning Centre 01452 428 667
Debenhams, Kings Square, Gloucester, GL1 1SH
The well-known specialist retailer of toys for pre-school children. Open 9am to 5.30pm. Located in Lower Ground Floor of the store, open 9am to 6pm five days a week, 11am to 5pm Sunday.

Early Learning Centre 01242 576 230
6-8 Pittville Street, Cheltenham, GL52 2LJ
The well-known specialist retailer of toys for pre-school children. Open 9am to 5.30pm.

Henrietta's House 01666 505 267
21 Market Place, Tetbury, GL8 8DD
Traditional shop specialising in educational toys from 0-8 years old. Brands stocked include Haba, Pin Toy, Plan Toys, Brio, Playmobile, Lucy Locket dressing-up clothes, Carolle Dolls, My Doll, Jelly-Cat, Kaloo, Moulin-Roty. Open 10am to 5pm Tues to Sat, and 10am to 1.30pm on Mon.

Hoggosaurus Toy Store 01454 326 566
3 West Walk, Yate, BS37 4AX
Broad range of both indoor and outdoor toys.

shopping

Jumblies   01453 520 394
42 Long Street, Wootton-Under-Edge, GL12 7BT
New traditional toy shop. Associate Member of Toymakers Guild. Specialises in hand crafted toys, wooden toys, Brio, John Crane, Jack-in-a-Box Company, Moulin-Roty. Small shop, packed to the gunnels! Open 10am to 5pm six days a week.

The Toy Shop   01608 650 756
High Street, Moreton-in-Marsh, GL56 0AD
Family-owned shop for last 56 years. Whole range of toys from over 250 invidividual stockists, including Vtech, Brio, Lego. Open 9am to 5pm five days a week (except Tuesday), closed 1pm to 2pm for lunch.

Toys 'R' Us   01452 311 315
St Ann Way, Winget Estate, Gloucester, GL1 5SF
Enormous toy superstore. Other branches Bristol, Cardiff. Open 9am to 10pm, Sunday 11am to 5pm.

Toyzone   01684 295 776
102 High Street, Tewkesbury, GL20 5JZ
Open 9am to 5pm five days a week. Small high street shop packed with products of all major brands, including Vtech, Mattel, Duplo, Fifi and the Flower Tots, dolls, dolls accessories, dressing-up clothes.

SOMERSET, BRISTOL & BATH

Chipper Toys Ltd   01373 464 141
82d Keyford, Frome, BA11 1JJ

Class Creations   01934 740 240
The Lippiatt, Cheddar Gorge, Cheddar, BS27 3QP
Quality Toys; traditional wooden toys, educational and nursery toys & children's books

Early Learning Centre
- 17 Old Market Centre,   01823 259 647
  Taunton, TA1 3TP
- 26 Vicarage Walk,   01935 471 741
  Quedarn Centre, Yeovil, BA20
- 7-8 Cheap Street, Bath   01225 466 321
- The Mall, Cribbs Causeway,   01179 50 8775
  Bristol, BS34 5GF
- 23 Broadmead Gallery,   01179 268 645
  Broadmead, Bristol, BS1
- Unit 8 The Sovereign Centre,   01934 643 474
  High Street, Weston-Super-Mare, BS23 1HL

Eastermead Activity Toys   01934 823 926
Eastermead Farm, Eastermead Lane, Banwell
Every sort of outdoor toy imaginable - trampolines, swings, slides, chess sets, climbing frames, playhouses, forts and dolls houses, ride-on toys and rocking horses.

GW Hurley   01278 789 281
27 High St, Burnham-on-Sea, TA8 1PA

Hurcott Toys   01460 240 160
Hurcott, Ilminster, TA19 0JS
Traditional wooden toys & jigsaw puzzles. Also stock outdoor toys - wooden climbing frames, trampolines & go-carts.

JJ's Toymaster   01934 418 151
44 Regent Street, Weston-Super-Mare, BS23 1SL

JJ's Toymaster   01275 341 819
4c Kenn Road, Clevedon, BS21 6EL

Just So   01179 743 600
12 Regent Street, Clifton, Bristol, BS8 9AU
Traditional toy shop stocking lots of wooden toys, Brio train sets, puzzles, soft baby shoes, children's crockery sets and books.

Little Imps   01458 830 099
8b Market Place, Glastonbury, BA6 9HW
Very traditional & quality toyshop specialising in wooden toys, spinning tops, games etc, also stock children's books

Pinocchio Toys   01643 822 123
13 High Street, Dunster, TA24 6SF
A classic, educational based toy shop, stocking 60% wooden toys and also Playmobil, Lego, ride-on toys, castles, forts, baby toys and educational books.

Small World   01984 641 122
Washford Mill, Abbey Road, Washford, Watchet
Traditional toy shop stocking a wide range of toys - lots of wooden toys, train sets, boats, ride-on toys etc.

Taunton Toys   01823 272 330
18 High Street, Taunton, TA1 3PJ

The Entertainer
Open 9.30am-5.30pm Mon-Sat. Until 8pm on Thurs. Closed Sun.
- 40 High Street, Keynsham   0870 905 5111
- 80 High Street, Midsomer Norton   0870 905 5112
- 30 Broadmead Gallery, Bristol   0870 905 5108
- Unit 1-3, 30-36 West Walk,   0870 905 5134
  Yate Shopping Centre, Bristol
- 36 Middle Street, Yeovil   0870 905 5118

The Gorge Bear Co   01934 743 333
Unit 9 Queens Row, 9 Cliff Street, Cheddar, BS27
Probably the UK's largest Specialist Teddy Bear Store - including many infamous and exclusive brands. Other branches: 20 Lower Middle Street, Taunton, Somerset, TA1 1SF. Tel 01823 332 050

The Toy Box   01275 851 516
61 High Street, Nailsea, BS48 1AW

The Toy Cupboard   01278 782 960
1 Pier St, Burnham-on-Sea, TA8 1BT
Beach Toys

Tick Top Toyshop   01823 257 070
4 St James Street, Taunton, TA1 1JH
A traditional toy shop specialising in toys for younger children and in particular under 3s. Large range of wooden toys, dolls houses, castles etc and other educational toys.

shopping 49

Totally Toys   01179 423 833
109 Gloucester Road, Bishopston, BS7 8AT

Toys R Us   01179 591 43 0
Centaurus House, Cribbs Causeway, Patchway, Bristol, BS34 5TU

Tridias Toys   0870 420 8630
124 Walcot Street, Bath, BA1 5BG

Watkin Toys   01823 272 549
6 East Reach, Taunton, TA1 3EN

Wells Toys   01643 705 550
45 The Avenue, Minehead, TA24 5BB
Extensive range of toys for all ages. Other branch: Union Street, Wells Tel: 01749 675 262.

WILTSHIRE

Aladdins Cave   01249 822 064
12 Phelps Parade, Calne, SN11 0HA
Range of toys from 0 upwards (incl. Wooden toys, soft toys, rattles)

Ducks Toyshop   01672 512 170
114 High St, Marlborough, SN8 1LT

Early Learning Centre   01793 831 300
1-2 Brunel Plaza, Swindon, SN1 1LF

Early Learning Centre   01722 337 551
16-18 High St, Salisbury, SP1 2NW

Early Learning Centre   01225 774 223
Unit 45 The Shires, Trowbridge, BA14 8AT

Hamleys of London   01793 538 500
Great Western Designer Village, Kemble Drive, Swindon, SN2 2DZ

Mad About Toys   01985 214 550
20 Three Horseshoe Walk, Warminster, BA12 9BT

Parfitts Books & Toys   01985 214 418
32 High St, Warminster, BA12 9AF
Wide range of toys, mainly wooden and children's books

Rainbows   01722 322 730
57 Estcourt Rd, Salisbury, SP1 3AS
Second hand toy shop

SPS   01249 813 560
1 William Street, Calne, SN11 9BB
Traditional toy shop stocking toys from the past plus wooden toys, pocket money toys, soft toys, board games.

SPS   01666 824 440
11 High St, Malmesbury, SN16 9AA

The Baby Carriage   01225 703 204
11 Bank St, Melksham, SN12 6LE
Stock a small range of goods - buggies, cloth nappies, moses baskets and toys.

The Disney Store   01793 617 771
Unit 2 The Lock, Canal Walk, Swindon, SN1 1LD

The Entertainer   0870 905 5110
45 Blue Boar Row, Salisbury, SP1 1DA
Open 9.30am-5.30pm Mon-Sat. Until 8pm on Thurs. Closed Sun.

The Entertainer   01722 327 333
45 Blue Boar Row, Salisbury, SP1 1DA
Pre-school section, arts & crafts, puzzles, jigsaws and range of sit-on toys

The Toy Shop   01225 768 415
Castle St, Trowbridge, BA14 8AS

Toys 'R' Us   01793 826 880
Oxford Rd, Swindon, SN3 4DG

toys: early development

Baby Einstein   020 8222 1571
www.babyeinstein.co.uk
Baby Einstein is an award-winning range of DVDs, videos, music CDs, books and toys that parents can share with their baby for early play and discovery.

Brainy Baby Company   01678 762 1100
www.brainybaby.com
Educational videos for children aged 6mths-5yrs.

Bright Minds   0870 442 2144
www.brightminds.co.uk
Educational toys for young children.

Child's Play   01793 616 286
www.childs-play.com
Child's Play has developed an award-winning series of baby books which help contribute to a lifelong love of reading.

Smart Baby Zone   0845 060 7786
www.smartbabyzone.co.uk
Smart Baby Zone is a new online company specialising in developmental and educational products for 0-5yrs.

Zapf Creation   0845 053 3333
www.zapf-creation.com
Every little girl's favourite, a real baby to wash, dress, feed and comfort – perfect toy when junior sibling arrives.

toys: online

Babyworld   01491 821 877
www.babyworld.co.uk
Babyworld stocks a massive range of cot, soft, wooden, ride-on and rocking toys. Order online for delivery within 2 working days.

Hippychick wheelybugs   01278 434 444
www.hippychick.com
Award-winning ride-on toys (see ad pg 41).

www.babydirectory.com

shopping

Loddon Valley Garden Toys 0845 644 1546
www.lvgt.co.uk
Leading brands of outdoor play equipment for all your family, including swings, slides, climbing frames, wooden playsets, sandpits, tampolines and more.

Wooden Train Sets 02380 898 085
& Accessories
www.woodentrainsets.co.uk
Brio-compatible train sets, bridges, tunnels, trains, track, buildings, competitive prices, fully secure website.

Win Green Company 01622 746 516
www.wingreen.co.uk
Little Gretels will be the envy of their pals with Win Green's Gingerbread Play House, made from appliquéd and embroidered cotton, with lace curtains. Perfect for bedrooms and playrooms, and can move outside for the summer. Many more designs.

travel and changing bags

Groovy Mummy 020 8650 1286
www.groovymummy.co.uk
Refreshingly stylish accessories including luxurious changing bags. We love their contemporary fabrics.

The Handbag Bar at Akino 020 7434 9999
www.handbagbar.com
The Handbag Bar is both a retail shop in London's fashionable Carnaby Street as well as offering a mail order service nationally. It's a unique proposition, representing choice and versatility, offering discerning women the opportunity to design their own handbags which are then tailored to their individual tastes. Their selection of baby travel and changing bags are crafted to look like designer bags and are made in various materials/fabrics such as cashmere, linen, silk brocade, suede. They vary in price range from £80-£150.

Hippychick Health Back 01278 434 440
Baby Bag
www.hippychick.com
A totally organised ergonomic shaped bag with contours to the body.

Caboodle Bags 01795 590 664
www.caboodlebags.co.uk
Nappy changing bags designed with great flair and practicality.

travel cots

You might ask whether this is a really necessary purchase, but everyone we've spoken to has one and has found it perfect during those early years, when you can take baby with you for the evening instead of hiring a babysitter. The pop-up models are even better for holidays as they weigh next to nothing and act both as a playpen and a cot

Graco 0870 909 0501
www.graco.co.uk
Two models, the Compact and the Contour. Very easy to assemble and relatively compact when folded away. Wheels help you manoeuvre them around and they can double-up as a playpen. The Contour comes with a bassinet which acts as a changing unit - very helpful for holidays abroad.

Nomad Travel Tent 01273 622 993
One of the lightest travel cots on the market, this is pricey compared to others. It squashes down into your suitcase and isn't bulky to store at home. It has side access which is great - because lifting a sleeping 3yr old is almost impossible.

Samsonite Pop-Up Bed 01746 769 676
www.baby-travel.com
From 0-6mths this pop-up travel cot is perfect for weekends or when dining with friends. It's very lightweight and folds away into its own hand carry bag.

twins and multiples

One of your major purchases will be a double pushchair where you will need to consider the needs of your lifestyle over the demands of the pushchair. But there is no doubt that you need to take advantage of all the special discounts that stores offer - ie join up to TAMBA (see helplines)

Lots of Babies 0161 740 9979
www.lotsofbabies.com
Specialists in prams, buggies and pushchairs for twins and triplets and more.

Twins Things 01600 715 146
www.twinsthings.co.uk
A wide range of poducts and gifts with an emphasis on things for Twins and Triplets and more.

United Twindom 07931 296 027
www.unitedtwindom.co.uk

The Handbag Bar
at Akino
Create the perfect baby changing bag for your new edition at the Handbag Bar at Akino or online at
www.handbagbar.com
2.15 Kingly Court, Carnaby Street London, W1B 5PW
Tel: 0207 434 9999

Every month we send out an e-newsletter reviewing new products with giveaways and competitions. So don't forget to register at www.babydirectory.com

childcare

Finding the right childcare is a potential minefield. Full-time nanny, mother's help or au pair? Through word of mouth, small ad in the local paper or a scribbled card in a shop window? While such methods of finding help may yield happy results, childcare is one area where you don't want to take risks. In this section we recommend professional agencies that will find you a nanny, maternity nurse or other carer with proper qualifications, experience and references.

52 childcare

au pair agencies

The majority of au pairs are aged between 17-25, and are admitted from non-EC countries, and work for around 6 months. Expect to pay between £35-£45 per week, in exchange for around 25hrs work of light houseworlk, childcare and babysitting. They are not suitable for sole care of babies and young children. The agencies below will do a lot of the hard work for you in terms of selecting suitable and reliable candidates and verifying all their details.

Bohemia Aupairs   01202 828 886
Au Pair agency specializing in placement of Czech and Slovak Au pairs. Also supply nannies, mothers help, housekeepers. Covers all parts of England, Wales, Scotland. Alexandra King, the director of the company speaks several languages inc. English. Czech, Slovak, Polish and Russian. Quality of staff is guaranteed. At interviews, referenceds, police, medical records checked.

A-One Au-Pairs & Nannies   01264 332 500
Karen Hopwood started A One Au Pairs and Nannies in 1997. The agency places aupairs nationwide, in Europe and the USA. It is a very professional agency which still manages to retain a personal feel. Karen is a founder of The British Au Pairs Agency Association, and also a member of The International Au Pairs Association, and all childcarers are CRB (Criminal Records Bureau) checked.

Genevieve Browne Au Pairs   01202 385 014
Genevieve Brown is an experienced and long-standing aupair agency selecting girls who want to come and stay with English families across various locations within the South of England, including (but not limited to) London, Oxford, Wiltshire, Avon, Dorset, Bath, Bournemouth and Poole.. They are very good at assessing both the needs of families as well as the aspirations of their girls which ensures a happy match.

Belaf   01249 812 551
www.belaf.com
Sisiter company of Genevieve Browne, Belaf puts English families in touch with girls (aged 17yrs+) who want to spend the holidays in England as part of their language studies. As an 'Aide-Maman' parents host the girls in exchange for help around the house and with the family. There is no cost to families.

babysitters

Reclaim your social life! We suggest that you develop between 3-4 babysitting contacts so that you can go out when a last-minute invitation arrives or when spontaneity strikes. For peace of mind you should check candidate references yourself to ensure that you are satisfied. Current rates are around £5-£7 per hr + taxi home after midnight.

Genevieve Browne Au Pairs

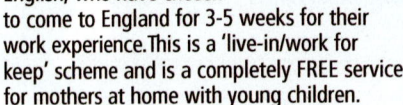

SUMMER HOLIDAY 'AIDE-MAMAN' SCHEME
French college or university students (17-19 yrs), studying English, who have chosen to come to England for 3-5 weeks for their work experience. This is a 'live-in/work for keep' scheme and is a completely FREE service for mothers at home with young children.

AU PAIRS FOR WORKING MOTHERS
Both long-term and also summer holiday (4-10 weeks) placements. Carefully vetted girls and modest placement fees.

Contact Carole to discuss your requirements:
Tel: 01249 812551
Email: Carole@genevievebrowne.co.uk

Au pairs ~ Nannies
Mother's helps ~ Babysitter
Couples ~ Live-in carers
Housekeepers ~ Cleaners

01202 828886
0800 0276829
24/7 Service

BOHEMIA KING
Discerning child & Homecare

Register on-line
www.bohemiaking.co.uk

Head office: 2 Holly Grove, Verwood, Dorset, BH31 6XA

childcare 53

Looking for Childcare?

We offer FREE, up to date, impartial advice and guidance on registered childminders, nurseries, playgroups, pre-schools, out of school clubs and holiday play schemes, creches and lots more

There is a shortage of childcare, play and youth workers, especially men, disabled people and those over 40

Have you thought about being a registered childminder, creche worker, play worker?

Do you have a young family and need a job that fits around them?

Need information on FREE early education places for 3 and 4 year olds?

Are you a parent or carer of a disabled child who would like support and advice?

Are you approaching retirement but still have a lot to give?

For more information please call the information service in the area you live, or work in.

Bath and North East Somerset Family Information Service **Tel: 0800 0731214**
www.bathnes.gov.uk/fis

Children's Information Service for Bristol **Tel: 0845 129 7217** www.cisbristol.co.uk

South Gloucestershire Children's Information Service **Tel: 01454 868008**
www.southglos.gov.uk/ed/cis

North Somerset Childcare Information Service **Tel: 01275 888778**

For other areas phone 08000 960296 or www.childcarelink.gov.uk

jobcentreplus

childcare

Alphabet Childcare   0117 959 1161
Provide regular babysitters in an around Bristol and Bath or for a one off occasion (weddings/hotels). Parents need to sign up with an initial fee and then they pay the babysitter direct. Temporary and permanent and all of them are vetted as they if were nannies.

councils & childminders

Your local council has the most up-to-date lists of childcare and vacancies for childminders in your area. Childminders usually offer childcare between 7.30am–7pm, in a homely environment with the added socialising benefits of a nursery.

CORNWALL
Cornwall Family Information Service   0800 587 8191
Main source for all Ofsted registered childcare and other family services and support organisations throughout the county, as well as holiday activities from 0-19yrs. They also work closely with employers and the childcare voucher scheme. You can get one-to-one advice either via their freephone number or at their drop-in shop at 61 Lemon Street, Truro.

DEVON
Devon & Torbay CIS   01392 385 535
www.devon.gov.uk/disc
Providing up-to-date information on all aspects of childcare in the Devon and Torbay areas (see ad pg 53).

Plymouth CIS   0800 783 4259
www.childcarelink.gov.uk/plymouth

DORSET
Bournemouth CIS	01202 456 222
Dorset CIS	01305 228 451
Poole	01202 261 999

GLOUCESTERSHIRE
Gloucestershire CIS	0800 5420 202
South Gloucestershire CIS	01454 868 666

www.southglos.gov.uk/ed/cis
Offering FREE, up-to-date, impartial advice and guidance on registered childminders, nurseries, playgroups, out of school clubs and holiday play schemes, creches and lots more.

SOMERSET, BRISTOL & BATH
Bath & NE Somerset CIS   0800 073 1214
www.bathnes.gov.uk/fis

Bristol CIS   0845 129 7217
www.cisbristol.co.uk

North Somerset CIS   01275 888 778
www.childcarelink.gov.uk

Somerset CIS   0845 600 7171

WILTSHIRE
Swindon CIS	01793 541 786
Wiltshire CIS	08457 585 072

doulas

Doulas, usually mothers themselves, have trained to help a mother before and after birth particularly with getting breastfeeding off to a good start as well as running the house and keeping things together generally. Like having your Mum but without the "in my day"…

British Doula Association   020 7244 6053
www.britishdoulas.co.uk
Provides a code of practice and training to British doulas.

maternity nurses and nannies

Specialising in the care of newborns, a maternity nurse will look after your baby on return from hospital, allowing you to rest. Normally, they are on call 24hrs a day with one day off per week

Rachel's Babies   01392 811 559
Rachel is just the sort of person you would want to ring up when you need a bit of guidance. Her many clients include Hollywood stars, London's elite as well as a number of MPs. Gwyneth Paltrow swears by her "flexible routine" approach drawn from over 30yrs as a maternity nurse. In addition to telephone calls and visits, she has recently published The Baby Book in which she unveils all her wise tips for mums during those early weeks with a new baby.

Mayfair Maternity   08704 423 262
www.mayfairmaternity.com
Maternity nurses, baby nurses, specialists in newborn infant and postpartum care - placing UK and overseas. All newborn care catered for including 1st babies, multiples and preemies 0+ .

Rachel's Babies
Exclusive Maternity Services

Rachel Waddilove NNEB
Experienced Maternity Nurse

- Will live in or visit daily
- Telephone advice
- Newborns to 1 year

Kingsford House, Longdown, Exeter EX6 7SE
Phone and fax   01392 811 559
Mobile   07974 743 303

childcare 55

midwives: independent

Sue Learner: 0117 927 6131
Independent Midwife
Sue's well-established midwifery practice of 17 years standing, based on 30 years midwifery experience, offers continuity of care at home for women throughout Bristol and outside the city. She has good links with obstetricians, health visitors, acupuncturists, homeopaths etc and will refer if necessary. Call her for a chat or to arrange a free informal meeting.

nanny agencies

ABC Poppins 01793 815 313
A professional, friendly, specialist nanny agency, established in 1994. They carefully place permanent and temporary, live-in and daily nannies, mothers helps, maternity nurses, nursery nurses and domestic staff (including couples) in the UK and overseas.

Alphabet Childcare 0117 959 1161
This agency, established for over 16 years, offers a fully comprehensive nanny service across Bath, Bristol, Somerset, Gloucestershire and Wiltshire. They have strong links with childcare colleges in Bristol and candidates return again and again. They can find temporary and permanent nannies, night nannies, maternity nannies, part-time and full-time nannies. They also provide Tax and NI services. But if you are looking for just a weekend requirement such as a wedding/conference then they have links with a creche company "The ABC childcare Crew" - see the website www.abcchildcarecrew.co.uk for more info.

Cheltenham Nannies 01242 680 999
www.cheltenhamnannies.co.uk
This agency was established in 1994 by Lynne Shrub and is both proactive and professional. They provide parents with a model employment contract and guidance for the job description to ensure a high quality response from candidates. And she only produces candidates for interview who meet the parent's specific experience and qualifications. All candidates are CRB checked and interviewed.

Eden Nannies 0845 128 4279
www.eden-nannies.co.uk
The complete childcare solution.

Sheila's Nannies 01392 256 203
A proactive and professional nanny agency. They provide parents with a model employment contract and guidance for the job description to ensure a high quality response from candidates. Oonly producing candidates for interview who meet the parent's specific experience so no time is wasted.

Tinies Childcare Head Office 020 7384 0322
Tinies Childcare: Bristol 01173 005 630
Tinies Childcare: Bath & Wilts 01672 564 744
Highly professional childcare agency supplying nannies, nursery nurses, maternity nurses as well as part-time and temporary nannies.in the South West. They also offer first aid courses and nanny training. You might also be interested in a new "emergency" childcare service which allows you to drop your children at a local asquith nursery - but you need to pre-register.

- No registration fees
- All applicants vetted with references

Carefully placing quality permanent and temporary staff

Live-in/out
Nannies • Mother's Help • Maternity Nurses • Nursery Staff • Babysitters
Couples: Housekeepers/Gardeners

01793 815 313

Email: poppins@mac.com
6 Beranburh Field,
Wroughton SN4 0QL

Providing Caring Hands

Helping little acorns become great oaks

Tel: 0845 230 1955
See our vacancies & register online:
www.cheltenhamnannies.co.uk

Sheila's Nannies

Providing: Nannies, Nanny shares, Maternity Nannies, Mother's helps, regular babysitters and a Wedding crèche service.

Qualified and experienced nannies available and required.

Telephone: 01392 256203
Email: sheilasnannies@hotmail.com

childcare

eden nannies
complete childcare solutions

Eden Nannies specialises in offering a wide range of childcare options to suit our client's individual needs. Our experienced consultants will listen to your requirements and offer professional advice and tailor made solutions. All of our candidates are personally interviewed by one of our consultants. We thoroughly vet and check all references and qualifications prior to registering any candidates.

Daily Nannies
Full time, Part time, Permanent, Temporary
In London and throughout the UK

Live-In Nannies
Full time, Part time, Permanent, Temporary
In London and throughout the UK

Mother's Help
Full time, Part time, Permanent, Temporary
In London and throughout the UK

Overseas Nannies
Experienced Nannies looking for opportunities to work in worldwide locations

Maternity Nurses
Full time, Nightly, Daily Temporary Care
In London and throughout the UK

Maternity Nannies
Full time, Nightly, Daily Temporary Care
In London and throughout the UK

Nursery Placements
In London and surrounding counties

118 Piccadilly, Mayfair,
London W1J 7NW
Tel: 0845 1284279
Fax: 0845 1284281
Email: info@eden-nannies.co.uk
www.eden-nannies.co.uk
Nearest Tube Station:
Green Park Tube

Why not visit our web site for more details or call...
0845 1284279

childcare 57

Tinies
Childcare for the modern world

Over 25 years experience, with more branches and more childcarers than anyone else

- Nannies
- Maternity Nannies
- Mothers Helps
- Emergency / Temporary Childcare

Tel: 0800 783 6070
www.tinies.co.uk

Unit 14, 126-128 New Kings Rd, London SW6 4LZ

nanny share

Sharing Care   020 7384 4971
www.sharingcare.co.uk
A website that puts families in touch with each other so they can share their childcare needs. You need to register for a small charge which then puts you in touch with neighborouging families.

nanny payroll services

If you've never seen the small binder that encompasses the PAYE tax tables then we do recommend you value your time highly and delegate all responsibility for calculating tax to one of the services below. Sanity could at least be your upside

NannyTax   0845 226 2203
PO Box 988, Brighton BN2 1BY
www.nannytax.co.uk
Nannytax is the UK's leading payroll service for parents employing a nanny.

Taxing Nannies   020 8882 6847
28 Minchenden Crescent, N14 7EL
www.taxingnannies.co.uk
London's leading payroll agency for employers of nannies.

nannytax⁺
Payroll **plus** for parents & nannies

- The UK's leading payroll support service for parents employing nannies
- Unlimited advice and guidance on all payroll and employment law issues
- Specialists in nannyshares
- Managed by the IPPM Manager of the Year
- Subscribe now and receive £250 tax rebate from the Inland Revenue

www.nannytax.co.uk • 0845 226 2203

58 childcare

HEALTHVISITORS.COM

Ask A Health Visitor

about

your infants, toddlers and small children

education

These days, education starts young. Here you'll find everything from day nurseries caring for almost-newborns, to formal nursery schools and pre-preps. We have listed all independent (ie private) nursery schools, day nurseries, Montessori and bilingual nurseries, in postcode order, to help parents find places that offer high-quality childcare and an early education. Compulsory education in the UK starts at 5yrs, but before that the following categories of care are on offer:

Day Nurseries: ages 3mths-5yrs; open 8am-6pm and for 48 or more weeks of the year. This includes catering for breakfast, lunch and tea, following the sleep routines set by parents, and gradually being introduced to a more structured day of music, play, painting, stories and outdoor games.

Nursery Schools: ages 2-5yrs; offer sessional care (ie 9am-12pm and/or 2pm-4pm), and are open on a termtime basis. Often attached to pre-prep schools.

Activities include music, play, painting, stories, games as well as early number and letter learning.

Montessori: many nurseries use Montessori methods, a system devised by Maria Montessori in 1907, which emphasises training of the senses and encouragement rather than a rigid academic curriculum

Bilingual Nurseries: these offer care either on a day nursery or nursery school basis, but have the additional advantage of your child being exposed to two languages. Children are gradually introduced to their second language through songs and simple instructions and within a term are happily conversing in either language.

Pre-Prep Schools, which prepare your child for big school at 7, have an S alongside their listing.

We have not listed **playgroups** as the parent or carer remains in attendance. For registered parent and toddler groups contact your local council (see page 204).

For nearly all nurseries and schools in the private sector, early registration is highly recommended, so ring, visit with babe in arms and register ahead of time, even if you later decide not to pursue that option. For a list of state-run nurseries, ie state primary schools with nursery classes, contact your local Council.

60 education (Cornwall postcodes)   S = SCHOOL

PAGES	
CORNWALL	pg 60-70
DEVON	pg 70-88
DORSET	pg 88-100
GLOUCESTERSHIRE	pg 100-115
SOMERSET, BATH & BRISTOL	pg 115-132
WILTSHIRE	pg 132-142

CORNWALL

EX22
Acorns Playgroup 01288 341 241
Oak Lane, Whitstone, Holsworthy, EX22 6TH
3-5yrs. 12.45-3.15pm. Termtime.

EX23
Berries Kindergarten 01288 353 237
Berries Avenue, Bude, EX23 8QE
2½-4yrs. 9am-1pm and 1.30-4pm.

Budehaven Day Nursery 01288 356 784
Valley Road, Bude, EX23 8DQ
8.30am-5.30pm.

Flexbury Park Pre-School 07792 979 686
Methodist Church Hall, Flexbury Park Road, Bude
2-5yrs. 9.30am-12.30pm. Termtime.

Happy Days South West 01840 230 507
Jacobstow, Bude, EX23 0BR
3mths-5yrs. 8am-6pm. 50wks.

Kilkhampton Pre-School 01288 321 621
Kilkhampton, Bude, EX23 9QU
2-5yrs. 9am-12pm. Termtime.

Marhamchurch Pre-School 07870 819 239
Marhamchurch, Bude, EX23 0HY
2-5yrs. 9am- 12pm. Termtime.

Morwenstow Under Fives
Community Centre, Morwenstow, Bude, EX23 9ST
0-5yrs. 9-11.30am. Termtime. 3 mornings.

Rainbows Day Nursery 01288 353 431
25 Downs View, Bude, EX23 8RG
3mths-5yrs.

S St Petrocs Pre-School 01288 352 876
Ocean View Road, Bude, EX23 8NJ
2½-5yrs. 8.30am-3pm. Termtime.

Stratton Playgroup 07790 819 424
New Road, Stratton, Bude, EX23 9AP
2-5yrs. 9-11.45am. Termtime.

PL24
Roselyon School Nursery 01726 812 110
St. Blazey Road, Par, PL24 2HZ
2½-5yrs. 9am -3.30pm. Termtime.

PL21
S The Plymouth College 01752 201 350
The Millfields, Plymouth, PL1 3JL
3-18yrs.

PL7
Kiddi Caru Day Nursery 01752 330 469
Ashleigh Way, Langage Park, Plympton, PL7 5JX
www.kiddicaru.com
3mths-5yrs. 8am-6pm. 51wks.

PL10
Kingfisher Playgroup 01752 822 259
Community Hall, Fore Street, Cawsand, Torpoint
2-4yrs. 9.30am-12pm. Termtime.

Little Monkeys 01752 822 287
Wringford Down Hotel, Hat Lane, Forder, Torpoint
6mths-4yrs. 8.30am-5.30pm. 50wks.

Millbrook Pre-School 01752 823 128
The Village Hall, Millbrook, Torpoint, PL10 1AY
2½-5yrs. 9.30am-12pm. Termtime.

PL11
Band Hut Playgroup 01752 812 771
Anthony Road, Torpoint, PL11 2JR
2-5yrs. 9.05-11.35am. Termtime.

Crafthole Pre-School 07900 553 116
Sheviock Memorial Hall, Crafthole, Torpoint, PL11
2½-5yrs. 9.30am-12pm. Termtime.

Downderry U5's Playgroup 01503 250 486
St. Nicholas Church, Downderry, Torpoint, PL11
9.15-11.45am. Termtime.

Sunshine Pre-School 07940 710 436
Cornerstone Church, Fore Street, Torpoint, PL11
2-5yrs. 9.15-11.45am. Termtime.

Trevorder R.N. Pre-School 01752 812 970
Trevorder Close, Torpoint, PL11 2NS
9.30am-12.15pm. Termtime.

PL12
Carclew Nursery 07870 431 619
Bethany Chapel, Bethany, Trerulefoot, Saltash
9am-12pm. Termtime.

China Fleet Under 5's 01752 854 669
North Pill, Saltash, PL12 6LJ
2-5yrs.

Cross Park Pre-School 01752 841 591
Long Park Road, Saltash, PL12 4AQ
2-5yrs. 9-11.30am and 12.40-3.10pm. Termtime.

www.babydirectory.com

Kiddi Caru Day Nursery
www.kiddicaru.com

Kiddi Caru - Plympton
Ashleigh Way
Langage Park
Plympton PL7 5JX
Telephone: 01752 330 469
Email: kiddiplympton@childcare.uk.com

Kiddi Caru - Torquay
The Willows
Nicholson Road
Torquay TQ2 7AZ
Telephone: 01803 615 400
Email: kidditorquay@childcare.uk.com

Kiddi Caru - Taunton
Blackbrook Business Park
Taunton
Somerset TA1 2PX
Telephone: 01823 444194
Email: kidditaunton@childcare.uk.com

Kiddi Caru - Exeter
Exeter Business Park
Honiton Road
Exeter EX1 3QS
Telephone: 01392 445 639
Email: kiddiexeter@childcare.uk.com

62 education (Cornwall postcodes)   S = SCHOOL

Daisy Chain Nursery 01752 848 938
Callington Road, Carkeel, Saltash, PL12 6HF
2-5yrs. 8am-6pm. 50wks.

Flying Start Nursery 01752 840 240
Church Road, Saltash, PL12 4AE
8am-6pm. 50wks.

Hemsley Ltd. 01752 849 227
54 Fore Street, Saltash, PL12 6JL
4½-5yrs. 8.15am-5.45pm. 50wks.

Issy Brunels Pre-School 01752 848 900
Callington Road, Saltash, PL12 6DX
2-4yrs.

Landulph Under Fives 01752 842 941
Memorial Hall, Landulph, Saltash, PL12 6NE
9.30am-3pm. Termtime.

Sir Robert Geffery's Pre-School 01752 851 343
School Road, Landrake, Saltash, PL12 5EA
2½-5yrs. 9am-3.15pm. Termtime.

St Germans Montessori Nursery 01503 230 830
Church Street, St. Germans, Saltash, PL12 5LG
15mths-5yrs. 8am-5.45pm. 50wks.

St Germans Under Fives 01503 230 133
The Old Telephone Exchange, Station Approach,
St. Germans, Saltash, PL12 5LX
2½-5yrs. 9.15-11.45am and 1-3.30pm. Termtime.

St Nicholas & St Faith Pre-School 01752 846 674
Alexandra Square, Saltash, PL12 6AN
2-5yrs. 9.10-11.40am and 12.20-2.50pm. Termtime.

PL13
Barbican Pre-School 01503 262 948
The Recreation Ground, Sunrising, East Looe, PL13
2½-5yrs. 9.30am-12pm and 12.45-3.15pm. Termtime.

Pelynt Pre-School 01503 220 251
The Village Hall, Summer Lane, Pelynt, PL13 2LP
2½-5yrs. 9.15-11.45am. Termtime.

Polperro Pre-School Playgroup 01503 272 890
The Village Hall, The Coombes, Polperro, Looe
2-5yrs. 9.30am-12pm. Termtime.

Tickles Day Nursery 01503 265 381
Methodist Church, Trewint Crescent, Looe, PL13
2mths-5yrs. 8am-6pm. 50wks.

West Looe Playgroup 01503 265 623
The Old School, Canteen, Downs Road, Looe, PL13
2-5yrs. 9-11.30am and 12.30-3pm. Termtime.

PL14
Braddock Acorns 01579 326 136
East Taphouse, Liskeard, PL14 4TB
3mornings. 9.15-11.45am. 36wks.

Bumbles Day Nursery 01579 343 767
Daromaba House, Clemo Road, Liskeard, PL14
0-5yrs. 7.30am-6pm. 50wks.

Dobwalls Pre-School 07848 444 293
4 Pendray Gardens, Dobwalls, Liskeard, PL14 4NT
9.15-11.45am. Termtime.

First Steps Pre-School 07739 388 630
St. Martin's Church, Church Street, Liskeard, PL14
2-5yrs. 9.30am-12pm. Termtime.

Liskeard Nursery 01637 875 672
Old Road, Liskeard, PL14 6HZ
0-8yrs. 7am-7pm. 51wks.

Liskeard Market Pre-School 01579 346 194
Varley Lane, Liskeard, PL14 4AP
8.30am-3.30pm. 50wks.

Liskeard School Nursery 01579 342 344
Luxstow, Liskeard, PL14 3EA
0-5yrs. 8.30am-3.30pm. Termtime.

Manuscript Day Nursery 01579 346 432
Moorswater, Liskeard, PL14 4LG
0-5yrs. 8am-5.30pm. 50wks.

Menheniot Playgroup Committee 07779 450 707
Old School House, Menheniot, Liskeard, PL14 3QS
2-5yrs. 9am-12pm. Termtime.

Pensilva Pre-School 07890 023 924
School Road, Pensilva, Liskeard, PL14 5PG
2½-5yrs. 9-11.30am. Termtime.

St Cleer Pre-School 07977 889 149
Memorial Hall, Well Lane, St. Cleer, Liskeard, PL14
2-5yrs. 9-11.30am and 12.45-3.15pm. Termtime.

PL15
Coombe Valley Nursery 01566 779 318
Hurdon Road, Launceston, PL15 9JR
8am-6pm. 50wks.

Coombe Valley Nursery 01566 777 036
Old Tree Lodge, Trebursye, Launceston, PL15 7ET
0-8yrs. 8.30am-5.30pm. 51wks.

Kingfisher Nursery 01566 772 484
Boyton CP School, Boyton, Launceston, PL15 9RJ
9am-12pm. 4mornings. Termtime.

Launceston Pre-School 01566 777 529
3 St. Thomas Hill, Launceston, PL15 8BL
no info

Lewannick Pre-School 01566 782 262
HawksTor Drive, Lewannick, Launceston, PL15
2½-5yrs. 12.45-3.15pm. Termtime.

Norht Pethewin Sunbeams Nursery 01566 785 207
Brazzacott, Launceston, PL15 8NE
2-5yrs. 8am-6pm. Termtime.

S = SCHOOL   (Cornwall postcodes) **education**   63

South Petherwin Pre-School 01566 779 476
South Petherwin, Launceston, PL15 7LE
2½-4yrs. 9.15-11.45am. Termtime.

S St Joseph's School 01566 772 580
St. Stephen's Hill, Launceston, PL15 8HN
3-16yrs.

St Stephen's Pre-School Playgroup 01566 777 109
Roydon Road, Launceston, PL15 8HL
9-11.30am and 12.45-3.15pm. Termtime.

Tregadillett Pre-School 01566 785 772
Community Centre, Tregadilett, Launceston, PL15
2-5yrs. 9.15-11.45am. Termtime.

PL17
Celliwic Nursery 01579 386 011
Launceston Road, Callington, PL17 7DR
2-5yrs. 8.30am-4pm. Termtime.

Cotton-tail Nursery 01579 370 983
South Coombeshead Barns, Stoke Climsland,
Callington, PL17 8PS
18mths-8yrs. 7.30am-6pm. 50wks.

Ducklings Venterdon Pre-School 07870 560 715
Methodist Chapel, Venterdon, Stoke Climsland,
Callington, PL17 8NY
2-5yrs. 9am-1pm. Termtime.

Flying Start Day Nursery 01579 371 004
Stoke Climsland, Callington, PL17 8PB
0-5yrs. 8am-6pm. 50wks.

Harrowbarrow & Metherell 01579 351 543
Pre-School Playgroup
The Village Hall, School Lane, Harrowbarrow,
Callington, PL17 8BE
9-11.45am and 1-3.515pm.

PL18
Calstock Under Fives 01822 834 418
The Village Hall, The Quay, Calstock, PL18 9QA
2½-5yrs. 9.30am-12pm. Termtime.

Calstock Under Fives 01822 834 908
Back Road, Calstock, PL18 9QL
3-5yrs. 9.15-11.45am. Termtime.

Delaware Pre-School 07891 031 786
Moorland Way, Drakewalls, Gunnislake, PL18 9EX
2-5yrs. 9-11.30am. Termtime.

Dimson Day Nursery & Kids Club 01822 832 900
Lower Dimson Farm, Gunnislake, PL18 9NS
1-5yrs. 8am-6pm.

Gunnislake Pre-School 07837 816 510
The School Room, Methodist Chapel, Chapel
Street, Gunnislake, PL18 9NA
2½-5yrs.4 mornings.

PL22
Kaleidoscope 01208 873 870
2, Restormel Industrial Estate, Liddicotte Road,
Lostwithiel, PL22 0HG
0-5yrs. 8am-6pm. 51wks.

Lostwithiel Pre-School Playgroup 01208 872 207
The Community Centre, Pleyber-Christ-Way,
Lostwithiel, PL22 0HE
2½-5yrs. Termtime. Mornings.

The Chimes Nursery 01208 873 815
8 Church Lane, Lostwithiel, PL22 0EQ
2-5yrs. 9.30am-3.30pm. Termtime.

PL23
Fowey Pre-School Playgroup 01726 833 188
Windmill, Fowey, PL23 1HE
9.15-11.45am and 12.30-3pm. Termtime.

Polruan Pre-School 01726 870 402
St.Saviours Hill, Polruan, Fowey, PL23 1PS
2-4½yrs. Mornings. 36wks.

PL24
Acorns Childcare Centre 01726 815 115
The Old St.Blazey, Church Street, St. Balzey, PL24
3mths-4yrs. 7am-6pm. 52wks.

Footsteps Childcare Centre 01726 816 911
Well Street, Tywardreath, Par, PL24 2QH
2-8yrs. 7.30am-6pm. 51wks.

Lollypop Pre-School Playgroup 07817 861 566
St. Blazey Cricket Pavilion, Phillip Varcoe Sports
Field, Middleway, St.Blazey, Par, PL24 2JX
2-4yrs. 9.30am-12pm. Termtime.

Rainbow Pre-School 07973 515 098
15 Moorland Road, Par, PL24 2PA
9.30am-1pm. Termtime.

St Austell Nursery 01637 875 672
Burrows Centre, Lamellyn Road, Par, PL24 2DD
0-8yrs. 7am-7pm. 50wks.

Tywardreath Pre-School 01726 813 356
Old Town Hall, Fore Street, Tywardreath, Par, PL24
2-4yrs. 9.15-11.45am and 1-3.30pm. Termtime.

PL25
Boscoppa Pre-School 0172 664 345
Scout Hut, Polmarth Close, Phynnisick Road,
Boscoppa, St.Austell, PL25 3TW
2-5yrs. 9.30am-12pm. Termtime.

Carlyon Bay Hotel 01726 812 304
Sea Road, Carlyon Bay, St.Austell, PL25 3RD
0-8yrs. 10am-6pm. 6wks in the holidays.

New Lawn Nursery 0172 674 133
Tregonissey Close, St. Austell, PL25 4DN
8.15am-5pm. 51wks.

education (Cornwall postcodes)

S = SCHOOL

Playtime Day Nursery 0172 663 528
Trevarthian Road, St.Austell, PL25 4BZ
3mths-5yrs. 8am-5.30pm. 50wks.

Stepping Stones Pre-School 077989 126 786
Carclaze Methodist Church, Treverbyn Road, St. Austell, PL25 4EW
2-4yrs. 9-11.30am. Termtime.

Stepping Stones Pre-School 0172 674 493
12-14 Wesley Place, Mount Charles, St. Austell, PL25 4QA
9.15-11.45am and 12.45-3.15pm. Termtime.

Woodland Kindergarten 07887 661 618
Old Church Hall, Church Road, Charlestown, St. Austell, PL25 3NS
2-5yrs. 8.30am-12.30pm and 2-4pm. Termtime.

PL26

Bugle Pre-School 07899 746 401
Methodist Sunday School Hall, Fore Street, Bugle, St.Austell, PL26 8PD
2-4yrs. 9am-12pm. Termtime.

Foxhole Pre-School 01726 822 022
Foxhole Centre, Foxhole, St. Austell, PL26 7XA
9.15-11.45am. Termtime.

Gorran Pre-School 07817 873 827
Gorran, St.Austell, PL26 6LH
2-5yrs. 9am-12pm. Termtime.

Goslings Pre-School 07919 878 694
Village Institute, Back Lane, Polgooth, St. Austell, PL26 7BP
2-5yrs. 9.15-11.45am. Termtime.

Happy Days Nursery 01726 71188
Penrice Hospital, Porthpean Road, St. Austell, PL26
0-8yrs. 7.30am-6pm.

Little Nippers Mevagissey 07792 505 264
Old Road, Trewinney, Mevagissey, PL26 6TD
2-5yrs. 9am-12pm. Termtime. 4 mornings.

Piccolo Early Years Group 01726 850 420
Bugle CPS, Fore Street, Bugle, St.Austell, PL26
3-5yrs. 8.45am-3pm. Termtime.

Roche Pebbles Day Nursery 01726 891 597
Fore Street, Roche, St. Austell, PL26 8EP
2-4yrs. 8am-6pm. 50wks.

Roche Pre-School Playgroup 01726 891 059
Victory Hall, Victoria Road, Roche, St.Austell, PL26
2-5yrs. 9-11.30am. Termtime.

St Mewan Pre-School 0172 674 887
St. Mewan CP School, St. Mewan, St. Austell, PL26
9-11.30am. Termtime.

St Mewan Under Fives 0172 673 496
St. Mewan Church Hall, St. Mewan, St. Austell, PL26 7DT
2½-5yrs. 9.15-11.45am. Termtime.

Whirleybobs Pre-School Playgroup 0172 676 068
Lanjeth and High Street Village Hall, Coombe Road, Lanjeth, St. Austell, PL26 7TL
2½-5yrs. 9.30am-12.15pm. Termtime.

PL27

Eglloshayle Pre-School Playgroup 07980 053 642
Egloshayle Playing Fields, Wadebridge, PL27 6AQ
9.15-11.45am. Termtime.

Happy Days 01208 815 727
Palmers Way, Trenant Ind. Est., Wadebridge, PL27
3mths-8yrs. 8am-6pm. 50wks.

St Breock Beacons 01208 815 900
Tremarren Road, Wadebridge, PL27 7XL
3-5yrs. 9-11.30am and 1-3.30pm. Termtime.

St Eval Pre-School 01841 540 076
Lincoln Row, St. Eval, Wadebridge, PL27 7TR
2-5yrs. 9.15-11.45am and 12.45-2.45pm. Termtime.

St Issey & Little Petherick Nursery 01841 541 110
The Church, St. Issey, Wadebridge, PL27 7QF
9-11.30am. Termtime.

Stay 'n' Play Pre-School 07950 239 171
Betty Fisher Centre, Southern Way, Wadebridge
2-5yrs. 9.15-11.45am. Termtime.

Wadebridge Nursery 01208 814 640
Fernleigh Road, Wadebridge, PL27 7AT
2½-5yrs. 9am-3.30pm. 50wks.

PL28

Happy Days 01841 533 894
Trecerus Industrial Estate, Padstow, PL28 8RW
0-8yrs. 7.30am-6.30pm.

Padstow Pre-School 01841 533 244
School Grounds, Grenville Road, Padstow, PL28
9.15am-3.15pm. Termtime.

St Merryn Under Fives 07980 393 497
The Parish Hall, St. Merryn, Padstow, PL28 8PJ
9-11.30am. Termtime.

PL30

Lanivet and District Under Fives 01208 831 297
Lanivet Village Hall, Lanivet, Bodmin, PL30 5HX
2-5yrs. 9-11.30am. 3mornings. Termtime.

Lanlivery Pre-School 07773 269 787
Lanlivery, Bodmin, PL30 5HX
9-11.30am and 1-3.30pm. Termtime.

www.babydirectory.com

S = SCHOOL (Cornwall postcodes) **education**

Luxulyan Smarties 01726 851 636
Luxulyan Village Hall, Luxulyan, Bodmin, PL30 5QA
2-5yrs. 9.15-11.45am. Termtime.

Nanstallon & District Playgroup 01208 832 230
Nanstallon Chapel, Nanstallon, Bodmin, PL30 5JY
2-5yrs. 9.30am-12pm. Termtime.

St Kew Pre-School 07970 284 875
St. Kew Parish Hall, Churchtown, St. Kew, Bodmin
2-8yrs. 9.15-11.45am. Termtime.

St Mabyn Pre-School 01208 841 659
St. Mabyn Village Hall, St. Mabyn, Bodmin, PL30
2-5yrs. 9.10-11.40am. 3 mornings. Termtime.

Happy Days 01208 269 101
Berrycoombe Vale, Bodmin, Pl31 2PH

St Tudy Pre-School Playgroup 01208 850 857
The Village Hall, Wadebridge Road, St. Trudy, Bodmin, PL30 3ND
2-5yrs. 9.30am-12pm. 3 mornings. Termtime.

PL31
Bodmin Pre-School 0120 879 825
Priory House, Bungalow, Priory Rd, Bodmin, PL31
2-5yrs. 9.15am-2.45pm. Termtime.

Flying Start Nursery 0120 877 233
Bodmin College, Lostwithiel Road, Bodmin, PL31
8am-6pm. 52wks.

Strawberry's Day Care Nursery 0120 878 093
Berryfields Community Centre, Bodmin, PL31 2EU
0-8yrs. 8am-6pm. 49wks.

Townend Cottage Pre-School 0120 879 686
Victoria Square, Bodmin, PL31 1EB
9.15-11.45am and 12.15-2.45pm. Termtime.

PL32
Camelford Pre-School 01840 212 114
Camelford Hall, Clease Road, Camelford, PL32 9PL
2-5yrs. 9.15-11.45am. Termtime.

Little Otters Children's Centre 01840 261 593
Marshgate, Camelford, PL32 9YN
3mths-4yrs. 50wks.

PL33
Delabole Pre-School Playgroup 07887 547 607
85A High Street, Delabole, PL33 9AH
2-5yrs. 9-11.30am and 1.45-3.15pm. Termtime.

Delatots Pre-School Playgroup 01840 212 814
120 High Street, Delabole, PL33 9AJ
2-5yrs. 9-11.30am and 1-3pm. Termtime.

PL35
Boscastle Pre-School 01840 250 171
Village Hall, Gunpool Lane, Boscastle, PL35 0AT
30mths-5yrs.

TR1
Chuckles Day Care Nursery 01872 261 277
Dereham Terrace, Truro, TR1 3DE
3mths-5yrs. 8am-6pm. 50wks.

Chyvelah House 01872 264 251
College Road, Truro, TR1 3XX
8wks-8yrs. 8am-6pm. 49wks.

Happy Days Day Nursery 01872 262 242
1 Oak Lane, Treliske Ind. Est., Treliske, Truro, TR1
0-8yrs. 7am-7pm. 50wks.

Hightertown Pre-School 01872 262 162
All Saints Church Hall, Tresawles Road, Truro
2-5yrs. 9.15am-12pm Termtime. Also mother and baby morning Tues 9.30 - 11 a.m

Leaps & Bounds Day Nursery 01872 260 797
Petherton House, Kenwyn Road, Truro, TR1 3SH
3mths-5yrs. 8am-6pm. 51wks.

Millpool Pre-School 07815 109 773
St. Clement School, Truro, TR1 1EQ
2-5yrs. 9.15-11.45am. Termtime.

Playbox Day Nursery 01872 222 571
9a Treyew Road, Truro, TR1 3AN
0-5yrs. 8am-6pm. 51wks.

Pottery Playgroup & Pre-School 01872 263 799
Chapel Hill, Truro, TR1 3BD
2-5yrs. 9am-3pm (Mon/Wed/Fri) 9-11.30am Tues/Thurs.

S St Michael's Catholic Small School 01872 242 123
Little Angels Nursery, St. George's Rd, Truro, TR1
2½-16yrs.

St Paul's Pre-School Playgroup 07808 818 989
Church Hall, Agar Road, Truro, TR1 1JU
2-5yrs. 9.15-11.45am. 4 mornings. Termtime.

S Treliske Preparatory School 01872 272 616
Pre-prep. Department, Willday House, Higher Town, Truro, TR1 3QN
3-5yrs. 8.15am-5pm. Termtime.

S Truro High School for Girls 01872 242 916
Falmouth Road, Truro, TR1 2HU
3-5yrs. 8.45am-3.15pm. Termtime.

TR2
Carlowen Day Nursery 01726 883 444
4 The Square Ind. Units, Grmapound Road, Truro, TR2 4DS
0-5yrs. 8am-5.50pm. 50wks.

Grampound Road Pre-School 01726 884 373
Sir Robert Harvey Memorial Hall, Grampound Road, Truro, TR2 4EE
2-5yrs. 9.15-11.45am. Termtime.

66 education (Cornwall postcodes)   S = SCHOOL

Probus Playgroup   07971 943 267
Ladock Road, Probus, Truro, TR2 4LE
3-4yrs. 9.15-11.45am. Termtime.

Probus Pre-School Playgroup   07977 320 599
The Village Hall, Forestreet, Probus, Truro, TR2 4LJ
2-5yrs. 9.15-11.45am. Termtime.

St Mawes & St Just Under Fives   07814 806 660
Recreation Ground, St.Mawes, Truro, TR2 5AR
2-5yrs. 9.30am-12pm. Termtime.

Tregony Playgroup   01726 884 474
Back Lane, Tregony, Truro, TR2 5RP
8.30am-6pm. Termtime.

Veryan & Portloe Playgroup   01872 501 733
Veryan Sports & Social Club, Veryan, Truro, TR2
2½-5yrs. 9.30am-12.30pm. Termtime.

TR3
Chuckles Nurseries Ltd.   01872 863 051
Station Road, Perranwelll Station, Truro, TR3 7PT
3mths-5yrs. 8am-6pm. 51wks.

Devoran Pre-School   01872 870 979
Methodist Church Hall, Devoran, Truro, TR3 6PY
2-5yrs.

Kea Pre-School   01872 260 299
Kea, Truro, TR3 6AY
2-5yrs.

Perran-ar-Worthal Pre-School   07974 484 841
The Village Hall, Perranwell Station, Truro, TR3 7LA
2-5yrs. 9-11.30am and 12.30-3pm. Termtime.

Ponsanooth Pre-School   01872 862 546
The Methodist Hall, St. Michael's Road,
Ponsanooth, Truro, TR3 7EB
2-4yrs. 9.15am-3.15pm. Termtime.

Stithians Pre-School Playgroup   07977 932 104
Village Hall, Church Road, Stithians, Truro, TR3
2-5yrs. 9-11.45am. Termtime.

Threemilestone Pre-School   01872 274 022
Polstain Road, Threemilestone, Truro, TR3 6DH
2-5yrs. Termtime.

S Trescol Vean School   01872 560 788
Baldhu, Truro, TR3 6EG
3-7yrs. 8.30am-3.30pm. Termtime.

TR4
Blackwater Pre-School   01872 560 570
North Hill, Blackwater, Turro, TR4 8ES
2-5yrs. 9-11.30am. Termtime.

Frogpool Pre-School Playgroup   07808 393 874
Frogpool Chapel, Frogpool, Truro, TR4 8RS
2-4yrs.

Goonhavern Pre-School   01872 573 384
Newquay Road, Goonhavern, Truro, TR4 9QD
2-5yrs. 9.15-11.45am. Termtime.

Little Acorns   07791 297 973
The Village Hall, St.Erme, Truro, TR4 9BJ
2-5yrs. 9-11.30am. Termtime.

Mount Hawke Pre-School   01209 891 505
Mount Hawke & Porthtowan Cricket Club, Towan
Cross, Mount Hawke, Truro, TR4 8DR
2-5yrs. 9-11.45am. Termtime.

Playtime@Porthtowan   01209 890 234
Village Hall, Beach Road, Porthtowan, Truro, TR4
2½-5yrs. 9.30am-12pm. 37wks.

S Polwhele House School   01872 273 011
Polwhele, Truro, TR4 9AE
3-13yrs. Termtime.

Shortlanesend Pre-School   07789 044 355
Villlage Hall, Shortlanesend, Truro, TR4 9DU
2 1/2 -5yrs. 9.15am-11.45. Termtime. Lunch club optional 11.45-12.45

Stepping Stones Pre-School   01872 561 542
Falmouth Road, Chacewater, Truro, TR4 8PZ

Tiggers Too Day Nursery   01872 560 128
The Old A30, Blackwater, Truro, TR4 8EY
1-4yrs.

TR5
St Agnes Pre-School   01872 554 005
Trelawney Road, St. Agnes, Truro, TR5 0TP
2-5yrs. 9.15-11.45am. Termtime.

TR6
Perranporth Pre-School   01872 572 021
Liskey Hill, Perranporth, TR6 0EU
2½-5yrs. 3mornings. 38wks.

TR7
Coral Early Years Unit   01637 876 060
Trenance Road, Newquay, TR7 2LU
3-5yrs. 9-11.30am and 12.45-3.15pm.

First Steps Childcare Centre   01637 877 073
Porth Bean Road, Newquay, TR7 3JF
0-8yrs. 7.30am-6.15pm. 50wks.

Happy Days South West Newquay   01637 852 085
Trevenson Road, Newquay, TR7 3BH
3mths-5yrs. 7.30am-5.30pm. 51wks.

Happy Days South West Treloggan   01637 879 977
Treninnick Hill, Newquay, TR7 2SR
0-5yrs. 8am-6pm. 51wks.

Kneehigh Nursery   01637 896 293
Tretherras Road, Newquay, TR7 2RE
2½-5yrs. 8am-4pm. 51wks.

S = SCHOOL (Cornwall postcodes) **education**

Newquay Pre-School Playgroup   01637 876 033
Clevedon Road, Newquay, TR7 2BU
2-5yrs. 8am-5pm. 51wks.

Rainbow Childcare Centre   01637 875 114
Elim Church, Seymour Avenue, Newquay, TR7 1BL
2½-5yrs. Mornings. Termtime.

St Michael's Under Fives   01637 874 133
Church Hall, St. Michael's Road, Newquay, TR7
2½-5yrs. 9.30am-12pm. 3 mornings. Termtimes.

TR8
Curlews Pre-School   07779 690 912
Chynowen Lane, Cubert, Newquay, TR8 5HE
2-5yrs. 9am-3pm. Termtime.

Happy Days   01726 861 412
School Road, Summercourt, Newquay, TR8 5EA
7.30am-6pm. 51wks.

The Valley Nursery   01637 830 680
Trevowah Road, Crantock, Newquay, TR8 5ES
3mths-5yrs. 8.00am-6pm. Termtime.

Quintrell Downs Pre-School   07792 228 908
Village Hall, North Way, Quintrell Downs, Newquay
2-4yrs. 9.30am-12pm. Termtime.

St Mawgan Pre-School   01637 860 924
Community Hall, St. Mawgan, Newquay, TR8 4ET
2-5yrs. 9-11.45am. Termtime.

St Newlyn East Pre-School   017765 564 162
The Cricket Pavilion, Cargoll Road, St. Newlyn East
2-5yrs. 9-11.30am. Termtime.

Summercourt Under Fives   07814 905 267
New Memorial Hall, School Road, Summercourt, Newquay, TR8 5DZ
2-5yrs. 9.15-11.45am. Termtimes. 3 days.

The Kindergarten   01637 877 696
6 West Road, Quintrell Downs, Newquay, TR8 4LD
0-8yrs. 7am-7pm. 51wks.

TR9
Indian Queens Under Fives   01726 862 919
St. Francis Road, Indian Queens, St. Columb, TR9
2-5yrs. 9.15-11.45am. Termtime.

St Columb Major Pre-School   07980 516 204
The Church Hall, St. Columb Major, TR9 6RW
9.15-11.45am. Termtime.

Wesley Pre-School   07979 741 506
Wesley Chapel Hall, St. Francis Road, Indian Queens, St. Columb Major, TR9 6DJ
2½-5yrs. 9.30am-12pm. Termtime.

TR10
Flying Start Day Nursery   01326 373 129
Penryn RFC, Kernick Road, Penryn, TR10 8NT
0-8yrs.

Penryn Pre-School Playgroup   01326 376 587
Methodist Chapel, The Terrace, Penryn, TR10 8EH
2-4yrs. 9.15-11.45am. Termtime.

Trelowan Pre-School   01326 378 377
Treverbyn Rise, Penryn, TR10 8RA
2½-5yrs. 4 mornings. Termtime.

Trevone Nursery   01326 372 929
Trevone Farm House, Mabe Burnthouse, Penryn
2-5yrs. 9am-3.30pm. Termtime.

TR11
Bouncers Day Nursery   01326 317 942
13 Trelawney Road, Falmouth, TR11 3LS
1-5yrs. 8am-6pm. 51wks.

Childs Play Day Nursery   01326 319 798
3 Dracaena Avenue, Falmouth, TR11 2EG
0-8yrs. 8am-6pm. 50wks.

Constantine Pre-School   07733 165 052
Trebarvah Road, Constantine, Falmouth, TR11 5AG
2½-5yrs. 9am-12pm Termtime. 4mornings.

Falmouth School U5's Centre   01326 372 428
Trescobeas Road, Falmouth, TR11 4LH
2-5yrs. 9.15am-3pm. Termtime.

Fit N Fun Kids   01326 379 428
10 Tregonigie Industrail Estate, Falmouth, TR11
3mths-8yrs.

Giggles and Wiggles Nursery   01326 313 271
Youth Club, Dracena Avenue, Falmouth, TR11 4ES
2-5yrs. 9.30am-12pm. Termtime.

Mawnan Playgroup   01326 250 662
MCA Hall, Carwinian Rd, Mawnan Smith, Falmouth
2-5yrs. 9.15-11.45am. Termtime.

Mylor Bridge Pre-School   07990 838 139
The School Room, Comfort Road, Mylor Bridge, Falmouth, TR11 5SE
2-5yrs. 8.30am-12.25pm. Termtime.

Smiling Faces Pre-School   07876 551 427
Longfield, Falmouth, TR11 4SU
2½-5yrs. 4 mornings. 38wks.

The Crypt Pre-School   07970 367 777
St. Mary's Church, Killigrew Street, Falmouth, TR11
2-5yrs. 9-11.30am and 12.30-3pm. Termtime.

The Garden Christian Pre-School   01326 315 249
Western Terrace, Falmouth, TR11 4QJ
9.15-11.45am. Termtime.

www.babydirectory.com

68 education (Cornwall postcodes) S = SCHOOL

TR12

Manaccan Pre-School Playgroup 01326 231 431
Manaccan, Helston, TR12 6HR
2-5yrs. 9.15-11.45am. Termtime.

Mullion Playgroup 07833 576 962
Methodist Church, Churchtown, Mullion, Helston
2-5yrs. 9.15am-12pm and 1-3.30pm. Termtime.

St Keverne Pre-School Playgroup 07891 291 214
School Hill, St. Keverne, Helston, TR12 6NQ
2-5yrs. 9-11.45am. Termtime.

St Martin Under Fives Group 01326 231 447
St. Martin, Helston, TR12 6BT
2-5yrs. 9-11.30am. Termtime.

TR13

Bright Sparks Playgroup 01326 573 641
Trewithick Road, Breage, Helston, TR13 9PZ
2-4yrs. 9.15am-12pm. Termtime. 3 mornings.

Flying Start Day Nursery 01326 573 400
Clies Yard, Meneage Street, Helston, TR13 8RG
0-5yrs. 8am-6pm. 51wks.

Gwari Lowen Pre-School 01326 572 100
Trannack, Helston, TR13 0DQ
2½-5yrs. Termtimes. Mornings.

Helston Day Nursery 01326 575 010
Church Hill, Helston, TR13 8NR
0-5yrs. 8am-5pm. Termtime.

Hillside Playgroup 01326 562 822
Community Centre, Penrose Road, Helston, TR13
2-4yrs. 9.15am-12pm. Termtime.

Little Merlins Pre-School 01326 562 894
Culdrose Community Centre, Hibernia Road,
Helston, TR13 8DJ
2-5yrs. 9.15-11.45am. Termtime.

Lizard CHILD Trust 01326 573 338
Penberthy Road, Helston, TR13 8AR
6mths-12yrs. 8am-6pm. 50wks.

Pathways Day Nursery 01326 560 287
Parc Eglos, Helston, TR13 8UP
3-8yrs. 7.45am-6pm. 50wks.

Puffins Day Nursery 01326 565 349
Water-Ma-Trout Ind. Estate, Helston, TR13 0LW
0-8yrs. 8.30am-6pm. 50wks.

Sithney Stepping Stones 01326 572 910
Sithney CPS, Crowntown, Helston, TR13 0AE
2-5yrs. 9-11.30am. Termtime.

Wendron Pre-School 07890 292 623
Church Hall, Trewennack, Helston, TR13 0BZ
1-4yrs. 3 mornings. Termtime.

TR14

Basset Pre-School 07814 643 039
7 Pendarves Road, Camborne, TR14 7QB
2½-5yrs. 9.15am-12.15pm. 39wks.

Basset Road Pre-School 01209 715 909
The Basset Centre, Basset Road, Camborne, TR14
2-5yrs. 9.15am-12.15pm. 39wks.

Beacon Pre-School 07881 586 806
Village Hall, Tolcarne Road, Beacon, Camborne
2½-4yrs. 9.30am-12pm. Termtime.

Camborne Nursery School 01209 713 607
The Glebe, Camborne TR14 7DT
3-5yrs. Termtime

Crofty Minors Pre-School 01209 717 611
Roskear Road, Camborne, TR14 8DJ
2-5yrs. 8.45-11.45am and 12.30-3.30pm. Termtime.

Flying Start Day Nursery 01209 715 543
1 Trelawney Road, Camborne, TR14 7LN
0-5yrs. 8am-6pm. 51wks.

Little Acorns 07768 108 325
Barripper Road, Higher Penponds, Camborne
2½-4yrs.

Little Monkey 01209 710 555
Mount Pleasant Road, Camborne, TR14 7RH
2-5yrs. 7.30am-6pm. 50wks.

Praze Pre-School 07763 173 797
Fore Street, Praze-an-Beeble, Camborne, TR14
2-4yrs. 9am-12pm. Termtime.

Rosemellin Gooseberry Bush 01209 713 119
Cliff View Road, Camborne, TR14 8QH
6wks-5yrs. 8am-6pm. 50wks.

St John's Pre-School 01209 718 803
Church Hall, Trevu Road, Camborne, TR14 7AE
2-5yrs.

TR15

Bugs Nursery 01209 211 757
Rear of 27 Clinton Road, Illogan Highway, Redruth
0-5yrs. 8am-5.30pm. 50wks.

Bumble Bears 07775 608 308
15 Chariot Road, Illogan Highway, Redruth, TR15
2-5yrs. 9am-3.30pm. Termtime.

Flying Start @ Cornwall 01209 611 609
College Camborne
Trevenson Campus, Poole, Redruth, TR15 3RD
0-8yrs. 8am-6pm. 50wks.

Flying Start Day Nursery 01209 217 171
24 Drump Road, Redruth, TR15 1LU
0-8yrs. 8am-6pm. 51wks.

(Cornwall postcodes) education

S = SCHOOL

Little Lambs Pre-School 01209 213 354
School Lane, Redruth, TR15 2ER
2½-4yrs. Termtime.

Treloweth Nursery 01209 313 080
Higher Broad Lane, Redruth, TR15 3JL
0-8yrs. 7am-7pm. 51wks.

Windmill Nursery 01209 214 884
West Park, Redruth, TR15 3AJ
3mths-8yrs. 8am-6pm. 50wks.

TR16

Buzy Bees Pre-School 01209 315 567
The Elliot, Treleigh CP School, Treleigh, Redruth
9.15-11.45am and 12.30-3pm. Termtime.

Illogan Pre-School Playgroup 01209 843 386
Churchtown, Illogan, Redruth, TR16 4SW
2-5yrs. 9-11.45am and 12.45-3.15pm. Termtime.

Noah's Ark Daycare Nursery 01209 842 586
7 Alexandra Road, Illogan, Redruth, TR16 4DY
3mths-5yrs. 8am-6pm. 50wks.

Portreath Pre-School 07773 123 297
The Institute, Penberthy Road, Portreath, Redruth
2-4yrs. 9-11.45am. Termtime.

St Day & Carharrack Pre-School 07799 511 829
School Hill, St. Day, Redruth, TR16 5LG
2-5yrs. 9.15-11.45am. Termtime.

Windmill Nursery School 01209 842 158
Railway Terrace, Portreath, Redruth, TR16 4LD
18mths-8yrs. 8.15am-5.30pm. 50wks.

TR18

Alverton School Day Nursery 01736 351 135
Toltuff Crescent, Penzance, TR18 4QD
0-5yrs. 8am-6pm. 50wks.

First Steps Nursery 01736 335 137
Penwith College, St.Clare Street, Penzance, TR18
0-4yrs. 8am-5.30pm. 51wks.

Gulval Little Learners 01736 364 747
School Lane, Gulval, Penzance, TR18 3BJ
2-5yrs. 9am-12pm and 12.30-3pm. Termtime.

Penzance Pre-School 01736 350 227
Old Tennis Pavilion, Penlee Park, Penzance, TR18
2-5yrs. 9am-12pm and 1-4pm. Termtime.

Redinnick Pre-School Playgroup 01736 363 292
Redinnick Place, Penzance, TR18 4HP
9-11.45am. Termtime.

St Peter's Under Fives 07803 557 334
Church Hall, Newlyn Coombe, Newlyn, Penzance
9am-12.30pm. Termtime.

S The Bolitho Nursery & School 01736 363 271
Polwithen Road, Penzance, TR18 4JR
3-18yrs. 9am-12pm. Termtime.

TR19

Ancarva Pre-School 01736 731 427
Foxes Lane, Mousehole, TR19 6QQ
2-5yrs. 9am-12pm. Termtime.

Pendeen Pre-School 07866 040 280
Church Hall, Church Road, Pendeen, Penzance
2-5yrs. 9.15am-12pm and 1-3pm. Termtime.

Sennen & Lands End Play 01736 871 863
Sennen, Penzance, TR19 7AE
2-5yrs. 9-11.30am and 12.45-3.15pm. Termtime.

St Buryan Busy Bees Pre-School 01736 810 480
Rectory Road, St.Buryan, Penzance, TR19 6BB
3-4yrs.

St Just Nursery Playgroup 01736 786 279
Bosorne Terrace, St. Just, Penzance, TR19 7LY
2-5yrs. 9-11.45am. Termtime.

St Just Pre-School Playgroup 07817 301 404
Bolitho Club Rooms, Cape Cornwall Street, St. Just
2-5yrs. 8.45-11.45am. Termtime.

TR20

Germoe Pre-School Nursery Group 01736 763 310
Germoe Lane, Germoe, Penzance, TR20 9QY
2-5yrs. 9am-12pm. Termtime.

Nancledra Pre-School 01736 740 021
Community Hall, Nancledra, Penzance, TR20 8NB
2-5yrs. 9-11.30am.Termtime.

Oasis Childcare Centre 01736 740 331
Lower Quarters, Ludgvan, Penzance, TR20 8EX
3-5yrs. Termtime.

St Madderns Pre-School 01736 364 845
Bellair Road, Madron, Penzance, TR20 8SP
2-5yrs. 9-11.30am. Termtime.

Sunny Corner Pre-School 01736 763 931
Chynoweth Lane, St. Hilary, Penzance, TR20 9DR
2-5yrs. 9-11.30am and 12.45-3.15pm. Termtime.

TR26

Montessori Nursery 01736 795 824
Old Lloyds Bank, Longstone Hille, Carbis Bay, St. Ives, TR26 2LJ
2-5yrs. Termtime.

St Christopher's Kindergarten 01736 797 643
10 Spernen Close, Carbis Bay, St.Ives, TR26 2QT
2-5yrs. 9.30am-1.15pm. Termtime.

The Barn Neighbourhood Nursery 01736 793 150
Higher Tregenna Road, St. Ives, TR26 2BB
3mths-5yrs. 8am-5.30pm. 50wks.

www.babydirectory.com

70 education (Cornwall and Devon postcodes)   S = SCHOOL

Tregenna Nursery   01736 793 150
Castle Hotel, St.Ives, TR26 2DE
3mths-5yrs. 8am-5.30pm. 50wks.

TR27
Busy Bodies Pre-School   07763 420 521
Gwinear Village Hall, Gwinear, Hayle, TR27 5LA
2-5yrs. 9.15-11.45am. Termtime.

Foundry Under 5's Pre-School   01736 755 511
Harbour View, Hayle, TR27 4LB
2-5yrs. 9.10-11.40am and 12.30-3pm. Termtime.

Hayle Montessori Nursery   07974 102 940
Methodist Church, Chapel Hill, Hayle, TR27 4JU
9.15-11.50am. Termtime.

Hayle Pre-School Playgroup   01736 755 346
Old Hopscotch Building, Bodriggy Street, Hayle
2-5yrs. 9am-12pm. Termtime.

Hopscotch Day Nursery   01736 755 600
Bodriggy Street, Hayle, TR27 4ND
0-8yrs.

Sandcastles Pre-School Playgroup   07976 315 692
Turnpike Road, Connor Downs, Hayle, TR27 5DT
2-5yrs. 9-11.30am. Termtime.

S St Piran's School   01736 752 612
Trelissick Road, Hayle, TR27 4HY
3-4yrs. 9am-12pm. Termtime.

DEVON
DT7
Uplyme Pre-School   07880 684 089
Lyme Road, Uplyme, Lyme Regis, DT7 3UY
3-5yrs. 9.15-11.45am. 36wks.

EX1
Kiddi Caru Day Nursery   01392 445 639
Emperor Way, Exeter Business Park, Exeter, EX1
www.kiddicaru.com
3mths-5yrs, 7.30am-6.30pm, 51 weeks per year (see ad pg 61).

S Bramdean School   01392 273 387
Richmond Lodge, Homerfield Road, Exeter, EX1
2-5yrs. 34wks.

Bumble Bees Day Nursery   01392 496 644
Uplands, 81 Heavitree Road, Exeter, EX1 2LX
0-5yrs. 8am-6pm. 51wks.

S Exeter Cathedral School   01392 255 298
The Chantry, Palace Gate, Exeter, EX1 1HX
2½-13yrs.

Fledglings Day Nursery   01392 405 258
Gladstone Road, Exeter, EX1 2ED
0-5yrs. 7.15am-6pm. 51wks.

Heavitree URC Pre-School   01392 660 274
United Reform Church, Fore Street, Heavitree,
Exeter, EX1 2QJ
2-5yrs. 9.30am-12pm. Termtime.

Kids & Co Pre-School Whipton   07970 175 868
Church Hall, Brookway, Whipton, EX1 3JJ
3-5yrs. 9.15-11.45am. Termtime.

S Maynard School   01392 273 417
Denmark Road, Exeter, EX1 1SJ
Girls. 7-18yrs.

Palace Gate Pre-School   01392 279 485
3 Palace Gate, Exeter, EX1 1JA
9.15am-3.15pm. Termtime.

Pip-Kins Day Nursery   01392 421 422
6 Barnfield Hill, Exeter, EX1 1SR
7.45am-6pm. 51wks.

Puffins in the City   01392 494 291
Keble House, Southernhay Gardens, Exeter, EX1
0-5yrs. 8am-6pm. 51wks.

Puffins of Exeter   01392 496 017
13 Mont le Grand, Exeter, EX1 2PD
0-5yrs. 8am-6pm. 51wks.

St Matthews Community Playgroup   01392 681 571
Clifton Road, Exeter, EX1 2EF
9.15-11.45am. Termtime.

EX2
Acorns Day nursery   01392 272 621
36 Alphington Road, Exeter, EX2 8HN
3mths-5yrs. 8am-6pm. 50wks.

Alphington Pre-School   01392 215 979
Community Centre, Church Road, Alphington
3-5yrs. 9-11.30am and 12.30-3pm. 38wks.

Busy Bears Day Nursery   01392 403 261
Royal Devon & Exeter Hospital, Barrack Road,
Exeter, EX2 5DW
0-5yrs. 7am-6pm. 51wks.

Countess Weir ABC Pre-School   01392 683 289
Glasshouse Lane, Exeter, EX2 7BS
3-5yrs. 9.15am-3.20pm. Termtime.

Dunsford Pre-School Playgroup   01647 253 251
Village Hall, Dunsford, Dunchideock, Exeter, EX2
3-5yrs. 9.30am-12pm. Termtime.

S Exeter Junior School   01392 258 712
Victoria Park Road, Exeter, EX2 4NS
7-11yrs.

Please say you saw the listings in the South West Baby Directory

S = SCHOOL   (Devon postcodes) **education**

Freshlings Nursery   01392 475 121
University of Plymouth: Faculty of Arts & Education, Earl Richards Road North, Exeter, EX2 6AS
0-5yrs. 8.15am-5.45pm. 50wks.

Hylton School   01392 254 755
13a Lyndhurst Road, Exeter, EX2 4PA
2-8yrs. 9am-3.30pm. Termtime.

Little Ones Day Nursery   01392 683 438
Burnthouse Lane, Exeter, EX2 6AY
8am-6pm. 51wks.

Ludwell Valley Centre   01392 678 785
Burnthouse Lane, Exeter, EX2 6AY
3-5yrs. 9am-3pm. Termtime.

S Magdalen Court School   01392 494 919
Mulberry House, Victoria Park Road, Exeter, EX2
2-18yrs. 9am-12pm and 1.15-3.15pm. Termtime.

Mary Poppins Day Nursery   01392 437 844
Wonford Street, Exeter, EX2 5DL
8wks-5yrs. 7.45am-6pm. 50wks.

Puffins at Clystheath   01392 496 017
The Chapel, Woodwater Lane, Exeter, EX2 7EX
8am-6pm. 50wks.

Puffins at Sowton   01392 496 017
Oak House, Falcon Road, Sowton Ind. Est, Exeter
0-5yrs. 8am-6pm. 50wks.

Shakespeare Road Pre-School   01392 219 876
68a Shakespeare Road, Exeter, EX2 6BU
2-5yrs. 9.15am-3.15pm. Termtime.

St Andrew's Playgroup   01392 424 952
Alphington Road, Exeter, EX2 8HP
3-5yrs. 9-11.30am and 12.30-3pm. Termtime.

St Leonard's Church Pre-School   07773 656 751
Roberts Road, Exeter, EX2 4HD
3-5yrs. 9.15-11.15am and 12.45-3.15pm. Termtime.

S St Margaret's School   01392 273 197
147 Magdalen Road, Exeter, EX2 4TS
Girls. 7-18yrs.

Start Right Nursery School   01392 877 330
74 Glasshouse Lane, Exeter, EX2 7BZ
2-4yrs. 9am-4pm. Termtime.

S The Montessori School   01392 201 303
3 St. Leonards Place, Exeter, EX2 4LZ
2½-7yrs. 8.30am-3.30pm. Termtime.

EX3
Hope House Montessori   01392 875 766
29 Monmouth Street, Topsham, Exeter, EX3 0AJ
2-5yrs. 9.15am-12.15pm. Termtime.

Topsham Pre-School   07979 711 329
Matthews Hall, Fore Street, Topsham, Exeter, EX3
9.30am-12pm and 1-3.30pm. Termtime.

EX4
Buttercups Montessori   01392 425 548
Community Hall, Mincinglake Valley Park, Exeter
9.15am-12.15pm. Termtime.

Exeter College Day Nursery   01392 205 534
Bishop Blackall Centre, Pensylvania Road, Exeter
0-8yrs. 8am-6pm. 50wks.

Exeter Steiner School   01392 427 200
Rear or Nr.1, Locarno Road, Exeter, EX4 1QD
9am-12.30pm. Termtime.

Exwick Parish Hall Pre-School   01392 491 068
Station Road, Exwick, Exeter, EX4 2EH
3-5yrs. 9.30am-12pm. Termtime.

First Steps Community Playgroup   01392 251 885
Stoke Hill, Exeter, EX4 7DB
3-5yrs. 9.05-11.35am and 12.35-3.05pm. Termtime.

Little Ones Day Nursery   01392 670 111
St. Boniface Hall, Pinhoe Road, Exeter, EX4 8AF
7.45am-6pm. 50wks.

Park Playgroup   01392 439 508
Methodist Church, 110-111 Cowick Street, Exeter
3-5yrs. 9.15-11.45am. Termtime.

Pinhoe Pre-School   01392 466 878
Harrington Lane, Pinhoe, Exeter, EX4 8PE
3-5yrs. 9am-3pm. Termtime.

St David's Hill Playgroup   01392 425 519
Community Centre, 17 St. David's Hill, Exeter, EX4
3-5yrs. 9am-12pm and 1-4pm. Termtime.

St Mark's Pre-School   07952 903 199
Pinhoe Road, Exeter, EX4 7HU
3-5yrs. 9am-12pm and 1-3.45pm.

St Thomas Methodist Pre-School   07939 048 948
Church Hall, Cowick Street, Exeter, EX4 1JE
9.30am-12pm. Termtime.

Stepping Stones Pre-School   07855 684 187
The Old School Building, Exwick Road, Exeter, EX4
3-8yrs. 9.30am-3.30pm. Termtime.

Stoke Hill Pre-School   01548 580 202
183a Mincinglake Road, Stoke Hill, Exeter, EX4
3-5yrs. 9.15am-3.30pm. Termtime.

Tic Tocs Day Nursery   01392 410 902
St. Wilfreds Court, Haldon Road, Exeter, EX4 4DZ
3mths-5yrs. 8am-6pm. 50wks.

University of Exeter Nursery   01392 264 416
Mardon Hall, Streatham Drive, Exeter, EX4 4QW
8.15am-5.30pm. 42wks.

www.babydirectory.com

education (Devon postcodes)

S = SCHOOL

EX5

Apple Blossom Day Nursery 01404 822 251
Honiton Road, Whimple, Exeter, EX5 2PT
8am-6pm. 50wks.

Brampford Area Pre-School 01392 841 414
School House, Brampford Speke, Exeter, EX5 5HE
2-5yrs. 9-11.30am. Termtime.

Broadclyst Pre-School 01392 466 743
School Lane, Broadclyst, Exeter, EX5 3JG
3-5yrs. 9am-3.15pm. Termtime.

Clyst Valley Pre-School 07870 482 459
Clyst St. Mary, Exeter, EX5 1BG
9.15-11.45am. Termtime.

Little Acorn Pre-School 01395 270 840
Village Hall, Stoney Lane, Woodbury, Salterton, Exeter, EX5 1PP
3-5yrs. 9.15-11.45am. Termtime.

Little Ones Day Nursery 01392 823 400
Budlake Hall, Budlake, Exeter, EX5 3JW
0-5yrs. 7.30am-6pm. 50wks.

Maytree Pre-School 07749 383 402
Village Hall, Flower Street, Woodbury, Exeter, EX5
2-5yrs. 9.15am-1.15pm. Termtime.

Newton St. Cyres Playgroup 01392 851 267
Newton St. Cyres, Exeter, EX5 5DD
0-4trs. Termtime. 3 mornings.

Puffins at Winslade 01392 445 094
Winslade Park, Clyst St.Mary, Exeter, EX5 1DS
0-5yrs. 8am-6pm.

Rockbeare Pre-School 01404 822 501
Rockbeare, Exeter, EX5 2EQ
8.50-11.40am. Termtime.

Silverton Pre-School Playgroup 01392 861 353
Evangelical Hall, School Road, Silverton, Exeter
3-5yrs. 9.10am-3.20pm. Termtime.

The Duchy Pre-School 07880 918 916
Millway, Bradninch, Exeter, EX5 4NL
3-5yrs. 9.15-11.45am. Termtime.

Thorverton Playgroup 07754 206 031
Memorial Hall, Silver Street, Thornverton, Exeter
3-5yrs. 9.30am-12pm. Termtime.

Whimple Pre-School Playgroup 07752 590 926
Victory Hall, Whimple, Exeter, EX5 2SU
3-5yrs. 9am-12pm and 12.30-3pm. Termtime.

EX6

Cheriton Bishop Playgroup 0164 724 314
Church Lane, Cheriton Bishop, Exeter, EX6 6HY
3-5yrs. 9am-12.50pm.

Cheriton Bishop Playgroup 07977 777 318
Village Hall, Cheriton Bishop, Exeter, EX6 6JA
9.30am-12pm. Termtime.

Christow Pre-School 01647 252 542
Dry Lane, Christow, EX6 7PH
3-5yrs. 9-11.30am. Termtime.

Cygnets Group 01392 824 340
Deepway Lane, Exminster, Exeter, EX6 8AJ
12.15-3.15pm. Termtime. 3 days.

Doddiscombsleigh Pre-School 01647 252 253
Doddiscombsleigh, Exeter, EX6 7PR
9-11.30am. 3 days.

Exminster Pre-School 01392 833 320
Deepway Centre, Deepway Lane, Exminster, EX6
3-5yrs. 9.15-11.45am.

Kennford Playbox 07745 116 486
Kenn Parish Hall, Kennford, Exeter, EX6 7TX
3-5yrs. 9.30am-12pm. Termtime. 4 days.

Kenton Pre-School 01626 891 770
The Victory Hall, Kenton, Exeter, EX6 8JA
3-5yrs. 9.30am-12pm.

Kenton Pre-School 01626 891 770
Mamhead Road, Kenton, Exeter, EX6 8LX
3-5yrs. 9.30am-12pm.

Starcross Pre-School 01626 890 188
Community Rooms, New Road, Starcross, EX6
9-11.30am and 12.30-3pm. Termtime.

Tedburn St Mary Playgroup 0164 761 494
Tedburn St. Mary, Exeter, EX6 6EZ
3-5yrs. 9.30am-12pm. Termtime.

S The New School 01392 496 122
The Avenue, Exminster, Exeter, EX6 8AT
3½-8yrs. 8.40am-3.20pm. Termtime.

EX7

Holcombe Pre-School & Nursery 07753 239 329
The Village Hall, Homcombe, Dawlish, EX7 0JT
3-5yrs.

Lanherne Nursery School 01626 863 091
18 Longlands, Dawlish, EX7 9NG
0-11yrs. 8am-6pm. 50wks.

Leonard Lamb Pre-School 07718 191 208
Community Centre, School Hill, Dawlish, EX7 9NL
3-5yrs. 37wks. Mornings.

The Secret Garden 01626 862 862
3 Barton Villas, Dawlish, EX7 9QJ
0-5yrs. 8am-6pm. 50wks.

Please say you saw the listings in the
South West Baby Directory

S = SCHOOL   (Devon postcodes) **education**   **73**

Tinky's Pre-School   07752 483 796
Community Centre, Sandy Lane, Dawlish, EX7 0AF
3-5yrs. 36wks.

EX8
ABC Day Nursery   01395 222 808
143 Exeter Road, Exmouth, EX8 3DX
7.30am-6pm.

All Saints Pre-School   07974 035 782
Church Hall, Church Road, Exmouth, EX8 1RZ
9.30-11.30am and 12.30-3pm. Termtime.

Bassetts Farm Pre-School   01395 267 451
St. John's Road, Exmouth, EX8 4EH
9am-3pm. 38wks.

Brixington Pre-School   01395 269 765
Ellwood Road, Exmouth, EX8 4LE
3-5yrs. 9.15-11.45am. 39wks.

Happy Days Nursery   01395 225 734
Gipsy Lane, Exmouth, EX8 3AF
0-5yrs. 8am-5pm. Termtime.

Lympstone Pre-School   01395 225 345
Lympstone Village Hall, Lympstone, EX8 5JY
3-5yrs. 9.05-11.45am. Termtime.

Pebbles Day Nursery   01395 272 049
15 Carlton Hill, Exmouth, EX8 2AJ
0-6yrs. 7.30am-6.15pm. 50wks.

Rainbow Nursery   01395 264 875
Long Causeway, Exmouth, EX8 1TS
3-5yrs. 8.55am-12pm. Termtime.

S St Peter's School   01395 272 148
Harefield, Lympstone, Exmouth, EX8 5AU
3-13yrs.

S The Dolphin School   01395 272 418
Raddenstile Lane, Exmouth, EX8 2JH
8.45am-3.30pm. 35wks.

The Sunshine Nursery School   07790 502 934
Gorfin Hall, Claremont Lane, Exmouth, EX8 2LE
3-5yrs. 9.15am-12.15pm. Termtime.

Tree House Pre-School   01395 272 935
41 Exeter Road, Exmouth, EX8 1PU
3-5yrs. 9am-3.15pm. Termtime.

Warren View Pre-School   01395 222 619
Sports Pavilion, Halsdon Avenue, Exmouth, EX8
3-5yrs. 9.30am-1.30pm. Termtime.

Withycombe Raleigh Playgroup   01395 273 626
Parish Church Hall, Withycombe Village Road, Exmouth, EX8 3AE
9.15-11.45am. Termtime.

EX9
Carousel Child Care   01395 446 195
Moor Lane, Budleigh, Salterton, EX9 6QF
0-8yrs. 7am-6pm.

Carousel Childcare   07792 927 278
Moor Lane, Budleigh Salterton, EX9 6QF
no info

Little Otters Pre-School   01395 445 825
Village Hall, Wynards Road, East Budleigh,
Budleigh Salterton, EX9 7DU
3-5yrs. 9.30am-12pm.

Saplings Children's Centre   01395 568 965
Bicton College, East Budleigh, Budleigh, Salterton
8am-6pm. 50wks.

EX10
Apple Tree Pre-School   01395 577 233
Manstone Avenue, Sidmouth, EX10 9TJ
3-5yrs. 9-11.45am and 11.50am-12.45pm. Termtime.

Bramscombe Nursery School   01297 680 339
Kingsdown Business Park, Kingsdown,
Branscombe, Sidmouth, EX10 0PD
0-5yrs. 8.30am-4pm. Termtime.

Rainbow Playgroup   01395 567 762
School Lane, Newton Poppleford, Sidmouth, EX10
3-4yrs. Termtime.

Sidford Playgroup   07812 776 952
Sidford Social Hall, Byes Lane, Sidford, Sidmouth
3-5yrs. 9.30am-12pm. Termtime.

Sidmouth Day Care Nursery   01395 515 510
All Saints Road, Sidmouth, EX10 8ES
0-5yrs. 8.30am-5.15pm. 51wks.

Sidmouth Pre-School Playgroup   01395 514 660
Vicarage Road, Sidmouth, EX10 8UG
3-5yrs. 9-11.45am.39wks.

S St John's School, Sidmouth   01395 513 984
Broadway, Sidmouth, EX10 8RG
2-13yrs. 8.30am-6pm. Termtime.

Tipton Owlets Playgroup   01404 813 220
Community Hall, Tipton St. John, Sidmouth, EX10
3-5yrs. 9.15-11.45am. Termtime.

EX11
Busy Otters Playgroup   07779 038 234
The Old Boys School, Yonder Street, Ottery
St.Mary, EX11 1EY
3-5yrs. 9.30am-12pm. Termtime.

Coleridge Pre-School Playgroup   01404 812 663
Old School, Jesu Street, Ottery-St-Mary, EX11 1EU
2-5yrs. 9.30am-12pm and 12.45-3pm. Termtime.

education (Devon postcodes)

S = SCHOOL

West Hill Pre-School   01404 814 386
Beech Park, West Hill, Ottery St. Mary, EX11 1UQ
2-5yrs. 9.15-3.15pm. Termtime.

EX12

Axmouth Pre-School   07754 431 705
Village Hall, Church Street, Axmouth, Seaton, EX12
3-5yrs. 9am-12pm. Termtime.

Branscombe Pre-School   01297 680 339
Branscombe, Seaton, EX12 3DA
3-5yrs. 8.55-11.30am. Termtime.

Nippers Day Nursery   01297 626 819
87 Harbour Road, Seaton, EX12 2NE
0-8yrs. 8.30am-4pm. 51wks.

Rupers Under 5's Pre-School   01297 625 621
Valley View, Seaton, EX12 2HF
3-5yrs. 9-11.30am and 12.30-3pm. Termtime.

EX13

All Saints Pre-School   01460 220 901
Cricket Club, All Saints, Axminster, EX13 7LX

Axminster Playgroup   07947 392 779
Stoney Lane, Axminster, EX13 5AZ
3-5yrs. 9am-12pm. Termtime.

Chardstock Pre-School   01460 221 714
The Old Kitchen, Chardstock, Axminster, EX13 7BX
3-5yrs. 9am-3.30pm. Termtime.

Kilmington Pre-School   07815 477 196
Village Hall, Kilmington, Axminster, EX13 7RG
3-5yrs. 9.15-11.45am. Termtime. 4days.

Rainbow Under 5's Playgroup   0129 733 005
Stoney Lane, Axminster, EX13 5BU
0-5yrs. 9.10am-12pm. Termtime.

Shute Little Acorns   0129 733 348
Shute, Axminster, EX13 7QR
2-5yrs. 9-11.40am. Termtime. 3 days.

Stepping Stones Nursery   0129 733 005
Stoney Lane, Axminster, EX13 5BU
3-5yrs. 1-3.30pm. Termtime.

EX14

Busy Bee Pre-School   0140 446 400
Clapper Lane, Honiton, EX14 1QF
2-3yrs. 9-11.30am and 12.30-3pm. Termtime.

Dunkeswell Pre-School   07905 550 482
6 Culme Way, Dunkeswell, Honiton, EX14 4JP
9.15am-12.15pm.

Guardian Angels Day Nursery   0140 442 503
Mountbatten Park, Ottery Moor Lane, Honiton
2-5yrs. 8am-5pm. 51wks.

Please say you saw the listings in the South West Baby Directory

Little Treasures Pre-School   07810 740 878
Village Hall, Gittisham, Honiton, EX14
9.15am-1pm. Termtime.

S Manor House School   0140 442 026
Springfield House, Honiton, EX14 9TL
3-11yrs.

Offwell Under Fives   07814 120 019
Village Hall, Wilmington, Honiton, EX14 9JH
3-5yrs. 9.15am-12.15pm. Termtime.

Payhembury Playgroup   01404 822 796
Village Hall, Payhemburgy, Honiton, EX14 3HT
3-5yrs. 12.45-3.15pm Mon/Tues/Thurs. Termtime.

Scallywags Pre-School   07812 859 080
Station Road, Feniton, Honiton, EX14 3EA
3-5yrs. 9.15am-12.30pm. Termtime.

Stockland & Yarcombe Pre-School   07890 347 631
Village Hall, Stockland, Honiton, EX14 9EF
3-5yrs. 9.15am-12pm. Termtime.

Upottery Pre-School   01404 861 705
Upottery, Honiton, EX14 9QT
2-5yrs. 9.15am-12pm. Termtime.

EX15

ABC Day Nursery   0188 438 039
Duke Street, Cullompton, EX15 1DW
0-5yrs. 8am-6pm. 51wks.

Cullompton Pre-School   0188 435 018
Brook Road, Cullompton, EX15 1DX
3-5yrs. 9.10-11.40am and 12.40-3.10pm. Termtime.

Culmstock Pre-School Playgroup   01884 841 038
The Methodist School Room, Mill Moor, Culmstock, Cullompton, EX15 3JJ
9.15-11.45am and 12.45-3.15pm. Termtime.

Hemyock Pre-School   01823 680 851
Parish Hall, Hemyock, Cullompton, EX15 3QW
9am-12pm. Termtime.

Kentisbeare Pre-School   07780 873 057
Village Hall, Kentisbeare, Cullompton, EX15 2AA
3-5yrs. 9am-12pm.

Noah's Ark Playgroup   0188 435 586
Baptist Church, High Street, Cullompton, EX15 1AA
3-5yrs. 9.15am-12pm. Termtime.

Plymtree Playgroup   07779 063 177
Village Hall, Cullompton, EX15 2JE
2-5yrs. 9.15-11.45am. Termtime.

Puddleducks Pre-School   01884 839 341
Village Hall, Clyst Hydon, Cullompton, EX15 2NH
3-5yrs. 9.30am-12pm. 3days.

S = SCHOOL (Devon postcodes) **education** 75

Teddybear Pre-School 07786 431 626
Church Hall, Langford, Cullompton, EX15 1SE
2-5yrs. 9.15am-3pm. Termtime.

Uffculme Pre-School 01884 840 282
Uffculme, Cullompton, EX15 3AY
3-5yrs. 9.15-11.45am and 12.45-3.15pm. Termitme.

Willand Pre-School 0188 433 711
School Drive, Gables Road, Willand, Cullompton
9.15-11.45am and 1-3pm. Termtime.

Young Ones Day Nursery 0188 435 001
28 Tiverton Road, Cullompton, EX15 1HT
8am-6pm. 51wks.

EX16
Bampton Pre-School 07759 946 388
School Close, Bampton, Tiverton, EX16 9NW
2-5yrs. 9.15-11.45am and 12.45-3.15pm. Termtime.

Bampton Street Nursery 01884 255 808
80-84 Bampton Street, Tiverton, EX16 6AL
3-5yrs. 9am-3pm. Termtime.

Bickleigh on Exe Pre-School 07773 639 353
Bell Meadow, Bicleigh, Tiverton, EX16 8RE
3-5yrs. 9.15am-3.15pm.

East Anstey Pre-School 01398 341 369
East Anstey, Tiverton, EX16 9JP
9-11.30am. Termtime.

Halberton Pre-School 01884 829 414
Church Path, Halberton, Tiverton, EX16 7AT
9am-12pm and 12.15-3.15pm. Termtime.

Park Hill Nursery 01884 258 995
Site Hut, Bolham Road, Tiverton, EX16 6SG
2-8yrs. 8am-5pm. 50wks.

Sampford Peverell Pre-School 07745 220 896
Memorial Hall, Lower Town, Sampford Peverell, Tiverton, EX16 7BJ
2-5yrs. 9.30am-12pm.

S St Aubyn's School 01884 252 393
Milestones House, Blundell's Road, Tiverton, EX16
3mths-11yrs.

St Paul's Day Nursery 01884 243 047
47 Barrington Street, Tiverton, EX16 6QP
0-8yrs. 8am-6pm. 50wks.

The Valley Nursery School 01823 672 521
Burlescombe, Tiverton, EX16 7JH
3-5yrs.

The Woodside Centre 01884 243 712
Lea Road, Tiverton, EX16 6SU
0-5yrs. 7.30am-6pm. 51wks.

Please say you saw the listings in the South West Baby Directory

Thornebuds Playgroup 01884 254 359
Village Hall, Chevithorne, Tiverton, EX16 7PU
3-5yrs. 9.30am-12.30pm and 1-3.30pm. Termtime.

Tiverton Opportunity Playgroup 01884 252 522
Old Heathcoat School Community Centre, King Street, Tiverton, EX16 5JJ
0-5yr.s 9.15-11.45am and 12.45-3.15pm. Termtime.

Witheridge Pre-School 01884 861 092
Fore Street, Witheridge, Tiverton, EX16 8AH
3-5yrs. 9-11.30am. Termtime.

Wooden House Nursery School 01884 252 161
The Wooden House, Chevithorne, Tiverton, EX16
2½-5yrs. 8.30am-3.15pm. 36wks.

EX17
Bow Playgroup 0136 382 503
Bow Village Hall, Bow, Crediton, EX17 6HS
3-5yrs. 9.30am-12pm. Termtime.

Cheriton Fitzpaine Playgroup 01363 866 188
Village School, Poughill, Crediton, EX17 4LD
9.30am-12pm and 12.15-1.15pm. Termtime.

Copplestone Busy Bees 0136 284 152
Bewsley Hill, Copplestone, Crediton, EX17 5NX
9am-1pm. Termtime.

S Crediton Preparatory School 01363 772 517
Searle Street, Crediton, EX17 2AT
3-8yrs. 9.15am-3.30pm. Termtime.

Early Birds 01363 773 837
Old Landscore, Greenway, Crediton, EX17 3LP
2-8yrs. 8am-6pm. 52wks.

East Worlington Playgroup 01884 860 567
Parish Hall, East Worlington, Crediton, EX17 4TS
2-5yrs. 9.15-11.45am. Termtime. 3 days.

Jolly Tots Pre-School 01363 772 410
Q.E. Community Centre, East Street, Crediton
9-11.45am. Termtime.

Lapford Pre-School 0136 383 069
Eastington Lane, Lapford, Crediton, EX17 6QE
3-4yrs. 9.30am-12pm Termtime.

Leapfrogs Day Nursery 01363 776 474
Old Haywards Courtyard, East Street, Crediton
0-8yrs. 8am-6pm. 50wks.

Morchard Bishop Playgroup 0136 382 708
Memorial Hall, Church Road, Morchard Bishop, Crediton, EX17 6PJ
3-5yrs. 9.30am-12pm. Termtime.

Morchard Bishop Stepping Up Playgroup 07816 967 140
Church Room, Church Street, Morchard Bishop
3-5yrs. 9.30am-12pm. Termtime.

education (Devon postcodes)   S = SCHOOL

Pippins Pre-School　01363 772 474
Methodist Church Hall, Union Road, Crediton, EX17
2-5yrs. 9am-4pm. Termtime.

Sandford & District Playgroup　01363 772 640
Parish Hall, Fanny Lane, Sandford, Crediton, EX17
3-5yrs. 9.30am-1pm. Termtime.

Sunflower Day Nursery　01363 777 020
82 High Street, Crediton, EX17 3LA
0-5yrs. 8am-6pm. 51wks.

Yeoford Four Plus Pre-School　01363 84 234
Staiton Road, Yeoford, Crediton, EX17 5HZ
3-4yrs.

EX18
Little Chums　01769 580 535
Beacon Road, Chulmleigh, EX18 7AA
3-5yrs. Termtime.

EX19
Dolton & Dowland Pre-School　01805 804 564
Village Hall, Dolton, EX19 8QS
9-11.30am. Termtime.

Winkleigh Pre-School　07970 558 793
Castle Street, Winkleigh, EX19 8HU
3-5yrs. 9.15-11.45am and 1.15-3.45pm. Termtime.

EX20
Bratton Clovelly Under Fives　07773 287 232
Parish Hall, Bratton Clovelly, Okehampton, EX20
0-5yrs. 10am-12.30pm. Termtime.

Bridestowe, Lydford and Sourton Pre-School　07751 814 955
Fore Street, Bridestowe, Okehampton, EX20 4EL
3-5yrs. 9.15-11.45am. Termtime.

Exbourne Pre-School　07929 286 823
Methodist Chapel School Room, The Methodist Church, Exbourne, Okehampton, EX20 3RX
9.15-11.45am and 12.30-3pm.

Hatherleigh Pre-School　01837 53770
Town Hall, Bridge Street, Hatherleigh, Okehampton
9-11.45am and 12.45-3.15pm. Termtime. 2-5 years

Lewtrenchard Pre-School Group　07817 030 805
Victory Hall, Lewdown, Okehampton, EX20 4BZ
3-5yrs. 10am-12.30pm. Termtime.

North Tawton Pre-School Busy Bees　0183 782 558
The Old Chapel, Barton Street, North Tawton, EX20
3-5yrs. Termtime.

Rainbow Pre-School　01805 603 300
Clinton Hall, Merton, Okehampton, EX20 3EQ
2-5yrs. 9.15-11.45am. Termtime.

Rainbow Pre-School Playgroup　07759 678 865
The Baptist Church Hall, Baptist Church, Fore Street, Okehampton, EX20 1NZ
9-11.30am. Termtime.

Stepping Stones Day Nursery　0183 755 111
83 North Road, Okehampton, EX20 1BD
4mths-5yrs. 7.45am-5.30pm. 50wks.

Toad Hall　0183 754 492
28 Station Road, Okehampton, EX20 1EA
8am-6pm. 50wks.

EX21
Ashwater Playgroup　01409 211 228
School House, Ashwater, Beaworthy, EX21 5EW
2-5yrs. 8-11am and 1-3.30pm.

Highampton Area Pre-School Group　01409 231 609
Village Hall, Church Road, Highampton, Beaworthy
1-5yrs. 9.30am-12pm and 12.45-3.15pm. Termtime.

Little Bears Pre-School　07890 814 564
Shebbear, Beaworthy, EX21 5SG
3-5yrs. 9.15-11.45am. Termtime. 3days.

Scallywags Pre-School　01409 281 838
The Parish Hall, Halwill Junction, Beaworthy, EX21
9.30am-12.30pm. Termtime.

S Shebbear College　01409 281 228
Shebbear, Beaworthy, EX21 5HJ
3-18yrs.

Tadpoles Pre-School　01409 231 609
Church Road, Highampton, Beaworthy, EX21 5LE
3-5yrs. 12.45-3.15pm. Termtime. 2 days.

EX22
Bradford Pre-School Nursery　07791 254 181
Village Hall, Bradford, Nr Holsworthy, EX22 7AB
2-5yrs. 9.15am-12.45pm. Termtime.

Bradworthy Pre-School Playgroup　01409 241 365
Mill Road, Bradworthy, Holsworthy, EX22 7RT
3-5yrs. 9am-12pm. Termtime.

Holsworthy Playgroup　07817 486 043
Badock Gardens, Bodmin Street, Holsworthy, EX22
2-5yrs. 9.30am-12pm. Termitme.

Pyworthy Under Fives　07771 881 851
Village Hall, Derriton Road, Pyworthy, EX22 6SX
2-5yrs. 9.15-11.45am. Termtime.

Thorne Manor Day Nursery　01409 255 444
Thorne Manor, Holsworthy, EX22 7JD
0-5yrs. 8am-6pm. 50wks.

Whitstone Pre-School　01288 341 241
Whitstone CPS, Oak Lane, Whitstone, Holsworthy, EX22 6TH
3-5yrs. 12.45-3.15pm. Termtime.

EX23
Berries Kindergarten　01288 353 237
Berries Avenue, Bude, EX23 8QE
2¹/₂-4yrs. 9am-1pm and 1.30-4pm.

S = SCHOOL　　　　　　　　　(Devon postcodes) **education**

Budehaven Day Nursery　　01288 356 784
Budehaven Community School, Valley Road, Bude,
EX23 8DQ
8.30am-5.30pm.

EX24
Colyton Caterpillars
St. Andrews Hall, Lower Church Street, Colyton
3-5yrs.

Farway Under 5's　　01404 871 239
Farway Primary School, Farway, Colyton, EX24
2-5yrs. 9am-12pm. Termtime.

EX31
Acorns Day Nursery Unit　　01271 329 936
Old Sticklepath Hill, Sticklepath, Barnstaple, EX31
8.30am-5.30pm.

BARN-A-B's Christian Pre-School　07775 565 912
Baptist Church, Boutport Street, Barnstaple, EX31
3-5yrs. 9.30am-12pm and 12.30-3pm.

Bratton Flemming Playgroup　07745 071 348
Bratton Fleming, Barnstaple, EX31 4TZ
3-5yrs. 9.30am-12.30pm. Termtime.

Bright Start Nursery　　01271 851 315
The Barracks, Chivenor, Barnstaple
1-3yrs. 9.15am-12pm. Termtime.

Chivenor Pre-School　　01271 857 728
The Barracks, Chivenor, Barnstaple, EX31 4AZ
3-5yrs. 9.15am-12pm. Termtime.

Christ Church Pre-School　　01271 379 988
Chrst Church, Bear Street, Barnstaple, EX31 7BU
3-5yrs. 9.30am-12pm.

Fremington Pre-School　　07808 386 424
Scout Hut, Beechfield Road, Fremington, EX31 3DD
3-5yrs. 9.10-11.40am. Termtime.

Marwood Pre-School　　01271 374 745
Marwood, Barnstaple, EX31 4HF
3-5yrs. 8.45-11.15am. 2 days.

Parracombe Pre-School　　07974 818 454
Buff Hall, Parracombe, Barnstaple, EX31 4QE
2-5yrs. 9.30am-12pm. 3 days.

Pilton Pre-School
Church Hall, Pilton Street, Barnstaples, EX31 1PQ
3-5yrs. 9.30am-12pm and 12.45-3pm. Termtime.

Scallywags Pre-School　　07890 681 045
St. Paul's Church Hall, Sticklepath Hill, Barnstaple
0-5yrs. 9.30am-12pm. Termtime.

Springfield Nursery　　01271 329 028
Springfield Farm, Marwood, Barnstaple, EX31 4DT
0-5yrs. 8am-6pm. 51wks.

St Andrews Playgroup　　01271 371 837
Church Hall, Bickington, Barnstaple, EX31 2JG
3-5yrs. 9.15am-12pm and 12.30-3pm. Termtime.

S **St Michael's School**　　01271 341 134
Tawstock Court, Tawstock, Barnstaple, EX31 3HY
3mths-13yrs. 8.30am-5.30pm. Termtime.

Sticklebricks Pre-School　　07789 890 693
1 & 2 Woodville, Crosslands, Barnstaples, EX31
3-5yrs. 9-11.30am and 12.30-3pm. Termtime.

EX32
1st Class Landlkey Pre-School　01271 831 023
Old School Centre, Landkey, Barnstaples, EX32
3-5yrs. 9am-3pm.

Bishops Tawton Playgroup　　07800 653 703
Village Hall, Exeter Road, Bishops Tawnton,
Barnstaple, EX32 0AB
9.15-11.45am. Termtime.

Brayford Boomerangs　　01598 710 718
Village Hall, Brayford, Barnstaple, EX32 7QH
2-5yrs. 9.30am-1pm. Termtime.

Flying Start Nursery　　01271 323 337
Trinity Street, Barnstaple, EX32 8HX
8.30am-5.30pm. 50wks.

Goodleigh Pre-School Playgroup　01271 831 593
Goodleigh Village Hall, Goodleigh, EX32 7LU
3-5yrs. 9.30am-12pm Termtime.

Kiddywinks　　01271 325 746
Barton Road, Barnstaple, EX32 8NG
7am-6pm. 51wks.

Ladybirds Childcare　　01271 830 118
Southcott, Newland, Landkey, Barnstaple, EX32
4mths-5yrs. 7.30am-6pm. 50wks.

Little Learners Pre-School　　01271 321 411
Victoria House Family Centre, Victoria Road,
Barnstaple, EX32 8NP
3-5yrs. 36wks. 4days.

Newport Nursery School　　01271 346 529
3 Trafalgar Lawn, Barnstaple, EX32 9BD
1-5yrs. 8am-6pm. 50wks.

Step by Step Pre-School　　01271 327 143
Landkey Road, Barnstaple, EX32 9BW
3-5yrs. 9-11.30am and 12.45-3.15pm. Termtime.

Sunflower Pre-School　　01271 375 429
Derby Road, Barnstaple, EX32 7HB
3-5yrs. 9-11.30am and 12.30-3pm.

Swimbridge Pre-School　　01271 830 357
Old School Room, Swimbridge, Barnstaple, EX32
9.30am-12pm.

77

education (Devon postcodes) S = SCHOOL

West Buckland Preparatory School   01598 760 629
West Buckland, Barnstaple, EX32 0SX
3-5yrs. 8am-6pm. 36wks.

S West Buckland School   01598 760 281
West Buckland, Barnstaple, EX32 0SX
3-18yrs.

EX33
Caen Catterpillars Pre-School   01271 812 786
Caen Street, Braunton, EX33 1AD
2-5yrs. 9-11.45am.

Croyde Bay Holiday Creche   01271 890 890
Holiday Village, Croyde, Braunton, EX33
9.30am-2pm. Termtime.

Kingsacre Community Pre-School
Greenacre, Braunton, EX33 1BN
3-5yrs. 9.30-11.45am.

Little Fishes Soft-Play Skool   01271 817 968
West Cross, Caen Street, Braunton, EX33 1AQ
0-8yrs. 7.30am-5.30pm. 50wks.

Southmead Pre-School   01271 813 511
Wrafton Road, Braunton, EX33 2BU
2-5yrs. Mornings. Termtime.

Stepping Stones Playgroup   07816 453 282
Putsborough Road, Georgeham, EX33 1JT
3-5yrs. 9am-12pm and 1.15-3.15pm. Termtime.

Westhill Nursery Pre-School   01271 812 938
West Hill House, Braunton, EX33 1AR
2-5yrs. 9am-12pm. Termtime.

EX34
Berrynarbor Pre-School   07787 712 106
Manor Hall, Berrynarbor, Ilfracombe, EX34 9SE
3-5yrs. 9am-12.30pm. Termtime.

Combe Martin Pre-School   01271 883 134
Rosea Bridge Lane, Combe Martin, Ilfracombe
3-5yrs. 9.15am-3.15pm. Termtime. Toddler playgroup 0-3yrs on Mon & Thurs 9.30-11.30am.

Darling Ones Kindergarten   01271 870 549
Moongold, Springfield Road, Woolacombe, EX34
0-8yrs. 8am-6pm. 50wks.

Ilfracombe Pre-School   07816 968 125
High Street, Ilfracombe, EX34 9QB
3-5yrs. 8.45am-2.45pm. Termtime.

Mayfield Kindergarten   01271 862 640
8 St. Brannocks Road, Ilfracombe, EX34 8EQ
0-8yrs. 8am-5pm. 50wks.

The Oak Tree
Old Medical Centre, Marlborough Road, Ilfracombe
3-5yrs. 9.30am-12pm and 12.45-2.45pm.

Tiny Tots Private Nursery   01271 867 067
19 Chambercombe Terrace, Ilfracombe, EX34 9QL
3-5yrs. 8am-5.30pm. Termtime.

Toad Hall Day Nursery   01271 862 475
2 Apsley Terrace, Illfracombe, EX34 9JU
0-5yrs. 8am-5.30pm. 51wks.

West Down Pre-School   01271 863 461
West Down, Ilfracombe, EX34 8NF
2-8yrs. 9am-12pm. Termtime.

Woolacombe & Mortehoe Busy Bees   01271 870 659
School House, Beach Road, Woolacombe, EX34
3-5yrs. 8.45-11.45am. Termtime.

EX35
Lyn Valley Playgroup   01598 753 336
Bottom Meadow, Sinai Hill, Lynton, EX35 6AR
2-5yrs. 9am-3.30pm. Termtime.

EX36
Bishops Nympton 'Little Owls'   01769 550 712
Parish Hall, Bishops Nympton, South Molton, EX36
9.10-11.40am and 12.40-3.15pm. Termtime.

Holly Oak House Nursery   01769 572 188
Mill Street, South Molton, EX36 4AS
2-5yrs. 8am-6pm. 51wks.

North Molton Little Deers   01598 740 111
The Portacabin, The Old School, The Square, EX36
2-5yrs.

South Molton Pre-School   01769 574 003
The PIP Centre, Central Park, South Molton, EX36
9.30am-12pm and 1-3.30pm. Termtime.

EX37
Chittlehampton Pre-School   01769 560 572
Village Hall, Chittlehampton, Umberleigh, EX37 9NS
9.30-11.30am. Termtime.

Kings Nympton Pre-School   07714 518 841
Kings Nympton, Umberleigh, EX37 9SP
2-5yrs. Sessions are offered during the week between 9am-3.30pm. Termtime.

Little Oaks Montessori   01769 520 601
Parish Hall, Burrington, Umberleigh, EX37 9JG
3-5yrs. 3mornings.

EX38
Jack & Jills Under Fives   07811 893 372
Methodist Church Rooms, Mill Street, Torrington
2-5yrs. 9.15-11.45am.

Torridge Pre-School   07870 509 674
Eric Palmer Community Centre, Castle Street, Torrington, EX38 8EZ
3-5yrs. 5mornings. Termtime.

S = SCHOOL   (Devon postcodes) education   79

EX39

Abbotsham & Alwington Nursery   07814 074 437
Village Hall, Abbotsham, Bideford, EX39 5BA
3-5yrs. 9.30am-12pm.

Bideford Baptist Pre-School   01237 471 893
Baptist Centre, Mill Street, Bideford, EX39 2JR
3-5yrs.

Claires Country Childcare   01271 858 601
Southfield, Horwood, Bideford, EX39 4PF
0-5yrs. 8am-6pm. 50wks.

S Edgehill College   01237 471 701
Northdown Road, Bideford, EX39 3LY
2½-19yrs.

S Grenville College Junior School   01237 472 208
Moreton House, Abbotsham Road, Bideford, EX39
2½-11yrs.

Hartland Pre-School   01237 441 258
North Road, Hartland, EX39 6BP
3-5yrs. 9am-12pm and 1-3.30pm.

Instow Pre-School   01237 473 779
The Parish Hall, Quay Lane, Instow, EX39 4JR
3-5yrs. Termtime. Mornings

Parkham Under Fives Playgroup   07786 675 260
Allardice Hall, Parkham, Bideford, EX39 5PL
3-5yrs. 9.15am-12.15pm. Termtime.

Pollyfield Pre-School   07773 459 290
Pollyfield Centre, Avon Road, Bideford, EX39 4BL
3-5yrs.

Sunflowers Pre-School   07786 675 260
Woolsery, Bideford, EX39 5QS
3-5yrs. 9-11.45 am and 12.50-3.20pm. Termtime.

PL1

Bambinos Day Nursery   01752 226 766
19 The Crescent, Plymouth, PL1 3AD
0-8yrs. 7.30am-6pm. 50wks.

Curious Kittens Day Nursery   01752 305 872
Kings Road, Devonport, Plymouth, PL1 5QG
0-5yrs. 8.30am-5.30pm. 51wks.

First Steps Pre-School   01752 660 997
Central Hall, Eastlake Street, Plymouth, PL1 1BA
2-5yrs. 9.45am-12.30pm. Termtime.

Margaret McMillan Nursery   01752 664 884
24 Hoe Street, The Barbican, Plymouth, PL1 2JA
2-5yrs. 8.15am-4pm. Termtime.

Pixieland 2 Day Nursery   01752 251 141
17 Hastings Street, Plymouth, PL1 5BA
7am-6pm. 50wks.

S St Dunstan's Abbey   01752 201 352
The Millfields, Plymouth, PL1 3JL
3-11yrs. Termtime.

Stoke Damerel Playgroup   01752 605 390
Stoke Damerel Church, Paradise Road, Stoke,
Plymouth, PL1 5QL
9am-3pm. Termtime.

PL2

Beanstalk Pre-School   01752 606 004
Smile Centre, St.Michael's Church, 37 Albert Road,
Devonport, Plymouth, PL2 1AB
2-5yrs. 9.30am-1.30pm. Termtime.

Curious Kitten Day Nursery   01752 305 872
Goschen Centre, Saltash Road, Keyham, Plymouth
3-5yrs. 8.15am-5.30pm. 51wks.

Get up and Go Nursery   01752 562 083
27 Wolseley Close, Ford, Plymouth, PL2 3BY
2-8yrs. 8.30am-5pm. 50wks.

Going Places Nursery   01752 776 633
Springhill Green, Pennycross, Plymouth, PL2 3RW
5-8yrs. 7am-6pm. 51wks.

Pelican Children's Centre   01752 551 191
66 Saltash Road, Keyham, Plymouth, PL2 1QS
3-5yrs. 8am-6pm. 48wks.

Peter Pan Playgroup   01752 605 259
The Presbytery, Ocean Street, Keyham, Plymouth
2-5yrs. 9-11.30am. Termtime.

Playbox Pre-School   01752 709 286
Pennycross Meth. Church Hall, Pridham Lane,
Peverell, Plymouth, PL2 3PZ
8.50-11.20am and 12.20-2.50pm. Termtime.

Roger's Burrow Day Nursery   01752 555 878
Woollcombe Block, HMS Drake, Devonport,
Plymouth, PL2 2BG
7am-6pm. 51wks.

YMCA Footsteps Pre-School   01752 780 626
Honicknowle Lane, Pennycross, Plymouth, PL2
2-5yrs. 9am-3.30pm. Termtime.

PL3

Bright Sparks   01752 294 029
Torridge Way, Efford, Plymouth, PL3 6JQ
2-11yrs. 9am-3pm. Open all year From Jan 2006 0-2 years

Compton Pre-School   01752 769 355
Higher Compton Road, Plymouth, PL3 5JB
9-11.30am and 12-3.15pm.

Kings School   01752 771 789
Hartley Road, Mannamead, Plymouth, PL3 5LW
3-5yrs. 8.55am-3.30pm. Termtime.

education (Devon postcodes)   S = SCHOOL

Little Teds Day Nursery Unit 2   01752 250 022
Laira United Church, Laira, Plymouth, PL3 6BP
0-5yrs. 9am-2.45pm. Termtime.

Nutkins Pre-School   01752 767 677
Hope Baptist Church, Peverell Park Road,
Plymouth, PL3 4QG
2-5yrs. 9am-2.45pm. Termtime.

Pathways Day Nursery   01752 700 164
194 Peverell Park Road, Plymouth, PL3 4QE
2-8yrs. 8am-6pm. 51wks.

Pixieland Mannamead   01752 770 550
162 Mannamead Road, Mannamead, Plymouth
0-8yrs. 7am-6pm. 50wks.

Pixieland Stoke   01752 511 007
10 Springfield Drive, Plymouth, PL3 4DU
0-5yrs. 7am-6pm. 50wks.

S Plantings Nursery   01752 265 171
33 Old Park Road, Peverell, Plymouth, PL3 4PY
3-16yrs. 9.15-11.45am. Termtime.

Playtots Childcare   01752 300 590
Blandford Road, Plymouth, PL3 6JA
2-5yrs. 8.30am-4pm. Termtime.

Plymouth College Prep School   01752 668 558
Seymour Road, Mannamead, Plymouth, PL3 5AS
3-18yrs. 8.45am-3.15pm.

S Plymouth College Prep School   01752 772 283
Munday House, Hartley Road, Plymouth, PL3 5LW
3-11yrs.

Sunbeams Day Nursery   01752 661 445
74 Peverell Park Road, Peverell, Plymouth, PL3
0-5yrs. 7.30am-6pm. 50wks.

Sunshine All Day Nursery   07890 869 164
Blandford Road, Efford, Plymouth, PL3 6JA
3-5yrs. 9.05-12.05pm.

Toad Hall Pre-School   07712 263 412
St Gabriel's Church Hall, Hyde Park Road,
Plymouth, PL3 4JN
3-5yrs. 9.15-11.45am and 12.45-3.15pm. Termtime.

Trinity Teddies Pre-School   01752 771 226
Torr Lane, Plymouth, PL3 5NY
9.15am-12pm. Termtime.

PL4

Bobtails Full Day Care   01752 225 271
Bernice Terrace, Lipson, Plymouth, PL4 7HW
2-5yrs. 8am-6pm. 50wks.

Fletewood School   01752 663 782
88 North Road East, Plymouth, PL4 6AN
3-5yrs. 9am-3.15pm. Termtime.

Freshlings Nursery   01752 232 338
University of Plymouth, Drake Circus, Plymouth
8.15am-5.45pm. 50wks.

Holding the Reins Nursery   01752 260 792
6 Ladysmith Road, Lipson, Plymouth, PL4 7NJ
2-5yrs. 8.15am-5.45pm. 50wks.

Kenleys Day Nursery   01752 664 734
7 Gordon Terrace, Mutley, Plymouth, PL4 6EP
8am-6pm. 51wks.

Kiddiewinks Pre-School   07779 336 475
Salisbury Road Baptist Church, Rosebery Avenue,
St. Judes, Plymouth, PL4 8SX
9.15am-1pm.

Little Angels Pre-School   01752 224 327
St. Matthias Lower Hall, North Hill, Plymouth, PL4
2-5yrs. 9.30am-12pm. Termtime.

Noah's Ark Childcare   0800 634 3867
30 Looe Street, Plymouth, PL4 0EA
0-5yrs. 7.30am-6pm. 50wks.

Noah's Ark Childcare   0800 634 3867
13-15 Brunswick Road, Plymouth, PL4 0NP
0-5yrs. 8am-6pm. 50wks.

Noah's Ark Childcare   0800 634 3867
20-24 Lucas Terrace, Plymouth, PL4 9LD
0-8yrs. 8am-6pm. 50wks.

Nomony Family Centre   01752 667 869
St.Johns Bridge Road, Cattedown, Plymouth, PL4
2-8yrs. 8am-6pm. 50wks.

Pixieland 1 Day Nursery   01752 272 304
Mount Gould Hospital, Mount Gould Road, Mount
Gould, Plymouth, PL4 7QD
7am-6pm. 50wks.

Bright Stars Pre-School   07946 096 588
Embankment Road, Plymouth, PL4 9JF
3-5yrs. 9.15-11.45am. Termtime.

Roundabout Day Care Nursery   01752 229 563
Embankment Road, Plymouth, PL4 9HP
0-5yrs. 7.30am-6pm. 51wks.

St Judes Pre-School   01752 302 245
St. Judes Vicarage, Knighton Road, Plymouth, PL4
3-5yrs. 8.45am-1.30pm.

PL5

Chaucer Pre-School   079101 800 900
Chaucer Way, Honicknowle, Plymouth, PL5 3EJ
2-5yrs. 9-11.30am and 12.45-3.15pm. Termtime.

Crownhill Kindergarten   01752 775 674
37 Meavy Avenue, Crownhill, Plymouth, PL5 3AH
3-5yrs. 9am-12pm and 1.15-3.45pm. Termtime.

S = SCHOOL   (Devon postcodes) **education**

Early Birds Pre-School 07788 527 814
Trelawney Avenue, St. Budeaux, Plymouth, PL5
3-5yrs. 9-11.30am and 12.30-3pm. Termtime.

Fletemoor Road Playgroup 01752 660 997
Fletemoor Road, St. Budeaux, Plymouth, PL5 1TF
2-5yrs. 9-11.30am and 12.30-3pm. Termtime.

Magic House Playgroup 01752 213 979
Trevithick Road, St. Budeaux, Plymouth, PL5 2AF
3-8yrs. 8am-3pm. Termtime.

Mary Dean Pre-School 07974 773 390
Mary Dean Avenue, Tamerton Foliot, Plymouth, PL5
8.45-11.15am and 12.30-3pm.

Squirrels Pre-School 07759 978 449
St Francis of Assisi Church, Little Dock Lane,
Plymouth, PL5 2LP
2-5yrs. 9.30am-12pm Mon/Wed/Thurs/Fri and 12-2.45pm
Tues. Termtime.

St Paul's Playgroup 01752 517 473
Barne Lane, St.Budeaux, Plymouth, PL5 1NE
3-5yrs. 9-11.30am and 12.30-3pm. Termtime.

PL6
Alexandra House 01752 718 888
20 Crownhill Fort Road, Plymouth, PL6 5BX
6mths-3yrs. 8am-4.30pm. 51wks.

Ark Childcare Centre 01752 766 711
Miller Way, Plymouth, PL6 8UL
4-11yrs. 8am-6pm. 50wks.

Bambinos Day Nursery 01752 696 616
School Drive, Woolwell, Plymouth, PL6 7JW
0-2yrs. 8am-6pm. Termtime.

Busy Bees Day Nursery 01752 792 844
Derriford Hospital, Derriford Road, Plymouth, PL6
8am-6pm. 52wks.

Crownhill Royal Naval Pre-School 01752 79 606
Crownhill Fort Road, Plymouth, PL6 5BX
3-5yrs. 9.15am-12pm. Termtime.

Eggbuckland Royal Naval Nursery 01752 796 079
29 Bellamy Close, Eggbuckland, Plymouth, PL6
2½-5yrs. 9.15am-12pm and 12.30-3pm. Termtime.

Eggbuckland Village Pre-School 07816 654 520
Church Hall, Church Hill, Eggbuckland, Plymouth
3-5yrs. 9-11.45am. 4 mornings. Termtime.

Fortview Day Nursery 01752 782 552
Crownhill Fort Road, Crownhill, Plymouth, PL6 5BX
0-5yrs. 8am-6pm. 50wks.

Frogmore Montessori Nursery 01752 769 704
Frogmore House, Frogmore Avenue, Eggbuckland
1-8yrs. 8am-12.30pm and 1.30-5.45pm. 50wks.

Happy Days Nursery 01752 791 271
Lulworth Drive, Widewell, Plymouth, PL6 7ER
3mths-5yrs. 8am-6pm. 50wks.

Jumping Jellybeans 01752 208 237
104 Tavistock Road, Plymouth, PL6 5EL
2-5yrs. 9.30am-1.25pm. Termtime.

Little Acorns Pre-School 01752 204 082
Pendeen Crescent, Plymouth, PL6 6QS
3-5yrs. 8.5-11.20am and 12.30-3pm. Termtime.

Mainstone Pre-School 01752 788 066
Pattinson Drive, Mainstone, Plymouth, PL6 8RU
2-5yrs. 9.15-11.45am and 12.15-2.15pm.

Marjon Playgroup 01752 777 327
Derriford Road, Plymouth, PL6 8BH
2-5yrs. 9.30am-12pm and 12.15-2.45pm. Termtime.

Marjons Day Nursery 01752 636 858
The College of St. Mark & St. John, Derriford Road,
Plymouth, PL6 8BH
8.45am-5pm. 50wks.

Roborough Pre-School 07944 076 272
Methodist Church Hall, Bickleigh Down Road,
Roborough, Plymouth, PL6 7BB
3-5yrs. Mornings. Termtime.

Tamerton Tots Pre-School 01752 707 707
Rolston Close, Southway, Plymouth, PL6 6PE
3-8yrs. 8am-5.30pm. Termtime.

Towerfield Tots Day Nursery 01752 726 318
Clearbrook House, Bickleigh Down Business Park,
Towerfield Drive, Woolwell, Plymouth, PL6 7TN
7.15am-5.45pm. 50wks.

Widey Court Pre-School 01752 701 187
Widey Court, Crownhill, Plymouth, PL6 5UB
3-5yrs.

Woolwell Under Fives Pre-School 01752 695 888
Community & Resource Centre, Darklake Lane,
Plymouth, PL6 7TR
9-11.30am and 12.15-2.45pm. Termtime

PL7
Bambinos Day Nursery 01752 348 088
Mudge Way, Plympton, Plymouth, PL7 2AQ
7.30am-6pm. U8's 51wks.

Buddies and Little Buddies 07855 172 321
Glen Road, Plympton, Plymouth, PL7 2DE
8am-6pm.

Chaddlewood Pre-School 01752 345 838
Hemerdon Heights, Plympton, Plymouth, PL7 2EU
2-5yrs. 9.15-11.45am and 12.45-3.15pm. Termtime.

Colebrooks Little Cherubs 01752 347 300
Methodist Church, Colebrook Road, Plympton,
Plymouth, PL7 4AA
2½-4yrs. 9-11.45am and 12.15-2.45pm. Termtime.

education (Devon postcodes)   S = SCHOOL

Cornwood & Lutton 07808 211 800
Under 5's Association
Sunday School Hall, Lee Mor, Plympton, Plymouth
2-5yrs. 9.15am-12pm.

Hobby Horse Day Nursery 01752 202 193
17 Branson Court, Plympton, Plymouth, PL7 2WU
0-8yrs. 8am-6pm. 50wks.

Newlife Children's Centre 01752 346 399
Station Road, Plympton, Plymouth, PL7 2AU
2-8yrs. 8am-6pm. Termtime.

Plympton Montessori Nursery 01752 343 127
Meadowfield Place, Plymouth, PL7 1XQ
2-5yrs. 8am-5.45pm. 50wks.

Plympton St. Maurice Pre-School 01752 343 085
Plympton Hill, Plymouth, PL7 1UB
2-8yrs. 7.40am-5.45pm. 50wks.

Rainbow Pre-School 01752 346 451
Harewood House, Ridgeway, Plympton, Plymouth
3-5yrs. 9.15am-12pm and 12.20-3pm. Termtime.

Rees Pre-School 01752 341 362
Community Centre, Mudge Way, Plympton,
Plymouth, PL7 2PS
2-8yrs. 9-11.30am and 12.30-3pm. Termtime.

Ridgeway Methodist Pre-School 01752 331 186
Mudge Way, Plympton, Plymouth, PL7 2PS
2-5yrs. 9.15-11.45am and 12.30-3pm. Termtime.

St Marys Pre-School 01752 348 525
Church Hall, 10 Market Road, Plymouth, PL7 1QW
2-5yrs.9.30am-12pm and 12.30-3pm. Termtime.

Woodford Methodist Pre-School 01752 337 335
Methodist Church, Greenway Avenue, Plymouth
2-5yrs. 9am-12pm.

Woodford Rascals Day Nursery 01752 347 170
Litchaton Way, Woodford, Plympton, Plymouth,
PL7
0-8yrs. 8am-6pm. 50wks.

PL8
Holbeton Pre-School Playgroup 1 01752 830 321
Village Hall, Brent Hill, Holbeton, Plymouth, PL8
9.30am-12pm. Termtime.

Ladybirds Day Nursery 01752 881 161
Steer Point Road, Brixton, Plymouth, PL8 2AH
0-8yrs. 7.30am-6.30pm. 50wks.

St Francis Pre-School Playgroup 078707 488 986
Village Hall, Noss Mayo, Plymouth, PL8 1EN
2-5yrs. 9.15am-12pm and 1-3.30pm. Termtime.

Yealmpton Pre-School 01752 881 810
Communit Centre, Stray Park, Yealmpton, PL8 2HF
9-11.45am and 12.45-2.45pm. Termtime.

PL9
Bramble Hedge Pre-School 01752 404 378
Hooe & Turnchapel Community Centre, Church Hill
Road, Hooe, Plymouth, PL9 9SE
9.15-11.55am. Termtime.

Kenleys Nursery School 01752 481 181
289 Dean Cross Road, Plymstock, Plymouth, PL9
3mths-8yrs. 8am-6pm. 51wks.

Ladybirds Pre-School 01752 408 966
Howard Road, Plymstock, Plymouth, PL9 7ES
3-5yrs. Termtime.

Little Deers Pre-School 01752 404 370
Morley Centre, Broadland Gardens, Stentaway
Drive, Plymouth, PL9 8TE
9.15am-12pm and 12.30-3pm. Termtime.

Oreston Pre-School 07968 045 836
Methodist Church Hall, Plymstock Road, Oreston,
Plymouth, PL9 7LL
2-5yrs. 9.15am-12pm. Termtime.

Plymstock Pre-School 01752 403 312
6 Memory Lane, Plymstock, Plymouth, PL9 9GH
9.15am-12pm and 12.30-3.15pm.

Radford Royal Naval Pre-School 01752 481 152
Stokingway Close, Plymstock, Plymouth, PL9 9JL
9.05-11.35am and 12.35-3.05pm. Termtime.

Seedlings Pre-School 01752 401 293
Shortwood Crescent, Plymstock, PL9 8QT
2-5yrs. 9am-3.30pm. Termtime.

St Mary's Pre-School 01752 404 767
Church Hall, Plymstock, Plymouth, PL9 9BD
2-5yrs. 9.15-11.45am. Termtime.

Stepping Stones Pre-School 07971 402 376
Church Hall, Springfield Road, Elburton, Plymouth
2-5yrs. 9.15am-12pm.

Toy Box Pre-School 01752 402 444
144 Staddiscombe Road, Staddiscombe, Plymouth
2-5yrs. 9.30am-12pm. Termtime.

Treetops Too 01752 406 541
Haye Road South, Plymouth, PL9 8HJ
2-8yrs. 8am-6pm. 51wks.

PL15
St Giles on the Heath Playgroup 01566 772 191
The Old School House, St. Giles-on-the-Heath,
Launceston, PL15 9SD
2-5yrs. 9am-12pm. Termtime.

PL16
Broadwoodwidger Pre-School 01409 211 366
Ivyhouse Cross, Broadwoodwidger, Lifton, PL16
0-5yrs. 36wks. 2 mornings.

S = SCHOOL   (Devon postcodes) **education**

Lifton Pre-School 01566 784 288
North Road, Lifton, PL16 0EH
3-5yrs. 9am-12pm. Termtime.

PL19

Gulworthy 0-5 Pre-School 01822 832 520
Parish Hall, Gulworthy, Tavistock, PL19 8JA
3-5yrs. 9.15am-12.15pm. Termtime. 2 days.

S **Kelly College Prep School** 01822 612 919
Parkwood Road, Tavistock, PL19 0JS
2½-11yrs.

Little Lambs Pre-School Playgroup 07812 918 236
Parish Hall, Lamerton, Tavistock, PL19 8QR
2-5yrs. 9.30am-12pm. Termtime.

Mary Tavy Pre-School 07818 024 628
Coronation Hall, Mary Tavy, Tavistock, PL19 9PB
1-4½yrs. 9.30am-12pm. Termtime. 3mornings.

Milton Abbot Under Fives 01822 612 842
Village Hall, Milton Abbot, Nr Tavistock, PL19 0PZ
3-5yrs. 9.45am-12.15pm. 3days.

S **Mount House School** 01822 612 244
Tavistock, Tavistock, PL19 9JL
3-13yrs.

Sunningdale Nursery 01822 613 416
54 Plymouth Road, Tavistock, PL19 8BU
3mths-5yrs. 8am-6pm. 50wks.

Tavistock Pre-School 01822 613 701
Alexander Centre, 62 Plymouth Road, Tavistock
2-8yrs. 9.15-11.45am and 12.45-3.15pm.

Tavistock Under Fives 07791 906 891
The Cabin, Courtlands Road, Tavistock, PL19 0EF
2-5yrs. 9.30am-2.30pm. Termtime.

The Old School Children's Centre 01822 612 362
Church Hill, Whitchurch, Tavistock, PL19 0ED
3-5yrs.

Whitchurch Montessori 01822 613 927
The Old Methodist Hall, Anderton Court,
Whitchurch, Tavistock, PL19 9EX
3-5yrs. 9.15am-12.15pm. Termtime.

Whitchurch Pre-School 07812 856 353
School Road, Whitchurch, Tavistock, PL19 9SR
3-4yrs. 9.15-11.45am. Termtime.

PL20

Bere Valley Playgroup 07733 181 080
The Parish Hall, Bere Alston, Yelverton, PL20 7EJ
9.30am-12pm. Termtime.

Bucland Monachorum 01822 853 291
Pre-School
Willowbank, 47 Chapel Meadow, Buckland,
Monachorum, Yelverton, PL20 7LR
2-5yrs. 9.15-11.45am. Termtime.

Edgemoor Nursery Centre 01822 855 644
Yelverton Business Park, Yelverton, PL20 7PE
3mths-5yrs. 8am-6pm. 51wks.

Penmoor ABC Nursery School 01822 855 175
War Memorial Hall, Meavy Lane, Yelverton, PL20
9am-1pm and 1-4pm. Termtime.

Princetown Pre-School Playgroup 01822 890 348
Tor Royal Lane, Princetown, PL20 6QT
2-5yrs. 9.01am-1pm. Termtime.

Walkhampton Pre-School 01822 853 277
Walkhampton, Yelverton, PL20 6JR
3-5yrs. 9am-12.30pm. Termtime.

Walkhampton Toddler Group 07866 841 532
Village Hall, Walkhampton, Tavistock, PL20 6JX
9am-12.30pm. Termtime.

Yelverton Pre-School 07969 767 817
St. Paul's Church Hall, Yelverton, PL20 6AA
3-5yrs. 9.30am-1pm.

PL21

Bittaford Under Fives 07814 525 787
Children's Centre, Moorhaven Village, Bittaford
9.30am-12pm. Termtime.

Cornwood & Lutton Under 5's 07808 211 800
Fore Street, Cornwood, Ivybridge, PL21 9PZ
3-5yrs.

Ermington Pre-School Unit 07771 712 597
Lower Reading Room, Church Street, Ermington
3-5yrs. 9-11.30am. Termtime.

Jays Day Nursery 01752 894 437
Children's Centre, Moorhaven Village, Ivybridge
0-5yrs.

Lee Mill Pre-School 07715 582 702
Church Hall, Lee Mill, Ivybridge, PL21 9EX
9.30am-12pm. Termtime. 3 days.

Manor Pre-School 01752 895 066
Manor Way, Ivybridge, PL21 9BG
8.45-11.45am and 12.30-3pm.

Millswood Nursery School 01752 894 737
St. Austins Priory, Cadleigh, Ivybridge, PL21 9HW
8.20am-3.30pm. Termtime.

Modbury Pre-School Playgroup 07810 195 925
Memorial Hall, Back Street, Modbury, Ivybridge
9.15-11.45am. Termtime.

Rocking Horse Day Nursery 01752 893 454
Abbots Road, Ivybridge, PL21 9TF
0-5yrs. 7.45am-5.30pm. 50wks.

Scallywags Pre-School 01752 893 924
Victoria Lane Hall, Victoria Lane, Ivybridge, PL21
3-5yrs. 9.30am-12pm. 33wks.

84 education (Devon postcodes) — S = SCHOOL

St John's Pre-School 01752 892 833
Church Hall, Blachford Road, Ivybridge, PL21 0AD
2-5yrs. 9am-1pm. Termtime.

Stowford Pre-School 01752 896 320
Exeter Road, Ivybridge, PL21 0BG
9-11.30am and 12.30-3.30pm.

The Old Fire Station Playgroup 01752 894 400
Wayside, Western Road, Ivybridge, PL21 9AU
3-5yrs. 9-11.30am. Termtime.

Ugborough Under Fives 07763 215 455
Village Hall, The Square, Ugborough, Ivybridge
9.30am-12.30pm. Termtime.

Woodlanders Nursery 01752 698 224
Woodland Road, Ivybridge, PL21 9HQ
0-5yrs. 8am-6pm. 51wks.

TQ1

S Abbey School 01803 327 868
Hampton Court, Fore Street, St. Marychurch,
Torquay, TQ1 4PR
3mths-11yrs, 9am-3pm, Termtime.

All Saints Pre-School 01803 323 702
Cary Avenue, Babbacombe, Torquay, TQ1 1QT
3-5yrs. 9.15am-12pm. Termtime.

Ellacombe Church Playgroup 07778 229 022
Church Hall, Ellacombe Church Road, Torquay
3-8yrs. 9am-3pm. Termtime.

Furrough Cross Pre-School 01803 324 226
Cross Church, Babbacombe Road, Torquay, TQ1
3-5yrs. 9am-3pm. Termtime.

Hatfield Nursery 01803 316 611
9 St. Margarets Road, Torquay, TQ1 4NW
7.30am-7.30pm. 50wks.

Noah's Ark Childcare Centre 0800 634 3867
133 Babbacombe Road, Torquay, TQ1 3SR
0-8yrs. 8am-6pm. 50wks.

Playplaces 01803 290 030
21 Carlton Road, Ellacombe, Torquay, TQ1 1NA
3-8yrs. 8am-6pm. Termtime.

St Marychurch Pre-School 01803 312 542
The Parish Hall, Church Road, Torquay, TQ1 4QY
2-5yrs. 9am-12pm. Termtime.

St Matthias Church Pre-School 01803 214 175
Babbacombe Road, Torquay, TQ1 1HW
3-4yrs. Termtime.

Stepping Stones Day Nursery 01803 328 449
69 Teignmouth Road, Torquay, TQ1 4ES
2-5yrs. 8.30am-5.30pm. 50wks.

S Stoodley Knowle School 01803 293 160
Ansteys Cove Road, Torquay, TQ1 2JB
2-18yrs. 33wks.

Sunbury Hill Nursery School 01803 292 732
Laurayne, Sunbury Hill, Torquay, TQ1 3EA
0-8yrs. 8am-6pm.

Thistledown Nursery 01803 316 511
Barewell Road, Torquay, TQ1 4PA
3mths-5yrs. 8am-6pm. 51wks.

TQ2

Kiddi Caru Day Nursery 01803 615 400
The Willows, Nicholson Road, Torquay, TQ2 7AZ
www.kiddicaru.com
3mths-5yrs, 8am-6pm, 51 weeks per year (see ad pg 61).

Acorns Pre-School 01803 200 588
All Saints Church Hall, Bampfylde Road, Torre,
Torquay, TQ2 5AR
3-5yrs. Termtime.

Acorns Pre-School 07773 752 525
Old Mill Road, Torquay, TQ2 6AP
8am-6pm. 51wks.

Chelston Methodist Playgroup 07816 987 236
Methodist Church, Old Mill Road, Chelston,
Torquay, TQ2 6HL
2.9-5yrs. 9.15am-3pm.

Holy Angels Pre-School 01803 605 415
Church Hall, Queensway, Chelston, Torquay, TQ2
2-5yrs. 9.15-11.45am and 12.30-3pm. Termtime.

Pea Pods Day Nursery 01803 407 262
20 Abbey Road, Torquay, TQ2 5NA
2-5yrs. 8.30am-5.30pm. 50wks.

Puffins at Newton Road 01803 612 446
156 Newton Road, Torquay, TQ2 7AQ
0-5yrs. 8am-6pm. 51wks.

Rainbow Day Nursery 01803 654 150
Torbay Hospital, Newton Road, Torquay, TQ2 7AA
3mths-4yrs. 7am-6pm.

Shiphay Day Nursery 01803 612 613
25 Courtland Road, Torquay, TQ2 6JU
2-5yrs.

Southernwood Nursery 01803 607 640
Greenway Road, Chelston, Torquay, TQ2 6JE
2-5yrs. 8.30am-5.30pm. 50wks.

Squirrels Pre-School 01803 328 819
Acorn Centre, Lummaton Cross, Torquay, TQ2 8ET
2-5yrs. 9am-4pm. Termtime.

St Andrews Pre-School 07803 654 286
Church Hall, Exe Hill, Shiphay, Torquay, TQ2 7NF
3-5yrs. 9-11.45am and 12.30-3pm.

(Devon postcodes) education

Tom Thumb Pre-School   01803 406 478
Newton Road, Torquay, TQ2 5BY
2-5yrs. 8.45am-5pm. Termtime.

TQ3
Collaton St Mary Playgroup   01803 668 810
Parish Rooms, Blagdon Road, Paignton, TQ3 3YA
2-5yrs. 9am-3.15pm. Termtime.

Marldon Pre-School Playgroup   07977 797 768
Village Hall, Village Road, Marldon, Paignton, TQ3
3-5yrs. 9.15-11.45am. Termtime.

Paignton Day Nursery   01803 559 941
Barum Close, Lower Polsham Road, Paignton, TQ3
8am-5.30pm. 50wks.

Preston Baptist Church   01803 522 541
Old Torquay Road, Paignton, TQ3 2RB
3-5yrs. 9.30am-12pm. 38wks.

St Paul's Second Steps Pre-School   07981 929 518
Church Hall, Torquay Road, Preston, Paignton, TQ3
3-5yrs. 9am-12pm. 38wks.

Torbay Opportunity Group   01803 558 194
Foxhole Clinic, 37 Smallcombe Road, Paignton
0-5yrs. 10am-12.30pm. 2 mornings. Termtime.

TQ4
Beehive Nursery   01803 557 077
Tower House School, Fisher Street, Paignton, TQ4
2-5yrs. 8.30am-5.30pm. 50wks.

Braeside Day Nursery   01803 557 012
1 Braeside Road, Paignton, TQ4 6BX
0-5yrs. 8am-6pm. 51wks.

Goodrington Pre-School   01803 846 020
Methodist Church, 1 Grange Road, Paignton, TQ4
2-5yrs. 9.30am-3pm. Termtime.

IMPS Day Nursery   01803 407 901
Hayes Road, Paignton, TQ4 5PJ
2-5yrs. 8.30am-5.30pm. 51wks.

Ladybirds Nursery   01803 551 578
Youth Centre, Dartmouth Road, Paignton, TQ4 6NX
8.30am-5.30pm. 50wks.

Little Angels Nursery   01803 526 200
Church Hall, St. Andrews Road, Paignton, TQ4 6HA
8.30am-4pm. 48wks.

Nippers Childcare Centre   01803 520 620
4 Midvale Road, Paignton, TQ4 5BD
8am-6pm. 50wks.

Roselands Community Nursery   01803 525 620
Porlock Way, Paignton, TQ4 7RH
0-8yrs. 8am-6pm. 50wks.

Whiterock Pre-School   01803 845 989
Freshwater Drive, Paignton, TQ4 7SB
3-5yrs. 9.15am-3pm. 39wks.

TQ5
Chestnut Heights Playgroup   01803 852 421
1-3 Poplar Close, Brixham, TQ5 0SA
2-5yrs. 9am-3pm. 37wks.

Galmpton Pre-School Limited   01803 845 547
Greenway Road, Galmpton, Brixham, TQ5 0LT
9.15am-12pm and 1.15-3.15pm. Termtime.

The Nest   01803 882 421
Higher Ranscombe Road, Brixham, TQ5 9HF
0-5yrs. 8am-6pm. 50wks.

TQ6
Dartmouth Pre-School   01803 834 449
South Ford Road, Dartmouth, TQ6 9QS
0-5yrs. Termtime.

Humpty Dumpty Day Nursery   01803 832 579
Milton Lane, Dartmouth, TQ6 9HW
3mths-5yrs. 8am-5.30pm.

Stoke Fleming Pre-School   01803 770 425
Stoke Fleming, Dartmouth, TQ6 0QA
9-11.30am and 12.30-3pm. Termtime.

TQ7
Aveton Gifford Pre-School   01548 550 888
Memorial Hall, Aveton Gifford, Kingsbridge, TQ7
9.15-11.45am. Termtime.

Loddiswell Pre-School   07939 221 653
Village Hall, Loddiswell, Kingsbridge, TQ7 4QJ
3-5yrs. Termtime. 4 mornings

Malborough & South Huish Playgroup   07817 741 562
Church Institute Hall, Marlborough, Kingsbirdge
9am-1pm. Termtime. 3days.

P.I.P's (Loddiswell Pre-School)   07939 221 653
Loddiswell, Kingsbridge, TQ7 4QJ
3-5yrs. 9-11.30am. Termtime.

St Malo Under Fives Centre   01548 854 308
Belle Cross Road, Kingsbridge, TQ7 1NL
3-5yrs. Termtime.

Stokenham Pre-School Centre   01548 580 202
Pre-School Building, Stokenham, Kingsbridge, TQ7
3-5yrs. 9.30am-12pm.

Treetops Pre-School Centre   01548 854 004
St. Johns House, Fore Street, Kingsbridge, TQ7
2-5yrs.

Tresillian Early Years   01548 857 663
Kingsbridge Community College, 112 Fore Street, Kingsbridge, TQ7 1AW
4mths-5yrs. 9.30am-12pm and 1-3.30pm. Termtime.

Please say you saw the listings in the South West Baby Directory

education (Devon postcodes)   S = SCHOOL

TQ8
Beehives Under Fives 01548 843 152
Young Salcombe Centre, Gould Road, Salcombe
9.15am-3.15pm. Termtime.

Salcombe Pre-School 01548 842 874
Onslow Road, Salcombe, TQ8 8AG
2-5yrs. 9am-12pm and 12.15-3.15pm. Termtime.

TQ9
Blackawton & Dittisham Playgroup 01803 772 363
School Lane, Blackawton, Totnes, TQ9 7BE
2-5yrs. 9am-3pm. Termtime.

Broadhempston Playgroup 07880 960 120
Village Hall, Broadhempston, Newton Abbot, TQ9
2-5yrs. 9.15am-12.45pm. 3days.

Daisy Pre-School 01803 864 737
Pathfields, Totnes, TQ9 5TZ
2-5yrs. 9.15am-3.15pm. Termtime.

Dartington Playgroup 01803 863 548
Foxhole, Dartington, Totnes, TQ9 6EB
2-5yrs. 9am-3pm. 37wks.

Humpty Dumpty Nursery 01803 868 414
Foxhole, Dartington Hall Estate, Totnes, TQ9 6EB
0-5yrs.

Mansion Community Nursery 01803 840 574
United Free Church, Fore Street, Totnes, TQ9 5RP
2-8yrs. 9.15am-3.30pm Termtime.

S Park School 01803 864 588
Park Road, Dartington Hall, Totnes, TQ9 6EQ
3-11yrs. 9am-3pm. Termtime.

Ready Steady Go 01548 521 615
East Allington, Totnes, TQ9 7RE
2-5yrs. 9am-3pm. Termtime.

St Christopher's School 01803 762 202
Mount Barton, Staverton, Totnes, TQ9 6PF
2-11yrs. 9am-3.30pm. Termtime.

Stoke Gabriel Pre-School 01803 782 155
Old School Room, Church Walk, Stoke Gabriel
2-5yrs. 9am-3pm. Termtime.

TQ10
Little Orchard Montessori Nursery 0136 473 131
Palstone Park, Exeter Road, South Brent, TQ10 9JP
2½-5yrs. 9am-3.30pm. Termtime. Setting is fabulous, located in Dartmoor National Parkland. Classroom divided into 6 Montessori Curiculum areas from Practical Life to Cultural. Also offer extra activities - each half term has a different subject.

Moorland Childhood Centre 0136 472 040
Little Orchard, Exeter Road, South Brent, TQ10 9JP
2-8yrs. 8am-6pm. 51wks.

South Brent Pre-School 0136 472 022
School House, Totnes Road, South Brent, TQ10
9.15-11.45am. Termtime.

TQ11
Playcentre Playgroup 01364 643 304
Garden Classroom, Bossel Road, TQ11 0DD
2-5yrs. 9-11.45am. Termtime.

Bagpuss Nursery 01364 642 816
Scout Hut, Duckpond Road, Buckfastleigh, TQ11
8.45am-3.30pm. 50wks.

TQ12
S Abbotsbury School 01626 352 164
90 Torquay Road, Newton Abbot, TQ12 2JD
2½-7yrs. 9am-12pm and 1-3.30pm. Termtime.

Abbotskerswell Pre-School 01626 336 326
Village Hall, Slade Lane, Abbotskerswell, Newton Abbot, TQ12 5YF
2½-5yrs. 9.45am-12.15pm. Termtime.

Ark in the Park 01626 324 800
20 Keyberry Park, Newton Abbot, TQ12 1BZ
0-5yrs. 8am-6pm. 51wks.

Cherubs Childcare 01803 405 011
Public Hall, Newton Road, Kingskerswell, TQ12
8am-6pm. 50wks.

Denbury Pre-School Playgroup 01803 813 149
Village Hall, West Street, Denbury, TQ12 6DP
2-5yrs. 9.15am-12.45pm. Termtime.

Happy Days Day Nursery 01626 334 070
Newton Abbot Racecourse, Kingsteignton Road, Newton Abbot, TQ12 2HD
0-5yrs. 8am-6pm. 50wks.

Happy Days Nursery 01626 333 323
1a Courtenay Park, Newton Abbot, TQ12 2HD
0-5yrs. 8am-6pm. 50wks.

Humpty Dumpty Nursery 01626 201 853
Coombeshead College, Lower Site, Highweek, Newton Abbot, TQ12 1TR
8am-6pm.

Kingskerswell Playgroup 01803 875 466
Church End Road, Kingskerswell, Newton Abbot
2-5yrs. 8.30am-3pm. Termtime.

Little Owls Nursery School
Village Hall, Bickington, Nr Newton Abbot, TQ12
3-5yrs. 9am-12pm. Termtime.

Liverton Pre-School 07792 375 914
Village Hall, Liverton, Newton Abbot, TQ12 6HW
9.30am-12pm. Termtime.

Magpie Pre-School 01626 360 400
Avenue Methodist Church, Newton Abbot, TQ12
9.30am-12pm. Termtime. 4days.

S = SCHOOL   (Devon postcodes) **education**

Newton Abbot Pre-School   07971 708 024
The Green Rooms, Fisher Road, Newton Abbot
9-11.30am-12.30-3pm. Termtime.

Ogwell Pre-School   07779 210 862
Memorial Hall, East Ogwell, Newton Abbot, TQ12
2-5yrs. 9.30am-2pm.

Puddleducks Pre-School   07949 365 468
Oaklands Barn, Stokeinteignhead, Newton Abbot
2-5yrs. Termtime.

Rackerhayes Pre-School   01626 352 030
Newton Road, Kingsteignton, Newton Abbot, TQ12
3-5yrs. 9.15am-12.15pm. and 12.45-3.15pm. Termtime.

Rydon Early Learners Pre-School   01626 369 848
Community Hall, Rydon Road, Kingsteignton, TQ12
2-5yrs. 9-11.30am and 12.30-3pm. Termtime.

Serendipity Day Nursery   01626 369 697
Oakymead Park, Newton Road, Kingsteignton,
Newton Abbot, TQ12 3AN
0-8yrs. 8am-6pm. 50wks.

St Joseph's Pre-School Unit   01626 352 559
Coombeshead Road, Newton Abbot, TQ12 1PT
3-5yrs. 9am-12pm and 1-3.30pm. Termtime.

St Michael's Church Pre-School   07808 620 794
Church Hall, Chudleigh Road, Kingsteignton,
Newton Abbot, TQ12 3JU
3-5yrs. 9.15am-12.15pm. Termtime.

S **Stover School**   01626 354 505
Newton Abbot, Newton Abbott, TQ12 6QG
3-18yrs.

The Centre Pre-School   01626 334 357
St. Pauls Parish Hall, Devon Square, Newton Abbot
2-5yrs. 9.30am-12pm. Termtime.

TQ13
Ashburton Pre-School   07866 087 151
The Cadet Hall, Love Lane, Ashburton, TQ13 7DD
3-5yrs. Termtime.

Bovey Busy Bees Pre-School   07909 576 422
Methodist Church Hall, Bovey Tracey, Newton
Abbot, TQ13 9AB
2-5yrs. 9.30am-12pm and 12.15-2.45pm. 3 days.

Bovey Tracey Pre-School   01626 834 835
The Church Rooms, Coombe Close, Bovey Tracey,
Newton Abbot, TQ13 9EN
0-5yrs. 9.30am-12pm. 33wks.

Chagford Montessori   01647 433 676
Lower Street, Chagford, Newton Abbot, TQ13 8BX
3-6yrs. 9am-3.45pm. Termtime.

Chagford Pre-School Playgroup   01647 281 137
Chagford, Newton Abbot, TQ13 8BZ
9.15am-12pm and 1.15-3.45pm. Termtime.

Chestnuts Day Nursery   01626 833 255
Abbey Road, Bovey Tracey, Newton Abbot, TQ13
0-5yrs. 8am-6pm. 50wks.

Chudleigh Knighton Pre-School   07977 315 773
Chudleigh Knighton, Chudleigh, Newton Abbot
2-5yrs. 9.30am-3pm.

Chudleigh Pre-School   01626 854 680
The School Room, Town Hall, Chudleigh, TQ13 0JT
3-5yrs. 9.15-11.45am. Termtime.

Chudleigh Pre-School   01626 854 680
Community Room, Lawn Drive, Chudleigh, TQ13
3-5yrs. 9.15-11.45am and 12-3pm. Termtime.

Hennock Pre-School   01409 231 609
Hennock, Bovey Tracey, Newton Abbot, TQ13 9QB
2-5yrs. 9.20-11.50am. Termtime.

Ilsington Pre-School   07779 691 992
Village Hall, Ilsington, Newton Abbot, TQ13 9RG
2½-5yrs. 9.30am-12pm. 3days.

Little Acorns Montessori   01626 832 137
Catholic Church Hall, Ashburton Road, Bovey
Tracey, TQ13 9BY
2½-5yrs. 9.30am-12.30pm. Termtime.

Moretonhampstead Pre-School   07940 271 722
Parish Hall, Fore Street, Moretonhampstead, TQ13
3-5yrs. 9.15-11.45am and 12.45-3.15pm. Termtime.

Sunshine Pre-School   01626 836 691
East Dartmoor Baptist Church, Hind Street, Bovey
Tracey, Newton Abbot, TQ13 9HT
3-5yrs. 9.30am-12pm. Termtime.

The Orchard Pre-School   07763 397 544
Village Hall, Lustleigh, Newton Abbot, TQ13
3-5yrs. 9.30am-12pm. 3mornings.

The Orchard Pre-School   01626 835 277
1st Bovey Tracey Scout Hall, Millmarsh Park, St.
John's Lane, Bovey Tracey, TQ13 9AL
2-5yrs. 9.30am-12pm. Termtime.

Widecombe Pre-School   01364 321 465
Church House, Widecombe-in-the-Moor, Newton
Abbot, TQ13 7TB
2.9-5yrs. 9am-12pm.

Woodlanders Kindergarten   01364 652 181
Woodland Road Centre, Woodland Road,
Ashburton, TQ13 7DR
3-5yrs. 9.15am-3.15pm. Termtime.

TQ14
Bishopsteignton Pre-School   07811 016 418
Horns Park, Bishopsteignton, Teignmouth, TQ14
3-5yrs. 9.30am-12pm and 1-3.30pm.

88 education (Devon and Dorset postcodes)   S = SCHOOL

East Teign Nursery   01626 770 066
Teignmouth United Reformed Church, Dawlish Street, Teignmouth, TQ14 8TB
0-5yrs. 8am-6pm. 50wks.

Our Lady & St. Patricks Roman   01626 773 905
Catholic Nursery
Fourth Avenue, Teignmouth, TQ14 9DT
3-5yrs. 9am-12pm and 1-3.30pm. Termtime.

Shaldon Pre-School - Lunch Club   07890 404 337
Victoria Hall, Bridge Road, Shaldon, TQ14 0DD
3-5yrs. 9.15am-3pm. Termtime.

Teignmouth Pre-School   01626 776 831
Richard Newton Hall, Higher Buckeridge Road, Teignmouth, TQ14 8QP
3-5yrs.

Treetops Neighbourhood Nursery   01626 777 886
Landscore Road, Teignmouth, TQ14 9JU
2-5yrs. 9.15-11.45am. Termtime.

S Trinity School   01626 774 138
Buckeridge Road, Teignmouth, TQ14 8LY
3mths-19yrs.

DORSET
BH1
Bournemouth Montessori   01202 780 010
81 Lansdowne Road, Bournemouth, BH1 1RP
3mths-5yr. 8am-5.30pm. 48wks.

Nuffield Day Nursery   01202 295 737
75 Landsdowne Road, Bournemouth, BH1 1RW
3mths-5yrs. 8.30am-6pm. 51wks.

Kinderworld Day Nursery   01202 290 103
6 Knyveton Road, Bournemouth, BH1 3QN
0-5yrs. 7.30am-6pm. 51wks.

Sunshine Nursery   01202 205 444
Bournemouth & Poole College, Lansdowne, Bournemouth, BH1 3JJ
2-6yrs. 8am-6pm. Termtime

Teddy's Place Day Nursery   01202 294 132
56 Westover Road, Bournemouth, BH1 2BS
2-5yrs. 8.30am-5.30pm. 50wks.

Toddlers Lodge Day Nursery   01202 303 229
4 Hamilton Road, Bournemouth, BH1 4EH
0-5yrs. 8am-6pm. 50wks.

Yavneh Kindergarten   01202 229 522
The Synagogue, Bournemouth Hebrew Congregation, Wootton Gardens, Bournemouth
2.9-5yrs. 9am-3pm. 46wks.

BH2
Tiny Tots Day Nursery   01202 299 415
D4 Wimborne Road, Bournemouth, BH2 6NG
0-5yrs. 8am-6pm. 51wks.

BH3
Carrie's Nursery   01202 516 928
55 Stirling Road, Talbot Woods, Bournemouth, BH3
2-6yrs. 8.15am-5.45pm. 51wks.

Little Acorns Pre-School   01202 533 420
St.Luke's Church Hall, St. Luke's Road, Winton, Bournemouth, BH3 7LT
2.9-5yrs. 9.15am-12pm. 36wks.

Little Gems   01202 533 911
80 Wimborne Road, Bournemouth, BH3 7AS
3mths-5yrs. 8am-6pm. 51wks.

BH4
Bushy Tails Day Nursery   01202 760 841
27 Burnaby Road, Westbourne, Bournemouth, BH4
0-5yrs. 8.15am-6pm. 51wks.

Schools Out Pre-School   01202 766 772
72 West Cliff Road, Bournemouth, BH4 8BE
3-5yrs. 9am-12.55pm. Termtime.

S Talbot Heath School   01202 761 881
Rothesay Road, Bournemouth, BH4 9NJ
3-18yrs.

Three Gables Day Nursery   01202 763 241
2 Snowdon Road, Westbourne, Bournemouth, BH4
0-8yrs. 8am-6pm. 50wks.

Wonder Years   01202 766 937
14 Herbert Road, Bournemouth, BH4 8HD
3mths-5yrs. 8.15am-6pm. 51wks.

BH5
Cats Whiskers Day Nursery   01202 396 453
35 Florence Road, Bournemouth, BH5 1HJ
3mths-5yrs. 8am-6pm. 51wks.

Corpus Christi Pre-School   07713 627 539
St. James Square, Bournemouth, BH5 2BX
3-5yrs. 8.45-11.30am and 12.30-3pm. Termtime.

Kinderworld Day Nursery   01202 428 880
5 Harcourt Road, Bournemouth, BH5 2JG
4mths-5yrs. 8am-6pm. 50wks.

S St Thomas Garnet School   01202 420 172
Parkwood Road, Bournemouth, BH5 2BH
3mths-5yrs. 8.45am-3.15pm. Termtime.

BH6
Badgers Pre-School Nursery   01202 418 281
4 Burtley Road, Bournemouth, BH6 4AP
2-5yrs. 8am-6pm. 51wks.

Bears Hideaway Day Nursery   01202 422 987
6A Stourwood Avenue, Bournemouth, BH6 3PN
0-5yrs. 8am-6pm. 51wks.

Belle Vue Day Nursery   01202 427 588
175 Belle Vue Road, Southbourne, Bournemouth
6mths-4yrs. 8.30am-5.30pm. 51wks.

(Dorset postcodes) education

Bobtails Day Nursery   01202 430 414
11 Kimberley Road, Bournemouth, BH6 5EX
8.30am-5.30pm. 51wks.

Cradlecare Day Nursery   01202 426 086
177 Cranleigh Road, Bournemouth, BH6 5JZ
0-5yrs. 8am-6pm. 51wks.

Fingers 'n' Thumbs Day Nursery   01202 423 044
6 New Park Road, Bournemouth, BH6 5AB
2-5yrs. 8.30am-5.30pm. 48wks.

Kings Castle Day Nursery   01202 422 235
31 Saxonbury Road, Bournemouth, BH6 5NB
2-5yrs. 8am-5pm. 51wks.

Kings Court Baby Nursery   01202 428 338
282 Iford Lane, Tuckton, Bournemouth, BH6 5NG
0-3yrs. 8am-6pm. 51wks.

Little People's Day Nursery   07792 663 041
New Church, 101 Tuckton Rd, Bournemouth, BH6
2-5yrs. 8.30am-5.30pm. 50wks.

Little People's Pre-School   07880 911 742
Denmead Hall, Denmead Road, Iford,
Bournemouth, BH6 5QH
2.9-5yrs. 8.30am-12.30pm. 48wks.

Littlebridges Day Nursery   01202 480 974
Old Bridge Road, Iford Lane, Bournemouth, BH6
2-5yrs. 8.30am-12.30pm and 1-5pm. 50wks.

Puffins Pre-School   01202 431 185
Immanuel United Reformed Church, 120
Southbourne Road, Bournemouth, BH6 3QJ
2-5yrs. 9.15am-12.15pm. Termtime.

Seaward Day Nursery   01202 424 655
61 Seaward Avenue, Bournemouth, BH6 3SJ
2-5yrs. 8.30am-5.30pm. 51wks.

St Nicholas Pre-School   01202 424 453
St. Nicholas Church Hall, Broadway, Southbourne,
Bournemouth, BH6 4EP
2-5yrs. 9am-12pm and 1-3.30pm. Termtime.

Tuckton Christian Pre-School   01202 431 223
306 Iford Lane, Bournemouth, BH6 5NG
3-5yrs. 9am-3pm. Termtime.

BH7
Alphabet Day Nursery   01202 720 111
St. Andrews Hall, 4c Wolverton Road, Boscombe,
Bournemouth, BH7 6HT
0-8yrs. 8am-7pm. 51wks.

Little Pines Day Nursery   01202 301 111
31 Kings Park Road, Bournemouth, BH7 7AE
3mths-5yrs. 8.30am-5.45pm. 50wks.

Platform One Day Nursery   01202 395 817
122 Wolverton Road, Bournemouth, BH7 6HX

St James Pre-School   01202 434 460
St. James Church, Pokesdown, Bournemouth, BH7
2-5yrs. 8.45am-12pm. Termtime.

St John's Pre-School   01202 303 686
St. John's Centre, 26 Shelley Road, Bournemouth
3-5yrs. 9.15-11.45am. Termtime.

St Saviours Pre-School   07719 403 482
St. Saviours Church Hall, Colemore Road,
Boscombe Gast, BH7 6RB
2.9-5yrs. 9am-1pm. Termtime.

Tops Day Nursery   01202 300 688
Castle Lane East, Bournemouth, BH7 7DW
6.45am-6.30pm. 50wks .

BH8
Barbara Rose Pre-School   01202 512 187
St. Paul's Church Hall, Landford Way,
Bournemouth, BH8 0AZ
2-5yrs. 9.30am-12pm and 1-3.30pm. Termtime.

Castle Lane Pre-School   01202 536 041
250 Castle Lane West, Bournemouth, BH8 9TT

Corner House Day Nursery   01202 553 108
62 Porchester Road, Bournemouth, BH8 8LA
8am-6pm. 51wks.

First Steps Nursery   01202 536 041
250 Castle Lane West, Bournemouth, BH8 9TT
2-4yrs. 8am-1pm and 1.30-6pm. 51wks.

Kingfisher Day Nursery   01202 302 412
12 Richmond Park Crescent, Bournemouth, BH8
5mths-4yrs. 8am-6pm. 51wks.

Mother's Care Day Nursery   01202 392 847
18 Lowther Road, Bournemouth, BH8 8NG
3mths-5yrs. 8.15am-6pm. 50wks.

S Park School   01202 396 640
45-49 Queens Park South Drive, Bournemouth
8.30am-3.10pm. 36wks.

Queens Park Montessori   01202 523 293
155 Richmond Park Road, Bournemouth, BH8 8UA
3mths-5yrs. 8am-5.45pm. 49wks.

Queen's Park Pre-School   01202 532 645
East Way, Bournemouth, BH8 9PU
2-5yrs. 8.50-11.30am and 12.20-3.10pm. Termtime.

The Original Queens   01202 396 635
Park Nursery
5 Richmond Park Crescent, Bournemouth, BH8
2-5yrs. 8.30am-4.30pm. 47wks.

S The Park School   01202 396 640
Queens Park South Drive, Bournemouth, BH8 9BJ
4-11yrs.

90 education (Dorset postcodes) S = SCHOOL

BH9
ABC Pre-School Nursery 01202 547 005
90 Edgehill Road, Bournemouth, BH9 2PH
8.30am-5.30pm. 51wks.

Bernets Day Nursery 01202 777 628
27 Bemister Road, Bournemouth, BH9 1LG
2-5yrs. 9am-4pm. 46wks.

Cherubs Pre-School Nursery 01202 531 515
St. Albans Church Hall, Linwood Road,
Bournemouth, BH9 1DW
2-5yrs. 9am-1pm and 1.30-5.30pm. 50wks.

Emma's Day Nursery 01202 773 816
46 West Way, Bournemouth, BH9 3EB
2-5yrs. 8am-6pm. 51wks.

Priory View Pre-School 07946 343 281
Moordown United Reform Church Hall, Priory View
Road, Bournemouth, BH9 3JG
9am-12pm. Termtime.

S Talbot House Prep School 01202 510 348
8 Firs Glen Road, Bournemouth, BH9 2LR

Talbot Park Day Nursery 01202 528 512
32 Talbot Road, Bournemouth, BH9 2JF
8.30am-6pm. 50wks.

BH10
Jack and Jill Pre-School 01202 571 655
Wimborne Road, Bournemouth, BH10 7AW
2¾-5yrs.

Jack-in-the-box Pre-School 07970 377 425
St. Bernadettes Church Hall, 46 Draycott Road,
Bournemouth, BH10 5AR
3-5yrs. 9am-12.30pm. Termtime.

Magic Roundabout Pre-School 01202 520 065
Methodist Church Hall, Beswick Avenue,
Bournemouth, BH10 4EX
2-5yrs. 9am-12pm. Termtime.

Northbourne House Day Nursery 01202 572 315
Northbourne House, 1262 Wimborne Road,
Northbourne, Bournemouth, BH10 7AQ
2-5yrs. 8am-6pm. 51wks.

St Mark's Mini Mice 07977 141 675
St. Mark's Church Hall, Alton Road, Wallisdown,
Bournemouth, BH10 4AA
2-5yrs. 9.15am-12pm. Termtime.

St Thomas Peter Pan Pre-School 07970 377 425
Western Avenue, Ensbury Pk, Bournemouth, BH10
2-5yrs. 9am-12.30pm. Termtime.

BH12
Baby Bibury 2 01202 737 393
Off Fortescue Road, Parkstone, Poole, BH12 2LH
3mths-5yrs. 8am-6pm. 51wks.

Busy Bodies Pre-School 01202 764 420
The Branksome, St. Aldhelm Centre, Poole Road,
Poole, BH12 1AD
3-5yrs. 9.30am-12pm. Termtime.

Cuddles Day Nursery 01202 747 198
Rossmore, Herbert Avenue, Poole, BH12 4HR
6wks-5yrs. 8am-6pm. 51wks.

Little Fish Playgroup 07951 154 770
Sunnyhill Community Church, Sunnyhill Road,
Parkstone, Poole, BH12 2DH
2-5yrs. 9-11.30am and 12.30-3pm. Termtime.

Little People Pre-School 01202 740 113
Bourne Valley Youth Centre, Northmere Road,
Parkstone, Poole, BH12 4DY
8.30am-3.30pm. Termtime.

Pinocchio Playgroup 07855 138 370
Newton Methodist Church Hall, Ringwood Road,
Poole, BH12 3JL
2-5yrs. 9.20am-12pm and 12.50-2.50pm. Termtime.

Talbot View Pre-School 07766 526 142
3 Alder Hillls Industrial Estate, Alder Road, Poole
2-5yrs. 9.30am-12pm and 1-3.30pm. Termtime.

Talbot Woods Day Nursery 01202 965 576
Bournemouth University, Talbot Campus, Fern
Barrow, Poole, BH12 5BB
3mths-5yrs. 8.00am-6.00pm. 51 weeks

Tiddlywinks Nursery 01202 380 103
Evering Avenue, Poole, BH12 4JG
2.9-5yrs. 9-11.30am. 38wks.

Tops Day Nursery 01202 716 130
104-106 Herbert Avenue, Poole, BH12 4HU
7am-6.30pm.

BH13
All Saints Nursery 01202 709 382
Church Hall, Western Road, Branksome Park,
Poole, BH13 7BP
2-5yrs. 9am-1pm. Termtime.

Bibury Day Nursery 01202 760 500
15 Wilderton Road, Branksome Park, Poole, BH13
0-5yrs. 8am-5.30pm. 50wks.

Little Rainbows Playgroup 01202 709 427
15 Banks Road, Poole, BH13 7PS
3mths-5yrs. 8.30am-4pm. 51wks.

Puss n Boots Day Nursery 01202 768 769
2 Lindsay Road, Branksome Park, Poole, BH13
3mths-5yrs. 8.30am-6pm. 51wks.

BH14
Ashley Cross Children's Nursery 01202 746 909
10 Charmouth Grove, Lower Parkstone, Poole
18mths-6yrs. 8am-6pm. 50wks.

S = SCHOOL (Dorset postcodes) **education**

Blue Penguin Montessori 01202 722 377
United Reformed Church, The Dickenson Hall,
Commercial Road, Poole, BH14 0JW
2-5yrs. 9am-12pm and 1-4pm. Termtime.

S Buckholme Towers School 01202 742 871
18 Commercial Road, Parkstone, Poole, BH14 0JW
3-5yrs. 8.50am-3.15pm. 33wks.

First Steps Play Nursery 07968 985 925
The Guide Hall, 12 Langdon Road, Parkstone,
Poole, BH14 9EH
2-4yrs. Termtime.

Flippers Day Nursery 01202 716 926
Oddfellows Hall, Chapel Road, Poole, BH14 0JU
3mths-5yrs. 8am-6pm. 50wks.

Little Stars Day Nursery 01202 741 437
39 Penn Hill Avenue, Poole, BH14 9LU
8am-5.45pm. 51wks.

Parkstone Pre-School 01202 742 966
10 Loch Road, Parkstone, Poole, BH14 9EX
2-5yrs. 9.am-11.30 and 12.30-3pm. Termtime. Also lunch club 11.30 -12.30

St John's Church Pre-School 01202 740 261
38a Ashley Road, Parkstone, Poole, BH14 0AA
2-5yrs. 9.15-11.45am and 12.45-3.15pm.

St Lukes Parkstone Pre-School 01202 735 685
37 Birchwood Road, Parkstone, Poole, BH14 9NW
3-5yrs. 9.30am-12.30pm. Termtime.

St Osmunds Playgroup 01202 380 509
Church Hall, Florence Road, Parkstone, Poole
3-5yrs. 9.15-11.45am and 12-2.30pm. Termtime.

St Peter's Pre-School 01202 736 474
Chapel Road, Poole, BH14 0JU
2.9-5yrs. 9.15-11.45am. Termtime.

Stepping Stones & Pebbles 01202 734 571
Montessori
105 Penn Hill Avenue, Parkstone, Poole, BH14 9LY
8am-6pm. 51wks.

Sunshine Nursery 01202 205 670
Bournemouth & Poole College, North Road, Poole
8am-6pm. Termtime.

S Uplands School 01202 742 626
40 St.Osmun's Road, Parkstone, Poole, BH14 9JY
2¹/₂-16yrs.

Wise Owl Playschool 07713 275 423
Methodist Church, Salterns Road, Poole, BH14 8BJ
2-5yrs. 9am-12pm. Termtime.

BH15
Buffer Bear 01202 684 064
Blandford Close, Poole, BH15 4BQ
8am-6pm. 50wks.

Little Angels Nursery 07837 303 294
St. Michaels Church Hall, Blandford Road,
Hamworthy, Poole, BH15 4HP
no info

Longfleet Lollipops 07748 633 097
St. Mary's Fellowship Centre, Poole, BH15 2LP
2-5yrs. 9.15-11.45am. Termtime.

Rainbow Nursery School 01202 673 581
14 Kingland Road, Poole, BH15 1TP
0-4yrs. 8am-6pm. 51wks.

St Clements Pre-School 01202 738 454
Church Hall, 55 Kinson Avenue, Poole, BH15 4PH
2.9-5yrs. 9.30am-12pm. 38wks.

St Georges Church Pre-School 01202 675 966
99 Darbys Lane, Oakdale, Poole, BH15 3EU
9.15-11.45am and 12.30-3pm. Termtime.

St Josephs Convent Nursery 01202 670 736
37 Parkstone Road, Poole, BH15 2NU
3-5yrs. 9am-3pm. Termtime.

Three Bears Pre-School 07973 898 150
211 Wimborne Road, Poole, BH15 2EG
2¹/₂-5yrs. 9.15am-2.30pm. Termtime.

Wombles Playgroup 07880 841 859
The Scout Hall, Beccles Close, Hamworthy, Poole
2-5yrs. 9am-3pm. Termtime.

BH16
S Yarrells Preparatory 01202 622 229
School
Yarrells House, Upton, Poole, BH16 5EU
www.yarells.co.uk
2-13yrs. 8.45am-3.30pm. Termtime. Quality education in a beautiful, loving environment. Wrap-around provision available (see ad pg 92).

Lytchett Matravers Pre-School 01202 623 915
Wareham Road, Lytchett Matravers, Poole, BH16
2-8yrs. 9am-3.30pm. Termtime.

Playbox 01202 622 877
Lytchett Park, Old Watery Lane, Lytchett Minster,
Poole, BH16 6JE
2-5yrs. 9am-3pm. Termtime.

St Gabriels Pre-School 01202 245 352
Keysworth Road, Turlin Moore, Poole, BH16 5BH
2-5yrs. 9am-3pm. Termtime.

Upton Methodist Pre-School 01202 631 915
Dorchester Road, Upton Poole, BH16 5NN
2-5yrs. 9-11.45am and 12.45-3.30pm. Termtime.

Willow Lodge Montessori School 01202 624 573
Dorchester Road, Lytchett Minster, Poole, BH16
3mths-7yrs. 8am-5.30pm. 48wks.

education (Dorset postcodes)   S = SCHOOL

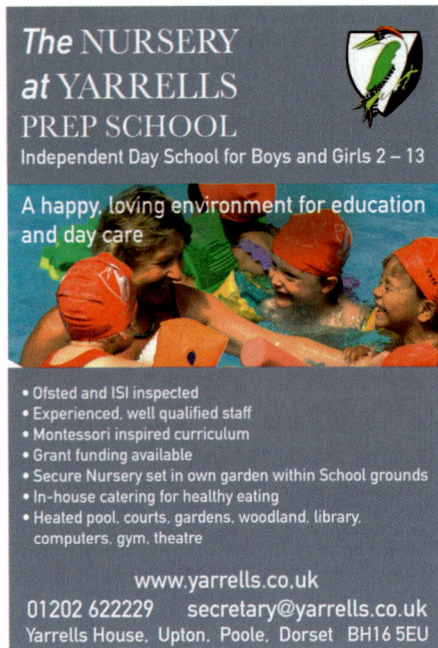

The NURSERY at YARRELLS PREP SCHOOL
Independent Day School for Boys and Girls 2 – 13

A happy, loving environment for education and day care

- Ofsted and ISI inspected
- Experienced, well qualified staff
- Montessori inspired curriculum
- Grant funding available
- Secure Nursery set in own garden within School grounds
- In-house catering for healthy eating
- Heated pool, courts, gardens, woodland, library, computers, gym, theatre

www.yarrells.co.uk
01202 622229   secretary@yarrells.co.uk
Yarrells House, Upton, Poole, Dorset BH16 5EU

BH17
Canford Heath Pre-School   01202 687 697
United Reformed Church, Mitchell Road, Canford Heath, Poole, BH17 8UE
2.9-5yrs. 9.15-11.45am. 37wks.

Christ Church Little Oaks   07761 861 603
Youth Centre, Northmead Drive, Poole, BH17 7XZ
2-4yrs. 9.30am-12pm. Termtime.

Dolphin Pre-School Playgroup   01202 388 205
Community Centre, Mithcell Road, Canford Heath, Poole, BH17 8SD
2-5yrs. 9.30am-1pm. Termtime.

Humpty Dumpty Pre-School   01202 770 012
Learoyd Road, Canford Heath, Poole, BH17 8PJ
2³/₄-5yrs. 9.15-11.45am. Termtime.

Ladybird Playgroup   01202 659 659
3 Canford Heath Road, Poole, BH17 9NG
9am-3pm. Termtime.

Postman Pat Pre-School   01202 698 649
Scout Hall, Canford Heath, Sherborn Crescent, Poole, BH17 8AP
2-5yrs. 9am-3pm. Termtime.

Twin Oaks Pre-School   01202 693 288
Waterloo Youth Centre, Kitchener Crescent, Poole
2-5yrs. 9-11.45am and 1-2.30pm.

BH18
Broadstone Christian Nursery   01202 601 748
161 Lower Blandford Road, Broadstone, BH18 8NU
2-8yrs. 8.30am-4.30pm. 48wks.

Hoppers Pre-School Playgroup   07950 505 539
St. John's Church Hall, Macaulay Road, Broadstone, BH18 8AR
8.55-11.30am and 12.45-3.15pm. Termtime.

Little People Kindergarten   07890 472 528
United Reformed Church Hall, Higher Blandford Road, Broadstone, BH18 9AB
2-5yrs. 8.15am-3.15pm. Termtime.

Playbox Playgroup   07810 767 494
Liberal Hall, York Road, Broadstone, BH18 8ET
2-5yrs. 9.15am-12.15pm. Termtime.

BH19
Langton Matravers Pre-School   07969 556 451
High Street, Langton Matravers, Swanage, BH19
2-5yrs. 8.45-11.45am. Termtime.

Mount Scar Cygnets Playgroup   01929 426 570
Mount Scar, Swanage, BH19 2EY
3-4yrs. 9-11.30am and 12.45-3.15pm. Termtime.

S Old Malthouse   01929 422 302
Langton Matravers, Swanage, BH19 3HB
Co-ed 3-13yrs. 8.15am-3.30pm.

Rainbows Nursery School   01929 421 928
5 Hillsea Road, Swanage, BH19 2QL
8am-5pm. 50wks.

St Mark's Pre-School   01929 424 539
The Reading Room, Bell Street, Swanage, BH19
2-5yrs. 9-11.30am and 12.30-3pm. Termtime.

St Mary's Pre-School   07817 102 555
Manor Road, Swanage, BH19 2BJ
9-11.30am. Termtime.

BH20
Bovington Nursery School   01929 403 602
Cox Close, Bovington Camp, Nr Wareham, BH20
2-5yrs. 9 - 3p.m. Term time only 39wks.

Corfe Castle Pre-School   07971 716 696
East Street, Corfe Castle, Wareham, BH20 5EE
2-5yrs. 9am-12pm. Termtime.

Focus Nursery School   01929 555 135
Worgret Road, Wareham, BH20 4PH
2-5yrs. 9am-1pm. Termtime.

Forest Pre-School   01929 553 984
Playschool Hall, Tantinoby Lane, Northmoor Park, Wareham, BH20 7PQ
2-5yrs. 9.30am-4pm.

S = SCHOOL   (Dorset postcodes) **education**   **93**

Ragamuffins Playgroup   01929 472 765
Rye Hill, Bere Regis, Wareham, BH20 7LP
2-5yrs. 9-11.30am and 1-3.30pm. Termtime.

Sandford Church Pre-School   01929 558 122
Wareham, BH20 7AJ
2-5yrs. 9-11.30am. Termtime.

Stoborough Nursery   01929 552 974
Corfe Road, Stoborough, Wareham, BH20 5AD
2.9-5yrs. 9.15-11.45am and 12.45-3pm. 39wks.

Three Bears Nursery   01929 405 777
Holt Road, Bovington, Wareham, BH20 6LE
6am-6pm. 48wks.

Tops Day Nursery   01929 555 051
1 Carey Road, Wareham, BH20 4AX
3mths-5yrs. 7.30am-6.30pm. 50wks.

Wool Pre-School   01929 405 144
Kids of Wool Building, Colliers Lane, Wool,
Wareham, BH20 6DL
2-5yrs. 9am-3pm. Termtime.

BH21

S Castle Court School   **01202 694 438**
Knoll Lane, Corfe Mullen, Wimborne, BH21 3RF
www.castlecourt.com
3-13yrs.

Chrysalis Montessori Nursery   01202 880 990
Cutlers Place, Colehill, Wimborne, BH21 2HN
2-5yrs. 9am-12pm and 1-4pm. Termtime.

Colehill Nursery   01202 889 724
Middlehill Road, Colehill, Wimborne, BH21 2HL
2.9-5yrs. 9.15am-12pm. 38wks.

Cranborne Pre-School   01725 517 439
Cecil Memorial Hall, Cranborne, BH21 5QB
2-5yrs. 9-11.45am. Termtime.

Down in the Woods Pre-School   07787 954 387
Merley Youth Centre, Chichester Walk, Merley
2-5yrs. 9am-1pm. Termtime.

S Dumpton School   01202 883 818
Deans Grove House, Deans Grove, Wimborne
2½-13yrs.

Jack & Jill Playgroup   07960 555 378
St. John's Church Hall, Legg Lane, Wimborne
2-5yrs. 9.05-11.50am. Termtime.

Jack and Jill Playgroup   01202 695 328
Methodist Church Hall, Wareham Road, Corfe
Mullen, Wimborne, BH21 3LB
3-5yrs. 9.15-11.45am. Termtime.

Lantern Playgroup   01202 840 836
The Lantern Church, Wimborne, BH21 1SQ
2-5yrs. 9-11.45am and 12.30-3pm. Termtime.

Castle Court School
Knoll Lane, Corfe Mullen,
Wimborne, Dorset, BH21 3RF

Castle Court welcomes boys and girls from the age of 3 into its Nursery "Badger" class, providing continuity of education in 35 acres of beautiful grounds until the age of 13. Within easy reach of Bournemouth and Poole, Ringwood and Dorchester, Castle Court has a strong tradition of music, sport and art, and a warm, friendly atmosphere.

T: 01202 694438   **www.castlecourt.com**

Meadow View Montessori   01202 657 847
Rear of St. Nicholas Church, Wareham Road, Corfe
Mullen, Wimborne, BH21 3LE
2-5yrs. 8.30am-4pm. 50wks.

Merley Community Pre-School   01202 841 330
Merley Community Centre, Harrier Drive, Merley,
Wimborne, BH21 1XE
9.15am-12pm. Termtime.

Moonacre Montessori Nursery   01202 822 338
Moonacre Potterne Way, Three Legged Cross,
Verwood, BH21 6RS
0-6yrs. 8am-6pm. 51wks.

Old Laburnum Montessori   01258 840 281
Old Laburnum Cottage, Gaunts Common,
Wimborne, BH21 4JR
2-5yrs. 8.30am-6pm. 44wks.

Pamphill Pre-School Nursery   01202 883 008
Pamphill, Wimbourne, BH21 4EE
2.9-5yrs. 9-11.45am. Termtime.

St Catherine's Kindergarten   01202 883 763
Cutlers Place, Colehill, Wimborne, BH21 2HN
9am-12pm. Termtime.

St James Cottage Nursery   01258 840 679
Gaunts Common, Wimborne, BH21 4JN
2-5yrs. 9am-12pm. Termtime.

Sturminster Marshall Pre-School   01258 858 395
78 High Street, Sturminster Marshall, Wimborne
2-5yrs. 9-11.45am. Termtime.

Tadpoles Pre-School Playgroup   01202 674 546
Hillside Road, Corfe Mullen, Wimborne, BH21 3TR
2-5yrs. 9-11.30am and 12.30-3pm. Termtime.

The Barn Nursery   01202 897 272
Stapehill Farm, Uddens Drive, Wimborne, BH21
2-5yrs. 9am-12pm and 12.45-3.15pm. Termtime.

The Children's House School   01202 690 800
Hanham Road, Corfe Mullen, Wimborne, BH21 3PX
2-5yrs. 8.30am-6pm. 48wks.

education (Dorset postcodes)   S = SCHOOL

Three Legged Cross Playgroup 07721 735 858
Church Road, Three Legged Cross, Wimborne
2-5yrs. 8.55-11.45am. and 12.30-3pm. Termtime.

Tops Day Nursery 01202 841 691
Tops House, Leigh Road, Wimborne, BH21 2BX
0-8yrs. 7.30am-6pm. 50wks.

Toy Box Pre-School 07949 734 773
The Pavilion, Badbury View Road, Corfe Mullen, Wimborne, BH21 3HU
2-8yrs. 8.30am-12pm. Termtime.

Wimbles Pre-School 07732 189 860
Colehill Methodist Church, Lonnen Road, Colehill, Wimborne, BH21 7AP
2-5yrs. 9.15am-12.15pm. Termtime.

Wimborne First Kindergarten 07778 597 709
School Lane, Wimborne, BH21 1HQ
2.9-5yrs. 9am-12pm. Termtime.

Wimborne St Giles Pre-School 01725 517 5347
Wimborne St.Giles, Wimborne, BH21 5LX
2-5yrs. 9.15-11.45am.

Witchampton Pals Pre-School 07931 491 581
Methodist Chapel School Room, Downley Road, Witchampton, Nr Wimborne, BH21 5AP
2-5yrs.9.30am-12pm. 50wks.

BH22
Busy Bees Pre-School 07704 107 692
Shaftesbury Close, West Moors, BH22 0DZ
2-5yrs 9-11.25am and 12.25-2.55pm

Ferndown Pre-School 01202 894 858
Community Centre, Pennys Walk, Ferndown, BH22
2-5yrs. 9.05-11.50am. Termtime.

Ickle Angels 01202 895 778
1 Carrol Avenue, Ferndown, BH22 8BW

Longham Community Pre-School 01202 572 210
United Reformed Church, Ham Lane, Longham, Ferndown, BH22 9DP
9-11.55am and 12.30-3.20pm. Termtime.

Pear Tree Montessori 01202 897 677
Glenmoor Road, Ferndown, BH22 8QE
2-4yrs. 8.30am-3.15pm. Termtime.

The Caterpillar Club 01202 893 272
Church Road, Ferndown, BH22 9ET
9am-12pm and 12.45-3.15pm. Termtime.

West Moors Pre-School 01202 871 744
The Avenue, West Moors, Ferndown, BH22 0JF
3-5yrs. 8.50-11.45am and 12-3pm. Termtime.

BH23
Burton Day Nursery 01202 490 506
131 Salisbury Road, Burton, Christchurch, BH23
0-5yrs. 8am-6pm. 51wks.

Burton Pre-School Playgroup 07967 150 275
The Village Hall, Salisbury Road, Burton, Christchurch, BH23 7JP
9am-12pm. Termtime.

Burton Pre-School 'Teddies' 077967 150 275
Burton Youth Centre, Sandy Plot, Burton, BH23
2-5yrs. 9am-12pm. Termtime.

Chewton Common Playgroup 07814 700 414
Chewton Common Road, Highcliffe, BH23 5AZ
3-5yrs. 9am-12pm. Termtime.

Christchurch Montessori 07971 621 470
Beauchamp Place, Reid Street, Christchurch, BH23
2-5yrs. 8am-5.30pm. 50wks.

Christchurch Montessori Baby-unit 01202 240 920
123 The Grove, Christchurch, BH23 2EZ
3mths-5yrs. 8am-5.30pm. 48wks.

Gundimore Pre-School Playgroup
HMS Orestes, Stanpit, Christchurch, BH23 3LY
2-5yrs. 9.15am-12.15pm and 12.30-3.30pm. Termtime.

S Homefield School 01202 479 781
Salisbury Road, Winkton, Christchurch, BH23 7AR
2-16yrs. 8.30am-3.30pm. Termtime.

Mudeford Pre-School 01202 488 125
Methodist Church hall, Christchurch, BH23 3HQ
8.45-11.45am and 12.15-2.45pm. Termtime.

Mudeford Wood Playgroup 01425 272 084
Community Centre, Pipers Drive, Christchurch
2-5yrs.

Nursery Rhyme 01202 482 648
26 River Way, Christchurch, BH23 2QP
2-5yrs.8.30am-12.30pm. 50wks.

Poppets Pre-School 01425 272 347
Regent Centre, 51 High Street, Christchurch, BH23
2-5yrs. 9am-12pm and 12.30-3pm. Termtime.

Rainbow Pre-School 01425 272 347
254 Lymington Road, Highcliffe, Christchurch, BH23
2-4yrs. 9.15am-12pm.Termtime.

Rainbow Pre-School 07796 107 540
St. Marks Church Hall, Hinton Wood Avenue, Christchurch, BH23 5AA
9.15am-12pm. Termtime.

BH24
Cherry Tree Montessori 01425 477 400
1 High Street, Ashley Heath, Ringwood, BH24 2HP
2-8yrs. 9am-3.45pm. Termtime.

Please say you saw the listings in the South West Baby Directory

S = SCHOOL (Dorset postcodes) **education**

St Ives Pre-School Playgroup 07799 188 712
Sandy Lane, St.Ives, Ringwood, BH24 2LE
2-5yrs. 9am-12.15pm. Termtime.

Hillside Pre-School 01202 820 679
Hillside Road, Verwood, BH31 7HE
2.9-4yrs. 9am-12pm and 1-3pm. 37wks.

BH31
Orchard Day Nursery 01202 820 124
Coopers Lane, Verwood, BH31 7PG
3mths-5yrs. 8am-6pm. 51wks.

St Michael's Playgroup 07718 372 211
Parish Centre, Manor Road, Verwood, BH31 2LE
2-3yrs. 9.30-11.30am. Termtime.

Trinity Pre-School 01202 825 025
Trinity First School, Coopers Lane, Verwood, BH31
2-5yrs. 9am-12pm and 12.30-3pm. Termtime.

Verwood First Pre-School 07890 168 152
Middle School, Howe Lane, Verwood, BH31 6JF
2.10-5yrs. 8.45-11.45am and 12.35-3.05pm. Termtime.

DT1
Chipmunks Day Nursery 01305 260 002
6 Herrington Road, Dorchester, DT1 2BS
3mths-5yrs. 7.45am-6pm. 51wks.

Dorchester Nursery School 01305 265 140
York Road, Dorchester, DT1 1QA
2-5yrs. 9.15-11.45am and 1-3.30pm. Termtime.

Dorchester Opportunity Group 01305 751 707
Prince of Wales Pre-School Centre, Maiden Castle Road, Dorchester, DT1 2HH
1-5yrs. 9.30am-2.30 pm. Termtime.

S Dorchester Prep School 01305 264 925
25/26 Icen Way, Dorchester, DT1 1EP
3-13yrs.

First Steps Pre-School 01305 250 600
Dorchester Youth & Community Centre, Kings Road, Dorchester, DT1 1NJ
2-5yrs. 9.15-11.45am and 12.30-3pm. Termtime.

Haycorns, St. Mary's 01305 257 393
Lucetta Lane, Dorchester, DT1 2DD
2½-5yrs. 9am-12pm and 1-3.30pm. Termtime.

Prince of Wales Pre-School 01305 751 940
Maiden Castle Road, Dorchester, DT1 2HH
2-5yrs. 9.30am-12.40pm and 1-3pm. Termtime.

S Sunninghill Prep School 01305 262 306
South Court, South Walks, Dorchester, DT1 1EB
3-13yrs.

Sunny Day Nursery 01305 268 577
Middle Farm Barns, Middle Farm Way, Poundbury Centre, DT1 3WA
3mths-5yrs. 7.30am-6pm. 51wks.

The Grove Pre-School 01305 266 766
The Bungalow, Damers Road, Dorchester, DT1 2LA
2-5yrs. 9.15-11.45am and 1-3.30pm. Termtime.

DT2
Bride Valley Fledglings 07967 400 385
Church Hall, Puncknowle, Dorchester, DT2 9BD
2-4yrs. 9.15-11.45am. 3 mornings.

Broadmayne & West 07815 606 841
Knighton Pre-School
Knighton Lane, Broadmayne, Dorchester, DT2 8PH
2-5yrs. 9-11.30am and 12.30-3pm. Termtime.

Buckland Newton Under 5's 07966 740 595
Village Hall, Buckland Newton, Dorchester, DT2
3-5yrs. 9.15am-1pm. Termtime.

Charminster Playgroup 01305 263 880
West Hill, Charminster, DT2 9RD
2-5yrs. 9-11.30am and 12.30-3pm. .Termtime.

Crossways Playgroup 01305 853 466
Village Hall, Moigne Combe Road, Crossways, Dorchester, DT2 8JA
2-5yrs. 9am-12pm. Termtime.

Ladybirds Playgroup 07751 577 567
Corscombe Village Hall, Corscombe, Dorchester
2½-5yrs. 9.15am-12.15pm Mon/Fri and 9.15am-2pm Wed.
Toddler session Tues 10am-2pm. Termtime.

Little Acorns 0798 543 958
Evershot Village Hall, The Common, Dorchester
0-8yrs. 9am-1pm. Termtime. 2 - 5 yrs

Maiden Newton Playgroup 01300 320 127
St.Mary's Youth Centre, Chilfrome Lane, Maiden Newton, Dorchester, DT2 0AX
2-5yrs. 8.45am-12pm. Termtime.

Puddletown Pre-School 01305 849 533
High Street, Puddletown, Dorchester, DT2 8RY
2-5yrs. 9am-3.15pm. Termtime.

Stepping Stones Pre-School 07765 341 673
Village Hall, Rectory Road, Piddlehinton, DT2 7TE
9.15-11.45am and 12.30-3pm. Termtime.

Sydling Springs Pre-School 07963 639 272
Village Hall, Sydling St. Nicholas, Dorchester, DT2
2-5yrs. 9.15am-12.15pm. Termtime .

Winfrith Day Nursery 01305 851 877
Winfrith Technology Centre, Dorchester, DT2 8JL
3mths-5yrs. 7.45am-5.30pm. 50wks.

education (Dorset postcodes)   S = SCHOOL

Winfrith Pre-School 01305 851 877
School Lane, Winfrith Newburgh, Dorchester, DT2
2-5yrs. 8.45am-3.15pm. Termtime.

DT3
Chesil Bank Pre-School 01305 871 932
The Square, Strangways Village Hall, Abbotsbury,
Weymouth, DT3 4JR
9.30am-12.30pm. 37wks.

Ducklings Pre-School 01305 766 920
Methodist Hall, North Square, Chickerell,
Weymouth, DT3 4DX
2-5yrs. 9am-12.15pm. Termtime.

Mulberry Bush Pre-School 01305 834 216
11 Eastdown Avenue, Weymouth, DT3 6QN
2.9-4yrs. 9am-12pm. 36wks.

Noah's Ark Playgroup
Church Hall, Higher End, Chickerell, DT3 4EQ
2-8yrs. 8.55am-3.30pm. Termtime.

Preston Playgroup 01305 832 973
Preston Road, Preston, Weymouth, DT3 6BH
2.9-5yrs. 9-11.45am. Termtime.

Radipole Pre-School 07966 736 919
Ratcliffe Hall, Queens Road, Weymouth, DT3 5EX
2-5yrs. 9-11.30am and 1-3.30pm. Termtime.

Roman Road Pre-School 07815 923 285
Spa Road, Weymouth, DT3 5EN
2-5yrs. 9am-3.30pm.

Scallywags 01305 813 038
Sports club, Dorchester Road, Weymouth, DT3
2-8yrs. 7.30am-6pm. 50wks.

Smarties Pre-School 01305 816 421
Dorchester Road, Weymouth, DT3 5DB
2-5yrs. 9am-12pm and 1-3.30pm. Termtime.

DT4
Allsorts Preschool 01305 786 357
Moose Lodge, 137 Chickerell Road, Weymouth
2-8yrs. 9am-3pm. Termtime.

Chipmunks Day Nursery 01305 760 060
34 Buxton Road, Weymouth, DT4 9PJ
0-8yrs. 7.45am-6pm. 51wks.

Chuckles Day Nursery 01305 761 232
Chickerell Road, Weymouth, DT4 9SY
0-6yrs. 8am-5.30pm. 51wks.

Humpty's House Pre-School 01305 780 857
Sycamore Road, Southill, Weymouth, DT4 9UF
9am-3pm.

Jelly Babies Day Nursery 01305 764 836
Weymouth College, Cranford Avenue, Weymouth
0-5yrs. 8am-5.30pm. 50wks.

Kidz are Us 01305 767 076
Southill, Weymouth, Dorset, DT4 9SF
2-5yrs. 8.30am-3pm.

Little Rascals Day Nursery 01305 363 495
1 Cumberland Drive, Granby Industrail Estate,
Weymouth, DT4 9TT
3mths-5yrs. 7am-6pm. 50wks.

Rodwell Pre-School 01305 788 270
Off Rodwell Avenue, Weymouth, DT4 8SG
2-5yrs. 9.30am-12.30pm and 1-3.30pm. Termtime.

St Paul's Pre-School 07771 948 662
St. Paul's Church Hall, Abbotsbury Road,
Weymouth, DT4 0BJ
3-5yrs. 9.15-11.45am. Termtime.

Sunny Days Nursery 01305 788 223
17 Glendinning Avenue, Weymouth, DT4 7QF
3mths-8yrs. 7am-7pm. 51wks.

S Thornlow Prep School 01305 785 703
Connaught Road, Weymouth, DT4 0SA
3-13yrs. 8.30am-4pm. 36wks.

Westhaven Pre-School 01305 782 727
Hereford Road, Weymouth, DT4 0QB
2-8yrs. 8am-6pm. Termtime.

Wyke Regis Pre-School 01305 789 222
Shrubbery Lane, Wyke Regis, Weymouth, DT4 9LU
2-6yrs. 9am-3.15pm. Termtime.

DT5
Easton Pre-School 07976 917 033
Clarence Road, Portland, DT5 2BD
9-11.45am. Termtime.

Haylands Pre-School 01305 822 625
83-85 Greenways, Portland, DT5 2LF
2-5yrs. 9-11.30am and 12.30-3pm. Termtime.

Jumping Beans Pre-School 0403 708 429
Weston Scout Hall, Weston, Portland, DT5 2DA
2-5yrs. 9am-3pm. Termtime.

Munchkins Day Nursery 01305 860 099
Brackenbury Centre, Fortuneswell, Portland, DT5
0-5yrs. 7.30am-6.30pm. Termtime.

Southwell Pre-School 07791 868 303
St. Andrews House, Church Lane, Southwell,
Portland, DT5 2EQ
9am-12.30pm. Termtime.

DT6
Bradpole Church Pre-School 01208 421 379
Middle Street, Bridport, DT6 3HS
2-5yrs. 9.15-11.45am. Termtime.

Bridport Montessori Pre-School 01308 456 362
Lynchetts, East Road, Bridport, DT6 4AE
8.30am-5.30pm. Termtime.

S = SCHOOL   (Dorset postcodes) **education**

Burton Bradstock Playgroup 07789 341 482
Women Institute Hall, Church Street, Burton
Bradstock, DT6 4QS
2-5yrs. 9.30am-12pm. Termtime.

Little Bees Nursery School 01308 424 578
Youth Centre, Gundry Lane, Bridport, DT6 3RL
0-5yrs. 9.15am-2.30pm. Termtime

Monkton Wyld Kindergarten 01297 560 342
Monkton Wyld Court, Monkton Wyld, Bridport, DT6
2-5yrs. 10am-12.30pm. Termtime.

St Andrews Pre-School 01308 458 151
St. Andrews Road, Bridport, DT6 3BJ
2-5yrs. 9-11.30am and 12.30-3pm. Termtime.

St Catherine's Pre-School 01308 425 870
Pymore Road, Bridport, DT6 3TR
3-5yrs. 8.50-11.20am. Termtime.

St Ronan's Pre-School 01308 422 128
1 Kings Square, Bridport, DT6 3QE
2-5yrs. 8.45-11.45am and 1-3pm. Termtime.

St Swithins Playgroup 01308 425 144
St.Swithins Church Vestry, North Allington, DT6
2-5yrs. 9.15-11.45am. Termtime

Stepping Stones Pre-School 07773 516 481
United Church Hall, West Street, Bridport, DT6 3LH
2-5yrs. 9.15-11.45am. Termtime.

Tick Tocks 01297 560 088
Riverdale, Charmouth, Bridport, DT6 6QZ
0-6yrs. 8.30am-5.30pm. 51wks.

Watercleaves Nursery School 01308 422 559
Watercleaves, Dottery, Bridport, DT6 5HW
2-5yrs. 8.50am-4pm. Termtime.

Whitchurch Canonicorum 01297 678 426
The Village Hall, Whitchurch Canonicorum, Bridport
2-5yrs. 9.45am-12.15pm .Termtime.

Wonderland Nursery 01308 421 731
The Old School, Gundry Lane, Bridport, DT6 3RL
5-8yrs. 9am-5.30pm.

DT7
Colway House Nursery 01297 443 701
Colway House, Uplyme Road, Lyme Regis, DT7
2-5yrs. 8.30am-4pm. Termtime.

Lyme Regis Playgroup 01297 442 623
Kingsway, Lyme Regis, DT7 3DY

Lyme Regis Pre-School 012974 413 285
Woodmead Halls, Hill Road, Lyme Regis, DT7 3PG
2-5yrs. 9-11.30am. Termtime.

DT8
Beaminster Playgroup 01308 863 959
Hogshill Street, Beaminster, DT8 3AE
2-5yrs. 9-11.30am and 12-2.30pm. Termtime.

Mosterton Playgroup 01935 891 678
Mosterton, Beaminster, DT8 3HG
2-5yrs. 9.15am-12pm. Termtime.

DT9
S Sherborne 01935 812 097
Preparatory School
Acreman Street, Sherborne, DT9 3NY
www.prep.sherborne.com
APS co-educational 3-13yrs day and boarding school.
A busy and happy place in which children thrive and
achieve excellent results in work, sport and a wide variety of
other activities. The pre-prep department takes children in
the nursery from 3yrs part or full-time, and children from 4-
6yrs in three classes full-time. Jumping Jack Toddler Group
meets every Wednesday between 2-3.30pm and Friday
mornings between 9-11am during termtime.

S St Antony's Leweston 01963 210 790
Nursery School
Sherborne, Dorset, DT9 6EN
www.leweston.co.uk
For children aged 2-4yrs. Stimulating and caring environment
in 46 acres of beautiful parkland. Outstanding staff including
music and language specialists. Morning and afternoon
sessions with lunch and after school creche available. Part of
Leweston Preparatory School educating from 4-11 years.

St Antony's Leweston 01963 210 790
Parent and Toddler Group
Free, friendly, weekly toddler group offering a wide-range of
activities to children aged newborn to 3 in a safe, secure
environment. Everyone welcome.

Bradford Abbas Pre-School 07779 215 686
Village Hall, Church Road, Bradford Abbas,
Sherborne, DT9 6RF
9am-12pm. Termtime.

Bright Start Playschool 07974 871 425
Scout Hut, Blackberry Lane, Sherborne, DT9 4DE
2-5yrs. 9am-12pm. Termtime.

Holwell Nursery School 016 323 368
Crouch Lane, Holwell, Sherborne, DT9 5LP
18mths-5yrs. 8.30am-4.30pm.

Lower Covey Day Nursery 01935 872 544
Lower Covey, Chapel Lane, Yetminster, DT9 6LJ
0-3yrs. 8am-6pm. 49wks.

Poyntington Playcentre 01963 220 651
Furlong, Pyntington, Sherborne, DT9 4LF
2-5yrs. 9.15am-12.15pm and 1.15-4.15pm. Termtime.

Please say you saw the listings in the South West Baby Directory

98 education (Dorset postcodes)   S = SCHOOL

WELL CARED FOR

LEWESTON NURSERY SCHOOL
Set in 46 acres of beautiful Dorset parkland Leweston Nursery caters for children aged 2½ to 4.

With small classes run by qualified staff and specialist teachers in Music and French the Nursery aims to foster a safe and happy environment where children can grow in confidence and develop as individuals.

Morning and afternoon sessions are offered, with after-school crèche facilities. Nursery Vouchers are accepted. A free parent and toddler group meets once a week for newborns to age 3.

For more information call Mrs Joanne Osborne on 01963 210790 or visit www.leweston.co.uk

LEWESTON
PREPARATORY

Part of St Antony's Leweston Schools educating boys aged 2½ to 11 and girls aged 2½ to 18
St Antony's Leweston is a registered charity number 295175

Sherborne Westend Pre-School 01935 814 190
West End Hall, Littlefields, Sherborne, DT9 6AU
2-5yrs. 9.15am-12pm. Termtime.

St Paul's Playgroup 01935 815 897
St. Paul's Play Group, The Horsa Block, Simosn Road, Sherborne, DT9 4DN
2-5yrs. 9am-12pm. Termtime.

Thornford Playgroup 07971 709 336
Village Hall, Pound Road, Thornford, DT9 6QB
2-5yrs. 9.30am-12.30pm. Termtime.

Wriggle Valley Pre-School 01935 873 830
Stonyacres, Yetminster, Sherborne, DT9 6LS
2-5yrs. 8.45am-12pm. Termtime.

DT10
Jungle Hut Pre-School 01258 820 634
New Street, Marnhull, DT10 1PZ
2-5yrs. 9.10am-12.10pm. Termtime.

Stalbridge Pre-School 01963 362 024
Stalbridge Community Hall, Stalbridge, DT10 2NJ
2-5yrs. 9.15am-12.15pm.

Stepping Stones Pre-School 01288 473 860
The Scout Hall, Ricketts Lane, Sturminster Newton
2-5yrs. 9.30am-12pm.

Sturminster Nursery 01258 473 753
Caddle House, Rixon, Sturminster Newton, DT10
3-8yrs. 8.30am-5.30pm. 5wks.

DT11
S Hanford School 01258 860 219
Childe Okeford, Blandford, DT11 8HL
www.hanfordschool.com
Girls. 7-13yrs.

Archway Nursery 01258 454 602
38 The Drive, Bryanston, Blandford Forum, DT11
0-5yrs. 8am-6pm. 50wks.

Blandford Camp Pre-School 01258 450 624
College Road, Blandford Camp, Blandford Forum
2-4yrs. 9am-3pm. Termtime.

Blandford Little Acorns 01258 458 265
Fairfield Road, Blandford Forum, DT11 7AB
2-5yrs. 9-11.30am and 12.30-3pm.

Capers 01258 456 797
Old School House, Spetisbury, Blandford Forum
3-8yrs. 8am-6pm. 50wks.

Child Okeford Pre-School 01258 861 007
Station Road, Child Okeford, DT11 8EL
2-5yrs. 9am-12pm. Termtime.

S Clayesmore Prep School 01747 811 707
Iwerne Minster, Blandford, DT11 8PH
2½-13yrs.

Fontmell Magna Under Fives 08456 014 771
The Village Hall, Fontmell Magna, Shaftesbury, DT11
3-5yrs. 9am-12pm. Termtime.

Larksmead Pre-School 01258 456 383
The Pavilion, Larksmead, Blandford Forum, DT11
2-5yrs. 9.30am-12.15pm.

Little Birch Pre-School 07929 363 291
Birch Avenue, Blandford St.Mary, DT11 9QD
2-5yrs. 9-11.45am. Termtime.

Milborne Ladybirds Playgroup 07989 029 365
Milborne St.Andrew Village Hall, Milborne St. Andrew, Blandford Forum, DT11 0JX
2-5yrs. 9.15-11.45am.

Okeford Fitzpaine Pre-School 07752 112 465
The Village Hall, Okeford Fitzpaine, Blandford Forum
3-5yrs. 9.15am-12.45pm.

Panda Pre-School 01258 458 151
The Milldown, Blandford Forum, DT11 7TX
2-5yrs. 9-11.30am and 12.25-2.45pm. Termtime.

Pimperne Pre-School 07780 976 654
Sports Pavilion, Old Bakery Close, Pimperne, Blandford Forum, DT11 8BS
2-5yrs. 9.30am-12pm.

Hanford School

Independent school for girls aged 7 to 13+

- full boarding
- no fixed exeats
- regular contact with parents
- genuine family atmosphere
- small classes
- school ponies
- specialist teachers for all subjects
- developing excellence
- encouraging free spirits
- coach service

For information please contact the Headmaster's secretary
Tel: **01258 860219** Fax: **01258 861255**
www.hanfordschool.com

Rainbow Pre-School 01258 881 547
Tregonwell Armshouses, Milton Abbas, DT11 0AX
2-5yrs. 8,50am-12.45pm Mon-Fri. Termtime. Also lunch club and August holiday club.

Scamps Pre-School 01258 452 107
Spetisbury First School, Spetisbury, DT11 9DW
3-5yrs. 9am-12pm. Termtime.

Shillingstone House Nursery 01258 861 599
Shillingstone House, Shillingstone, DT11 0RZ
0-8yrs. 8am-6pm. 50wks.

Shillingstone Playgroup 01258 861 433
Portman Hall, Blandford Road, Shillingstone, DT11
2-5yrs. 9.30am-12pm. Termtime.

Tadpoles Day Nursery 01929 471 846
The Cricket Club, Recreation Ground, Winterbourne Kingston, Blandford, DT11 9BL
2-5yrs. 9am-1pm. Termtime.

The Old School Nursery 01258 857 922
West Street, Shapwick, Blandford Forum, DT11
0-5yrs. 7.45am-6pm. 50wks.

The Winterbornes Montessori 01258 881 728
St. Mary's Church Rooms, Winterborne Whitechurch, Blandford Forum, DT11 9BP
2-5yrs. 8am-6pm. 45wks.

SP5
The Chase Nursery 01725 552 388
Common Road, Sixpenny Handley, SP5 5NJ
2.9-5yrs. 9.30am-12pm. 3mornings.

SP6
Kingswood Day Nursery 01425 656 451
The Old School, Daggons Road, Alderholt, Fordingbridge, SP6 3DN
6mths-5yrs. 8am-5.30pm. 50wks.

SP7
Enmore Green Pre-School 01747 854 621
Enmore Green Church Hall, Church Hill, Shaftesbury, SP7 8QR
2 1/2 - 5yrs. 9am-12pm. Termtime.

First Steps Pre-School 07813 465 467
Lindlar Hall, Lindlar Close, Shaftesbury, SP7 8PS
2-4yrs. 9.15am-12.15pm and 1-3.30pm. Termtime.

Flying Start Nursery 01747 852 666
35 Bell Street, Shaftesbury, SP7 8AE
1-5yrs. 9am-3pm. 38wks.

Little Acorns Pre-School 01747 854 993
Christys Lane, Shaftesbury, SP7 8PH
2.9-5yrs. 9.30am-12.15pm.

Please say you saw the listings in the South West Baby Directory

100 education (Dorset and Gloucestershire postcodes) S = SCHOOL

Motcombe Pre-School   07905 083 279
Motcombe, Shaftesbury, SP7 9NT
2-5yrs. 9am-12.45pm. Termtime.

Port Regis Preparatory School   01747 855 572
Motcombe, Shaftesbury, SP7 9QA
3-13yrs. 8.30am-3.30pm. Termtime.

Tiddleywinks   01747 850 665
Shaftesbury Youth Club, Coppice Street,
Shaftesbury, SP7 8PF
23/4-5yrs. 9.15-11.45am and 12.30-3pm. 37wks.

SP8
Bourton and Zeals Playgroup   07746 775 990
Bourton Village Hall, Bourton, Gillingham, SP8 5DH
2.9-5yrs. 9.15am-12pm. Termtime.

Stower Vale Pre-School   01747 839 942
Stower Provost School, Woodville, Gillingham, SP8
2.9-4yrs. 10am-12.30pm. 38wks.

Topsie Rabbit Kindergarten   01747 821 565
Gillingham Leisure Centre, Hardings Lane,
Gillingham, SP8 4HX
2-5yrs. 9.15am-12pm and 1-3.30pm. 49wks.

Youth Centre Nursery School   07803 693 793
Cemetery Road, Gillingham, SP8 4AZ
2-5yrs. 9am-12pm and 12.30-3pm. Termtime.

TA20
Thorncombe Jumping Beans   0146 030 389
Toddler and Playgroup
The Community Room, Village hall, Thorncombe,
Chard, TA20 4NE
2-5yrs. 9.45am-12.15pm. Termtime.

GLOUCESTERSHIRE
BS12
Abbeywood Tots Day Nursery   0117 969 3990
97 Station Road, Filton, BS12 7JK
3mths-5yrs 8am-6pm

BS15
Christchurch Pre-School   07752 918 789
Christchurch Hall, Church Road, Hanham, BS15
3-5yrs. 9.15-11.45am and 12.30-3pm.

Courtney Ladybirds   01173 308 049
Courtney Road, Kings Wood, Bristol, BS15 9RD
8.45-3pm. Termtime.

Hillside Day Nursery   01179 604 330
Potterswood, Britannia Road, Kingswood, BS15
2-5yrs. 8am-6pm. 50wks.

Kingswood Foundation Day Nursery   01179 352 222
43 Britannia Road, Kingswood, Bristol, BS15 8DB
6mths-5yrs. 8am-5.30pm. 50wks.

Lees Hill Pre-School Playgroup   01179 604 285
Lees Hill Pavilion, Lees Hill, Kingswood, Bristol
2-5yrs. 9.45-11.45am and 12.30-3pm. Termtime.

Made for Ever Playgroup   01179 080 015
Fisher Road, Kingswood, Bristol, BS15 4RQ
3-5yrs. 9.15am-3.30pm. Termtime.

Our Lady of Lourdes Playgroup   01179 872 027
2 Court Road, Kingswood, Bristol, BS15 9QB
9am-12pm and 12.45-3.15pm. Termtime.

BS15
Potterswood Pre-School   07977 484 496
Potterswood Methodist Church, Pows Road,
Kingswood, Bristol, BS15 9QA
2½-5yrs. 9.15am-12pm. Termtime.

Rag Dolly Pre-School Playgroup   07890 097 213
Holy Trinity Church Hall, High Street, Kingswood
2½-5yrs. 9-11.30am. Termtime.

Step by Step Day Nursery   01199 096 267
43 Lees Hill, Kingswood, Bristol, BS15 4TN
2-5yrs. 8.30am-5.30pm. 50wks.

Sydenham House   01179 673 942
11 High Street, Kingswood, Bristol, BS15 4AA
3mths-5yrs. 7.30am-6pm.50wks.

The Park Nursery   01454 862 614
Old Park School, High Street, Kingswood, BS15
8am-6pm. 50wks.

Tiny Tots Day Nursery   01179 475 436
128/130 High Street, Hanham, Bristol, BS15 3EJ
6wks-8yrs. 7.30am-6pm. 50wks.

Warmley Playgroup   01179 674 282
20 Deanery Road, Kingswood, Bristol, BS15 9JB
9.30am-12pm. Termtime .

BS16
Leapfrog Day Nursery   01179 568 222
St. Lukes Close, Emersons Green, BS16 7AL
www.leapfrogdaynurseries.co.uk
3mths-3yrs. 7am-7pm. 50wks (see ad pg 124).

Apple Tree Pre-School   07765 436 634
Deers Lodge Scout Hut, Deershurst, Soundwell
2-5yrs. 9am-1pm. Termtime.

Badminton Road Playgroup   01179 562 347
Badminton Road Methodist Church, Downend
2-4yrs. 9.15-11.45am and 12.30-2.30pm. Termtime.

Barn Owl Nursery   01179 562 222
The Old Barn, Old Gloucester Road, Hambrook
2-4yrs. 8am-6pm. 51wks.

www.babydirectory.com

S = SCHOOL   **(Gloucestshire postcodes) education**

Crossways Pre-School   01179 573 923
B.C.F. Blackhorse Building, Blackhorse Road, Mangotsfield, BS16 9DB
2-5yrs. 9.30am-12pm. Termtime.

Frenchay Pre-School Playgroup   01179 572 484
Village Hall, Cleeve Road, Frenchay, BS16 1JE
2½-5yrs. 9.30am-12pm and 12.30-2.30pm. Termtime.

Great Expectation Nursery   01179 561 632
7 Baugh Road, Downend, Bristol, BS16 6PL
8am-6pm. 50wks.

Great Expectations Day Nursery   01179 561 632
26 Baugh Gardens, Downend, Bristol, BS16 6PP
2-5yrs. 8am-6pm. 50wks.

Hillside Day Nursery   01179 047 106
23 Gladstone Street, Staple Hill, Bristol, BS16 4RF
2-5yrs. 8am-6pm. 50wks.

Lincombe Barn Playgroup   01179 562 367
Lyncombe Barn, Overndale Road, Bristol, BS16
2½-5yrs. 9.15-11.45am. Termtime.

Mangotsfield Pre-School   01179 074 347
The Scout Hut, Northcote Road, Mangotsfield, Bristol, BS16 9HF
2½-5yrs. 9.15am-12.15pm.

Mangotsfield Pre-School   01179 561 642
St.James Parish Hall, Richmond Road, Mangotsfield, BS16 9HB
2½-5yrs. 9.15am-12.15pm.

Page Park Pre-School   07790 346 176
Sports Pavilion, Page Park, Staple Hill, BS16 5LB
2½-5yrs. 9.15-11.45am and 12.15-2.45pm.

Pucklechurch Playgroup   07790 683 311
Community Centre, Abson Road, Pucklechurch
9.15-11.45am. Termtime.

Quakers Road Playgroup   07884 455 901
Christchurch Hall, Quakers Road, Downend, Bristol
3-5yrs. 9-11.45am. Termtime.

Stanbridge County Playgroup   01179 575 152
Stanbridge Road, Downend, BS16 6AL
3-5yrs. 9-11.30am and 12.30-3pm. 38wks.

Sunbeams Day Nursery   01179 566 060
33-35 Dibden Road, Downend, Bristol, BS16 6UE
3mths-5yrs.

The Squirrel Tree Nursery   01179 753 862
Frenchay Hospital, Frenchay Park Road, Bristol
6mths-5yrs. 7.30am-6pm. 50wks.

Tower Playgroup   07855 023 461
Church Room, Thomas A. Beckett Church, Pucklechurch, BS16 9RB
2-4yrs. 9.15-11.4am and 12.45-3pm. Termtime.

Willow Tree Day Nursery   01173 125 800
St. Stephens Road, Soundwell, Bristol, BS16 4RL
0-5yrs. 8am-6pm. 48wks.

BS17
S Overndale School   01454 310332
Chapel Lane, Old Sodbury, BS17 6NQ
co-ed 1-11yrs

BS30
Bitton Playgroup   01179 326 042
St. Marys Church Hall, Church Lane, Bitton, BS30
3-5yrs. 9.30am-12pm. Termtime.

Busy Bee Playgroup   01179 083 387
United Church, Bath Road, Longwell Green, BS30
3-5yrs. 9.15-11.45am and 12.30-3pm. Termtime.

Cadbury Heath Pre-School   07813 502 833
Park Road, Cadbury Heath, Warmley, Bristol, BS30
2-5yrs. 9.15-11.45am. Termtime.

Footprints Pre-School Playgroup   01179 873 395
The Mustard Tree, Watsons Road, Longwell Green, Bristol, BS30 9DW
3-5yrs. 9.15am-1.10pm. Termtime.

Hanham Toddlers Pre-School   01179 082 406
Methodist Church, Chapel Road, Hanham, BS30
2½-5yrs. 9-11.30am and 12.30-3pm. Termtime.

Just Learning Nursery   01179 677 840
Stoneleigh Drive, Barrs Court, Bristol, BS30 7EJ
0-8yrs. 7am-7pm. 50wks.

Longwell Green Playgroup   01179 325 111
Shellards Road, Longwell Green, Bristol, BS30 9DU
9.15-11.45am and 12.30-3pm. Termtime.

North Common Pre-School   01179 322 256
Methodist Church, Mill Lane, Warmley, BS30 8BJ
3-4yrs. 9.30am-12pm. 38wks.

Oldland Pre-School   01179 328 411
10 School Road, Oldland Common, Bristol, BS30
3-5yrs. 9.15-11.45am and 12.45-3.15pm. Termtime.

Redfield Edge Playgroup   01454 865 756
Oldland Youth Club, High Street, Oldland Common, Bristol, BS30 9TL
3-5yrs. 9.15am-1.15pm. Termtime.

Redroofs   01179 492 700
24 Poplar Road, North Common, Warmley, Bristol
3mths-5yrs. 8am-6.30pm. 50wks.

The Rocking Horse Day Nursery   01179 476 218
Tower Road North, Bristol, BS30 8XQ
6mths-4yrs. 8am-6pm. 50wks.

Wick Pre-School   07884 477 392
The Church Room, Church Road, Wick, BS30 5PD
3-5yrs. 9.15-11.45am. Termtime.

102 education (Gloucestershire postcodes) S = SCHOOL

BS32

Bright Horizons Day Nursery   01454 202888
Ferndene, Bradley Stoke, BS32 9DF
6wks-5yrs 7.30am-6.00pm

Christ the King Pre-School   01179 312 304
Mautravers Close, Bradley Stoke, Bristol, BS32 8EE
3-5yrs. 9.15-11.45am. Termtime.

Covey Pre-School Playgroup   01179 311 999
4 Baileys Court, Webbs Wood Road, Bristol, BS32
2-4yrs. 8.30am-12.45pm and 1-3.45pm. 45wks.

Little Acorns   01454 616 745
New Community Building, Savages Wood Road, Bradley Stoke, BS32 4BN
2½-4yrs. 9.15am-12pm and 12.30-3pm. 36wks.

Olveston Pre-School   07790 246 588
Parish Hall, Upper Tockington Road, Tockington
3-5yrs. 9.15am-12pm. 36wks.

Play Pitch Pre-School   07905 474 942
Baileys Court Activity Centre, Baileys Court Road, Bradley Court, BS32 8BH
2½-5yrs. 9.15am-1.10pm. Termtime.

Princess Christian Day Nursery   01454 202 888
Ferndene, Bradley Stoke, BS32 9DF
2-5yrs. 7.30am-6pm. 50wks.

The Covey Nursery   01179 794 190
6 Baileys Court, Webbs Wood Road, Bradley Stoke, Bristol, BS32 8EJ
8am-6pm. 50wks.

Trinity Pre-School   01454 620 976
Holy Trinity Church, Broad Croft, Bradley Stoke
3-5yrs. 9-11.30amand 12.30-3pm. Termtime.

BS34

Abbeywood Tots Day Nursery   0117 931 5072
Filton College Campus, Filton Avenue, Filton, BS34
3mths-5yrs 8am-6pm

Acorns Nursery   01179 899 000
Axa Centre Bristol, Brierly Furlong, Stoke Gifford, Bristol, BS34 8SW
6wks-5yrs. 8am-6pm. 50wks.

Ambourne House Day Nursery   01454 615 352
233 Gloucester Road, Patchway, Bristol, BS34 6ND
3mths-5yrs 8.30am-5.45pm. 51wks. Also holiday clubs for up to 8yrs.

Bluebells Pre-School   07855 645 708
Filton Folk Centre, Elm Park, Filton, BS34 7PS
2-5yrs. 9.15am-12.45pm. Termtime.

Filton Park Pre-School   01454 866 580
Charborough Road Centre, Charborough Road, Filton, Bristol, BS34 7RA
3-5yrs. 9.15-11.45am and 12.45-3.15pm. Termtime.

Flying Start Pre-School   01454 202 283
The Pavilion, The Avenue, Patchway, BS34 6BD
2½-5yrs. 9.15-11.45am and 1-3pm. Termtime.

Holy Family Playgroup   01173 771 027
Amberley Road, Stoke Lodge, BS34 6BY
3-5yrs. 9.15-11.45am. Termtime.

Little Rainbows Pre-School   01179 409 693
172 Rodway Road, Patchway, Bristol, BS34 5ED
9.05am-1pm. Termtime.

Little Sunbeams   01179 311 927
Coniston Community Centre, The Parade, Coniston Road, Patchways, BS34 5LP
6wks-5yrs. 8am-6pm. 51wks.

North Patchway Pre-School   07791 663 230
North Patchway Hall, Gloucester Road, Patchway
2-5yrs. 9.15-11.45am and 12.45-3pm. Termtime.

Patchway Centre Playgroup   01179 751 850
Community Centre, Rodway Road, Patchway
2-5yrs. 9.15am-12pm and 1.15-3.45pm. Termtime.

Play Station Day Nursery   01454 610 101
5 Station Road, Little Stoke, BS34 6LP
0-8yrs. 7.45am-6.15pm. 50wks.

Princess Christian Day Nursery   01179 799 977
Hunts Ground Road, Stoke Gifford, Bristol, BS34
3mths-5yrs. 7.30am-6pm. 50wks.

Priory Day Nursery   01179 692 503
99 Gloucester Road North, Filton, Bristol, BS34 7PT
0-5yrs. 7.30am-6pm. 50wks.

Priory Day Nursery School   01179 692 503
99 Gloucester Road North, Filton, Bristol, BS34 7PT
6wks-5yrs. 8am-6pm. 50wks.

Startrite Pre-School Playgroup   01454 865 730
Youth Centre, Little Stoke Lane, Little Stoke, BS34
3-5yrs. 9.15-11.45am. Termtime.

Stoke Gifford Playgroup   07759 595 714
Poplar Rooms, North Road, Stoke Gifford, Bristol
3-5yrs. 9.15-11.45am. 37wks.

The Priory Day Nursery   0117 969 2503
99 Gloucester Road North, Filton, BS34 7PT
6wks-5yrs 8am-6pm

Woodpeckers Day   01179 694 300
Nursery - Bright Horizons
DPA, Abbeywood, Stoke Gifford, BS34 8JH
9mths-4yrs. 7.30am-6pm. 50wks.

BS35

First Step Pre-School   01454 858 580
Easton Hill Road, Thornbury, BS35 1AX
2-5yrs. 9.15-11.45am and 12.30-3pm. Termtime.

S = SCHOOL   (Gloucestshire postcodes) **education**

First Step Pre-School Playgroup   01454 867 283
Knapp Road, Thornbury, Thornbury, Bristol, BS35
2-5yrs. 9.15am-1.15pm. Termtime.

Oldbury Busy Bee Playgroup   01454 411 993
Oldbury on Severn Memorial Hall, Camp Road,
Oldbury on Severn, BS35 1PX
3-4yrs. 9.15am-1pm. Termtime.

Pilning Pips Pre-School Playgroup   07748 053 730
Trinity Hall, 3 Redwick Road, Pilning, BS35 4LG
2-5yrs. 9.30am-12pm and 1-3pm. Termtime.

Rainbow Teddies 2   01454 867 239
Rock Street, Thornbury, Bristol, BS35 2BL
9-11.30am and 1-3pm. Termtime.

Rainbow Teddies   01454 867 231
Manorbrook Primary School, Park Road, Thornbury,
9-11.30am and 1-3pm. Termtime.

Severn Beach Playgroup   01454 632 745
Emmaus Church Centre, Gorse Cover Road,
Severn Beach, Bristol, BS35 4NR
3-5yrs. 9.15-11.45am. Termtime.

Severnside Opportunity Group   07963 776 342
St. Mary's Church Hall, Eastbury Road, Thornbury
3mths-5yrs. 10am-1pm. Termtime.

Stepping Stones Playgroup   07764 495 463
The Methodist Hall, Main Street, Olveston, BS35
9.15-11.45am and 12.40-3.15pm. Termtime.

The Wishing Well Day Nursery   01454 413 056
22 Eastland Road, Thornbury, BS35 1DS
8am-6pm.

BS36

Coalpit Heath Pre-School   01454 771 821
The Manor Hall, Henfield Road, Coalpit Heath
2^1/$_2$-5yrs. Mornings. Termtime.

Cottage Day Nursery   01454 777 900
3 Lower Stone Close, Frampton Cotterell, Frampton
Cotterell, Bristol, BS36 2LG
2-5yrs. 7.30am-6pm. 50wks.

Crossbow Pre-School   01454 316 638
Zion Church Hall, Woodend Road, Frampton
Cotterell, BS36 2HX
2.10-5yrs. 9.15am-12pm. 39wks.

Crossbow Pre-School   07713 829 887
St Peters Church Hall, School Road, Frampton
Cotterell, BS36 2DA
3-5yrs. 9.15am-12pm. Termtime.

Pooh Corner Day Nursery   01454 857 529
Bethseda Methodist Church, Down Road,
Winterbourne Down, Bristol, BS36 1BN
8am-6pm. 52wks.

St Michael's in Greenfield   01454 777 604
Pre-School Group
Greenfield Centre, Park Avenue, Winterbourne,
BS36 1NJ
2-5yrs. 9-11.30am and 12.30-3pm. Termtime.

Winterbourne Down Pre-School   07974 652 285
All Saints Church Hall, Church Road, Winterbourne
Down, BS36 1BX
9.15am-12pm.

BS37

Abbotswood Playgroup   01454 313 648
St. Nicholas Family Centre, Chargrove,
Abbotswood, Yate, BS37 4LG
2^1/$_2$-5yrs. 9.30am-12 pm and 1-3.30pm. Termtime.

Cherry Tree Day Nursery   01454 228 665
7 Lodge Road, Yate, Bristol, BS37 7LE
0-5yrs. 8am-6pm. 51wks.

Chipping Sodbury Pre-School   01454 327 328
Baptist Church Centre, Hounds Road, Chipping
Sodbury, Bristol, BS37 6EE
9.15-11.45am and 12.45-3.10pm. Termtime. 4 days.

Cornerways Day Nursery   01454 318 183
The Old School, Broad Lane, Westerleigh, Bristol
2-5yrs. 9am-3pm. Termtime.

Frome Opportunity Group   01454 326 673
Cranleigh Court, 130 Cranleigh Court Road, Yate
9.30am-12pm. Termtime.

Jack in the Box Nursery   01454 850 122
84 Firgrove Crescent, Yate, BS37 7AG
8am-6pm. 50wks.

Overndale School   01454 310 332
19 Chapel Lane, Old Sodbury, BS37 6NQ
2^1/$_2$-5yrs. 9.15am-3.15pm. Termtime.

Phase 5 Pre-School Playgroup   01454 311 459
Kelston Close, Yate, BS37 8SZ

Playaway Pre-School   07890 698 867
Hanham Road, Kingswood, Bristol, BS37 4PQ
3-5yrs. 9.15am-3pm. Termtime.

Playmates Day Nursery   01454 320 928
104 Station Road, Yates, Bristol, BS37 4PQ
2^1/$_2$-5yrs. 9am-12pm and 1-4pm.

Rangeworthy Playgroup   01454 228 326
King George V Memorial Hall, New Road,
Rangeworthy, BS37 5QF
2^1/$_2$-5yrs.

Raysfield Pre-School Playgroup   01454 324 688
Dodington Parish Hall, Finch Road, Chipping
Sodbury, Bristol, BS37 6JE
2^1/$_2$-5yrs. 9.15-11.45am and 12.30-3pm. Termtime.

education (Gloucestershire postcodes)

S = SCHOOL

Ridgewood Pre-School Playgroup 01454 868 645
244 Station Road, Yate, Bristol, BS37 4AF
9.15-11.45am. Termtime.

St Nicholas Nursery 07989 113 460
Chargrove, Yate, Bristolg, BS37 4LG
2½-5yrs. 9.15-11.45am. Termtime.

Stanshawes Court 01454 327 670
4 Stanshawes Court Drive, Yate, Bristol, BS37 4EA
0-5yrs. 8am-6pm. 50wks.

The Time Out Creche 01454 865 801
Kennedy Way, Yate, BS37 4DQ
9.45-11.50am. 50wks.

GL1

Leapfrog Day Nursery 01452 506 161
Pullman Court, Great Western Road, Gloucester
www.leapfrogdaynurseries.co.uk
3mths-3yrs. 7am-7pm. 50wks (see ad pg 124).

Birchwood Day Nursery 01452 477 123
8 Heathville Road, GL1 3DS
3mths-5yrs. 8am-5.30pm. 51wks.

Brunswick Day Nursery 01452 563 226
Gloscat Media Studies Building, Brunswick Road, Gloucester, GL1 1HH
1-8yrs. 8.30am-5.30pm. 49wks.

Calton Road Playgroup 01452 522 202
Calton Road, Gloucester, GL1 5ET
2.9-5yrs. 9-11.30am and 12.30-3pm.

Colwell Community Nursery 01452 380 912
Widden Primary School, Sinope Street, Gloucester
0-8yrs. 8am-6pm. 50wks.

Gloucestershire Islamic Nursery 01452 503 533
Sinope Street, Gloucester, GL1 4AW
9-11.30am and 12.30-3pm. Termtime.

Grey Gables Day Nursery 01452 306 269
38 Herbert Street, Gloucester, GL1 4AD
8am-6pm. 50wks.

Ivy House Day Nursery 01452 331 444
94 Eastgate Street, Gloucester, GL1 1QN
0-8yrs. 8am-5.45pm. 50wks.

Jack & Jill Kindergarten 01452 412 220
162 Stroud Road, Gloucester, GL1 5JX
2-4yrs. 9.15am-12.15pm and 12.45-3.45pm.

Kingsholm Early Years Centre 01453 828 977
Guinea Street, Gloucester, GL1 3BN
9-11.30am and 1-3pm. Termtime.

Day Nursery 01452 506 161
Pullman Court, Gloucester, GL1 3PZ
0-5yrs. 7.30am-6pm. 52wks.

Linden Nursery 01452 527 020
Linden Road, Gloucester, GL1 5HU
9-11.30am and 1.15-3.15pm. Termtime.

Little Footsteps Day Nursery 01452 380 599
106 Stroud Road, Gloucester, GL1 5JN
0-5yrs. 8am-5.45pm. 50wks.

Little Oaks Day Nursery 08454 225 095
Gloucester Royal Hospital, Great Western Road, Gloucester, GL1 3NN
3mths-5yrs.

Mount Lands Day Nursery 01452 506 880
36 Vicarage Road, Gloucester, GL1 4LD
18mths-8yrs. 8am-5.30pm. 50wks.

My Day Nursery Ltd. 01452 525 666
10 Denmark Road, Gloucester, GL1 3HW
5mths-4yrs. 8am-6pm. 50wks.

Patti Cakes Day Nursery 01452 415 355
45 Tuffley Avenue, Gloucester, GL1 5LU
6wks-5yrs. 8am-5.45pm. 50wks.

St Luke's Under Fives 07985 783 159
Methodist Church, Stroud Road, Gloucester, GL1
2.9-5yrs. 9.30am-12pm. Termtime.

St Paul's Playgroup 01452 507 505
New Street, Gloucester, GL1 5BD
2-5yrs. 9am-12pm Termtime.

St Peter's Under 5's Playgroup 07816 223 995
St Peter's Social Centre, Blackdog Way, Gloucester, GL1 3EQ
2½-5yrs. 9.30am-12pm and 12.30-2.30pm. Termtime.

Sunnyside Day Nursery 01452 416 613
119 Stroud Road, Gloucester, GL1 5AH
0-5yrs. 8am-5.30pm. 50wks.

Sure Start Day Nursery 01452 308 536
2 Furlong Road, Gloucester, GL1 4UT
6mths-4yrs. 8.30am-5.30pm. 50wks.

The Family Haven 01452 422 971
31 Spa Road, Gloucester, GL1 1UY
0-8yrs. 10am-1pm. and 1.30-3.30pm. 52wks.

Tredworth Early Years Centre 01452 311 793
Paul Street, Tredworth, Gloucester, GL1 4NY
2-4yrs. 9-11.30am and 12.40-3.10pm. Termtime.

GL2

Leapfrog Day Nursery 01452 725 533
Merlin Drive, Quedgley, GL2 4NJ
www.leapfrogdaynurseries.co.uk
3mths-3yrs. 7am-7pm. 50wks (see ad pg 124).

Acorns 01452 750 467
Churcham Primary School, Churcham, GL2 8BD
9.30am-12.15pm. Termtime.

S = SCHOOL (Gloucestshire postcodes) **education**

Beech Green Nursery 01452 729 326
St James, Quedgeley, GL2 4WD
2-5yrs. 8am-6pm. 50wks.

Chestnuts Day Nursery 01452 386 888
82 Church Road, Longlevens, Gloucester, GL2 0AA
3mths-8yrs. 7.30am-7.30pm. 50wks.

Elmscroft Under Fives 07779 892 318
Barnwood Road, Gloucester, GL2 0RX
23/4-5yrs. 9.30am-12pm. Termtime.

Fieldcourt Fieldmice 07833 987 439
Courtfield Road, Quedgeley, Gloucester, GL2 4UF
3-4yrs. 9-11.30am and 12.30-3pm. Termtime.

Hardwicke Playgroup 01452 721 115
Hardwicke Village Hall, Green Lane, Hardwicke
9.30am-12pm. Termtime.

Hempsted Playgroup & Toddlers 01452 527 188
St Swithuns Road, Hempsted, Gloucester, GL2 5LH
2½-5yrs. 9.15-11.45am and 12.30-2.45pm.

Highnam Day Nursery 01452 525 872
Lassington Lane, Highnam, Gloucester, GL2 8LW
3-4yrs. 9am-12pm. Termtime.

Into Play Day Nursery 01452 380 662
Paygrove Lane, Longlevens, Gloucester, GL2 0AU
0-8yrs. 7.30am-6.15pm. 50wks.

Ladybirds Playgroup 01452 720 257
Courtfield Road, Quedgeley, Gloucester, GL2 4UF
3-5yrs. 9-11.30am. Termtime.

Little Rascals Day Nursery 01452 741 014
Coach House, Framilode, Gloucester, GL2 7LH
3mths-5yrs. 8.30am-4.45pm. 50wks.

Longlevens Early Years Centre 01452 304 464
Paygrove Lane, Longlevens, Gloucester, GL2 0AX
3-5yrs. 9.15-11.45am and 12.45-3.10pm. Termtime.

Longlevens Tiny Tots Playgroup 07944 737 072
Clinic Hall Church Road, Longlevens, GL2 0AJ
2.7-5yrs. 9.10-11.40am and 12.20-2.50pm. Termtime.

Longney School Pre-School Group 01452 720 461
Chatter Street, Longney, Gloucester, GL2 3SL
3-4yrs. 9.15am-12pm and 1-3pm. Termtime.

Lonsdale Under Fives 01452 526 553
Lonsdale Road, Gloucester, GL2 0TA
2-5yrs. 9.30am-12pm. Termtime.

Norton Playgroup 07816 568 108
Village Hall, Old Tewkesbury Road, Norton, GL2
2.9-5yrs. 9.30am-12pm. Termtime.

Playdays Playgroup 01452 530 570
Community Centre, Church Road, Longlevens, Gloucester, GL2 0AJ
2-5yrs. 9.15-11.45am and 12.30-3pm. Termtime.

Puddleducks Hall Day Nursery 01452 728 095
The Old Rectory, Church Lane, Hardwick, GL2 4RP
2-5yrs. 8am-4pm. Termtime.

Saul Under Fives Playgroup 07986 721 452
Saul Memorial Hall, Saul, GL2 7JD
2.9-5yrs. 9.30am-12pm. Termtime.

Scallywags Nursery 01452 724 303
303 Bristol Road, Quedgeley, Gloucester, GL2 4QP
0-4yrs. 8am-6pm 50wks.

Seedlings Pre-School Playgroup 07796 345 919
The Community Centre, School Lane, Quedgeley, Gloucester, GL2 4PJ
2-4yrs. 9.30am-12pm. Termtime.

Slimbridge Playgroup 01453 890 561
Slimbridge Villlage Hall, St. Johns Road, Slimbridge, Gloucester, GL2 7DF
2-5yrs. 9.30am-12pm. Termtime. 3 days.

Twigworth Under 5s 01452 730 420
Tewkesbury Road, Twigworth, Gloucester, GL2
3-4yrs. 8.50-11.30am. Termtime.

Whitminster Little Tigers 07960 836 922
Village Hall, School Lane, Whitminster, GL2 7NT
2yrs 9 mnths. 9.30am-12pm. Termtime. Wed 12.30 -3pm

GL3

Abbeymead Under 5s Playgroup 07792 947 030
The Church Centre, Larkhay Road, Hucclecote
2½-5yrs. 9.15-11.45am [Sept-Dec] and 11.55am-2.40pm [Jan-July]. Termtime.

Brockworth Pre-School 01452 862 809
Moorfield Road, Brockworth, GL3 4JL
2.9-5yrs. 9am-12pm and 12.15-3.15pm. Termtime.

Busy Bees Playgroup 01452 541 183
Abbotswood Road, Brockworth, Gloucester, GL3
2-4yrs. 9.15am-12pm and 1-2.45pm. Termtime.

Chapel Hay Playgroup 01452 859 317
Methodist Church Hall, Chapel Hay Lane, Churchdown, GL3 2ET
2-4yrs. 9.15am-12pm. Termtime.

Churchdown Day Nursery 01452 531 105
46 Parton Road, Churchdown, Gloucester, GL3 2AF
0-8yrs. 8am-6pm. 50wks.

Churchdown Pre-School 01452 714 178
Station Road, Churchdown, Gloucester, GL3 2NB
3-5yrs. 9am-3.15pm. Termtime.

Hillview Playgroup 07960 593 220
Hillview Road, Hucclecote, GL3 3LQ
2-5yrs. 9.15-11.45am. Termtime.

Hucclecote Playgroup 01452 616 289
Hucclecote Road, Gloucester, GL3 3RT
2-4yrs. 9.30am-12pm and 12.30-3pm. Termtime.

106 education (Gloucestershire postcodes) S = SCHOOL

Larkfield Playgrou   01452 739 090
Luke Lane, Innsworth, Gloucester, GL3 1HJ
2-5yrs. 9.15-11.45am and 12.15-2.45pm. Termtime.

Little Gems Under 5's Playgroup   07811 716 123
Scout Hut, Clyde Road, Brockworth, GL3 4JN
2-4yrs. 9.30am-12pm. Termtime.

Little People Day Nursery   01452 610 477
165 Hucclecote Road, Hucclecote, Gloucester, GL3
8.30am-5.30pm. 50wks.

Parton Manor Family Centre   01452 714 392
Craven Drive, Churchdown, Gloucester, GL3 2AG
0-5yrs. 9am-3pm. Termtime.

Prickles Childcare   01452 535 463
18 Ermin Street, Brockworth, Gloucester, GL3 4HJ
9mths-3yrs. 8.30am-5pm. 50wks.

Red Sparrows Day Nursery   01452 730 018
RAF Innsworth, 54-56 Mottershead Drive,
Innsworth, Gloucester, GL3 1EH
11mths-4yrs. 7.30am-6pm. 50wks.

Ridgemount Cottage Nursery   01452 864 107
73 Ermin Street, Brockworth, Gloucester, GL3 4EH
0-8yrs. 8am-6pm. 50wks.

St Mary's Playgroup   07749 713 742
Cheltenham Road East, Churchdown, Gloucester
2.9-5yrs. 8.55-11.30am. Termtime.

Tiddlywinks Day Nursery   01452 613 987
104 Hucclecote Road, Gloucester, GL3 3RX
0-5yrs. 8am-6pm. 50wks.

Tree Tops Day Nursery   01452 613 674
141 Hucclecote Road, Hucclecote, Gloucester, GL3
3mths-5yrs. 8am-6pm. 50wks.

GL4

Teddies Nursery   0800 980 3801
Esporta Health Club, Unit 1 Centre Seven,
Barnwood, Gloucester, GL4 3HR
www.teddiesnurseries.co.uk
3mths-5yrs. 8am-6pm. 51wks (see ad pg 142).

Abbeydale Playgroup   01452 301 492
Glevum Way, Abbbeydale, GL4 4BL
2-5yrs. 9.15-11.45am and 12.15-2.45pm. Termtime.

Barnwood Playgroup   01452 614 775
Colin Road, Barnwood, GL4 3JP
9.20-11.40am. Termtime. Friday only

Best Friends Day Nursery   01452 523 305
3 Grange Road, Tuffley, GL4 0PY
0-5yrs. 8.30am-5.20pm. 50wks.

Best Friends Too   01452 384 921
28 Tuffley Lane, Tuffley, GL4 0DU
0-5yrs. 8.30am-5.30pm. 50wks.

Brimpsfield & Birdlip Playgroup   01452 863 240
The Village Hall, Birdlip, GL4 8JH
3-5yrs. 9-11.30am.

Chipmunks Day Nursery   01452 613 828
The Old Primary School, Churchfield Road, Upton
St.Leonards, Gloucester, GL4 8AE
0-8yrs. 8am-5.45pm. 50wks.

Coney Hill Early Years Centre   01452 541 033
Coney Hill Road, Gloucester, GL4 4NA
9am-3.15pm. Termtime.

Finlay Early Years Centre   01452 530 312
Finlay Road, Gloucester, GL4 6TR
3-4yrs. 9-11.30am.

Haresfield Playgroup   07952 622 263
Brookthorpe Village Hall, Brookthorpe, GL4 0UJ
2.9-5yrs. 9.15am-12pm. Termtime.

Robinswood Early Years Centre   01452 530 440
Matson Avenue, Matson, Gloucester, GL4 6HE
0-6yrs. 9-11.30am and 12-3pm.

St Augustines Playgroup   01452 384 442
Matson House, Matson Lane, Matson, Gloucester
2.9-5yrs. 9.15-11.45am and 12.15-2.45pm. Termtime.

St Georges Playgroup   07759 101 247
St. George's Church Hall, Grange Road, Tuffley
2-5yrs. 9.15-11.45am. Termtime.

Sunshine Corner Under 5's   01452 541 637
Evenlode Road, Tuffley, Gloucester, GL4 0JY
2-8yrs. 9am-3pm. Termtime.

Tadpoles Sessional Care   01452 541 457
7a Highfield Place, Gloucester, GL4 4PB
10mths-4yrs. 9.30-11.30am and 12.30-2.30pm. Termtime.

The Acorn Centre   01452 541 351
Grange Road, Tuffley, Gloucester, GL4 0PH
2-5yrs. 9-11.30am and 12.30-3pm.

The Moat Pre-School   01452 384 234
Juniper Avenue, Matson, Gloucester, GL4 6AP
3-5yrs. 9-11.30am. Termtime.

Tuffley Playgroup   07903 336 257
Murray Hall, Tuffley Lane, Tuffley, GL4
2.9-5yrs. 9.30am-1.15pm.

Twin Gables Day Nursery   01452 417 488
102 Eastern Avenue, Gloucester, GL4 4LW
9mths-4yrs. 8am-6pm. 50wks.

Upton St Leonards Playgroup   07906 495 998
10 Bondend Road, Upton St.Leonards, Gloucester
2.9-5yrs. 9.30am-12pm and 1-2.45pm.

Please say you saw the listings in the
South West Baby Directory

S = SCHOOL   (Gloucestshire postcodes) **education**

GL5

Amberley Playgroup 01453 872 571
The Parish Rooms, Amberley, Stroud, GL5 5AA
2-5yrs. 9.30am-12.15pm. 3 days. Termtime.

Beanstalk Day Nursery 01453 761 171
Stratford Road, Stroud, GL5 4AH
3mths-5yrs. 8.30am-5.30pm. 50wks.

Brimscombe Playgroup 01453 882 474
Brimscombe Hill, Brimscombe, Stroud, GL5 2QR
9.30am-12pm. 40wks.

Bumble Bees Playgroup 07817 468 732
Trinity Rooms, Field Road, Stroud, GL5 2HX
2.9-5yrs. 9.15-11.45am and 1-3.30pm.

Callowell Caterpillars 01453 762 962
Barrowfield Road, Farmhill, Stroud, GL5 4DG
2-5yrs. 8.50am-12pm and 12.45-3pm. Termtime.

Cashes Green Playgroup 07855 031 973
Hillcrest Road, Cashes Green, Stroud, GL5 4NL
2-5yrs. 9-11.45am and 12.45-3pm. Termtime.

Jane Arnolds Nursery School 01453 753 045
Church Lane, Rodborough, Stroud, GL5 3NF
2-5yrs. 9am-12pm and 1-3.30pm. Termtime.

Polly's Day Nursery 01453 835 113
Gydynap Lane, Inchbrook, Stroud, GL5 5EZ
9mths-5yrs. 8am-6pm. 51wks.

Rodborough Playgroup 01453 758 179
Rodborough Tabernacle, Tabernacle Walk,
Rodborough, Stroud, GL5 3UJ
3-4yrs. 9.15am-12pm. Termtime.

St Matthew's Playgroup 01453 756 057
Church Hall, Church Road, Cainscross, Stroud, GL5
2.9-5yrs. 9.15-11.45am and 12.45-3.15pm.

The Shambles Nursery School 01453 765 626
The Old Library, Lansdown Stroud, Gloucester, GL5 1BB
9am-12pm and 1-3.30pm. Termtime.

Thrupp School Nursery 01453 883 586
Thrupp Primary School, Thrupp Lane, Thrupp,
Stroud, GL5 2EN
3-5yrs. 9am-12pm. Termtime.

Tigger's @ Downfield 01453 750 957
Downfield Road, Cainscross, Stroud, GL5 4HL
0-5yrs. 8am-6pm. 50wks.

Uplands Playgroup 01453 762 205
Thompson Road, Uplands, Stroud, GL5 1TE
2.9-5yrs. 9am-12pm. Termtime.

Woodchester Playgroup 01453 873 004
Woodchester Primary School, Church Road, North
Woodchester, Stroud, GL5 5PD
2.9-4yrs. 9-11.45am. 39wks.

GL6

S **Beaudesert Park School** 01453 832 072
Minchinhampton, Nr Stroud, GL6 9AF
4-13yrs. 8.10am-3.30pm. Termtime.

Bisley Pre-School Playgroup 01452 770 102
Bisley School, School Lane, Bisley, Stroud, GL6 7BE
2-5yrs. 9am-12.40pm. Termtime.

Bussage Nursery School 01453 731 241
Bussage House, Bussage, Stroud, GL6 8BB
9am-12pm. Termtime.

Bussage Playgroup 01453 883 205
Bussage Village Hall, The Ridge, Bussage, Stroud,
GL6 8BB
9.30am-12pm. Termtime.

Coigne Playgroup 01453 882 479
Youth Centre, Tobacconist Road, Minchinhampton,
Stroud, GL6 9JJ
2.9-5yrs. 9am-12pm. Termtime.

Eastcombe Playgroup 01452 770 227
Eastcombe Villlage Hall, Eastcombe, Stroud, GL6 7ED
2.9-5yrs. 9.30am-12pm. Termtime.

Horsley Playgroup 01453 833 625
Horsley Cofe School, The Street, Horsley, GL6 0PU
3-5yrs. 12.30-3pm. Termtime.

Horsley Playgroup 07929 974 982
Horsley Village Hall, Priory Fields, Horsley, GL6 0PT
2-5yrs. 9.30am-12pm. 2 mornings.

Keyhole Nursery 01285 821 275
Kilmory, Whiteway, Stroud, GL6 7ER
0-5yrs. 8am-6pm. 51wks.

Minchinhampton Nursery Group 01453 882268
Scout Hall, Dr.Brown's Road, Minchinhampton,
Stroud, GL6 9BT
2-5yrs. 9am-12pm. Termtime.(Fri 9- 3pm)

Minchinhampton School 01453 883 273
Nursery Unit
Bell Lane, Minchinhampton, Stroud, GL6 9BP
3-4yrs. 8.50-11.45am. Termtime.

Nailsworth Town Hall Day Nursery 01453 834 531
Nailsworth Tow Hall, Old Bristol Road, Nailsworth,
Stroud, GL6 0JF
9am-3.30pm. Termtime.

Painswick Playgroup 01452 813 316
c/o The Croft School, Churchill Way, Painswick,
GL6 6RQ
2.9-5yrs. 9am-12pm.

Phoenix Playmates 01453 754 335
Nailsworth Primary School, Nympsfield Road,
Nailsworth, GL6 0ET
2-5yrs. 9am-3.30pm. Termtime.

108 education (Gloucestershire postcodes)   S = SCHOOL

Polly's Day Nursery　　01453 731 101
Brownshill Road, Brownshill, Stroud, GL6 8AS
8am-6pm. 51wks.

Puddleducks Playgroup　　01453 884 214
The Sports & Social Club, Highfield Road, Chalford Hill, GL6 8LZ
2.9-5yrs. 9.30am-12pm and 12.30-3pm. Termtime.

Whiteshill Pre-School Playgroup　　01453 762 949
Whiteshill County Primary School, Main Road, Whiteshill, Stroud, GL6 6AU
2.9-5yrs. 9-11.45am. 3 days.

GL7

Acorns Nursery School　　01285 655 505
10 Park Street, Cirencester, GL7 2BN
2.9-5yrs. 8.30am-3.30pm. Termtime.

Bingham Kindergarten　　01285 651 310
Bingham Hall, King Street, Cirencester, GL7 1JT
2-5yrs. 8.30am-12pm. Termtime.

Cirencester Opportunity Group　　01285 659 117
Beeches Road, Cirencester, GL7 1BW
3-5yrs. Termtime.

Daisychain Day Nursery　　01285 654 000
64 Victoria Road, Cirencester, GL7 1ES
0-8yrs. 8am-6pm. 50wks.

Down Ampney Pre-School　　07753 440 644
The Village Hall, Down Ampney, Cirencester, GL7
2.9-5yrs. 9am-12pm. 3 mornings.

Fairford Playgroup　　01285 713 176
The Park, Leafield Road, Fairford, GL7 4JQ
2-4yrs. 8.45-11.45am. Termtime.

S Hatherop Castle School　　01285 750 206
Hatherop, Nr. Cirencester, GL7 3NB
9am-3.30pm. Termtime.

S Ingleside School　　01285 654 046
Beeches Rd, Cirencester, GL7 1BN
2.9-11yrs. 8.30am-3.15pm. 50wks.

Kemble and District Playgroup　　07746 951 417
Village Hall, School Road, Kemble, Cirencester
2-5yrs. 9-11.45am. Termtime.

Kempsford Pre-School Playgroup　　0778 3032 320
The Village Hall, High Street, Kempsford, GL7 4EY
2 1/2 - 5yrs. 9.15-11.45am and 12.30-2.55pm. Termtime.

Lechlade Little Learners　　07989 037 981
Wharf Lane, Lechlade, GL7 3AU
2-5yrs. 9am-12pm and 1-3.10pm. Termtime.

Lewis Lane Playgroup　　07816 623 298
47 Lewis Lane, Cirencester, GL7 1EB
2-5yrs. 9.30am-12pm. Termtime.

Mrs Berry's Montessori Nursery　　01285 643 959
10 Berry Hill Road, Cirencester, GL7 2HE
9am-4pm. Termtime.

Phoenix Pre-School Playgroup　　01285 655 982
Fosse Close Community Rooms, Arnolds Way, Cirencester, GL7 1TA
2.9-5yrs. 9.30am-12pm. Termtime.

Siddington Playgroup　　01285 652 866
Coach Road, Siddington, Cirencester, GL7 6HL
2.9-5yrs. 9-11.30am. Termtime.

South Cerney Pre-School　　01285 860 340
School Site, Berkeley Close, South Cerney, Cirencester, GL7 5UW
2.9-4yrs. 9-11.45am. Termtime.

St Peter's Nursery　　01285 642 473
St. Peter's Road, Cirencester, GL7 1RE
2-5yrs. 9am-12pm. Termtime.

Stepping Stones Day Nursery　　01285 642 460
Ashcroft Road, Cirencester, GL7 1RA
3mths-5yrs. 8am-6pm.51wks.

Stratton Playgroup　　01285 640 576
Stratton Village Hall, Thessaly Road, Stratton, GL7
2-4yrs. 9-11.30am. Termtime.

S The King's Junior School　　01452 337 337
Pitt Street, Gloucester, GL7 3EX
2.10-18yrs. 8.20am-3.15pm. 35wks.

The Manor Farm Nursery　　01367 253 821
Manor Farm Estate, Burford Road, Lechlade, GL7
7.30am-6pm. 51wks.

Avening Playgroup　　01453 832 695
Sunground, Avening, Tetbury, GL8 8NW
3-5yrs. 9.15am-12pm. Termtime.

S Querns Westonbirt School　　01666 881 390
Westonbirt, Tetbury, GL8 8QG
4-11yrs. 8.50am-3.30pm. Termtime.

Roundabout Nursery Group　　01666 503 858
Dolphins Hall, New Church Street, Tetbury, GL8
2-5yrs. 9.15am-12.15pm. Termtime.

St Mary's Playgroup
Christchurch Hall, The Chipping, Tetbury, GL8 8EU
2.9-5yrs.

Tetbury Nursery Playgroup　　01666 504 855
Carrie Kitkat Clinic, The Ferns, Tetbury, GL8 8JE
2.9-5yrs. 9-11.30am and 12.30-3pm. Termtime.

The Stables Nursery　　01666 502 830
The Old Stables, Upton Grove, Tetbury, GL8 8LR
3mths-5yrs. 8am-6pm. 51wks.

S = SCHOOL (Gloucestshire postcodes) **education**

GL9
Cotswold Nursery 01454 218 100
Tormarton Village Hall, High Street, Tormarton, Badminton, GL9 1HZ
2-5yrs. 8.30am-4pm. Termtime.

Didmarton Playgroup 01454 238 831
The Village Hall, Didmarton, GL9 1DT
2½-5yrs. 9.30am-12pm. Termtime.

Hawkesbury Playgroup 01454 238 682
The Village Hall, High Street, Hawkesbury Upton
2½-5yrs. 8.45-11.45am. Termtime.

GL10
Kings Stanley Playgroup 01453 828 977
Kings Stanley Village Hall, Marling Close, Kings Stanley, GL10 3JA
2½-5yrs. 9.30am-12pm. Termtime. 3 mornings.

Little Angels Day Nursery 01453 828 292
Hollybrooke House, Newtown, Stonehouse, GL10
3mths-5yrs. 8am-6pm. 50wks.

Quietways Playgroup
Douglas Morley Hall, Methodist Church, Elms Road, Stonehouse, GL10 2NP
9-11.30am. 3 mornings. Termtime.

St Joseph's Hilltots 01453 860 311
Front Street, Nympsfield, Stonehouse, GL10 3TY
9am-12pm. Termtime.

The Park Early Years Centre 01453 821 361
Elms Road, Stonehouse, GL10 2NP
2-5yrs. 8.45am-3pm.

GL11
Coaley Village Playgroup
The Street, Coaley, Dursley, GL11 5EB
2-5yrs. 8.45am-12pm. Termtime.

Dursley Early Years Centre 01453 543 151
School Road, Highfields, Dursley, GL11 4NZ
2-5yrs. 9.30-11.45am and 1-3pm. Termtime.

Funbusters @ Everlands 01453 548 781
Birch Road, Norman Hill, Dursley, GL11 5SF
2.9-5yrs. 9.30am-12pm. Termtime.

Hopton School House 01453 542 489
18 Hopton Road, Cam, Dursley, GL11 5PB
2.9-5yrs.

Imagine Co-operative Childcare 01453 544 111
22 Woodfield Road, Cam, Dursley, GL11 6HE
6mths-4yrs. 8am-6pm. 50wks.

Lower Cam Under 5's 07932 180 272
Arthur Winterbotham Memorial Hall, Cam, GL11
2.9-5yrs. 9.30am-12pm. Termtime.

Nibley House Nursery 01453 519 538
Nibley House, North Nibley, Dursley, GL11 6DL
2-5yrs. 8.30am-4.30pm. Termtime.

North Nibley Playgroup
Village Hall, Innocks Estate, North Nibley, GL11
2-5yrs. 9-11.30am. Termtime.

St Bartholomews U5's Playgroup
St. Bartholomews Church Hall, Cam Pitch, Cam, Dursley, GL11 5HL
2½-5yrs. 9.30-11.30am. Termtime.

Stepping Stones Playgroup 01453 544 588
Highfields, Dursley, GL11 4NZ
9.30am-12pm. Termtime.

The Woodfield Nest Pre-School 01453 543 535
Elstub Lane, Dursley, GL11 6JJ
9.10am-3.10pm. Termtime.

Treetops Nursery 01453 543 712
Third Avenue, Highfields, Durlsey, GL11 4NZ
0-5yrs. 7.30am-6pm. 50wks.

Uley Playgroup 01453 861 024
Village Hall, The Street, Uley, Dursley, GL11 5AL
2.9-5yrs. 9.15am-1pm. Termtime.

Upper Knapp Farm Day Nursery 01453 543 661
Manor Avenue, Lower Cam, Nr. Dursley, GL11 5LS
6wks-5yrs. 50wks.

GL12
Active Tots Day Nursery 01453 845 569
Waterloo Mill Cottage, Wotton-on-Edge, GL12 7JN
2-5yrs. 8am-6pm. 51wks.

Blue Coat Pre-School 01453 525 022
Symn Lane, Wotton under Edge, GL12 7BD
2-4yrs. 9.15-11.45am. Termtime.

Charfield Pre-School 0786 604 915
Wotton Road, Charfield, GL12 8TG
2.9-5yrs. 9.15-11.45am. Termtime.

Kingswood Village Playgroup 01453 843 862
Village Hall, Wickwar Road, Kingswood, Wotton-under-Edge, GL12 8RF
2-5yrs. 9.15-11.45am. Termtime.

Little Acorns Pre-School 07816 236 818
The Log Cabin Club, Tortowrth, Wotton-under-Edge, GL12 8HG
3-4yrs. 9-11.30am. Termtime.

S Rose Hill School 01453 843 196
Alderley, Wotton-under-edge, GL12 7QT
2½-13yrs. 8.45am-3.25pm. Termtime.

The Kindergarten, 01453 843 371
The British School
Wortley Road, Wotton-on-Edge, GL12 7JU
2-5yrs. 9-11.30am and 12.30-3pm. Termtime.

education (Gloucestershire postcodes)

S = SCHOOL

Tytherington Pre-School 07813 530 790
Village Hall, Itchington Road, Tytherington, Wotton-under Edge, GL12 8UP
2½-5yrs. 9.30am-1pm. Termtime.

Wickwar Playgroup 01454 294 946
Community Hall, Honeybourne Way, Wickwar, Wooton under Edge, GL12 8NB
2-5yrs. 9.05-11.05am and 1.15-3.15pm. Termtime.

GL13
Berkeley Playgroup 01453 819 328
Marybrook Street, Berkeley, GL13 9AZ
2.9-5yrs. 9-11.45am and 12.30-3.10pm. Termtime.

Sharpness Playgroup 07759 308 427
Newtown, Berkeley, GL13 9NU
2.9-5yrs. 9.15-11.45am and 12.30-3pm. Termtime.

Stone with Woodford Playgroup 07800 851 236
The Village Hall, Stone, Nr Berkeley, GL13 9LE
2.9-5yrs. 9.15am-12pm. Termtime.

GL14
Bright Horizons 01452 760 303
Pre-School and Playgroup
Westbury-on-Severn, GL14 1PA
2-4yrs. 9-11.30am and 12.-3pm. Termtime.

Earlybirds Pre-School Group 01594 822 311
St. Whites Road, Cinderford, GL14 3DH
3-5yrs. 12.30-3pm. Termtime.

Forest View Early Years Centre 01594 822 430
Latimer Road, Cinderford, GL14 2QA
2.9-8yrs. 9am-3.15pm. 50wks.

Langdons Day Nursey 01594 510 404
Lower High Street, Newnham-on-Severn, GL14 1BE
3mths-5yrs. 7.30am-6pm. 50wks.

Little Acorns Nursery 01594 822 171
Church Street, Littledean, Cinderford, GL14 3NL
3-5yrs. 8.45-11.15am. Termtime.

Lunaland Children's Daycare 01594 844 269
Whimsey Industrial Estate, Steam Mills Road, Cinderford, GL14 3JA
3mths-8yrs. 7am-6pm. 50wks.

Newnham Early Birds 01594 510 522
Station Road, Newnham, GL14 1AT
2-5yrs. 9.15-11.45am. Termtime.

Ruspidge Playgroup 07803 829 270
Ruspidge Memorial Hall, Ruspidge Road, Ruspidge, Cinderford, GL14
2-5yrs. 9.30am-12pm. 2days.

S St Anthony's Convent 01594 823 558
93 Belle Vue Road, Cinderford, GL14 2AA
3-5yrs. 9am-3.15pm. Termtime.

St John's Playgroup
St. John's Cricket Club, Forest Vale Road, Cinderford, GL14 2PH
2.9-5yrs. 3days.

Steam Mills Playgroup 01594 827 353
Steam Mills School, Steam Mills, Cinderford, GL14
2-5yrs. 9-11.30am. Termtime. 3 days.

GL15
Blakeney Under Fives 01594 510 367
Church Rooms, Church Way, Blakeney, GL15 4DT
2.9-5yrs. 9.30am-12pm. Termtime. 2 days.

Bream Early Learners 01594 564 535
The Beverlery Casey Building, High Street, Bream, Lydney, GL15 6JW
2.9-5yrs. 9-11.30am and 12.30-3pm. Termtime.

Lydney Early Years Centre 01594 844 269
Bream Road, Lydney, GL15 5JH
2-5yrs. 9-11.30am and 12.30-3pm. Termtime.

Lydney Playgroup & Nursery 01594 841 779
Bream Road, Lydney, GL15 5JW
3-5yrs. 9am-12pm. Termtime.

Nutkin Nursery
Lydney Park Estate, Old Park, Lydney, GL15 6BU
8am-5.30pm. 50wks.

Pillowell Early Years Group 01594 562 244
School Road, Pillowell, Nr Lydney, GL15 4QT
2.9-4yrs. Termtime.

Primrose Hill Nursery 07979 662 193
School Crescent, Lydney, GL15 5TA
2.9-5yrs. 8.55-11.30am and 12.15-2.45pm. 40wks.

St Briavels Playgroup 01594 530 428
High Street, St. Briavels, GL15 6TD
2½-5yrs. 9-11.30am. Termtime.

Woolaston Playgroup
Village Hall, Knapp Lane, Alvington, Lydney, GL15 6BJ
2.9-4yrs. 9.15-11.45am. Termtime.

Yorkley Playgroup 01594 510 212
Lydney Road, Yorkley, Lydney, GL15 4RR
2-4yrs. 9-11.30am. Termtime.

GL16
Berry Hill Under 5's Group 01594 810 808
Nine Wells Road, Berryhill, Coleford, GL16 7AT
2½-5yrs. 9.05-11.45am and 12.05-2.45pm. Termtime.

Christchurch Nursery School 01594 836 192
Ross Road, Christchurch, Coleford, GL16 7NS
2-5yrs. 9.15am -3pm.Termtime.

Coleford Early Years Centre 01594 837 552
Bowens Hill Road, Coleford, GL16 8DU
2-5yrs. 9-11.30am and 12.30-3.pm. Termtime.

S = SCHOOL   (Gloucestshire postcodes) **education**

Coleford St Johns Playgroup 07833 912 453
Bowens Hill Road, Coleford, GL16 8DU
2.9-5yrs. 9.15am-12.15pm. 39wks.

Ellwood Nursery 01594 835 624
Old School House, Bromley Road, Ellwood,
Coleford, GL16 7LY
2-8yrs. 8.30-11.30am and 12.30-3pm. Termtime.

The Rose Day Nursery 01594 835 824
Market Place, Coleford, GL16 8AJ
8am-6pm.

GL17

Drybrook Ducklings 01594 541 221
Old School House, Drybrook Road, Drybrook, GL17
2-5yrs. 9-11.30am. Termtime.

Longhope Playgroup 07949 289 366
Latchen Room, Latchen, Longhope, GL17 0QE
2-5yrs. 9.15am-12.15pm. Termtime.

Mitcheldean Early Learners 01594 543 231
Community Centre, The Playing Fields, Townsend,
Mitcheldean, GL17 0BA
2.9-5yrs. 9.30am-12pm. Termtime.

Pippins Creative Childcare Centre 01452 831 104
Squirrel Lodge, School Lane, Longhope, GL17 0LJ
2-5yrs. 9am-3.30pm. Termtime.

Pips Nursery 01594 860 344
Lydbrook, Gloucester, GL17 9PX
3-5yrs. 9am-2.55pm. Termtime.

Ruardean Under Fives 01594 541 267
Ruardean Memorial Hall, Ruardean, GL17
Mother and Toddler Group 0-5yrs. 10am-12.30pm. Mon-Thurs.

Sunbeams Day nursery 01594 541 054
Hawkers Hill, Mitcheldean, GL17 0BS
5mths-8yrs. 7.30am-5.30pm. 50wks.

Woodside Squirrels 01594 542 287
Ruardean Woodside, Ruardean, GL17 9XP
2.9-5yrs. 9.15-11.45am and 12.30-3pm. Termtime. 3 days.

GL18

Ann Cam Pre-School Nursery 07905 726 756
Ann Cam School, Bayfield Gardens, Dymock, GL18
3-5yrs. 9.05-11.45am. Termtime.

Happy Days Nursery 01531 822 242
11 Glebe Close, Newent, GL18 1BQ
3mths-10yrs. 7.45am-6pm. 50wks.

Little Pickles Playgroup 01531 828 076
Early Years Centre, Bradfords Lane, Newent, GL18
2-5yrs. 9-11.30am and 12.30-3pm. Termtime.

Newent Opportunity Group 01531 822 745
Bradfords Lane, Newent, GL18 1QT
0-5yrs. 9.15-11.45am and 12.30-3pm. Termtime.

GL19

Apperley & Deerhurst Nurser 07931 447 596
Apperley, GL19 4DW
2-5yrs. 9.15-11.45am. 1 day a week.

Countryside Day Nursery 01452 840 026
Barn Lane, Corse, GL19 3RH
1-11yrs. 8am-5.45pm. 50wks.

Huntley Playgroup 01452 830 510
Ross Road, Huntley, GL19 3EX
9.15am-12pm. Termtime.

Huntley Playgroup 01452 831 285
Village Hall, North Road, Huntley, Gloucester, GL19
2.9-5yrs. 9.30am-12pm. Termtime.

Orchard Nursery School 01452 790 121
Orchard Rise, Tibberton, Gloucester, GL19 3AQ
2.9-5yrs. 9.05am-12pm. 3 mornings.

Pauntley Playgroup
Village Hall, Brand Green, Redmarley, GL19 3JD
2-4yrs. 9.15am-12pm. Termtime. 3 mornings.

Redmarley Playgroup
Village Hall, Redmarley, Gloucester, GL19 3NQ
2.9-5yrs. 10am-12.30pm. Termtime.

Tibberton & Taynton Under 5s 01452 790 469
Orchard Rise, Tibberton, Gloucester, GL19 3AQ
2-5yrs. 9.15am-12pm. Termtime.

GL20

Alderton Playgroup 01242 620 386
Village Hall, Dibden Lane, Alderton, GL20 8NT
2-5yrs. 9.30am-12pm. Termtime.

Ashchurch Village Playgroup 01684 273 820
St. Nicholas Church Hall, Ashchurch Road,
Ashchurch, Tewkesbury, GL20 8LH
2-5yrs. 9-11.30am. Termtime.

Little Foxes Playgroup 07950 752 417
Wheatpieces Community Centre, Columbine Road,
Walton Cardiff, GL20 7SP
2-5yrs. 9.15-11.45am and 12.15-2.45pm. Termtime.

Mitton Manor Playgroup 07799 757 345
Carrant Road, Twekesbury, Gloucester, GL20 8AR
2.9-5yrs. 9-11.30am and 12.30-3pm. Termtime.

My Day Nursery 01684 276 279
7 Ashchurch Road, Tewkesbury, GL20 8DS
12wks-8yrs. 8am-6pm. 50wks.

Newtown Playgroup 07790 798 242
Brensham Road, Tewkesbury, GL20 8EW
2-5yrs. 8.50-11.20am and 12.45-2.45pm. Termtime.

Northway Pre-School Playgroup 01684 273 750
Playgroup Building, Northway Infant School,
Virginia Road, Tewkesbury, GL20 8PT
2-5yrs. 9am-12pm and 1-3pm.

112 education (Gloucestershire postcodes)   S = SCHOOL

Priors Park Playgroup   07773 017 755
St.John's Ambulance HQ, Links Road, Tewkesbury
2½-5yrs. 9.30am-12pm. Termtime. 3 days.

Queen Margaret EYC   01684 292 198
York Road, Tewkesbury, GL20 5HU
2-5yrs. 9-11.30am and 12.30-3pm. Termtime.

Rainbow Corner Playgroup   01684 296 779
18 Hardwicke Bank Road, Northway, Tewkesbury
3-4yrs. 9.15am-12pm and 1-3.45pm. Termtime.

Skallywags Day Nursery   01684 294 244
1 Conigree Lane, Abbots Road, Tewkesbury, GL20
3mths-8yrs. 8am-5.45pm. 50wks.

Tewkesbury Early Years Centre   01684 294 174
Chance Street, Tewkesbury, GL20 5RQ
0-4yrs. 9.15am-3.15pm. Termtime.

S The Abbey School   01684 294 460
Church Street, Tewkesbury, GL20 5PD
2½-13yrs. 9am-3.30pm. 34wks.

Tredington Playgroup   07730 889 231
Tewkesbury, GL20 7BU
2.9-5yrs. 9-11.30am. Termtime. 3 days.

Twyning Playgroup   01684 292 816
Village Hall, Fleet Lane, Twyning, GL20 6DG
9.30am-12pm.

GL50

Bright Eyes Day Nursery   01242 702 772
Knapp Villa, 6 Knapp Road, Cheltenham, GL50
0-5yrs. 8am-6pm.

Brightlands Day Nursery   01242 230 938
107 St. Georges Road, Cheltenham, GL50 3ED
8am-6pm. 50wks.

Christ Church Pre-School   01242 578 163
Church Hall, Malvern Road, Cheltenham, GL50
2-5yrs. 9-11.45am. Termtime.

Churchill Gardens Playgroup   01242 774 861
Nieghbourhood Resource Centre, 340 High Street, Cheltenham, GL50 3JF
2-5yrs. 9.30am-12pm. Termtime.

Dunalley Ducklings Nursery   01242 512 391
West Drive, Cheltenham, GL50 4LB
9.15-11.45am and 12.45-3.15pm. Termtime.

Hickory Dickory Day Nursery   01242 574 362
19 Cambray Place, Cheltenham, GL50 1JS
0-5yrs. 8.15am-5.45pm.

Primary Colours Day Nursery   01242 250 550
57 Montpellier Terrace, Cheltenham, GL50 1UX
3mths-4yrs. 8.30am-5.30pm. 50wks.

St Gregory's Child Care Trust   01242 515 387
Knapp Road, Cheltenham, GL50 3QH
2.9-5yrs. 9.15am-12pm. 36wks.

St Phillip's & St James Playgroup   01242 250 212
60 Painswick Road, Cheltenham, GL50 2ER
2-5yrs. 9-11.45am. Termtime.

Tree Tops Cheltenham   01242 241 349
1 Queens Road, Cheltenham, GL50 2LR
0-5yrs. 8am-6pm. 50wks.

University of Gloucestershire   01242 578 813
Pre-School Centre
53 Christchurch Road, Cheltenham, GL50 2PR
8am-6pm. 50wks.

GL51

S Dean Close Prep School   01242 512 217
Lansdown Road, Cheltenham, GL51 6QS
2-18yrs.

Early Birds Day Nursery   01242 693 200
156 Arle Road, Cheltenham, GL51 8LH
6.50am-6pm.51wks.

Elfin Nursery Pre-School group   07711 578 619
Cold Pool Lane, Up Hatherley, Cheltenham, GL51
2-5yrs. 9.15-11.45am and 12.45-2.45pm. Termtime.

Foxcubs Day Nursery   01452 857 449
Chapel House, Old Reddings Road, The Reddings, Cheltenham, GL51 6SA
0-5yrs. 8am-6pm.

Gardners Lane Early Years Centre   01242 252 185
Gardners Lane, Cheltenham, GL51 9JW
2.9-5yrs. Termtime.

Gloscat Day Nursery   01242 532 016
Cheltenham Campus, Princess Elizabeth Way, Cheltenham, GL51 7SJ
0-8yrs. 8am-6pm.

Gloucester Road Playgroup   01242 512 792
Gloucester Road, Cheltenham, GL51 8PB
9.15-11.45am and 12.30-3pm.

Little Smarties   01242 577 581
Two Cedars, Fairmount Road, Cheltenham, GL51
0-5yrs. 8am-6pm. 50wks.

Mary Godwin Under Fives   01242 263 746
The Pavilion, Wymans Lane, Swindon Village, Cheltenham, GL51 9QF
9.15-11.45am. Termtime.

Meadows Day Nursery   01242 862 040
Windrush, Little Shurdington, Shurdington, Cheltenham, GL51 4TX
0-5yrs. 8am-6pm. 50wks.

s = SCHOOL   **(Gloucestshire postcodes) education**

Playhouse Day Nursery   01242 253 212
287 Hatherley Road, Up Hatherley, Cheltenham
0-5yrs. 8am-6pm. 50wks.

Ron Smith Pavilion Under Fives   01242 224 407
Springbank Way, Springbank, Cheltenham, GL51
2-5yrs. 9.30am-12pm and 12.30-3pm.

Rowanfield Nursery   01242 515 334
Alstone Lane, Cheltenham, GL51 8HY
3-5yrs. 8.55-11.25am and 12.25-2.55pm. Termtime.

Shurdington Playgroup   07860 370 355
Bishop Road, Shurdington, Cheltenham, GL51 4TB
2-5yrs. 9.30am-12pm. Termtime. 3 days.

Sir Charles Playgroup   07765 410 835
Shelley Road, Cheltenham, GL51 7DP
2-5yrs. 9-11.30am. Termtime.

St Barnabas Church Playgroup   01242 222 219
Orchard Way, Cheltenham, GL51 7JY
2-5yrs. 9-11.30am and 1-3.30pm. Termtime.

St Christopher's Playgroup   07808 835 681
St. Christopher's Church Hall, Lincoln Avenue,
Warden Hill, Cheltenham, GL51 5DD
9-11.45am and 12.55-3.10pm.

St Mark's & Hesters Way   01242 690 025
Playgroup
Community Centre, Brooklyn Road, Cheltenham
21/2-5yrs. 9.30am-12pm. Termtime.

St Mark's Playgroup   01242 580 022
Church Road, St.Marks, Cheltenham, GL51 7AL
2-5yrs. 9.30am-12pm. Termtime. 4days.

St Silas Playgroup   01242 525 454
Hester's Way Road, Cheltenham, GL51 0SE
2.9-5yrs. Termtime.

Swindon Village Early Years   01242 692 760
Church Road, Swindon Village, Cheltenham, GL51
2.9-5yrs. 3 mornings. Termtime.

The Reddings Playgroup   01452 857 607
The Reddings & District Association Centre, North
Road West, The Reddings, Cheltenham, GL51 6RF
2.9-5yrs. 9.30am-12pm. Termtime.

Winton House Private Day Nursery 01242 511 417
11 Warden Hill Road, Cheltenham, GL51 3AU
1-5yrs. 8am-5.30pm. 50wks.

Young Explorers Day Nursery   01242 705 645
5 Arle Avenue, Cheltenham, GL51 8JP
0-5yrs. 8am-5.45pm. 50wks.

GL52

Abbotts Day Nursery   01242 515 702
49 All Saints Road, Cheltenham, GL52 2HF
0-8yrs. 8am-5.30pm. 49wks.

All Saints Playgroup   07801 889 541
John Wood Room, All Saints Church, All Saints
Road, GL52 2EY
2-5yrs. 9.15-11.45am and 1-3.30pm. Termtime.

Battledown Kids Club   01242 525 472
Harp Hill, Charlton Kings, Cheltenham, GL52 6PZ
2-5yrs. 10am-3pm.

Battledown Lodge Day Nursery   01242 525 374
77 Hales Road, Cheltenham, GL52 6SR
0-6yrs. 8am-5.45pm. 50wks.

Bushbabies Day Nursery   01242 578 908
213 Prestbury Road, Cheltenham, GL52 3ES
8am-12.45pm and 1-5.45pm. 50wks.

Butterflies Day Nursery   01242 679 664
Lacon House, Millham Road, Bishops Cleeve, GL52
8.15am-5.45pm. 51wks.

Circus Day Nursery   01242 253 222
Haddo, Pittville Circus Road, Cheltenham, GL52
0-8yrs. 8am-6pm.

Elmtree Playgroup   01684 294 490
The Youth & Community Centre, Church Road,
Bishops Cleeve, Cheltenham, GL52 8LR
2-5yrs. 9.15-11.45am and 12.15-2.45pm. Termtime.

Garden House Nursery School   01386 881 886
Gotherington Rex Rhodes Building, Gotherington,
Nr. Cheltenham, GL52 9ET
3-5yrs. 9am-3pm. Termtime.

Garden House Nursery School   07754 949 509
Village Hall, Gotherington, Cheltenham, GL52 9ET
2-3yrs. 9.15am-12.15pm. Termtime.

Glenfall Pre-School   01242 234 055
Glenfall Way, Charlton Kings, Cheltenham, GL52
2.9-5yrs. 9am-12.30pm. Termtime.

Holy Apostles Playgroup   01242 526 858
Battledown Approach, Cheltenham, GL52 6QZ
2.9-5yrs. 8.50am-12pm and 12.30-3pm. Termtime.

Kiddiewinks Day Nursery Limited   01242 672 215
42 Evesham Road, Bishops Cleeve, Cheltenham
8am-6pm. 50wks.

Little Treasures   01242 573 712
19 Lynworth Exchange, Mendip Road, Cheltenham
18mths-4yrs. 9am-3.30pm. 50wks.

Lynworth Kindergarten   01242 244 462
Cotswold Road, Cheltenham, GL52 5HD
2.9-5yrs. 8.45-11.30am and 1.30-3pm. Termtime.

Prestbury Pavilion Playgroup   07765 436 730
New Barn Close, Prestbury, Cheltenham, GL52 3LP
2-5yrs. 9.15am-12pm. Termtime.

education (Gloucestershire postcodes)

S = SCHOOL

Kingfishers offers a homely caring environment during the foundation years at school.
Freshly cooked food
Acres of grounds for play
French & music within core curriculum
Ballet and After School Care

Cheltenham College Junior School
Kingfishers Girls & Boys (3-7)
Contact us on:
01242 522697
ccjs@cheltcoll.gloucs.sch.uk
www.cheltcoll.gloucs.sch.uk

Prestbury Playmates Pre-School
St. Mary's Church Hall, Bouncers Lane, Prestbury, Cheltenham, GL52 5JF
9am-2.45pm. Termtime.

S St Edward's Junior School   **01242 538 910**
252 London Road, Charlton Kings, Cheltenham, GL52
2½-5yrs. 9.15-11.45am. Termtime.

Tythe Barn Playgroup   **01242 672 732**
Tithe Barn, Cheltenham Road, Bishops Cleeve, Cheltenham, GL52 8LU
2-5yrs. 9.15-11.45am and 12.15-2.45pm. Termtime.

Whaddon Early Years Centre   **01242 513 010**
Clyde Crescent, Cheltenham, GL52 5QH
0-4yrs. 9am-3pm. Termtime.

Woodmancote Pre-School   **01242 675 855**
Village Hall, Bushcombe Close, Woodmancote
3-4yrs. 9.30am-12pm and 12.30-3pm. Termtime.

GL53

S Cheltenham College Junior School   **01242 522 697**
Thirlestaine Road, Cheltenham, GL53 7AB
3-7yrs. 9am-3.30pm.Termtime. 2 Sessions in pre-school 20 per class

Angel Day Nursery   **01242 574 093**
16 Keynsham Road, Cheltenham, GL53 7PX
5mths-5yrs. 8am-5.30pm. 51wks.

Charton Kings Kindergarten   **01242 814 483**
Lyefield Road East, Charlton Kings, Cheltenham,
3-5yrs.

Falcon Day Nursery   **01242 576 170**
Rosewood, Salterley Grange, Leckhampton Hill, Cheltenham, GL53 9QW
0-5yrs. 8am-5.45pm. Termtime.

Leckhampton Road Playgroup   **07879 201 439**
207 Leckhampton Road, Leckhampton, Cheltenham, GL53 0BX
2-5yrs. 9.15am-12pm. Termtime.

Little Apples, Delancey Hospital   **08484 222 260**
Charlton Lane, Cheltenham, GL53 9DU
7am-6pm. 52wks.

Naunton Park Pre-School Playgroup   **01242 573 491**
Naunton Lane, Leckhampton, Cheltenham, GL53
2-5yrs. 9am-12pm and 1-3.30pm. Termtime.

Nursery Rhymes   **01242 260 550**
Peace Croft, Kidnappers Lane, Cheltenham, GL53

The Nursery School, Charlton Kings   **01242 521 944**
Church Street, Charlton Kings, Cheltenham, GL53 8AP
2-5yrs. 8.45am-3pm.

S The Richard Pate School   **01242 522 086**
Southern Road, Leckhampton, Cheltenham, GL53 9RP
9am-3.30pm. 36wks.

Westfield Day Nursery   **01242 245 307**
121 Leckhampton Road, Cheltenham, GL53 0DQ
0-5yrs. 8.30am-5.30pm. 51wks.

Barn Day Nursery & Nursery School   **07986 094 464**
1 Willow Court, Bourton Industrial Park, Bourton-on-the-Water, Cheltenham, GL54 2HQ
0-8yrs. 7.45am-6pm. 50wks.

GL54

Bourton Playgroup & Toddlers   **07950 048 066**
Bourton Primary School Grounds, Bourton-on-Water, GL54 2AU
2-5yrs. 9.15-11.45am and 12.30-3pm. Termtime.

Chedworth Playgroup   **01285 720 689**
The Village Hall, Chedworth, Cheltenham, GL54
2-5yrs. 9am-12pm Termtime.

Condicote Playgroup   **07796 987 173**
Condicote Village Hall, Condicote, Cheltenham, GL54 1EY
2.9-5yrs.

Gretton Nursery Playgroup   **07765 040 654**
The Village Hall, Gretton, GL54 5EY
2-5yrs. 9am-12pm. Termtime.

Guiting Manor Nursery School   **01451 850 907**
Church Lane, Guiting Power, Cheltenham, GL54 5TY
2-8yrs. 9am-4pm. Termtime.

Guiting Power Playgroup   **01451 850 399**
The Village Hall, GL54 5TY
9.30am-12pm.

Please say you saw the listings in the
South West Baby Directory

S = SCHOOL (Gloucestershire Somerset, Bath & Bristol postcodes) **education**

Jack & Jill Paygroup   07771 898 608
Cowl Lane, Winchcombe, Cheltenham, GL54 5RA
2-5yrs. 9am-3.45pm. Termtime.

Northleach Playgroup   01451 860 019
School House, Mill End, Northleach, Cheltenham, GL54 3HJ
2.9-5yrs. 9am-12pm.

Sherborne Playgroup   01451 844 833
The Old Telephone Exchange, Sherborne, Nr Cheltenham, GL54 3DH
2-5yrs. 9am-12pm and 12.30-3pm. Termtime.

Stepping Stones Day Nursery   01451 820 345
Manor Farm, Upper Slaughter, Cheltenham, GL54 2JJ
8am-6pm. 50wks.

Sunny Playschool   07950 594 380
Village Hall, Hawker Square, Cheltenham, GL54 2NT
2.9-5yrs. 9.30am-12pm. Termtime.

Winchcombe Playgroup   01242 603 631
Back Lane, Winchcombe, Gloucester, GL54 5QJ
2.9-5yrs. 9-11.45am and 1.45-3.15pm. Termtime.

Withington Playgroup   01242 890 505
Withington Primary School, Withington, Cheltenham, GL54 4BQ
2-5yrs. 9.45am-12.15pm. Termtime.

Chipping Campden Playgroup   01386 841 699
Old Telephone Exchange, Littleworth, Chipping Campden, GL55 6BD
2-5yrs. 9am-1pm and 1.30-3pm. Termtime.

Kiddywinks Pre-School   07989 037 679
The Old Police Station, High Street, Chipping Campden, GL55 6HB
2-5yrs. 9am-3.30pm. Termtime.

Mickleton Playgroup   01386 438 844
King George's Hall, Chapel Lane, Mickleton
9am-12pm. Termtime.

Rompers Day Nursery   01386 842 000
Station Road, Chipping Campden, GL55 6LD
3mths-5yrs. 8.30am-5.30pm.

Blockley Nursery School   01386 701 104
The Old Coach House, Bell Lane, Blockley, Moreton-in-Marsh, GL56 9BB
18mths-4yrs. 9am-4pm.

Blockley Playgroup   01386 701 358
The Jubilee Centre, Park Road, Blockley, Moreton-on-Marsh, GL56 9BY
2-4yrs. 9am-12.45pm. Termtime.

Moreton-in-Marsh Playgroup   01608 651 948
St. David's Centre, Church Street, Moreton-on-Marsh, GL56 0LT
9-11.45am. Termtime.

Walkers Private Day Nursery   01608 651 334
St. David's Walk, Church Street, Moreton-in-Marsh, GL56 0LT

Woodlands Nursery   01453 873 004
Fire Service College, Moreton-in-Marsh, GL56 0RH
3-4yrs. 8.15am-5.45pm. 51wks.

Beachley Barracks (Little Scamps) 01291 645 381
Families Office, Beachley, Chepstow, NP16 7YG
9.15am-12.15pm. Termtime.

Penguins Pre-School Centre   01291 624 356
King Alfreds Road, Sedbury, Chepstow, NP16 7AG
23/4-5yrs. 9.30am-12pm. Termtime.

Riverside Nursery   01291 625 783
Powder House Farm, Tutshill, Chepstow, NP16 7PT
0-5yrs. 8am-6pm. 51wks.

St John's on the Hill Day Nursery
Tutshill, Chepstow, NP16 7LE
2-13yrs. 8.30am-6.30pm. 34wks.

Tutshill Playgroup   01291 629 134
War Memorial Hall, Coleford Road, Tutshill, Chepstow, NP16 7BN
9.15am-12.10pm.

Brockweir Playgroup   01291 689 799
Mackenzie Hall, Brockweir, NP25 4LZ
9.30am-12pm. Termtime. 3 mornings.

Marshfield Pre-School   01225 891 900
The Community Centre, Hayfield, Marshfield, Chippenham, SN14 8RA
2-8yrs. 8am-6pm. 50wks.

Manor Kindergarten and Nursery   01386 852 866
Dumbleton Village Hall, Dairy Lane, Dumbleton, WR11 7TS
1-8yrs. 8.30am-5.30pm. Termtime.

SOMERSET, BATH & BRISTOL
BA1
Apple Tree Day Nursery   01225 318 744
Spring Lane, Bath, BA1 6NY
0-5yrs. 8am-6pm. 50wks.

Busy Bees Pre-School   01225 317 786
Room 14, St. Mark's School, Baytree Road, Fairfield Park, Bath, BA1 6ND
2½-5yrs. 9am-12pm. Termtime

Caterpillars Day Nursery   01225 824 462
Royal United Hospital, Combe Park, Bath, BA1 3NG
0-5yrs. 715am-6pm. 50wks.

Combe Park Pre-School   01225 332 088
16 Combe Park, Bath, BA1 3NP
3-4yrs. 9.15am-12pm and 12.3-3pm. Termtime.

education (Somerset, Bath & Bristol postcodes)   S = SCHOOL

Jabberwocky Montessori 01225 330 070
7 Lansdown Crescent, Bath, BA1 5AX

S King Edward's Preparatory School 01225 421 681
Weston Lane, Bath, BA1 4AQ
3-7yrs.

S Kingswood Prep School 01225 310 468
College Road, Lansdown, Bath, BA1 5SD
2½-11yrs.

Noah's Ark Weston 07941 611 417
All Saints Centre, High Street, Weston, Bath, BA1 4BX
3-5yrs. 9.30am-12pm and 12.30-3pm. Termtime.

Pepper Pot Pre-School 01225 852 555
Dovers Park, Bathford, Bathford, BA1 7UB
2-5yrs. 9.15-11.45am. Termtime.

Pinocchio Day Nursery 01225 336710
The Scout Hall, High Street, Weston, BA1 7BJ
18mths-5yrs 7.30am-5.30pm

Playbox Day Nursery 01225 332579
20 Gloucester Road, Bath, BA1 7BJ
16mths-5yrs 8am-6pm

S Royal High School 01225 313 877
Lansdown Road, Bath, BA1 5SZ
Girls. 3-18yrs.

Snapdragons Nursery 01225 426 255
Henley Lodge, Weston Road, Bath, BA1 2XT
7.30am-6.30pm. 50wks.

Snapdragon's Nursery 01225 483660
4 Grosvenor Place, Bath, BA1 6AX
0-5yrs 8am-6pm

The Kinder Garden 01225 426 857
12 Catherine Place, Bath, BA1 2PR
2-5yrs. 8.30am-6.15pm. 46wks.

The Royal High Junior School 01225 422 931
Hope House, Lansdown Road, Bath, BA1 5ES
3-11yrs. 8.15am-3.15pm. 308days.

Weston Park Nursery School 01225 492439
Weston Park House, Bath, BA1 4AL
2½-5yrs 9am-4pm

YMCA Day Nursery 01225 325 911
International House, Broad Street Place, Bath, BA1
1 1/2 - 5yrs. 8.30am-5.30pm. 51wks.

Zebedees Day Nursery 01225 316 639
Avon Street, Bath, BA1 1UP
1-5yrs. 8am-6pm. 50wks.

BA2

Barnaby Pre-School 07980 486 977
St Barnabus Church Hall, Mount View, Southdown, Bath, BA2 1JX
0-5yrs. 9.30am-12pm. Termtime.

Bathampton Playgroup 01225 463 060
Village Hall, Holcombe Lane, Bathampton, BA2 4ET
9.15am-12pm. 4 mornings.

Bear Flat Pre-School 01225 445 694
Beechen Cliff Methodist Church Hall, Bruton Avenue, Bath, BA2 4ET
2-5yrs. 9.30am-12pm. Termtime.

Foxtots Nursery 01225 884 648
Bradford Park, Fox Hill, Bath, BA2 5PS
3-5yrs. 8am-6pm. 50wks.

Hopscotch Nursery School 01225 448 191
98 Wellsway, Bath, BA2 4SD
2-5yrs. 8.30am-5.45pm

Magic Box Pre-School 01373 472 877
Wellow Village Hall, Wellow, Bath, BA2 4ET
2 1/2 -4yrs. 9.15am-2.45pm. Termtime. Mon/Wed/Fri.

Mews Day Nursery 01225 332593
Carfax Garden, Henrietta Mews, Bath, BA2 6LR
18mths-5yrs 8.30am-5.30pm

Mogghill Annex Pre-School 01761 232 176
St. Johns Church Hall, Peasedown St. John, Bath
2-5yrs. 9.30am-12.30pm. Termtime.

S Monkton Combe School 01225 833158
159 Church Road, Combe Down, Monkton Combe, Bath, BA2 7ET
co-ed 3-13yrs

Mulberry House 01225 339843
High Street, Bathampton, BA2 6SY
3mths-5yrs. 8.15am-6pm

Nursery Times 01761 472266
The Drumway, Markbury, Bath, BA2 9HS
2-5yrs 8am-6pm

Oak Tree Day Nursery 01225 875 590
Newton Park, Newton, St. Loe, Bath, BA2 9BN
0-5yrs. 8am-6pm. 50wks.

Oldfield Park Baptist Pre-School 07799 271 853
Triangle, Bath, BA2 3JD
2-5yrs. 9.30am-12pm. Termtime.

Paragon School 01225 310 837
Lyncombe House, Lyncombe Vale, BA2 4LT
3-11yrs. 8.45am-3pm.

S = SCHOOL   (Somerset, Bath & Bristol postcodes) education

Rainbow Pre-School Playgroup   01761 434 898
The Methodist Church Hall, Bath Road, Peasedown
St. John, Bath, BA2 4ET
2-5yrs. 9.15-11.45am. Termtime.

Single Hill Nursery   01761 431073
Ashgrove Baptist Chapel, Eckweek Road,
Peasedown St John, Bath, BA2 8EQ

Stepping Stones Pre-School   07811 973 568
Ascension Church Hall, Claude Avenue, Oldfield
Park, Bath, BA2 1AG
9.30am-12pm.

Sunflower Pre-School   01761 471 987
Camerton Recreation Centre, Camerton, Bath, BA2
2-5yrs. 9.30am-12pm. Termtime.

Sunshine Pre-School   01225 837 202
United Reform Church, Frome Road, Bath, BA2
2-4yrs. 9.15am-1.15pm. Termtime.

Tadpoles Nursery   01225 837717
The Avenue, Combe Down, Bath, BA2 5EQ
2½-5yrs 8.30am-5.30pm

The Mews Nursery   01225 332 593
Carfax Gardens, Henrietta Mews, Bath, BA2 6LR
2-5yrs. 8am-6pm.

S The Paragon School   01225 310 837
Lyncombe House, Lyncombe Vale, Bath, BA2 4LT
3-11yrs.

Widcombe Acorns Pre-School   01225 445 446
St. Marks Community Centre, St. Marks Road,
Witcombe, Bath, BA2 4ET
0-5yrs. 9.30am-12pm and 1-3.30pm. Termtime.

Writhlington Playgroup   01761 437 694
Village Hall, Writhlington, Radstock, BA2 4ET
2-5yrs. 9-11.30am. Termtime.

BA3
Chatterbox Day Nursery   01761 411 595
The Annexe, Grove Bungalow, Welton Grove,
Midsomer Norton, Bath, BA3 2TS
50wks.

Little Learners   01761 438 509
Norton Radstock College, South Hill Park, Wells
Road, Radstock, BA3 3RW
0-8yrs. 8.45am-5.15pm. 50wks.

Longvernal Nursery School   01761 418 226
Clapton Road, Midsomer Norton, Radstock, BA3
3-5yrs. 9am-12pm and 3-6pm. Termtime.

Mogghill House Nursery   01761 232 176
Mogg Hill House, Abbey Road, Stratton-on-the-
Fosse, Radstock, BA3 4QW
2-5yrs. 9.30am-12.30pm. Termtime.

Moorewood Nursery   01761 232 774
9 Stockhill Road, Chilcompton, Radstock, BA3 4JL
2-5yrs. 9am-12pm. Termtime.

Noah's Ark Nursery School   01761 416 157
71 North Road, Midsomer Norton, Radstock, BA3
8.45am-2.45pm. Termtime.

Red Room Pre-School   07969 957 671
Green Street, ston Easton, Radstock, BA3 4BZ
2-5yrs. 9.15am-12pm. Termtime.

St Peter's Church Playgroup   07759 859 025
St. Peter's Church Hall, Long Fellow Road,
Radstock, Bath, BA3 3YZ
2-5yrs. 9-11.45am. Termtime.

Sunflowers Day Nursery   01761 419997
St Peters Park, Wells Road, Radstock, BA3 3XU
2-5yrs 8.30am-5.30pm

BA4
Acorns Pre-School   01749 831 338
Paradise Crescent, Evercreech, BA4 6EH
2½-5yrs. 39wks.

S All Hallows School   01749 880 227
Cranmore Hall, Shepton Mallet, Somerset, BA4 4SF
4-13yrs.

First Steps Day Nursery   01749 346 733
44 Compton Road, Shepton Mallet, BA4 5QT
0-8yrs. 8am-6pm. 50wks.

Next Steps Nursery   01749 346 808
The Bath and West Showground, Shepton Mallet
7.30am-6.30pm.

Puddleducks Pre-School   01373 836 881
Upton Noble Village Hall, Church Street, Upton
Noble, BA4 6AS
2½-5yrs. 9.15am-12.15pm. 38wks.

Southill Nursery   01749 880640
Southill House, West Cranmore, Shepton Mallet
1-5yrs 8.30am-5.30pm

The Bush Nursery   01749 899 010
Pilton, Shepton Mallet, BA4 4HP
1-5yrs. 8.30am-5.30pm. 50wks.

BA5
Horrington House Pre-School   01749 673 516
Bath Road, West Horrington, Wells, BA5 3EB
2-5yrs. 9-11.30am. Termtime.

Tree House Day Nursery   01749 679637
School Lane, South Horrington, Wells, BA5 3DL
1-5yrs

S Wells Cathedral Junior Sch   01749 834 400
8 New Streets, Wells, BA5 2LQ
3-10yrs.

education (Somerset, Bath & Bristol postcodes) S = SCHOOL

BA6

Baltonsborough Pre-School 01458 851 218
Ham Street, Baltonsborough, Glastonbury,
BA6 8PX
2-5yrs. 9am-12pm. Termtime

Bouncing Bens Pre-School 07813 517 929
Benedict Street, Glastonbury, BA6 9EX
3yrs. 8am-3.30pm. Termitme.

Butleigh Nursery School 07974 675 310
Butleigh Youth Club, Backtown, Butleigh, BA6 9PB
2-4yrs. 9am-3.30pm. Termtime. 3 days.

Fairfield Montessori 01458 834 294
76 Benedict Street, Glastonbury, BA6 9DN
3mths-5yrs. 8am-6pm. 50wks.

S Millfield Preparatory School 01458 832 446
Edgarley Hall, Glastonbury, BA6 8LD
2-13yrs.

Playaways Nursery 01458 830 838
High Street, Glastonbury, BA6 9DZ
2-5yrs. 8am-6pm. 50wks.

St Dunstans Honeybees 07767 895 696
Wells Road, Glastonbury, BA6 9BY
2-5yrs. 9am-1.30pm.

BA7

Toybox Pre-School 01963 351 523
Ansford Park, Castle Cary, BA7 7JJ
2-5yrs. 9.30am-12pm. Termtime.

BA8

Explorers 07890 886 613
Ash Walk, Henstridge, BA8 0QD
2½-5yrs. 9am-12pm. Termtime.

Marsh Meadows Nursery School 01963 370 607
Feltham Farm, Horsington Marsh Horsington,
Templecombe, BA8 0EN
2-5yrs. 8am-5.30pm. Termtime.

Sunnyside Nursery School 01963 362 454
Whitechurch Lane, Henstridge, BA8 0PA
2-5yrs. 9am-4pm. Termtime.

BA9

Busy Kids Pre-School 01963 31842
Balsam Centre, Balsam Park, Wincanton, BA9 9HB
2-5yrs. 8.30am-3.30pm.

Little Ark Pre-School 0196 332 660
The Priory, Tout Hill, Wincanton, BA9 9DH
2-5yrs. 9am-12pm and 1-3pm.

Westhill Nursery 0196 333 246
Westhill, Wincanton, BA9 9BX
2-5yrs. 9.15-11.45am. Termtime.

BA10

S Bruton School for Girls 01749 814 400
Sunnyhill, Bruton, BA10 0NT
Girls and boys from 3yrs. Nursery open 8.15am-5.30pm.
Termtime. Also parent & toddler sessions.

S Meadow School 01749 813 176
18-20 High Street, Bruton, BA10 0AA
3-11yrs. 9am-1pm. Termtime.

BA11

ABC Nursery 01373 473 361
Christchurch Hall, Park Road, Frome, BA11 1EU
2-5yrs. 9.30am-12pm. Termtime.

Ark Nursery 01373 462 408
41 Lower Keyford, Frome, BA11 4AR
9.30am-12pm. Termtime.

Beckington Pre-School 01373 831 492
Baptist Church Hall, Beckington, Frome, BA11 6TD
2½-4½yrs. 9.30am-12.30pm. Termtime.

Busy Bees Nursery School 01373 451 619
Green Lane, Frome, BA11 4JW
3mths-5yrs. 8am-6pm. 52wks.

Butterfly Pre-School 01373 451 734
Manor Road, Marston Trading Estate, Frome, BA11
2-5yrs. 9.15-3.30pm. 46wks.

Garden Nursery Childcare Centre 01373 453 345
St. Mary, Innox Hill, Frome, BA11 2LN
2-5yrs. 9.15am-3.15pm. Termtime.

Littleoaks Day Nursery 01373 453 838
Frome Community College, Bath Road, Frome
2-5yrs. 8am-6pm. 50wks.

Mells Nursery 01373 812 380
School House, Mells Green, Mells, Frome, BA11
9.15am-12pm. Termtime.

Pyramid Children's Centre 01373 471 606
The Wesley Methodist Church, Wesley Slope, Butts
Hill, Frome, BA11 1HP
2½-5yrs.

Rainbow Nursery 01373 462553
44b Portway, Frome, BA11 1QR
8am-6pm

Springmead School 01373 831 555
Castle Corner, Beckington, Somerset, BA11 6TA
2-11yrs.8am-6pm. 50wks.

Sunflower Montessori 01373 453853
9 Palmer Street, Frome, BA11 1DS
2.75-5yrs

BA16

Jabberwocky Nursery 01458 446 999
Unit 2, 3 Tanyard, Leigh Road, Street, BA16 0HU
0-5yrs. 8am-6pm. 50wks.

S = SCHOOL (Somerset, Bath & Bristol postcodes) **education**

Kickers and Dribblers   01458 445 987
Tannery Ground, Middle Brooks, Street, BA16 0TA
3mths-5yrs. 8am-6pm. 50wks.

Overleigh Pre-School Group   01458 448 655
45 Overleigh, Street, BA16 0TR
2½-5yrs.

Rainbow Pre-School   07876 322 763
United Reformed Church, Orchard Road, Street
2-5yrs. 9.15-11.45am. Termtime.

Strode College Day Nursery   01458 844 412
Church Road, Street, BA16 0AB
2-5yrs. 8.45am-5pm. 36wks.

Appletree Nursery   01935 433301
51 The Park, Yeovil, BA20 1DF
3mths-5yrs 6.30am-7pm

BA20
First Steps Childrens Day Nursery   01935 474314
148 Hendford Hill, Yeovil, BA20 2RG
8am-5.45pm

New Life Pre-School   01935 433 146
The Gateway, Addlewell Lane, Yeovil, BA20 1QN
2-5yrs. 9.15am-12pm. Termtime. 3 days.

Parcroft Playgroup   07811 627 607
Summerleaze Park, Yeovil, BA20 2BR
2½-5yrs. 9am-12pm and 1-3.30pm.

Safe and Sound Day Nursery   01935 474 897
59 Preston Road, Yeovil, BA20 2BW
0-5yrs. 7.45am-6pm. 50wks.

S The Park School   01935 423 514
The Park, Yeovil, BA20 1DH
3-18yrs.

Toybox Nursery   01935 428 244
8 Linden Road, Yeovil, BA20 2BH
0-5yrs. 8am-6pm. 50wks.

BA21
Abbey Pre-School   07773 463 791
The Community Centre, The Forum, Yeovil, BA21
2-5yrs. 9.15am-12pm.

Buckler's Mead Pre-School   01935 424 454
1 St. Johns Road, Yeovil, BA21 4NH
6mths-5yrs. Mon-Wed 9am-4pm.Thur-Fri 9am-12pm. T/time.

Elim Church Day Nursery   01935 431 625
Elim Church Hall, Southville, Yeovil, BA21 4JA
3mths-8yrs. 8am-6pm. 50wks.

Elim Church Pre-School   01935 424 816
Larkhill Christian Centre, Larkhill Road, Yeovil
2-5yrs. 9am-3.30pm. Termtime.

Marsh Lane Day Nursery   01935 410 563
64 Marsh Lane, Yeovil, BA21 3BX
3mths-5yrs. 8am-6pm. 51wks.

Scalliwags Day Nursery   01935 384 503
Yeovil District Hospital, Higher Kingston, Yeovil
0-8yrs. 6.45am-6pm. 52wks (not bank holidays).

St Nicholas Nursery   07971 043 725
St. Michaels Road, Yeovil, BA21 5AG
3mths-5yrs. 8.30am-5.30pm. 50wks.

The Centre Pre-School   01935 472 439
64 Chelston Avenue, Yeovil, BA21 4PU
2-5yrs. 9.15am-12pm. Termtime.

The Honey Pot Nursery   01935 420 255
St. Michael's Avenue, Yeovil, BA21 4LW
0-5yrs. 8am-6pm. 50wks.

The Honeypot Pre-School   01935 427 643
32 Fairmead Road, Yeovil, BA21 5SE
2-5yrs. 9.15am-12pm. Termtime.

Westfield Pre-School Playgroup   07773 095 071
Stiby Road, Yeovil, BA21 3EP
2-5yrs. 9am-12pm and 12.40-3.10pm. Termtime.

Young Ones Childcare Centre   01935 433 365
Monks Dale, Yeovil, BA21 3JD
2½-8yrs. 9am-6pm. 50wks.

BA22
S Chilton Cantelo School   01935 850 555
Chilton Cantelo, Yeovil, BA22 8BG
7-18yrs.

East Chinnock Under Fives   07798 812 540
The Church Room, Weston St., East Chinnock,
Yeovil, BA22 9EL
2-5yrs. 9.15am-12pm and 1-3.30pm. Termtime.

S Hazelgrove   01963 440 314
King's Bruton Preparatory School, Hazelgrove
House, Yeovil, BA22 7JA
Co-ed 3-13yrs

Heron Pre-School   01935 840 562
Tall Trees Community Centre, Taranton Hill,
Illchester, BA22 8JP
2-5yrs. Mon - Fri 9-11.45am and 12.45-3.30pm. Termtime.
Lunch Club Mon - Thurs 11.45 - 12.45

St Mary's Pre-School   07813 474 953
Church Rooms, Church Street, Ilchester, Yeovil
2-5yrs. 9.15-11.45am and 12.45-3.45pm. Termtime.

Yeovilteenies Day Nursery   01935 453 731
RNAS Yeovilton, Ilchester, Yeovil, BA22 8HL
3mths-5yrs. 7.30am-5.30pm. 50wks.

BS1
Golden Valley House Day Nursery   01275 853 304
18 Oaksey Grove, Nailsea, BS48 2TP
2-5yrs 8am-6pm

120 education (Somerset, Bath & Bristol postcodes)   S = SCHOOL

Inwood Nursery   01934 876 674
Wrington Road, Congresbury, BS49 5AR
2-5yrs 8am-6pm

BS1
Buffer Bear Nursery   01179 079 935
British Empire and Commonwealth Museum, Clock Tower Yard, Temple Meads, Bristol, BS1 6QH
3mths-5yrs. 8am-6pm. 50wks.

BS2
Bristol University Nursery   01179 276 077
34 St Michaels Park, Kingsdown, BS2 8BW
3mths-5yrs

Jumoke Day Nursery   01179 447 514
20-22 Hepburn Road, Bristol, BS2 8UD
2-5yrs. 8.30am-5.30pm. 50wks.

St Paul's Day Nursery   01173 772 278
Little Bishop Street, St. Pauls, Bristol, BS2 9JF
2-6yrs. 9.30am-3pm. 51wks.

BS3
Teddies Nursery   **01179 531 246**
Clanage Road, Bower Ashton, BS3 2JX
www.teddiesnurseries.co.uk
3mths-5yrs. 8am-6pm. 51wks (see ad pg 142).

Ashton Vale Pre-School   07980 065 799
Ashton Vale Church, Risdale Road, Ashton Vale
termtime. Mornings.

First Steps Day Nursery   01179 533 043
Southville Centre, Bealey Road, Southville, Bristol, BS3 1QG
1-5yrs. 8am-5.30pm. 50wks.

Magic Roundabout Nursery   01179 639 800
141 Coronation Road, Southville, BS3 1RE
0-5yrs 7.30am-7.30pm

Windmill Hill City Farm Pre-School 01179 633 299
Philip Street, Bedminster, Bristol, BS3 4EA
3-5yrs. Termtime. 3 mornings.

BS4
Abacus Day Nursery   **01179 772 868**
6 Emery Road, Brislington, BS4 5PF
3mths-5yrs. 8am-6pm. 51wks plus a holiday club.

S Cleve House School   01179 777 218
254 Wells Road, Bristol, BS4 2PN
co-ed 3-11yrs

Court House Day Nursery   01179 772 210
270/272 Wells Road, Knowle, Bristol, BS4 2PU
6wks-5yrs 7.30am-6pm

Hamilton Pre-School   01179 144 471
Holymead Junior School Annexe, Wick Road, Brislington, Bristol, BS4 4HP
3-5yrs. 9-11.30am and 12.30-3pm. Termtime.

Knowle West Playcentre   01179 631 737
Filwood Broadway, Knowle, Bristol, BS4 1JL
2-5yrs. 9.30-11.30am. Termtime.

Village Pre-School   01179 715 222
St. Luke's Church Hall, Church Parade, Brislington, Bristol, BS4 5AZ
9.15-11.45am. Termtime.

BS5
Bristol Children's Playhouse   01179 510 037
Berkeley Green Road, Eastville, Bristol, BS5 6LU
9am-12.45pm. Termtime.

Busy Bee Day Nursery   01179 775 357
268 Wells Road, Knowle, Bristol, BS5 2PN
6mths-4yrs. 8am-5.30pm. 50wks.

Dhek Bhal   01173 772 080
All Hallows Road, Easton, BS5 0HR
10am-5pm.

Hillside Pre-School   01179 478 371
Hillside Road, Bristol, BS5 7PB
3-5yrs. 9.15-11.45am and 12.50-3.20pm. Termtime.

Little Haven Day Nursery   01179 414 484
261 Crews Hole Road, St George, Bristol, BS5 8BE
0-5yrs 8am-6pm

Redroofs Day Nursery   01179 492 600
227 Kingsway, St George, BS5 8NT
Birth-5yrs 8amam-5.00pm

Springwoods Nursery School   01179 030 269
Bannerman Road, Easton, BS5 0RR
6wks-5yrs. 8am-6pm. 48wks.

Tiny Happy People   01179 554 255
Easton Christian Family Centre, Beaufort Street, Easton, Bristol, BS5 0SQ
0-5yrs. 9.30am-12pm and 12.3-3pm. Termtime.

Whitehall Day Nursery   01179 030 496
81 Whitehall Road, Whitehall, Bristol, BS5 9BG
9.15am-2.45pm. 52wks.

BS6
Archfield House Nursery   01179 422 120
2 Archfield Road, Cotham, BS6 6BE
0-5yrs. 8am-6pm. 51wks.

Art Raft Piglets Nursery   01179 046 358
St. Saviours Hall, Woodfield Road, Redland, BS6 6PQ
1-4yrs. 8am-6pm. 50wks.

S Bristol Steiner Waldorf   0117 973 4399
School (The Rowan Tree)
12d Cotham Road, Cotham, Bristol, BS6 6DR
0-3yrs parent and toddler sessions. 3-4yrs playgroup and then 3^1/$_2$-6yrs kindergarten.

S = SCHOOL   (Somerset, Bath & Bristol postcodes) **education**

Candle Playgroup 01179 424 607
6 Ashley Road, Bristol, BS6 5NL
9.30am-12pm. Termtime.

Daisychain Nursery 01179 706 828
Vining Hall, Etloe Road, Westbury Park, Bristol, BS6
6wks-5yrs 7.30am

Downs Park Day Nursery 01179 628 526
46 Downs Park West, Westbury Park, Bristol, BS6
0-5yrs. 8am-6pm. 50wks.

Green Door Day Nursery 01179 853 267
35 Belvoir Road, St. Andrews, Bristol, BS6 5DQ
0-5yrs. 8am-5.45pm. 50wks.

Hampton Road Day Nursery 01179 467 054
118-120 Hampton Road, Redland, Bristol, BS6 6JD
0-5yrs 8am-6pm

Harcourt Pre-School 07887 771 912
St. Albans Church Hall, Bayswater Avenue,
Westbury Park, Bristol, BS6 7NS
2½-5yrs. 9am-12pm. Termtime.

Noah's Ark Pre-School 01179 446 229
Cairns Road Baptist Church, Cairns Road, Bristol
9.15-11.45am and 12.45-3.15pm. Termtime.

Pooh Corner Day Nursery 01179 466 178
46 Lower Redland Road, Redland, Bristol, BS6 6FT
3mths-5yrs

Redhouse Day Nursery School 01179 428 293
1 Cossins Road, Westbury Park, Bristol, BS6 7LY
2-5yrs 8am-5.30pm

S Redland High School for Girls 01179 244 404
1 Grove Park, Redland, Bristol, BS6 6PP
Girls 3-11yrs.

Redland Pre-School 01179 080 455
126 Hampton Road, Bristol, BS6 6JE
2-5yrs. 9.15am-1.15pm. Termtime.

Rocking Horse Day Nursery 01179 240 431
34 Northumberland Road, Bristol, BS6 7BD
8am-6pm. 52wks.

Rowan Tree Kindergarten 01179 734 399
12d Cotham Road, Cotham, BS6 6DR
3-7yrs. 8.30am-3.30pm. 35wks.

St Matthews Playgroup 01179 441 598
St. Matthews Church, Clare Road, Kingsdown, BS6
3-5yrs. 9.15-11.45am and 12.30-3pm. Termtime.

The Green Door Nursery 01179 853 267
35 Belvoir Road, St Andrews, Bristol, BS6 5DQ
Birth-5yrs 8am-6pm

The Rocking Horse Day Nursery 01179 240 431
34 Northumberland Road, Redland, Bristol, BS6
18mths-5yrs 8am-6pm

Tin Drum Nursery 01179 247 175
32 Redland Grove, Redland, Bristol, BS6 6PR
8am-6pm. 51wks.

S Torwood House School 01179 735 620
27-29 Durdham Park, Redland, Bristol, BS6 6XE
co-ed 0-7yrs

White Tree Pre-School 01179 731 562
4 North View, Westbury Park, Bristol, BS6 7QB
3-5yrs. 9.15am-12pm. Termtime

BS7

Ashgrove Park Day Nursery 01179 513 123
60 Ashgrove Road, Ashley Down, Bristol, BS7 9LQ
6wks-5yrs 8.15am-5.45pm 51wks.

Brunel Nursery 07977 926 346
City of Bristol College, Ashley Down Road, Bristol, BS7
2mths-5yrs 8am-6pm

Clyde House Day Nursery 01179 247 488
1 Nevil Road, Bishopston, BS7 9EG
6wks-5yrs 8.15am-5.45pm

Eden Grove Playgroup 07765 204 751
Eden Grove, Horfield, Bristol, BS7 0PQ
2½-5yrs. 9.30am-12pm. Termtime.

Honey Tree Day Nursery 01179 314 650
Filton Road, Horfield, Bristol, BS7 0XZ
6wks-5yrs. 8am-6pm. 52wks.

Horfield Playgroup 07977 348 850
Churchways Avenue, Horfield, Bristol, BS7 8SN
9.30am-12pm. Termtime. 4 days.

Horfield Welly Pre-School 07837 133 925
Wellington Hill, Bristol, BS7 8ST
9.30am-12pm. Termtime. 4days.

Magic Dragon Pre-School 07791 659 967
Church of Good Shepherd Hall, Bishop Road,
Bishopston, Bristol, BS7 8NA
2½-5yrs. 9.30-11.45am. Termtime. 4 days.

Peter Pan Nursery 01179 355 410
1 Churchways Crescent, Horfield, Bristol, BS7 8SW
6mths-5yrs 8am-6pm

Pied Piper Playgroup 01179 425 104
Bishopston Methodist Church, 245 Gloucester
Road, Bishopston, Bristol, BS7 8NY
3-5yrs. 9.15am-12pm. Termtime.

Rainbow Nursery 01179 243 000
26 Sommerville Road, Bristol, BS7 9AA
2-5yrs 8.15am-5.45pm

St Bonaventures Pre-School 07905 463 621
St. Bonaventures Church, Greyfriars Hall, Friary
Lane, Bishopston, Bristol, BS7 8HN
3-5yrs. 9-11.30am. Termtime.

education (Somerset, Bath & Bristol postcodes)   S = SCHOOL

The Honeytree Day Nursery 01179 314 650
Filton Road, Horfield, Bristol, BS7 0NX
3mths-5yrs 8am-6pm

BS8

Amberley Hall Nursery 01179 741 550
21 Richmond Dale, Clifton, Bristol, BS8 2UB
0-5yrs. 8am-6pm. 51wks.

S Bristol Grammar Lower School 01179 736 109
Elton Road, Bristol, BS8 1SR
7-11yrs.

Butcombe 01173 157 591
Clifton College Pre-Prep School, Guthrie Road,
Clifton, BS8 3EZ
3-8yrs 8am-6pm

Children's House 01179 096 761
Catholic Pre-School
Clifton Cathedral House, Clifton Park, Bristol, BS8
9.30am-12pm. Termtime.

Christchurch Clifton Pre-School 01179 733 750
Christchurch, Clifton Park, Bristol, BS8 3BN
3-5yrs. 9.15-11.45am. Termtime.

S Clifton College Preparatory 01173 157 502
School
The Avenue, Clifton, Bristol, BS8 3HE
3-13yrs.

S Clifton High Lower School 01179 738 096
College Road, Clifton, Bristol, BS8 3JD
3-11yrs.

Clifton Tots Day Nursery 01179 237 416
8 St.Paul's Road, Clifton, Bristol, BS8 1LT
6wks-5yrs. 8am-6pm. 50wks.

Mornington House Day Nursery 01179 733 414
Mornington Road, Clifton, BS8 2UU
0-5yrs 8am-6pm

Oakfield Road Day Nursery 01173 772 270
17 Oakfield Road, Clifton, Bristol, BS8 2AW
2-4yrs. 8.30am-4.30pm. 50wks.

Rocking Horse Day Nursery 01179 467 145
1 Woodland Road, Clifton, BS8 1AU
6wks-5yrs 7am-6pm

The Clifton Children's House 01179 237 578
2 York Gardens, Clifton, BS8 4LL
2½-4.5yrs, 9.15am-12.00, 1.00-3.15pm

BS9

S Badminton Junior School 01179 055 200
2 Hyde Park Avenue, North Petherton, Bridgwater
Girls 4-11yrs.

Busy Bees Pre-School Playgroup 07949 225 350
St. Peter's Hall, St.Peter's Church, The Drive,
Henleaze, Bristol, BS9 4LD
2½-5yrs. 9.15-11.45am. Termtime.

Jack & Jill Pre-School 01179 622 888
Northcote, Great Brockeridge, Westbury on Trym,
Bristol, BS9 3TY
9am-12pm and 12.45-2.45pm. Termtime.

Little Monsters Pre-School 01179 685 167
Sea Mills Boys & Girls Club, Bluebell Close, Off
Woodleaze, Bristol, BS9 2HX
2-5yrs. 9.30am-12pm. Termtime.

Once Upon a Time Day Nursery 01179 625 203
2-4 Downs Cote Drive, Westbury on Trym, Bristol
6wks-5yrs 8am-6pm

St Mary's Church Pre-School 01179 687 449
Church Rooms, Mariners Drive, Stoke Bishop, BS9
3-4yrs. Termtime.

S St Ursula's High School 01179 622 616
Brecon Road, Westbury-on-Trym, Bristol, BS9 4DT
3-16yrs.

Stoke Bishop Montessori 01179 686 960
70 Parrys Lane, Stoke Bishop, Bristol, BS9 1AQ
8am-6.15pm. 50wks.

Stoke Bishop Pre-School 07814 222 525
The Village Hall, 42 Stoke Hill, Stoke Bishop, BS9
9am-12.55pm. Termtime.

S The Red Maids' Junior School 01179 629 451
Grange Court Road, Westbury-on-Trym, Bristol
Girls. 7-11yrs.

The Toy Box Nursery 01179 623 010
11 The Drive, Henleaze, Bristol, BS9 4LD
3mths-5yrs 8am-6pm

Toybox Day Nursery 01179 623 010
11 The Drive, Henleaze, Bristol, BS9 4LD
3mths-7yrs. 8am-6pm. 51wks.

Westbury Baptist Pre-School 01179 629 990
Reedley Road, Westbury on Trym, Bristol, BS9 3TD
9am-12pm. Termtime.

BS10

Ecole Francaise De Bristol 01179 593 311
Henbury Village Hall, Church Lane, Henbury,
Bristol, BS10 7QG
2-5yrs. 8am-5.30pm. Termtime.

Lake House Nursery 01179 622 948
2 Lake Road, Bristol, BS10 5HG
2-5yrs. 8am-5.45pm. 50wks.

Please say you saw the listings in the South West Baby Directory

S = SCHOOL   (Somerset, Bath & Bristol postcodes) **education**

Manor House Day Nursery 01179 629 620
145 Southmead Road, Westbury-on-Trym, Bristol, BS10 5DW
2-5yrs. 8am-6pm. 51wks.

Southmead Day Nursery 01173 772 343
Doncaster Road, Southmead, Bristol, BS10 5PW
2-4yrs. 8am-4pm. 50wks.

Southmead Saplings 01179 592 070
Southmead Hospital, Southmead Road, Westbury-on-Trym, Bristol, BS10 5NB
3mths-5yrs. 7am-6pm. 50wks.

The Manor House 01179 629 620
145 Southmead Road, Westbury on Tyrm, Bristol, BS10 5DW
3mths-5yrs 8am-6pm

BS11
Mama Bear's Day Nursery 01179 823 345
112-116 Grove Leaze, Shirehampton, Bristol, BS11
3mths-6yrs. 7.30am-3pm. 51wks.

Sansway House Day Nursery 01179 829 609
A89 Saltmarsh Drive, Lawrence Weston, Bristol, BS11 0NL
2-5yrs. 8am-6pm. 50wks.

Step Ahead Day Nursery 01179 045 695
College of Further Education, Broadlands Drive, Bristol, BS11 0NT
2-5yrs. 8am-5pm. 50wks.

BS13
Bishopsworth Playgroup 07970 716 884
Old School Rooms, Church Road, Bishopsworth, Bristol, BS13 8JR
2-5yrs.9.30-11.30am. Termtime.

Four Acres Nursery 01179 030 476
Four Acres, Bristol, BS13 8RB
2-8yrs. 8am-6pm. 50wks.

Gatehouse Nursery 01179 781 708
Gatehouse Centre, Hareclive Road, Hartcliffe, Bristol, BS13 9JN
0-5yrs. 8.45am-5pm. 50wks.

BS14
Abbeywood Tots Day Nursery 01179 693 990
Stockwood Lane, Bristol, BS14 8SJ
7.30am-6pm. 50wks.

Christ Church Playgroup 01179 754 616
Petherton Road, Hengrove, Bristol, BS14 9BP
2yrs 10 mnths-5yrs. 9-11.30am. Termtime. Mon, Tues Thurs.

St Nicholas Pre-School 01275 892 633
Church Hall, Church Road, Whitchurch, BS14 0PR
3-5yrs. 9-11.30am and 12.30-3pm. Termtime.

Sunshine Pre-School 07952 929 661
School House, East Dundry Road, Whitchurch, BS14 0LL
2-5yrs. 9.15am-12.15pm and 1.10-4.30pm. Termtime.

BS15
Hillside Day Nursery 01179 604 330
Potterswood, Britannia Road, Kingswood, Bristol, BS15 8EB
3mths-5yrs 8am-6pm

Kingswood Foundation Day Nursery 01179 352 222
43 Bitannia Road, Kingswood, Bristol, BS15 8DB
6wks-5yrs

Kingswood Methodist Church Playgroup 01179 613 488
Grantham Road, Kingswood, Bristol, BS15 1JR
3-5yrs. Termtime.

Little Acorns 01179 606 537
55 New Cheltenham Road, Kingswood, Bristol
2-5yrs 8.30am-5.30pm

Orchard Lea Day Nursery 01179 353 803
165a Burchells Green Road, Kingswood, Bristol, BS15 1DX
6mths-5yrs. 8am-6pm. 50wks.

St George Pre-School 07977 386 134
Cherry Orchard Lane, Off Summerhill Road, St. George, BS15 1HG
2½-5yrs. 9-11.30am. Termtime.

St Michael's Pre-School 07746 499 252
St. Michael's Church Hall, Two Mile Hill, Kingswood, BS15 1AP
2-5yrs. 9-11.45am. Termtime.

Tiny Tots Day Nursery 01179 475 436
128-130 High Street, Hanham, Bristol, BS15 3EJ
0-5yrs 7.30am-6pm

BS16
Leapfrog Day Nursery 01179 568 222
St Luke's Close, Emersons Green, Bristol, BS16
www.leapfrogdaynurseries.co.uk
3mths-5yrs. 7am-7pm. 52 wks (see ad pg 124).

Bambinos 01173 305 300
63 Downend Road, Downend, Bristol, BS16 5UF
2-5yrs. 8.30am-5.30pm

Barn Owl Nursery 01179 562 222
Old Gloucester Road, Hambrook, Bristol, BS16
2-5yrs. 8am-6pm. 51wks.

Colstons Lower School 01179 655 297
Park Road, Stapleton, Bristol, BS16 1BA
3-11yrs. 8.15am-5.25pm. Termtime.

124 education (Somerset, Bath & Bristol postcodes) **S** = SCHOOL

Leapfrog Day Nurseries... For the BEST Care and Education for your child!

We offer fantastic facilities and an outstanding service to mums and dads!

- Fun educational learning and facilities
- Safe, secure environments with individual play areas
- Places available for 0-5 year olds
- Flexible opening hours Monday - Friday
- OFSTED registered and inspected

Come and see for yourself!

Bristol
Bradley Stoke - 01454 202888
Emersons Green - 0117 956 8222
Portishead - 01275 847275
Stoke Gifford - 0117 979 9977

Gloucestershire
Gloucester - 01452 506161
Quedgeley - 01452 725533

Somerset
Weston Super Mare - 01934 519850

Wiltshire
Chippenham - 01249 463000
Salisbury - 01722 417272
Swindon (Abbeymeads) - 01793 702233
Swindon (Broome) - 01793 422202
Swindon (Peatmoor) - 01793 887602
Swindon (St Andrew's Ridge) - 01793 726919

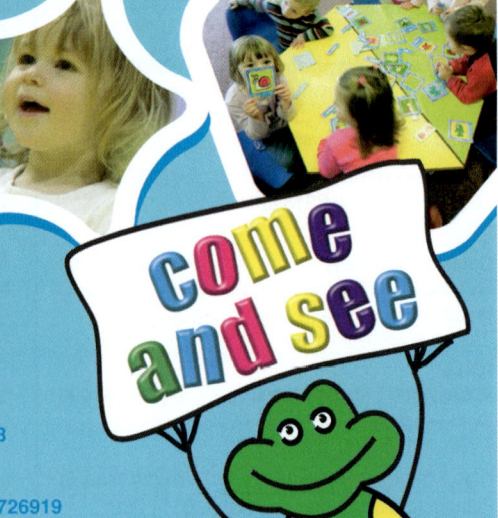

www.leapfrogdaynurseries.co.uk

S = SCHOOL   (Somerset, Bath & Bristol postcodes) **education**   **125**

Fishponds Pre-School 07947 231 086
St. John's Church Hall, Lodge Causeway,
Fishponds, Bristol, BS16 3NW
3-5yrs. 9.15-11.45am and 1-3.30pm.

Fledglings Day Nursery 01179 393 398
25 Oldbury Court Road, Fishponds, Bristol, BS16
18mths-3yrs 8am-5.30pm

S Gracefield Prep School 01179 567 977
266 Overndale Road, Fishponds, Bristol, BS16 2RG
co-ed 4-11yrs

Hillside Day Nursery 01179 047 106
23 Gladstone Street, Staple Hill, Bristol, BS16 4RF
3mths-5yrs 8am-6pm

St Joseph's Pre-School 01179 147 173
St. Joseph's Church Hall, Forest Road, Fishponds
10mths-5yrs. 9-11.30am. Termtime.

Stepping Stones Day Nursery 01179 657 269
1 Hawkesbury Road, Fishponds, Bristol, BS16 2AP
2-5yrs 8am-6pm

Stickyfish Pre-School 01179 584 075
Baptist Church, Downend Road, Fishponds, Bristol
9.30am-12pm. Termtime.

BS20
Leapfrog Day Nursery **01275 847 275**
Serbert Road, Gordano Gate, Portishead, BS20
www.leapfrogdaynurseries.co.uk
0-5yrs. 7.30am-6pm. 50wks.

Brampton Pre-School 01275 817 834
Brampton Way, Portishead, Bristol, BS20 6YN
3-5yrs. 9.15-11.45am and 12.30-3pm. Termtime.

Honey Tree Day Nursery 01275 843 752
13 Stoke Road, Portishead, Brisol, BS20 6BQ
3mths-5yrs. 7.30am-6pm. 50wks.

The Coach House Nursery 01275 840 000
49 Nore Road, Portishead, Bristol, BS20 6JY
6wks-5yrs. 7.45am-6.15pm. 50wks.

The Honey Tree Day Nursery 01275 843752
Stoke House, 13 Stoke Road, Portishead, BS20
3mths-5yrs 8am-6pm

BS21
Bognor House Day Nursery 01275 872 706
114 Old Church Road, Clevedon, BS21 7XP
2-4yrs. 8.30am-4.30pm. 50wks.

Clevedon Montessori 01275 877 743
34 Albert Road, Clevedon, BS21 7RR
2-5yrs.

Folly Farm Day Nursery 01275 854 597
Clevedon Road, Tickenham, Nailsea, BS21 6RY
2-5yrs 8am-6pm

Highdale Day Nursery 01275 872 345
School Lane, Highdale Avenue, Clevedon, BS21
2-5yrs. 8am-6pm. 50wks.

Little Clowns Day Nursery 01275 340069
10 Queens Road, Clevedon, BS21 7TH
0-5yrs 8am-6pm

Rydal Day Nursery 01275 342352
11 Albert Road, Clevedon, BS21 7RP
2-5yrs 8.30am-5.30pm

St Andrew's Sunbeams 01275 874 591
St. Andrew's Church Centre, Old Church Road,
Clevedon, BS21 7UB
3-5yrs. Mornings. Termtime.

BS22
Busy Bees Day Nursery 01934 522 521
7 Nightingale Court, Weston-super-Mare, BS22 8SX
6wks-5yrs. 8am-6pm. 50wks.

Early Birds Day Nursery 01934 522 713
89 Ebdon Road, Worle, Weston-super-Mare, BS22
2-5yrs. 8am-6pm. 50wks.

Honey Tree Day Nursery 01934 641 588
8 Martindale Road, Weston-super-Mare, BS22 8QE
6wks-5yrs. 7.30am-6pm. 52wks.

Kewstoke Pre-School 01934 520 159
Kewstoke Village Hall, Crookes Lane, Kewstoke
3-4yrs. 9am-12pm. Termtime.

Little Acorns Pre-School 01934 514 735
500 Locking Road, Weston-super-Mare, BS22 8QY
9.15-11.45am. Termtime.

Milton Baptist Pre-School 01934 641 574
Milton Baptist Church, Baytree Road, Weston-
Super-Mare, BS22 8HJ
3-4yrs. 9am-12pm. Termtime.

Peekaboo Day Nursery 01934 510 046
106 New Bristol Road, Worle, Weston-super-Mare
8am-6pm. 50wks.

Priory Pre-School 01934 511 411
Queensway, Worle, Weston-super-Mare, BS22 6BP
3-5yrs. 9-11.30am and 12.30-3pm. Termtime.

Ready Steady Go 01934 519 525
Bishop Avenue, Worle, Weston-super-Mare, BS22
3-4yrs. 9.30am-12pm and 12.30-3pm. Termtime.

St Georges Pre-School 01934 521 454
St. Georges Community Centre, Willow Close, St.
Georges, Weston-super-Mare, BS22 7XF
3-5yrs. 9am-12pm. Termtime.

The Honey Tree Day Nursery 01934 641588
8 Martindale Road, Weston Super Mare, BS22 8QE
3mths-5yrs 8am-6pm

education (Somerset, Bath & Bristol postcodes)   S = SCHOOL

BS23

Apple Orchard Day Nursery   01934 629 558
6 Orchard Place, Weston Super Mare, BS23 1QP
2-5yrs. 8am-6pm. 51wks.

Chatterboxes Pre-School   01934 416 300
39a Swiss Road, Weston-super-Mare, BS23 3AY
3-4yrs. 9am-12pm. 3 days. Termtime.

Funny Bunnies   01934 621 041
All Saints Road, Weston-super-Mare, BS23 2NN
2-5yrs. 9.30am-12pm. Termtime.

Green Umbrella Day Nursery   01934 633 021
A114 Milton Road, Weston-super-Mare, BS23 2UW
1-5yrs. 8am-6pm. 51wks.

Little Clowns Day Nursery   01934 641 381
92 Moorland Road, Weston Super Mare, BS23 4HT
3ths-5yrs. 8am-6pm. 51wks.

Little Clowns Nursery   01934 641 381
92 Moorland Road, Weston-super-Mare, BS23 4HT
8am-5.45pm. 50wks.

Little Dumplings   01934 415 155
15 Orchard Street, Weston-super-Mare, BS23 1RG
2-5yrs. 8.30am-6pm.50wks.

Little Scallywags Day Nursery   01934 414 471
Weston General Hospital, Grange Road, Uphill,
Weston-super-Mare, BS23 4TQ
3mths-5yrs. 7am-5pm. 50wks.

Mendip House Nursery & Pre-School   01934 629 584
17a Bedford Road, Weston-super-Mare, BS23 4EJ
6wks-5yrs. 8am-6pm. 51wks.

Rainbow Smiles Nursery   01934 629727
39 Charlton Road, Weston Super Mare, BS23 4HG
6wks-5yrs 8am-6pm

Stanger Montessori Nursery   01934 626 546
2a Hamilton Road, Weston-Super-Mare, BS23 2DH
3-5yrs. 9am-3pm. Termtime.

Swiss House Nursery School   01934 621 576
36 Swiss Road, Weston-Super-Mare, BS23 3AZ
1-5yrs. 8am-6pm. 51wks.

The Green Umbrella Day Nursery   01934 633021
114a Milton Road, Weston Super Mare, BS23 2UW
0-5yrs 8am-6pm

The Secret Garden Nursery   01934 621576
Swiss House, 36 Swiss Road, Weston Super Mare,
BS23 6UW
2-5yrs 8.30am-5.30pm

Tiny Toes Day Nursery   01934 412 779
The Old Barn, Uphill Road South, Weston-super-
Mare, BS23 4TU
3mths-5yrs. 8am-6pm. 50wks.

Worley Birds   07958 394 205
Meadvale Community Hall, c/o 15 Ashleigh Road,
Weston-super-Mare, BS23 2XG
3-5yrs. 9-11.50am. Termtime.

BS24

Leapfrog Day Nursery   01934 519 850
Bransby Way, Locking Castle, Weston-Super-Mare,
www.leapfrogdaynurseries.co.uk
3mths-3yrs. 7am-7pm. 52wks (see ad pg 124).

Around 3 Day Nursery   01934 814 364
Monkton Avenue, Old Mixon, Weston Super Mare,
BS24 9DA
3mths-5yrs 8.30am-5.30pm. 51wks.

Locking Pre-School Playgroup   01934 823 162
Locking Village Hall, Grenville Avenue, Locking,
Weston-super-Mare, BS24 8AR
3-5yrs. 9.15am-12.15pm and 1.15-3.45pm. Termtime.

Princess Christian   01934 519 850
District Centre, Bransby Way, Locking Castle,
Weston-super-Mare, BS24 7EU
6wks-5yrs. 8am-6pm. 50wks.

BS25

Churchill Pre-School   07977 878 512
Memorial Hall, Ladymead Lane, Churchill,
Winscombe, BS25 5NH
2-4yrs. 9-11.45am and 12.45-3.15pm. Termtime.

Rainbow Montessori Nursery   01934 863 165
The United Reform Chapel, Lynch Road,
Winscombe, BS25 1AR
9.15am-4pm. Termtime.

Shipham Pre-School   01934 844 571
The Pre-School Unit, Turnpike Road, Shipham, BS25
2-5yrs. 9-11.30am and 12.30-3pm. Termtime.

S Sidcot Pre-Prep School   01934 843 102
Winscombe, North Somerset, BS25 1PD
3-11yrs.

BS26

Notting Hill Day Nursery   01934 733 393
Notting Hill Way, Weare, Axbridge, BS26 2JU
3mths-5yrs. 7.30am-6pm. 51wks.

The Cottage Nursery   01454 777900
3 Lower Stone Close, Frampton Cotterell, BS26
2-5yrs 7.30am-6pm

Yew Tree Nursery   01934 750 556
Yew Tree Farm, Tarnock, Axbridge, BS26 2SA
2^1/$_2$-4yrs. 7am-7pm. 39wks.

BS27

Early Birds Pre-School   01934 740 123
Cheddar First School, The Hayes, Cheddar, BS27
2-5yrs. 9am-3.15pm. Termtime.

S = SCHOOL (Somerset, Bath & Bristol postcodes) **education**

Tiny Tots Day Nursery 01934 742851
Grassmead, Station Road, Cheddar, BS27 3AE
2-5yrs 9am-3.15pm

BS28
Wedmore Playgroup 01934 713 824
Blackford Road, Wedmore, BS28 4BS
9-11.45am. Termtime.

BS30
Red Roofs Nursery 01179 492 700
24 Poplar Road, Warmley, Bristol, BS30 5JU
0-5yrs 8am-5.30pm

The Rocking Horse Day Nursery 01179 476 218
The Grange School, Tower Road North, Bristol, BS30
6wks-5yrs 8am-6pm

BS31
Queens Road Methodist 01179 877 753
Church Pre-School
Queens Road, Keynsham, Bristol, BS31 2NN
2½-5yrs. 9.30am-12pm and 12.30-3pm. Termtime.

St Francis Pre-School 01179 861 560
St. Francis Church Hall, Warwick Road, Keynsham, Bristol, BS31 2PW
2-5yrs. 9.30am-12pm and 12.15-2.45pm.

Tiddlers Day Nursery 01225 872088
480 Bath Road, Saltford, BS31 3DJ
3mths-5yrs 8am-6pm

BS32
Leapfrog Day Nursery 01454 202 888
Ferndene, Bradley Stoke, Bristol, BS32 9DF
www.leapfrogdaynurseries.co.uk
3mths-3yrs. 7am-7pm. 52wks (see ad pg 124).

S Tockington Manor School 01454 613 229
Tockington, Bristol, BS32 4NY
2-13yrs.

BS34
Leapfrog Day Nursery 01179 799 977
Hunts Ground Road, Stoke Gifford, Bristol, BS34
www.leapfrogdaynurseries.co.uk
3mths-5yrs 7.30am-6.00pm (see ad pg 124).

Nutfield Grove Pre-School 01179 315 169
The Scout Hut, Nutfield Grove, Filton, Bristol, BS34
2-5yrs. 9.15-11.45am and 12.25 -2.55pm. Termtime.

BS39
Acorn Pre-School Group 01761 416 767
Paulton Village Hall, Farrington Road, Paulton, Bristol, BS39 7LW
2½-4yrs. 9-11.45am. Termtime.

Beanstalk Day Nursery 01761 452 267
Croft Cottage, Main Street, Farrington Gurney, Bath, BS39

Bishop Sutton Pre-School 07971 330 577
Methodist Hall, Bishop Sutton, Bristol, BS39 5TR
2-5yrs. 9.15am-1pm. Termtime.

Bo Peep Pre-School 07971 914 659
The Methodist Church Hall, High Littleton, Bristol
9.15am-12pm. Termtime.

Little Fidgets School 01761 452 719
The Memorial Hall, Farrington Gurney, Bristol, BS39
2-5yrs. 9.30am-12pm. Termtime. 3 days.

Montessori Kindergarten 01761 451 460
Village Hall, Litton Lane, Hinton Blewett, Temple Cloud, Bristol, BS39 5AY
2-5yrs. 9am-12pm and 12-3pm. Termtime.

Noah's Ark Pre-School 01761 413 529
The Wooden Classroom, Farrington Road, Paulton, Bristol, BS39 7LW
2-5yrs. 9-11.45am and 12.45-3.20pm. Termtime.

Pied Piper Day Nursery 01791 453109
The Methodist School Room, Upper Bristol Road, Clutton, BS39 5TE
2-5yrs 8.30am-5.30pm

Stanton Drew & Pensford Nursery 07803 875 775
The Village Hall, Sandy Lane, Stanton Drew, Bristol
2-5yrs. 9.30am-12pm. Termtime.

BS40
Blagdon Under 5's Pre-School 07748 367 257
Bath Road, Blagdon, Bristol, BS40 7RW
9-11.45am. Termtime.

East Harptree Nursery 01934 744 593
East Harptree Theatre, Middle Street, East Harptree, BS40 6AZ
2-5yrs. 9am-3.30pm. Termtime.

Jigsaws 01275 333155
2 High Street, Chew Magna, BS40 8PW
3mths-5yrs 6am-6pm

Langford Day Nursery 01934 853237
Langford House, Langford, BS40 5DT
3mths-5yrs am-6pm

Magna Minor Day Nursery 01275 333 900
2 High Street, Chew Magna, Bristol, BS40 8PW
3mths-8yrs. 8am-6pm. 50wks.

S Sacred Heart Prep School 01275 332 470
Winford Road, Chew Magna, Bristol, BS40 8QY
3-11yrs.

BS48
Church Lane Pre-School 07776 401 178
Holy Trinity Church Hall, Church Lane, Nailsea, BS48 4NG
3-4yrs. 9.15am-12pm and 1-3.30pm. Termtime.

education (Somerset, Bath & Bristol postcodes) S = SCHOOL

S Fairfield Pneu School 01275 462 743
Fairfield Way, Backwell, BS48 3PD
Co-ed 3-11yrs.

Happy Hours Nursery 01275 790 433
9 Worcester Gardens, Nailsea, BS48
3mths-5yrs 8am-6pm

Rainbow Pre-School 01275 462 795
W.I. Hall, Station Road, Backwell, BS48 3NW
2½-5yrs. 9.15am-12pm. Termtime.

S The Downs School 01275 852 008
Wraxall, Bristol, BS48 1PF
3-13yrs.

BS49

Happy Hours Nursery 01934 876 973
Hereward House, North End Road, Yatton, Bristol
3mths-5yrs. 8am-6pm. 50wks.

Secret Garden Nursery 01934 853 350
The Barns, Elms Farm, Brinsea Road, Congresbury
3-5yrs. 8am-6pm. 50wks.

Stepping Stones Pre-School 07977 808 132
The Scout Hut, High Street, Claverham, BS49 4NE
2-4yrs. 9.15am-12.15pm.Termtime.

Stonecroft Day Nursery 01934 833 717
11 High Street, Yatton, Bristol, BS49 4JD
2-5yrs. 8am-6pm. 51wks.

The Secret Garden Day Nursery 01934 853350
The Little Barn, Brinsea Road, Congresbury, BS49
5mths-5yrs 8am-6pm

SK9

House of Rompa 01625 548399
Holly Rd, Wilmslow, SK9 1LZ

TA6

First Class Nurseries 01278 424 450
St. Mary's School, Oakfield Road, Bridgwater, TA6
2-5yrs. 8am-5.30pm. 50wks.

TA1

Kiddi Caru Day Nursery 01823 444 194
Blackbrook Park Avenue, Blackbrook Business Park, Taunton, TA1 2PX
www.kiddicaru.com
3mths-5yrs, 8am-6pm, 51 week per year (see ad pg 61).

Albys Childcare 01823 252 945
Albemarle Road, Taunton, TA1 1BA
2½-4yrs. 8am-6pm. 50wks.

Bizzi-Kids 01823 288 556
51 Manor Road, Taunton, TA1 5BQ
1-5yrs. 8.30am-5.30pm. 50wks.

Circles Neighbourhood Nursery 01823 282 691
Outer Circle, Taunton, TA1 2BU
2½-5yrs. 9-11.40am and 12.20-3pm. 39wks.

Doddys Pre-School 01823 252 667
Dodson Hall, Upper Holway Road, Taunton, TA1
2½-5yrs. 9.15am-12pm plus an optional lunchtime session until 1.15pm. Termtime.

Mini Mariners 01823 323 513
Creechbarrow Road, Taunton, TA1 2DU
0-5yrs. 8.30am-5.30pm. 52wks.

Park View Nursery 01823 271841
57 Hamilton Road, Taunton, TA1 2EL
3mths-5yrs 8am-6pm

Primary Colours Day Nursery 01823 334 507
The Trident Youth Hut, Galmington Road, Taunton
2-4yrs. 8am-5.45pm. 50wks.

S Queens College Prep School 01823 272 990
Trull Road, Taunton, TA1 4QP
3-7yrs.

Railway Runabouts Pre-School 07812 644 067
Railway Club, Station Approach, Kilkenny, Taunton
2-5yrs. 9am-12.15pm. Termtime.

Silver Street Day Nursery 01823 283 355
30 Silver Street, Taunton, TA1 3DL
1-5yrs. 8am-6pm. 49wks.

St Johns Pre-School Group 01823 326 722
Church Hall, St. John's Road, Taunton, TA1 4AZ
9.15am-3.15pm. Termtime.

The Elms Children's Nursery 01823 331 932
126 Staplegrove Road, Taunton, TA1 1DP
1-5yrs. 8.30am-5.30pm. 50wks.

The Mount Pre-School 07748 535 659
St. George's Youth Centre, The Mount, Taunton
2½-4yrs. 9am-1pm. Termtime.

Tops Day Nursery 01823 342 038
Taunton & Somerset Hospital, Musgrove Park, Taunton, TA1 5DA
0-8yrs. 7am-6pm. 50wks.

YMCA Pre-School 01823 283 899
Lisieux Way, Taunton, TA1 2LB
2-5yrs. 9.15am-3.15pm. Termtime.

TA2

Abacus Day Nursery 01823 288 681
293 Cheddon Road, Taunton, TA2 7BA
18mths-5yrs 8amam-5.30pm

Busy Beavers Pre-School 01823 253 331
Greenway Road, Rowbarton Methodist Church Hall, Taunton, TA2 6LA
3-5yrs. 9am-12pm. Termtime.

S = SCHOOL (Somerset, Bath & Bristol postcodes) **education**

S King's Hall 01823 285 920
Kingston Road, Taunton, TA2 8AA
3-13yrs.

Lyngford Park Pre-School 01823 354 495
Bircham Road, Taunton, TA2 8EX
3-4yrs.

Priorswood Pre-School 01823 282 169
Wedlands, Taunton, TA2 7AD
2-5yrs. 9am-12pm. Termtime.

S Taunton School First 01823 349 200
Steps & Pre-Prep
Staplegrove Road, Taunton, TA2 6AE
co-ed 2½-13yrs

Wyvern Day Nursery 01823 336 175
Ladymead Community School, Cheddon Road,
Taunton, TA2 7QP
3mths-5yrs. 8am-5.45pm. 50wks.

TA3
Bushy Cross Day Nursery 01823 442 476
Bushy Cross Lane, Ruishton, Taunton, TA3 5JT
3mths-5yrs 8am-5.45pm. 51wks.

Churchinford Pre-School 01460 234 160
Village Hall, Churchinford, Taunton, TA3 7RG
2½-4yrs. 3mornings. Termtime.

Creech St Michael Pre-School 07977 224 412
Hyde Lane, Creech St. Michael, Taunton, TA3 5QQ
2-5yrs. 9am-3.30pm.

Lemon Tree Nursery School 01823 251 307
The Old Rectory, Orchard Portman, Taunton, TA3
1-5yrs. 8.15am-4pm.

Little Acorns Pre-School 01823 491 615
The Playing Fields Pavilion, Greenway, North Curry
2-5yrs. 9am-3pm.

Ruishton Woodland Pre-School 01823 480 768
Huish Wood Scout Campsite, West Hatch, Taunton
2-5yrs. 9am-3pm.

The Lemon Tree Nursery School 01823 251307
The Old Rectory, Orchard Portman, Taunton, TA3
2-5yrs 8.15am-4pm

Thornwick Day Nursery 01823 335803
Thornwick Shoreditch, Taunton, TA3 7BL
18mths-5yrs 8am-5.45pm

Trull Pre-School Group 07816 971 010
The Old Village Hall, Church Road, Trull, Taunton
3-5yrs. 9am-12pm and 12.30-3pm. Termtime.

Willow Set Pre-School 07989 289 872
The Church Rooms, Stoke St. Gregory, Taunton
2-5yrs. 9-11.30am. Termtime.

TA4
Bishops Lydeard Pre-School 07754 502 478
Village Hall, Bishops Lydeard, Taunton, TA4 3LH
3-5yrs. 9.15am-12pm.

Rainbow Playgroup 07816 387 488
The Base, Hartswell, Wiveliscombe, Taunton, TA4
2-4yrs. 9-11.30am and 12.30-3pm.

St Peter's Pre-School 01984 639 182
Doniford Road, Williton, Taunton, TA4 4SF
2½-5yrs. 9am-3.15pm.

TA5
Cannington College Nursery 01278 655 130
Cannington, Bridgwater, TA5 2LS
1-5yrs. 8am-5.30pm. 50wks.

Cannington Pre-School 07704 644 135
Village Hall, Cannington, Bridgwater, TA5 2HP
2-5yrs. 9am-1pm. Termtime. 3days.

Goathurst Pre-School 01278 671 710
Village Hall, Goathurst, Nr Bridgwater, TA5 2DF
2-5yrs. 9.30am-12pm. Termtime.

North Petherton Pre-School 07949 423 565
Church Rooms, Church Walk, North Petherton,
Bridgwater, TA5 2QR
9am-3pm. Termtime.

Stowey Bears Pre-School 01278 733 660
Nether Stowey Village Hall, Lime Street, Nether
Stowey, Bridgwater, TA5 1NH
2-4yrs. 9.30am-3.30pm. Termtime.

Wendy House Nursery 01278 653 775
28 Rydon Crescent, Cannington, Bridgwater, TA5
3mths-5yrs. 7.30am-6.30pm. 50wks.

TA6
Avenue Nursery School 01278 663 040
2 Hyde Park Avenue, North Petherton, Bridgwater
2½-5yrs. Termtime.

Bridgwater New Horizons 07971 717 223
Bridgwater Methodist Church, Monmouth Street,
Bridgwater, TA6 5EQ
2-5yrs. 8.30am-3.30pm. Termtime.

Butterflies Day Nursery 01278 431 868
East Bower Farm, East Bower, Bridgewater, TA6
3mths-5yrs 8am-5.30pm

Green Dragon Montessori School 01278 429 951
Green Dragon Hall, Green Dragon Lane,
Bridgwater, TA6 3AJ
9am-1pm. Termtime.

Greenfields Pre-School 01278 458 817
Sure Start House, 130 Taunton Road, Bridgwater
2½-4yrs. Termtime.

education (Somerset, Bath & Bristol postcodes) S = SCHOOL

Kids & Co Dragons Playgroup 07960 862 934
St. Georges Hall, Kendale Road, Bridgwater, TA6
9.30am-12pm and 12.15-2.45pm.

Little Gems 01278 661 466
85 Fore Street, North Petherton, Bridgwater, TA6
0-8yrs. 8am-6pm.

Pawlett Village Playgroup 07867 727 369
The Methodist Church, Chapel Road, Pawlett,
Bridgwater, TA6 4SH
2½-5yrs. 9.30am-12pm. Termtime.

Salvation Army Pre-School 01278 445 682
The Crest, Moorland Road, Bridgwater, TA6 4JS
9.15-11.45am and 12.15-2.45pm.

Sunbeams Day Care Nursery 01278 446919
Parkway House, Bath Road, Bridgwater, TA6 4PT
0-5yrs 8amam-5.30pm

The Garden's Children's Centre 01278 457 581
Westonzoyland Road, Bridgwater, TA6 5HT
3mths-5yrs. 8am-6pm. 52wks. Afterschool and Holiday clubs also available.

TA7
Chedzoy Pre-School 07989 034 180
Morganians R.F.C., Chedzoy Lae, Bridgwater, TA7
2½-5yrs. 9.15-11.45am. Termtime.

Cherrytrees Montessori School 01458 210436
6 Church Close, Shapwick, Bridgwater, TA7 9LS
2½-5yrs

Hunny Bears Day Nursery 01278 683 512
A3 Riverton Road, Puriton, Bridgwater, TA7 8BW
2-4yrs. 8am-6pm. 50wks.

Little Steps Pre-School 07754 301 286
The Village Hall, Church Road, North Newton, TA7
2-5yrs. 9.15am-12pm. Termtime.

Middlezoy Pre-School 01823 690 204
Methodist Church, Church Road, Middlezoy,
Bridgwater, TA7 0NZ
2-4yrs. 9-11.30am and 12.30-3pm. Termtime.

Polden Hills Pre-School
Village Hall, Middle Road, Cossington, TA7 8LH
2½-4yrs. 9.15am-12pm. 36wks.

Stepping Stones Pre-School 01278 691 187
Cheer Lane, Westonzoyland, Bridgwater, TA7 0EY
3-5yrs. 9.30am-3.30pm. Termtime.

TA8
Allsorts Childcare Nursery 01278 785 974
2 The Grove, Burnham-on-Sea, TA8 2PA
8am-6pm. 48wks.

Burnham Infants Pre-School 01278 793 331
Winchester Road, Burnham-on-Sea, TA8 1JD
9am-3pm. Termtime.

Fair Start Nursery 01278 795 165
6 Princess Street, Burnham-on-Sea, TA8 1EH
3-5yrs. 9am-3.30pm. Termtime.

Southleigh Kindergarten 01278 783 999
11 Rectory Road, Burnham-on-Sea, TA8 2BY
2-7yrs. 8am-5.30pm. Termtime.

TA9
Brent Knoll Kindergarten 07721 742 005
Brent Street, Highbridge, TA9 4EQ
2-5yrs. 9.05am-1pm.

Mark Harvest Pre-School 01278 641 691
The Causeway, Mark, Highbridge, TA9 4QA
2-5yrs. 9.15am-12pm. Termtime.

Rose Cottage Baby Nursery 01278 793 103
Rose Cottage Farm, Burnham Moor Lane,
Edithmead, Burnham-on-Sea, TA9 4HE
3mths-5yrs. 8am-6pm. 50wks.

Rossholme Nursery 01278 760 219
East Brent, Highbridge, TA9 4JA
2½-5yrs. 9am-1pm or 2-4pm. Termtime

West Huntspill School 01278 789 234
New Road, West Huntspill, Highbridge, TA9 3QE
2½-5yrs. 9am-3pm. Termtime.

TA10
Acorn Day Nursery 01458 274 848
Pitney Village Hall, Pitney, Langport, TA10 9AS
2-5yrs. 8.30am-12pm and 1-4.30pm. 50wks.

TA11
Barton St David Pre-School 07803 751 900
The Village Hall, Church Street, Barton St. David
9am-12pm.

Charltons Pre-School 07714 494 497
Bonfire Lane, Charlton Mackrell, Somerton, TA11
2-5yrs. 9am-12pm. 30wks.

Roundabout Pre-School 01458 274 382
Etsome Terrace, Somerton, TA11 6LY
2½-5yrs. 9am-12pm and 1-3.30pm. Termtime.

TA12
Acorns Pre-School 01935 824 971
United Reformed Church Hall, Bower Hinton, Nr
Martock, TA12 6LN
2½-5yrs. Mon-Thurs 9.15am-12pm and Wed pms. T/time.

Kingsbury Episcopi Pre-School 01460 241 004
Stembridge, Martock, TA12 6BP
2-5yrs. 9am-12pm. Termtime .

Martock Pavilion Pre-School 07703 785 000
Stoke Road, Martock, TA12 6AF
2-5yrs. 9.30am-12pm and 12.20-2.50pm. Termtime.

S = SCHOOL   (Somerset, Bath & Bristol postcodes) education

TA15
Montacute Pre-School   01935 822 022
Baptist School Rooms, South Street, Montacute
2-5yrs. 9.15am-12pm and 1-3.30pm. Termtime.

TA16
Merriott Pre-School   0146 077 922
Church Street, Merriott, TA16 5PT
9-11.30am and 12.30-3pm.

TA17
St George's Pre-School   0146 073 033
The School House, West Street, Hinton St. George
2-5yrs. 9am-12pm.

TA18
Jigsaw Pre-School   07767 770 745
West One Youth Centre, West Street, Crewkerne
0-5yrs. 9am-12pm. Termtime.

Jigsaw Too   07767 770 745
Beech Centre, Maiden Beech School, Crewkerne
2-4yrs. 9am-12pm. Termtime.

Misterton Pre-School   07974 699 519
Village Hall, Unity Lane, Misterton, Crewkerne
2-5yrs. 9am-1pm. Termtime. 4 days.

S Perrot Hill School   0146 072 051
North Perrot, Crewkerne, Somerset, TA18 7SL
3-13yrs.

St Martins Day Nursery   01460 73265
18 Abbey Street, Crewkerne, TA18 7HY
3mths-5yrs. 8am-6pm. 50wks.

TA19
Ashill Pre-School   07929 394 923
School House, Ashill, Ilminster, TA19 9ND
2-5yrs. 9.15-11.45am. Termtime.

First Steps Montessori   01460 241 266
Millenium Hall, Water St, Sevington, TA19 0QH
2½-5yrs

Merryfield Pre-School   0146 052 574
Frist School, Copse Lane, Ilton, TA19 9EX
9am-1.15pm. Termtime.

Miniatures Day Nursery   01460 55488
Church Road, Ilton, Ilminster, TA19 9EY
0-5yrs 8am-5pm

Shepton Beauchamp Nursery   07765 437 301
The Village Hall, Shepton Beauchamp, Ilminster
2-5yrs. 9.15am- 1pm.

St Mary's Pre-School   07881 713 926
Village Hall, Barrington, Ilminster, TA19 0JF
2-5yrs. 9.15am-12.15pm. Termtime.

TA20
Buckland St Mary Pre-School   01460 234 303
Buckland St. Mary, Chard, TA20 3SJ
9-11.45am. Termtime. 3 days.

Chard Methodist Pre-School   01460 67855
Methodist Church Hall, Fore Street, Chard, TA20
2-5yrs. 9.15-1.45am. Termtime. 4 days.

S Chard School   01460 63234
Fore Street, Chard, TA20 1QA
Co-ed day school from 2-11yrs. Termtime.

Honeycomb Nursery   0146 063 211
Pollard House, Crimchard, Chard, TA20 1JT
2-5yrs. 9am-12pm and 12.3-3.30pm. Termtime.

Winsham Pre-School   0146 030 441
Jubilee Hall, Church Street, Winsham, Chard, TA20
3-5yrs. 9.15am-12pm. Termtime.

TA21
Acorns Day Nursery   01823 664 865
Spypost House, 3 Exeter Road, Rockwell Green,
Wellington, TA21 9DH
3mths-5yrs 8.30am-5.30pm

Oakfield Day Nursery   01823 665172
Oakfield, Pyles Thorne Road, Wellington, TA21 8DX
3mths-5yrs 8.30am-5.30pm

Sampford Arundel Pre-School   07837 482 554
Sampford Arundel Parish Rooms, Sampford
Arundel, Wellington, TA21 9EN
9am-3pm. 3days.

Stawley Under 5's   01823 663 292
Stawley School, Appley Cross, Wellington, TA21
2-5yrs. 9.30-3pm. Termtime.

Stawley Under 5's Playgroup   01823 672 867
The Cricket Pavilion, Appley Cross, Stawley,
Wellington, TA21 0HH
3-5yrs. 9am-12pm.

The Apple Tree Pre-School   07818 835 143
Community Centre, White Hart Lane, Wellington
2-5yrs. 9.15am-12pm. Termtime.

Waterloo Road Pre-School   01823 661 676
Methodist Church, Waterloo Road, Wellington
2-5yrs. 9am-3.15pm. Termtime.

TA22
S Wellington Junior School   01823 668 700
South Street, Welllington, TA21 8NT
3-10yrs.

The 'Rocking Horse'   01398 323 696
Dulverton Childcare Centre, Barns Close West,
Dulverton, TA22 9EE
0-4yrs. 8.30am-6pm. 50wks.

TA23
Buckland School   01984 631 314
7 St Decumans Road, Watchet, Watchet, TA23 0HR
8.15am-4pm. 41wks.

132 education (Somerset, Bath & Bristol and Wiltshire postcodes)   S = SCHOOL

Little Vikings Nursery School 01984 633 655
Liddymore Road, Watchet, TA23 0EX
23/4-5yrs. 9-11.30am and 12.45-3.15pm.

TA24
Cheeky Cherubs Nursery 01643 707 658
27 Irnham Road, Minehead, TA24 5DW
8am-6pm. 50wks.

Dunster Pre-School 01643 822 233
St. Georges Street, Dunster, Minehead, TA24 6RX
2½-5yrs. 9-11.45am and 1-3.30pm. Termtime.

Nextsteps Nursery 07977 542 778
Carhampton Recreational Hall, Minehead, TA24
8am-6pm. 50wks.

Red Deer Nursery School 01643 813 673
Gallon House, Simonsbath, Minehead, TA24 7JY
2-5yrs. 9am-12pm. Termtime.

WILTSHIRE
BA2
Little Folks Nursery 01225 722 604
76 Murhill, Limpley Stoke, Bath, BA2 7FB
9am-3pm. Termtime.

BA12
Barney Lodge Day Nursery 01985 214 286
5 Westbury Road, Warminster, BA12 0AN
3mths-5yrs. 8am-6pm. 51wks.

Codford Caterpillars Pre-School 01985 851 030
The Cocoon, Codford School, Cherry Orchard,
Codford, Warminster, BA12 0PN
2-4yrs. 9am-2.45pm. Termtime.

Elm Hill Pre-School 01985 212 339
96 Elm Hill, Warminster, BA12 0AZ
3-5yrs. 9.15am-12pm. Termtime.

First Steps Nursery 0198 584 494
School House, 68 Church Street, Horningsham,
Warminster, BA12 7LW
1-4yrs. 9am-3pm. Termtime.

Garrison Pre-School 01985 222 488
The Community Centre, Firbank Crescent,
Warminster, BA12 0BY
3-5yrs. 9.15am-12pm. Termtime.

Heytesbury Hedgehogs 07870 472 091
Heytesbury, Warminster, BA12 0EA
2-5yrs. 9am-3pm. Termtime.

Leaping Frogs Kindergarten 01747 830 074
The Walton Building, The Square, Mere,
Warminster, BA12 6DL
2-4yrs. 9.30am-12.30pm. Termtime.

Little Cuckoos Pre-School 01373 832 298
Lyes Green, Corsley, Warminster, BA12 7QH
2-4yrs. 9am-3pm. Termtime.

Mere Playgroup 01747 861 817
The Youth Centre, Queens Road, Mere,
Warminster, BA12 6EP
2-5yrs. 9-11.45am. Termtime.

Noah's Ark Pre-School 07759 21 172
Princecroft Lane, Warminster, BA12 8NT
2-5yrs. Mornings.

S Stourbridge House School 01747 860 165
Castle Street, Mere, Warminster, BA12 6JQ
2½-8yrs. 9am-3.30pm. 34wks.

Sunnyhill Nursery 01985 215 317
16 Bath Road, Warminster, BA12 8PD
2-8yrs. 8am-5.30pm. 48wks.

Sutton Veny Pre-School 01985 840 428
Village Hall, High Street, Sutton Veny, Warminster
3-5yrs. 9am-12pm. Termtime.

Teddybear Montessori 01985 212 204
The Lakeside Centre, Weymouth Street,
Warminster, BA12 9NP
9.15am-1.10pm. Termtime.

The Owlets Pre-School 07761 049 886
Village Hall, High Street, Maiden Bradley,
Warminster, BA12 7JG
2-5yrs. 9.30am-12.30pm.

The Rainbow Pre-School 07876 111 365
The Pratton Hut, Youth Centre, The Close,
Warminster, BA12 9AL
2-5yrs. 9am-1pm. Termtime.

Toad Hall Nursery School 07761 467 111
St. John's Parish Hall, Boreham Road, Warminster
18mths-5yrs. 9am-3pm. Termtime.

S Warminster Preparatory School 01985 224 800
11 Vicarage Street, Warminster, BA12 8JG
3-11yrs.

Warminster Pre-School Nursery 07977 740 264
Greenland Hut, Weymouth Street, Warminster
3-5yrs. 9am-3pm. Termtime.

BA13
Acorn Nursery School 07941 417 606
Heywood & Hawkeridge Village Hall, Church Road,
Heywood, Westbury, BA13 4LP
2-5yrs. 9am-3pm. 43wks.

Bratton Pre-School 07949 286 991
The Church Institute, Tynings Lane, Bratton, Westbury
2-5yrs. 9.15am-12pm. Termtime.

Busy Bees Pre-School 07749 257 608
Chapmanslade School, High Street,
Chapmanslade, Westbury, BA13 4AN
2½-5yrs. Mon/Wed/Fri 8.45am-12pm and Tues/Thurs
8.45am-3pm. Termtime.

S = SCHOOL (Wiltshire postcodes) **education**

Courtleigh Nursery School 01373 824 134
The Old Church Hall, The Churchyard, Market Place, Westbury, BA13 3BZ
2-4yrs. 8am-6pm. 51wks.

Cygnets Pre-School 01373 827 555
Sandalwood Road, Westbury, BA13 3UR
2-5yrs. 9.15-11.45am and 12.30-3pm. Termtime.

Daisy Chain Pre-School 07890 864 347
Methodist Church Hall, Station Road, Westbury
2-5yrs. 9.15-11.45am. Termtime.

Dilton Marsh Pre-School 01373 826 693
High Street, Dilton Marsh, Westbury, BA13 4DY
2-5yrs. 9am-12pm. Termtime.

Eden Vale Pre-School 01373 822 335
Westbury Youth Development Centre, Eden Vale Road, Westbury, BA13 3NY
3-5yrs. 9.15-11.45am. Termtime.

Hobby Horse Day Nursery 07970 656 311
117 Eden Vale Road, Westbury, BA13 3QG
0-5yrs. 8am-6pm. 51wks.

Kingfisher Pre-School 07803 548 406
Arundell Close, Westbury, BA13 3UA
9am-12pm. Termtime.

The Rainbow Playschool 01373 826 599
All Saints Church Hall, Church Lane, Westbury
2-5yrs. 9.30am-12pm. Termtime.

BA14

Busy Bees Pre-School 01225 753 085
Southwick Village Hall, Frome Road, Southwick, Trowbridge, BA14 9QD
2-5yrs. 9.15-11.45am. Termtime.

Court Mills Pre-School 01225 776 772
Community Centre, Polebarn Road, Trowbridge
3-5yrs. 9.30am-12pm. Termtime.

Holbrook Park Pre-School 01225 774 478
Holbrook Lane, Trowbridge, BA14 0PS
2-5yrs. 9-11.30am and 12.30-3pm. Termtime.

Holt Pre-School 01225 782 808
Village Hall, The Street, Holt, Trowbridge, BA14
3-5yrs. 9.30am-12pm. 3 mornings. Termtime.

Just Learning Nursery 01225 768 510
19 Hackett Place, Hilperton, Trowbridge, BA14
0-5yrs. 7.30am-6.30pm.

Ladybirds Pre-School 01225 358 612
Broadcloth Lane, Trowbridge, BA14 7HE
3-5yrs. 9.15-11.45am and 12.30-3.30pm. Termtime.

Little Stars Pre-School 01225 355 412
Broadcloth Lane, Trowbridge, BA14 7HE
2-5yrs. 9am-3pm. Termtime.

Longscroft Children's Nursery 01225 777 698
Longscroft Farm, Trowle, Trowbridge, BA14 9BL
7.30am-6pm.

Nestlings Pre-School 07796 017 703
Pratten Hut, School Lane, Staverton, Trowbridge
2-5yrs. 9-11.30am and 12.30-3pm. Termtime.

Playtime Pre-School 07946 023 013
Bethesda Church Hall, Gloucester Road, Trowbridge, BA14 0AD
9.30am-12pm and 1.15-2.45pm.

Seesaw at Newtown 01225 774 647
Newtown School, Newtown, Trowbridge, BA14 0BB
2-8yrs. 8am-6pm. Termtime.

Seesaw Nursery 01225 767 006
12 Wingfield Road, Trowbridge, BA14 9EB
1-8yrs. 8am-6pm. 50wks.

Seesaw Nursery 2 01225 776 049
1 Eastbourne Road, Trowbridge, BA14 7HW
0-5yrs. 8am-6pm. 51wks.

St Michaels Pre-School 01225 769 765
Village Hall, Whaddon Lane, Hilperton, Trowbridge
2-5yrs. 9.30am-12pm. Termtime.

St Thomas Pre-School 07898 302 662
Church Hall, York Buildings, Trowbridge, BA14 8PT
9.15-11.45am and 12.15-2.45pm.

Steps Ahead Day Nursery 01225 719 110
Bradley Road, Trowbridge, BA14 0RG
0-8yrs. 8am-6pm. 50wks.

Upper Studley Playgroup 07796 933 359
Baptist Church Hall, Frome Road, Trowbridge
2-5yrs. 9.30am-12pm. Termtime.

Woodleigh Nursery 01225 753 041
1 Green Lane, Trowbridge, BA14 7DA
2-5yrs. 8.30am-5.30pm. 51wks.

BA15

Castle Gardens Nursery Group 07759 929 588
The Lambert Rooms, Mount Pleasant, Bradford on Avon, BA15 1SJ
2-5yrs. 9-11.45am. Termtime.

Catkins Nursery 01225 867 819
169 Trowbridge Road, Bradford-on-Avon, BA15 1ET
2-5yrs. 9.15-11.45am and 1-3.30pm. Termtime.

Hollyhocks Kindergarten 07790 948 111
Monkton Farleigh Village Hall, Monkton Farleigh, Bradford-on-Avon, BA15 2QD
3-6yrs. 9.30am-12.30pm. Termtime.

134 education (Wiltshire postcodes)   S = SCHOOL

Oakfield Nursery School 01225 866 649
Bradford-on-Avon Sports and Social Club,
Trowbridge Road, Bradford-on-Avon, BA15 1EW
9.15-11.45am. 38wks.

Westview Day Nursery 01225 864 544
35 St.Margarets Street, Bradford-on-Avon, BA15
0-5yrs. 7am-7pm. 51wks.

Westwood Nursery School 01225 863 117
Upper Westwood, Bradford-on-Avon, BA15 2DP
9.15-11.45am and 12.30-2.30pm. Termtime.

Winsley Acorns Pre-School 07891 164 644
Winsley Village Hall, Winsley, Bradford-on-Avon
3-5yrs. 9.30am-1pm. Termtime.

SN1
Central Playgroup 07720 874 076
Central Community Centre, Emlyn Square, Railway
Village, Swindon, SN1 5BL
2-5yrs. 9.30am-12pm. Termtime.

Childrens Nursery 01793 463 573
Civic Offices, Euclid Street, Swindon, SN1 2JH
8am-5.30pm. 51wks.

Clifton Street Pre-School 01793 491 187
Clifton Street Social Hall, Clifton Street, Swindon
2-5yrs. 9.15am-12pm. Termtime.

King William Playgroup 07811 649 355
Savernake Street Community Centre, Savernake
Street, Swindon, SN1 3LZ
3-5yrs. 9.15-11.45am. Termtime.

Noah's Ark Kindergarten 01793 434 155
55 Okus Road, Old Town, Swindon, SN1 4LE

Queens Park Playgroup 07961 813 219
Queens Park Social Hall, Euclid Street, Swindon
3-5yrs. 9.15-11.45am. Termtime.

Playsteps 01793 0619 406
The Hub, Church Place, Swindon, SN1 5EH

Toad Hall Nursery 01793 436 432
Trinity Hall, Victoria Road, Swindon, SN1 3AL
0-5yrs. 8am-6pm. 50wks.

Trees Day Care Nursery 01793 480 780
Trees, Quarry Road, Old Town, Swindon, SN1 4EN
0-8yrs. 8am-6pm. 50wks.

Westbourne Pre-School 07793 861 268
Westbourne Youth Centre, Westcott Street,
Swindon, SN1 5QS
9-11.45am. Termtime.

SN2
Even Swindon EYC 01793 523 681
Hughes Street, Swindon, SN2 2ER
3-5yrs. 12.30-3pm. Termtime.

Ferndale Pre-School 07817 981 011
All Saints Church Hall, Southbrook Street, Swindon
2-4yrs. 9.15-11.45am. Termtime.

Green Road Pre-School 07816 614 973
Upper Stratton Baptist Church, Green Road,
Stratton St.Margaret, Swindon, SN2 7JD
2-4yrs. 9am-3.15pm. Termtime.

Kids Create Nursery 01793 825 047
Lower Stratton Methodist Hall, Swindon, SN2 6JS
9-11.30am and 12.15-2.45pm. 4 days, Termtime.

Little Pinetrees 01793 707 147
Pinehurst Community Centre, Beech Avenue,
Swindon, SN2 1JT
3-5yrs. 9.15-11.45am and 12.15-2.15pm. Termtime.

Little Stars 01793 498 430
The Swindon College Nursery, North Star Avenue,
Swindon, SN2 1DY
8am-5.30pm. 50wks.

Next Step Montessori Nursery 01793 825 941
ST.Phillip's Road, Swindon, SN2 7QH
2-5yrs. 9.15-11.45am and 12.45-3.15pm. Termtime.

North Star Nursery 01793 411 994
Polaris House, Polaris Way, Swindon, SN2 1UH
3mths-4yrs. 8am-5.45pm. 50wks.

St Mary's Playgroup 01793 523 371
Bessemer Road East, Rodbourne, Swindon, SN2
9-11.30am and 12.30-3pm. Termtime.

St Philip's Pre-School 01793 705 769
Beechcroft Road, Upper Stratton, Swindon, SN2
2-4yrs. 9-11.40am and 12.40-2.40pm. Termtime.

Sunshine Kids 01793 525 831
Rear Hall, Elim Pentecostal Church, Osbourne
Street, Swindon, SN2 1DA
2-5yrs. 9.15-11.45am and 12.45-3.15pm. Termtime.

Sunshine Pre-School 01793 723 677
Alton Close, Swindon, SN2 5HF
2-4yrs. 9.05-11.35am and 12.35-3.05pm. Termtime.

White Cottage Day Nursery 01793 435 534
St. Paul's Street, Gorse Hill, Swindon, SN2 1AY
0-8yrs.

SN3
Jigsaw Day Nursery 01793 422 202
Pipers Way, Broome, Swindon, SN3 1RG
www.leapfrogdaynurseries.co.uk
0-5yrs. 8am-6pm. 51wks (see ad pg 124)

Buffer Bear at the Great Western Hospital 01793 605 861
Marlborough Road, Swindon, SN3 6BB
3mths-4yrs. 6.45am-7pm. 52wks.

S = SCHOOL (Wiltshire postcodes) **education**

Carousel Pre-School Playgroup 0793 488 799
Dome Community Centre, Burghley Close, Walcot, Swindon, SN3 3BS
3-5yrs. 9.15am-12pm. Termtime.

Coleview Pre-School 01793 828 688
Towcester Road, Swindon, SN3 4AS
3-4yrs. 9.10-11.40am and 12.15-2.45pm. Termtime.

Covingham Kingfishers 01793 434 221
St. Paul's Church Centre, Lovell Close, Covingham, Swindon, SN3 5EJ
2-8yrs. 8am-3pm. Termtime.

Covingham Roundabout 01793 529 952
Martinfield, Covingham, Swindon, SN3 5EJ
2-5yrs. 9am-12pm and 1-3pm. Termtime.

Croft Playgroup 01793 526 622
Marlborough Lane, Swindon, SN3 1RA
9.15-11.45am. Termtime.

Eldene Pre-School 01793 488 802
Eldene Centre, Swindon, SN3 3RZ
3-5yrs. 9-11.30am and 12.45-3.15pm. Termtime.

Hand in Hand Nursery 01793 831 304
Kingsdown Scout Hall, Taylor Crescent, Kingsdown Park, Swindon, SN3 4UY
2-5yrs. 9.15-11.45am. Termtime.

Hector's Playgroup 01793 342 347
Goddard Park Centre of Early Excellence, Welcombe Avenue, Swindon, SN3 2QN
0-5yrs. 8am-6pm. Termtime.

Holy Family Pre-School 07732 704 560
Marlowe Avenue, Swindon, SN3 2PT
2-5yrs. 8.50-11.30am and 12.30-3pm. Termtime.

Holy Rood Playgroup 07986 714 548
Upham Road, Swindon, SN3 1DH
3-5yrs. 9.15-11.45am and 12.15-2.45pm. Termtime.

Kidsunlimited 0845 850 0222
Greenbridge Road, Swindon, SN3 3LD
3mths-5yrs. 7.30am-6pm. 51 wks.

Lawn Pre-School 01793 613 504
Pratten Huts, Cleeve Lawn, Swindon, SN3 1LE
9-11.30am and 12.40-3.10pm. Termtime.

Liden Pre-School 01793 485 392
Liden Junior School, Liden Drive, Liden, Swindon
3-5yrs.

Nythe Pre-School 01793 642 424
Nythe Annexe, The Drive Nythe, Swindon, SN3
2½-4yrs. 9-11.30am and 12.30-2.30pm. Termtime.

Resolution Day Nursery 01793 532 059
Sea Cadets Hall, Upham Road, Old Walcot, Swindon, SN3
2-5yrs. 7.30am-5.30pm. Termtime.

South Marston Pre-School 0773 189 601
Old Vicarage Lane, South Marston, Swindon, SN3
9am-12pm and 1.10-3.10pm. Termtime.

St Margaret's Pre-School 07816 547 752
St. Margaret's Centre, Kenwin Close, Stratton St. Margaret, Swindon, SN3 4XF
2-5yrs. 9.15-11.45am. Termtime.

Sunrise Nursery 01793 820 858
Delamere Drive, Stratton St.Margaret, Swindon
2-4yrs. 7.30am-6pm. 50wks.

SN4

Allsorts Pre-School 01793 849 955
The Rosary, Wootton Bassett, Swindon, SN4 8AF
2-5yrs. 9.15am—3pm. Termtime. They also offer a mums and tots group from 0-5yrs on Wed pms.

Amesbury Methodist Church Pre-School 01980 622 840
High Street, Amesbury, Salisbury, SN4 8AF
9.am-12pm Termtime.

Asquith Nursery Ridgeway 01793 845 572
Inverary Road, Wroughton, Swindon, SN4 9DL
3mths-5yrs. 8am-6pm. 51wks

Broad Town Pre-School 01793 731 395
Broad Town School, Broad Town, Swindon, SN4
2-4yrs. 9.15am-1pm. Termtime.

Hopscotch Pre-School 07956 163 015
Chiseldon Methodist Church, Turnball, Chiseldon, Swindon, SN4 0LJ
3-5yrs. 8.50-11.45am. 39wks.

Learning Curve 01793 851 495
Garabrecan, Brinkworth Road, Wootton Bassett, Swindon, SN4 8DS
0-5yrs. 8am-6pm. 50wks.

Longleaze Nursery 01793 848 978
Byron Avenue, Wootton Bassett, Swindon, SN4
9am-3pm. Termtime.

Old Court Community Pre-School 01793 849 783
Station Road, Wootton Bassett, Swindon, SN4 8QY
2-8yrs. 9.15am-3.45pm. Termtime.

Poplars Daycare Nursery 01793 790 774
Poplars, Lower Wanborough, Swindon, SN4 0AA
7.30am-6.30pm. 50wks.

Tick Tock Nursery Playgroup 01793 814 191
School Lane, Markham Road, Wroughton, Swindon
2-4yrs. 9am-12pm and 12.45-3.15pm. Termtime.

Wanborough Playgroup 07711 054 015
St. Andrews Village Hall, Lower Wanborough, High Street, Wanborough, Swindon, SN4 0AD
3-5yrs. 9-11.45am. Termtime.

136 education (Wiltshire postcodes) S = SCHOOL

Wroughton Pre-School 0778 750 2245
The Church Hall, Priors Hill, Wroughton, Swindon
2-5yrs. 9-11.45am and 1-2.45pm. Termtime.

SN5
Leapfrog Day Nursery 01793 887 602
Peatmoor Village Centre, Shearwood Road,
Peatmoor, Swindon, SN5 5DJ
12wks-4yrs. 7.30am-6pm. 50wks (see ad pg 124).

Freshbrook Playgroup 01793 879 178
Community Centre, Worsley Road, Freshbrook,
Swindon, SN5 8LY
9.15-11.45am and 12.15-2.45pm. Termtime.

Greendown Playgroup 01793 882 234
Grange Park Way, Grange Park, Swindon, SN5
9.15am-12pm and 12.15-2.45pm. 37wks.

Headstart Nursery 01793 877 779
1403 Delta Office Park, Welton Road, Swindon
0-5yrs. 8am-6pm. 50wks.

Holy Trinity Playgroup 07743 321 163
Shaw Village Centre, Ramleaze Drive, Shaw,
Swindon, SN5 5PY
2-5yrs. 9am-12pm and 12.30-2.30pm. Termtime.

Jellytots Playgroup 07718 028 621
Brookfield School, Cartwright Drive, Shaw,
Swindon, SN5 5SB
3-5yrs. 9-11.45am and 12.30-3pm. Termtime.

Link & Learn Pre-School 01793 465 464
Link Centre, Ike Gradwell Community Suite, Link
Centre, Whitehill Way, SN5 7DL
3-5yrs. 9am-12pm. Termtime.

Lydiard Millicent Pre-School 07967 121 199
The Butts, Lydiard Millicent, Swindon, SN5 3LR
3-5yrs. 9.15am-12.15pm. Termtime.

Playclose Playgroup 01793 778 141
Methodist Church, Purton, Swindon, SN5 4DP
2-5yrs. 9.10am-12.45pm. 51wks.

Sparklers Pre-School 01793 887 473
Pepperbox Hill, Peatmoor, Swindon, SN5 5DP
2-5yrs. 9.15-11.45am and 12.15-2.45pm. Termtime.

Upper Shaw Farm Playgroup 07712 713 369
Community Centre, Ridge Green, Shaw, Swindon
9-11.45am and 12.15-2.45pm. Termtime.

Westlea Pre-School 07876 485 516
Langstone Way, Swindon, SN5 7BT
2-4yrs. 9.05-11.45am and 12.30-3pm. Termtime.

Windmill Hill Day Nursery 01793 877646
Windmill Business Park, Whitehill Way, Swindon
6wks-5yrs, 8am-6pm, 52 week per year.

SN6
Cricklade Pre-School 01793 750 817
The Old Library, Bath Road Cricklade, Swindon
9-11.45am and 1-3.30pm. Termtime.

Highworth Pre-School 01793 766 646
Newburgh Place, Highworth, Swindon, SN6 7DN
9.15-11.45am and 12.45-3.15pm. Termtime.

Hillsborough Day Nursery 01793 790 271
Hillsborough, Bishopstone, Nr Swindon, SN6 8PW
1-7yrs. 8am-6pm. Termtime.

Kirkland Day Nursery 01285 862 060
Coxs Hill, Ashton Keynes, SN6 6NY
6mths-5yrs. 7.30am-6pm. 51wks.

Meadow Park Nursery and 01793 752 600
Preparatory School
Manor House, Calcutt Street, Cricklade, Swindon
3mths-4yrs. 7.50am-6pm. 47wks.

S Pinewood School 01793 782 205
Swindon, Swindon, SN6 8HZ
3-13yrs.

Thames Pre-School 01793 750 635
Bath Road, Cricklade, Swindon, SN6 6AX
2-5yrs. 9-11.30am and 12.30-3pm. Termtime.

Vorda Pre-School 01793 763 668
British School Building, Brewery Street, Highworth,
Swindon, SN6 7AJ
9.15-11.45am and 12.45-3.15pm. Termtime.

Westgate Nursery School 01793 861 268
82 Cricklade Road, Highworth, Swindon, SN6 7BL
0-8yrs. 8am-6pm. 50wks.

SN8
Aldbourne Pre-School 07919 808 641
Back Lane, Aldbourne, Marlborough, SN8 2BP
2-5yrs. 8am-3pm. Termtime.

Baydon Under 5's Pre-School 01672 540 752
Youth Centre, Manor Road, Baydon, Marlborough
2-4yrs. 9am-12pm. Termtime.

Bluebell Nursery 01672 861 276
Lockeridge, Marlborough, SN8 4EL
3-5yrs. 9am-12.15pm. Termtime.

College Fields Montessori 01672 515 486
College Fields, Marlborough, SN8 1UA
2-5yrs. 9.15am-3.15pm. 48wks.

Grafton Pre-School 01672 810 478
East Grafton, Marlborough, SN8 3DB
9.15am-1.15pm. Termtime.

Little Dragons Pre-School 07855 026 083
Village Hall, Ogbourne St. George, Marlborough
2-5yrs. 9.15am-12.15pm. Termtime.

S = SCHOOL (Wiltshire postcodes) **education**

Manton Pre-School 07776 006 000
Manton Village Hall, Preshute Lane, Manton, Marlborough, SN8 4HQ
3-5yrs. 9.15-11.45am and 12.30-3pm. (Times decided at beginning of each term, depending on intake) Termtime.

Oare Kids Pre-School 07816 564 429
Rudge Lane, Oare, Marlborough, SN8 4JH
9.15am-12.45pm. Termtime.

Pebbles Pre-School 01672 539 215
The Social Centre, High Street, Avebury, Malrborough, SN8 1RF
2-5yrs. 9.15am-12.45pm. Termtime.

Ramsbury Pre-School 01672 520 901
Methodist Church Hall, Oxford Street, Ramsbury, Marlborough, SN8 2PG
3-5yrs. 9.30am-12.45pm. Termtime.

Sixpenny Daycare 01672 541 730
Smiths Barn, West Street, Aldbourne, Marlborough
8wks-8yrs. 8am-6pm. 51wks.

Snowdrops Pre-School 01488 668 610
The Village Hall, Ham, Malrborough, SN8 3RB
2-5yrs. 9.15am-2.45pm. Termtime.

St Mary's Under Fives 01672 516 098
The Church Hall, Silverless Street, Marlborough
3-5yrs. 9.15-11.45am and 12.15-2.45pm. Termtime.

S Stepping Stones Nursery 01488 681 067
Oakhill Farmhouse, Upper Oakhill, Froxfield, Marlborough, SN8 3JT
2-4yrs. 9am-3.30pm. Termtime.

SN9
Barn Nursery School 01672 851 148
Nursery Farm, Woodborough, Pewsey, SN9 5PF
2-5yrs. 9am-6pm. 48wks.

Bubbles Pre-School 01672 562 099
Wesley Hall, North Street, Pewsey, SN9 5ES
9.30am-12pm. Termtime.

Busy Bees Nursery 01672 851 891
Woodborough Church Rooms, Church Road, Woodborough, Pewsey, SN9 5PH
2-5yrs. 9am-1.15pm. Termtime.

Chatterbox Pre-School 01980 615 275
Building 35, Trenchard Lines, Upavon, Pewsey
2-4yrs. 9.10am-12.10pm. Termtime.

Puddleducks 01672 562 469
Pewsey Sports Centre, Wilcot Road, Pewsey, SN9
2-5yrs. 9.15am-12.15pm.

S St Francis School 01672 563 228
Marlborough Road, Pewsey, SN9 5NT
2-13yrs.

SN10
All Cannings Pre-School 01380 860 761
Village Hall, The Street, All Cannings, Devizes, SN10 3PA
2-5yrs. 9.15am-12.45pm.

Bishops Cannings Pre-School 01380 860 661
The Mobile, Bishops Canning, Devizes, SN10 2LD
2-5yrs. 9-11.5am. Termtime.

Cedar House Nursery School 01380 728 385
London Road, Devizes, SN10 2DU
2-5yrs. 9am-3.30pm. Termtime.

Cheverell Old School Nursery 01380 812 418
The Old School, High Street, Great Cheverell, Devizes, SN10 5XZ
8.30am-3.15pm. Termtime.

Chirton Pips Pre-School 01380 840 684
The Street, Chirton, Devizes, SN10 3QS
9.15am-12pm. Termtime.

Devizes Pre-School Playgroup 01380 728 894
The Green, Devizes, SN10 5AA
0-5yrs. 9am-12.30pm. 50wks.

Heathcote House Nursery School 01380 725 080
The Green, Devizes, SN10 5AA
3mths-5yrs. 8am-6pm. 50wks.

Lavington Pre-School 07730 285 998
Sandfields, West Lavington, Devizes, SN10 4HJ
2-5yrs. 9am-12pm and 12.40-3.15pm. Termtime.

Little Bears Playgroup 01380 724 044
Estcourt Crescent, Devizes, SN10 1LR
2-5yrs. 9.15-11.45am. Termtime.

S Mill School 01380 723 011
Five Lanes, Potterne, Devizes, SN10 5TE
9am-3.30pm. Termtime.

Noah's Ark Nursery School 01380 727 203
Downlands Road, Devizes, SN10 5EF
2-4yrs. 9am-3.15pm.

Potterne 'Bright Sparks' 07815 038 738
Blackberry Lane, Potterne, Devizes, SN10 5NZ
2-5yrs. 9am-12pm. Termtime.

St Barnabas Pre-School 01380 816 016
Drove Lane, Market Lavington, Devizes, SN10 4NT
2-5yrs. 9am-3pm. Termtime.

St Joseph's Nursery 07814 481 740
St. Josephs Place, Devizes, SN10 1DD
2-5yrs. 9am-3.15pm. Termtime.

Taylor Made Childcare 01380 739 039
Bath Road, Devizes, SN10 2AP
0-5yrs. 8am-6pm. 51wks.

138 education (Wiltshire postcodes)

S = SCHOOL

The Trees Day Nursery 01380 739 888
The Mews, London Road, Devizes, SN10 2DH
2-8yrs. 8am-6pm. 50wks.

Urchfont Pre-School 01380 848 444
Cuckoo Corner, Urchfont, Devizes, SN10 4RA
2-5yrs. 9am-3.15pm. Termtime.

SN11
Appletree Nursery 01249 819 082
Prince Charles Drive, Calne, SN11 8TG
2-8yrs. 8am-5.50pm. 51wks.

Buttercups Kindergarten 01249 812 231
Calstone Wellington, Calne, SN11 8PY
8am-5.30pm. Termtime.

Heddington Under 5's 01380 850 885
Paddock Farm, Stockley Road, Heddington, Calne
2-4yrs. 9.15-11.45am. Termtime.

Humpty Dumpty Pre-School 01249 811 491
Methodist Church Hall, Silver Street, Calne, SN11
9.45am-12.15pm. Termtime. 4 days.

Jack and Jill Pre-School 07970 043 775
Pratten Hut, William Street, Calne, SN11 9BD
2-4yrs. 9.15-11.45am. Termtime.

Key Day Nursery 01249 815 307
38-40 Lickhill Road, Calne, SN11 9DF
0-2yrs. 7.30am-pm. 51wks.

Rub a Dub Pre-School 01249 818 974
Lansdowne Hall, Derry Hill, Calne, SN11 9QY
9.30am-3pm. Termtime.

S St Margaret's 01249 857 220
Preparatory School
Curzon Street, Calne, SN11 0DF
3-11yrs.

SN12
S ABaCus Nursery 01225 701 742
Cottles Park, Atworth, Melksham, SN12 8NT
www.stonarschool.com
2-5yrs. 8am-6pm. Termtime.

Atworth Pre-School 07840 704 451
Village Hall, Bath Road, Atworth, Melksham, SN12
3-5yrs. 9am-12pm. Termtime.

Broughton Gifford Pre-School 07817 968 141
The Village Hall, The Street, Melksham, SN12 8PR
8.45am-12.15pm. 3 mornings. Termtime.

Broughton Road Pre-School 01225 707 594
Old Broghton Road, Melksham, SN12 8BX
9.15am-12pm and 12.30-3pm. Termtime.

Canberra Pre-School 07889 660 714
56 Spa Road, Melksham, SN12 7NY
2-5yrs. 9.15am-12pm. Termtime.

ABaCus@Stonar

ABaCus is a nursery for children from 2 - 4yrs

- **Beautiful** Scenic Location
- **Term Time & Holiday** Sessions Available
- **Hot** Lunches
- **Easily** Accessible

For Further Information Please Contact
Karen Ibbott, Stonar School, Cottles Park, Atworth, Wiltshire, SN12 8NT
Telephone: 01225 701742
Facsimile: 01225 790830
www.stonarschool.com
email: admissions@stonarschool.com

Please Quote Ref BD 1

Cloverlead Day Nursery 01225 791 742
19 Lancaster Road, Bowerhill, Melksham, SN12
3mths-5yrs. 8am-6pm. 50wks.

Cloverleaf Day Nursery 01225 707 220
160 West Hill, Whitley, Melksham, SN12 8RD
3mths-5yrs. 8am-6pm. 50wks.

Forest Methodist Nursery 01225 705 351
Forest Road, Melksham, SN12 7AA
2-5yrs. 8.30am-3.30pm.

Kingfisher Nursery 01225 790 296
2 Kingfisher Drive, Bowerhill, Melksham, SN12 6FJ
2-5yrs. 9.30am-1pm. Termtime.

Page One Nursery 07977 260 456
St. Michael's Church Hall, Church Street, Melksham,
9am-3pm. Termtime.

Queensway Chapel Pre-School 01225 351 922
Queensway, Melksham, SN12 7LQ
0-8yrs. 8am-6pm. 51wks.

Rocking Horse Nursery 01225 700 894
The Old Brewery House, Bath Road, Shaw, Melksham
0-8yrs. 8am-6pm. 51wks.

Seend Playgroup 07803 403 356
Irene Usher Pavilion, Rusty Lane, Seend, Melksham, SN12
2-5yrs. 9-11.45am and 12-2.30pm.

S = SCHOOL (Wiltshire postcodes) **education**

Snapdragons Atworth 01225 707 009
Prospect Farm, Atworth, Melksham, SN12 8JW
7.30am-6.30pm. 51wks.

Snapdragons Sandridge 01225 899 488
3 St. Margarets Gardens, Melksham, SN12 7BT
8am-6pm. 51wks.

S Heywood Preparatory School 01249 713 379
The Priory, Priory Street, Corsham, SN13 0AP
3-11yrs.

Magic Dragon Nursery 01225 744 892
The Cricket Pavilion, The Recreation Ground, Corsham,
8am-6pm. 51wks.

Neston Pre-School Playgroup 01225 811 299
Village Hall, Pool Green, Neston, Corsham, SN13
2-5yrs. 9.15-11.45am. Termtime.

Rudloe Pre-School 07970 323 131
Broadwood Avenue, Rudloe, Corsham, SN13 0LX
9am-3pm.

SN14

Leapfrog Day Nursery 01249 463000
Bath Road, Chippenham, SN14 0FL
3mths-5yrs. 7am-7pm. 52 wks (see ad pg 124).

Azimghur Tots Pre-School 01225 745 323
Azimghur Barracks, North Colerne, Chippenham, SN14 8QY
1-8yrs. 9.15am-12pm. Termtime.

S Grittleton House School 01249 782 434
Grittleton House, Grittleton, Chippenham, SN14
2-5yrs. 9am-3.20pm. Termtime.

Happy Caterpillars Pre-School 07762 113 030
The Street, Hullavington, Chippenham, SN14 6EF
9.10am-12.10pm. Termtime.

Moonbeams 01249 652 363
Kingsley Road, Chippenham, SN14 0AS
3-5yrs. 9.10-11.40am and 12.20-2.50pm.

North Wraxall Pre-School 01225 891 550
The New Hall, North Wraxall, Chippenham, SN14
2-4yrs. 4mornings. Termtime.

Yatton Keynell Under 5's 01249 783 185
Village Hall, Biddestone Lane, Chippenham, SN14
2-5yrs. 9.15am-12.15pm. Termtime.

SN15

Benger Bears 07791 896 683
Village Hall, Chestnut Road, Chippenham, SN15 4RP
3-4yrs. 9am-3pm.

Brinkworth Butterflies 07814 567 960
Village Hall, Brinkworth, Chippenham, SN15 5AF
2-5yrs. 9.30am-12.15pm. 4 mornings. Termtime.

Bromham Pre-School 01380 720 283
Social Centre, New Road, Bromham, Chippenham,
3-4yrs. 9.30am-1pm.

Busy Bees Nursery 01249 444 371
Lowden Avenue, Chippenham, SN15 1LH
2-5yrs. 8.30am-3.30pm. Termtime.

Dodford Farm Nursery 01249 891 349
Dodford Farm House, Dodford Lane, Christian Malford, Chippenham, SN15 4DE
0-5yrs. 8am-6pm. 51wks.

Happy Days Nursery 07971 106 479
St. Paul's Church Hall, Malmesbury Road, Chippenham, SN15 1QA
2-5yrs. 9.15am-2.45pm. Termtime.

Key Day Nursery School 01249 653 547
47-49 London Road, Chippenham, SN15 3AJ
0-5yrs. 8.30am-5.30pm. 50wks.

Little Albert's Pre-School 01249 896 440
24-26 Teal Avenue, Lyneham, Chippenham, SN15
2-5yrs. 9-11.5am and 12.30-3.20pm. Termtime.

Little Alberts Pre-School 01249 890 381
24 Teal Avenue, Lyneham, Chippenham, SN15
9am-12pm and 12.30-3.20pm. Termtime.

Lodge Farm Nursery 01249 750 210
Malmesbury Road, Kington St. Michael, Chippenham, SN15 5PY
8am-6pm. 51wks.

Lyneham Village Pre-School 01249 891434
Preston Lane, Lyneham, Chippenham, SN15 4QJ
2½-5yrs. 9-11.45am and 12.45-3.30pm. Termtime.

Minnows Pre-School 01249 465 432
St Andrew's Church, Market Place, Chippenham
2-5yrs. 9.30am-12pm. Termtime.

New Road Nursery 01249 652 004
37 New Road, Chippenham, SN15 1HP
0-5yrs. 51wks.

Seagry Playgroup 07773 011 321
Village Hall, Upper Seagry, Chippenham, SN15
2-5yrs. 9.15am-12.15pm.Termtime.

St Mary's Nursery 07702 416 484
Rowden Hill, Chippenham, SN15 2AH
9am-2.35pm. Termtime.

Walter Powell Pre-School 01249 263 909
Dauntsey Road, Great Somerford, Chippenham
3-5yrs. 9.15am-12.15pm. 39wks.

Wiltshire College Pre-School 01249 465 308
9 Wiltshire College, Cocklebury Road, Chippenham
2-5yrs. 8.50am-4.30pm. Termtime.

140 education (Wiltshire postcodes) S = SCHOOL

Salisbury Cathedral School

where boys and girls play together

Mother & Toddler Group
Pre - Prep from 3 years
Prep School up to 13 years

27 acres in the heart of the city of Salisbury

Telephone 01722 555300 for a prospectus

www.salisburycathedralschool.com

Wise Owls Pre-School 07984 386 948
The Manor Room, The Village Hall, Chippenham,
3-5yrs. 33wks.

SN16
Busy Hands Pre-School 01666 840 952
Sherston Village Hall, High Street, Malmesbury
2-5yrs. 9.15-11.45am. Termtime.

Cross Hayes Pre-School 07884 284 897
Malmesbury Town Hall, Cross Hayes, Malmesbury
2-5yrs. 9.15am-1.15pm. Termtime.

Crudwell Pre-School 01666 577 764
Village Hall, Crudwell, Malmesbury, SN16 9SS
2-5yrs. 9.15am-12pm. Termtime.

King's Day Nursery 01666 824 987
4 Silver Street, Malmesbury, SN16 9BU
0-5yrs. 7.30am-6.30pm. 51wks.

Malthouse Nursery 01666 825 227
Charlton Park, Malmesbury, SN16 9DG
9.15am-3pm. 36wks.

Noah's Ark Day Nursery 01666 840 105
Firlea, Tetbury Road, Sherston, Malmesbury, SN16
0-5yrs. 7.45am-6pm. 50wks.

Rainbow Nursery 01666 575 081
Chelworth Manor Farm, Chelworth, SN16 9SG
9.15am-3pm. Termtime.

St Mary's Pre-School 07714 109 235
St. Mary's Hall, The Triangle, Malmesbury, SN16
2-5yrs. 9.30am-2pm. Termtime.

SN25
Leapfrog Day Nursery 01793 726 919
Highdown Way, St.Andrews Ridge, Swindon, SN25
0-5yrs. 7am-7pm. 50wks (see ad pg 124).

Princess Christian Day Nursery 01793 702 233
Elstree Way, Abbeymeads, Swindon, SN25 4YX
0-5yrs. 8am-6pm. 52wks (see ad pg 124).

Haydon Meadow Pre-School 01793 706 696
The Haydon Centre, Thames Avenue, Swindon, SN25
3-4yrs. 9-11.30am and 12.15-2.45pm. 39wks.

Learning Tree Pre-School 07876 735 206
St. Andrews Methodist Church, Swindon, SN25
3-5yrs. 9.15-11.45am and 12.30-3pm. Termtime.

Little Scholars 01793 762 037
Hugo Drive, Abbey Meads, Swindon, SN25 4GY
3-5yrs. 9-11.30am and 12-2.30pm. 35wks.

Little Sunshine Pre-School 07940 510 840
Church of Christ the Servant, Abbey Meads Village
Centre, Elstree Way, Swindon, SN25 4YX
3-5yrs. 9-11.45am and 12.30-3.15pm. Termtime.

Moredon Pre-School 01793 434 155
1 The Street, Moredon, SN25 3ER
2-5yrs. 9.15-11.45am and 1-2.30pm. Termtime.

St John's Pre-School 07879 623 507
Thames Avenue, Haydon Wick, Swindon, SN25
2½-5yrs. 9.15-11.45am and 12.45-2.45pm. Termtime.

SN26
Blunsdon Nursery School 01793 721 451
Village Hall, High Street, Blunsdon, SN26 7AR
9am-12pm. 35wks.

SP1
Leapfrog Day Nursery 01722 417 272
London Road, Salisbury, SP1 3YU
0-5yrs. 7am-7pm. 51wks (see ad pg 124).

S Salisbury Cathedral 01722 555 300
School Nursery
The Old Palace, 1 The Close, Salisbury, SP1 2EQ
www.salisburycathedralschool.com
3-13yrs.

S Chafyn Grove School 01722 333 423
Bourne Avenue, Salisbury, SP1 1LR
3-13yrs.

First Steps Day Nursery 01722 410 456
41 Brown Street, Salisbury, SP1 2AS
1-8yrs. 8am-6pm. 51wks.

Please say you saw the listings in the
South West Baby Directory

S = SCHOOL   (Wiltshire postcodes) *education*

S Godolphin Prep School   01722 430 652
Laverstock Road, Salisbury, SP1 2RB
Girls. 3½-11yrs.

Griffin School   01722 416 82
154 Castle Road, Salisbury, Salisbury, SP1 3SA
2-5yrs. 8am-7pm. 51wks.

S La Retraite Swan   01722 333 094
19 Campbell Road, Salisbury, SP1 3BQ
Co-ed. 2½-16yrs.

Ladybird Pre-School   07951 919 737
St. Francis Church Hall, Beatrice Road, Salisbury
3-5yrs. 9.15am-12pm. 39wks.

S Leaden Hall School   01722 334 700
70 The Close, Salisbury, SP1 2EP
Girls. 3-11yrs.

York House Nursery   01722 324 008
31 New Street, Salisbury, SP1 2PH
0-5yrs. 8am-6pm. 51wks.

SP2
Kingfisher Montessori   07702 815 894
South Street, Wilton, Salisbury, SP2 0JS
2-yrs. 9am-3pm. Termtime.

Little Fishes Day Nursery   01722 503 777
Dews Road, Salisbury, SP2 7SN
3mths-5yrs. 8am-6pm. 51wks.

Manor Farm House Nursery   01722 743 978
Netherhampton, Salisbury, SP2 8PU
2-5yrs. 8.30am-3pm. Termtime.

South Hills Nursery School   01722 744 971
Home Farm Road, Wilton, Salisbury, SP2 8PJ
0-8yrs. 8am-6pm. 36wks.

Toybox Day Nursery   01722 336 262
Odstock Road, Salisbury, SP2 8BJ
0-5yrs. 7am-6pm. 51wks.

SP3
Dinton Pre-School   01722 716 011
Park Farm, Teffont, Salisbury, SP3 5RR
2-4yrs. 9.15-11.45am and 12.15-2.45pm. Termtime.

Hindon Childrens Centre   01747 820 260
Hindon School, School Lane, Hindon, SP3 6EA
2-5yrs. 9am-1pm. Termtime.

Little Steeple People   07810 661 522
The Mobile Classroom, Steeple Langford School,
Steeple Langford, Salisbury, SP3 4NQ
2-4yrs. 9-11.30am. Termtime.

Shrewton Pre-School   07946 575 866
High street, Shrewton, Salisbury, SP3 4DB

St Thomas A Becket Nursery   01980 621 194
Tilshead, Salisbury, SP3 4RZ
2-5yrs. 9am-12pm. Termtime.

Tisbury Community Pre-School   07815 648 068
Elizabeth Hall, Park Road, Tisbury, Salisbury, SP3
2-5yrs. 9.15am-12pm. Termtime.

Wardour Pre-School   07790 930 494
Wardour, Tisbury, Salisbury, SP3 6RF
3-5yrs. 9am-12.15pm. Termtime.

SP4
Acorns Nursery School   01980 652 107
25 Stonehenge Road, Durrington, Salisbury, SP4
2-5yrs. 9.15am-12pm and 1-3.30pm. Termtime.

Airfield Camp Pre-School   01980 678 259
Netheravon, Salisbury, SP4 9SF
2.9-5yrs. 9am-12pm. Termtime.

Allington Pre-School   07817 761 238
Newton Tony Memorial Hall, Newton Tony,
Salisbury, SP4 0HF
3-5yrs. 9.30am-12pm and 12.30-3pm. 39wks.

Amesbury Pre-School   07749 826 503
High Street, Amesbury, Salisbury, SP4 7ET
u5's 9am-12pm. Termtime.

S Avondale School   01980 632 387
High Street, Bulford, Salisbury, SP4 9DR
3-11yrs. 8.40am-12pm. 36wks.

Boscombe Down Chipmunks   01980 663 938
Families Activities Centre, Boscombe Down,
Amesbury, Salisbury, SP4 0JF
1-3yrs. 9.15am-12pm. Termtime.

Durley Nursery   01980 623 563
71 London Road, Amesbury, Salisbury, SP4 7EQ
3-5yrs. 4 mornings. 9am-3pm. Termtime.

Durrington Pre-School   0781 062 8135
High Street, Durrington, SP4 8AD
2yrs 9mnths –5yrs. 9.15-11.45am. Termtime.

Hickory House Nursery   01980 612 634
HPA, Porton Down, Salisbury, SP4 0JG
0-5yrs. 8.15am-5.30pm. 51wks.

Little Orchards Pre-School   01722 782 878
Village Hall, Middle Woodford, Salisbury, SP4 6NR
9am-1pm. Termtime.

The Avon Playgroup   01980 670 207
Phoenix Hall, Hight Street, Netheravon, Salisbury
2-5yrs. 9am-12pm. Termtime .

The Haig Day Nursery   01980 672 331
The Haig Centre, Ward Road, Bulford, SP4 9NJ
3mths-5yrs. 8am-6pm. 51wks.

142 education

S = SCHOOL

Teddies Nurseries, part of BUPA, is one of the UK's leading providers of quality nursery care. Teddies provide nurturing care for children aged three months to school age.

- Qualified, experienced and caring staff
- Foundation stage curriculum
- Healthy menus, freshly prepared each day
- Fees include pampers, nappy cream, bottles, formula baby milk and free settling in sessions
- All registered parents can feel better with the reassurance of the free 24hr BUPA HealthLine providing medical advice 365 days a year

Open 8am-6pm flexible hours Mon-Fri

"Over 85% of the parents who view our nurseries choose Teddies childcare"

For more information please visit **www.teddiesnurseries.co.uk** or call **0800 980 3801**

BUPA Childcare

Teddies Nurseries

Your child at the heart of our care

SP5

Alderbury Pre-School   01722 711 226
School Hill, Alderbury, Salisbury, SP5 3DR
2-4yrs. 9.15am-2.45pm. Termtime.

Bright Sparks Nursery School   01722 781 069
Ebbesbourne Wake Village Hall, Ebbesbourne Wake, Salisbury, SP5 5JF
2-5yrs. 9am-3pm. Termtime.

Downton Community Pre-School   01725 511 178
The Band Hall, 28-30 Gravel Close, Downton, Salisbury
2½-5yrs. 9.30am-12.30pm. Termtime.

Lover and Redlynch Pre-School   01725 510 295
School Road, Lover, Salisbury, SP5 2PW
35wks.

Nomansland Pre-School   01794 390 108
Methodist Chapel, Forest Road, Nomansland, Salisbury, SP5 2BP
2-5yrs. 9.30am-1pm. Termtime.

S Norman Court   01980 862 345
West Tytherley, Salisbury, SP5 1SY
3-13yrs.

S Sandroyd   01725 516 264
Rushmore, Tollard Royal, Salisbury, SP5 5QD
7-13yrs.

Windrush Nursery   01794 884 888
2 Windrush Cottages, West Dean, Salisbury, SP5
2-5yrs. 9.15am-3pm. Termtime.

Winterslow Pre-School   01980 863 337
Village Hall, Midleton Road, Winterslow, Salisbury
3-4yrs. 9.15am-12pm. Termtime.

Semley Montessori Nursery   07971 423 299
Semley, Shaftesbury, SP7 9AU
2-5yrs. 9am-12.10pm. Termtime.

SP9

Caterpillas Pre-School   01980 602 460
Nadder Road, Tidworth, SP9 7QN
9.15am-12.15pm and 12.30-3pm. Termtime.

Poppies Day Care Nursery   01980 844 310
Tidworth College, Ordnance Road, Tidworth, SP9
0-5yrs. 8am-5.30pm. 50wks.

St Andrews Pre-School   01980 602 539
1-2 St. Andrews Road, Tidworth, SP9 7EP
2-5yrs. 9.15am-1.15pm. Termtime.

SP11

Ludgershall Pre-School   01264 790 999
Short Street, Ludgershall, Andover, SP11 9RB
2-5yrs. 9-11.30am and 12.15-2.45pm. Termtime.

toddler activities

As every mother will know, idle little hands and minds need channelling. A mix of physical and creative activities will help develop confidence, co-ordination, concentration, creativity and individual skills, Our listings will give you loads of inspiration and guide you to the multifarious classes, clubs and centres that abound. For active kids, we list gym clubs, dance classes, swimming classes, football and more; for creative youngsters there are arts and crafts clubs, drama classes, musical activity groups and ceramic cafes. Add a soupçon of French language here and a shot of football there, and your toddler will be the most accomplished in town

toddler activities

Age Range	Activity ideas and when to introduce them
First **6** weeks	Lots of **physical contact**, **gentle voices**, **faces** to look at.
6 weeks to **3** months	Put toys within **touching** distance; use **bouncing** chairs; **massage**; **stretching** exercises and kicking; holding **rattles** (soft so they don't bash themselves); and **rolling** over onto tummy. Encourage baby **babble** by repeating the sounds they make/peek-a-boo.
3 months to **6** months	Looking at picture **books**, **sitting** and **bouncing** on your knee, introduce an **activity mat** with dangling toys with interesting textures/colours; if good head control introduce **baby bouncers**. Start socialising within **music** groups (see pg 153) and **baby swimming** (see pg 154).
6 months to **10** months	Encourage **sitting** up with support and getting more **active** (see gym groups on page 148). Provide interestingly shaped **objects** (ie keys that rattle) and encourage **passing** from one hand to another. Introduce **signing actions** with songs.
10 months to **1** year	Practise **waving bye-bye** and **clapping hands**; encourage use of **finger** and **thumb** to pick up small objects (such as string attached to a toy); encourage **standing up** with your support; **dropping** things and seeing where they go; **filling** and **emptying** containers.
1 year to **18** months	First real **words** appear at this stage so continue with nursery rhymes; play with **sand** and **water**; **copying** games (such as making faces in a mirror); introduce push-along toys, **ball** throwing, **stacking** bricks and shape **sorting**; begin to **stand** and **walk** or **cruise** between furniture.
18 months to **2** years	Provide **ride** on toys; go **climbing** and **sliding** in the playground or in indoor activity playcentres (see pg 148); jigsaws (lift-out and inset); introduce **playdough** (see our recipe opposite); encourage **colouring** and continue going to **music** clubs.
2 years to **3** years	Introduce ball games such as **football** or **skittles** (and emphasise **taking turns**); help with **construction** toys; encourage **sentences** and **remembering songs**; develop **turning** one page at a time whilst **reading books**. Practise **cutting** out with scissors.
3 years to **5** years	Hold a **crayon** between **first two fingers and thumb** and draw **shapes** not scribble; encourage **dressing up** (see pg 27) and **make believe**. Introduce **numbers** and **letters** (particularly in their name); try **listening games** or **cooking** (eg decorating biscuits); encourage **swimming** without aids; start **dance**, **drama** classes or **foreign** language clubs.

toddler activities   145

art and crafts
Check out these websites for lots of good art and craft projects that you can do at home.

Messy Monsters 0161 798 4518
www.messymonsters.co.uk
Messy Monsters has launched, and will be launching more, art and craft clubs for babies and children over the next 12 months. If you would like to see if they have a club near you, or you are interested in starting one yourself then check out their website or call for an information pack. They have lots of good craft materials for sale for home use as well.

Preschool Express
www.preschoolexpress.com
We love this site which is a US on-line activity newsletter for parents and grandparents of preschool children. It has daily suggestions of easy to do craft activities (themed seasonally), plus a very helpful "pattern station" which are shapes that you can print out and use for the projects. It then has lots of suggestions for activities with the shapes.

Mucky Pups 01625 537 219
www.muckypups.com
Another online site for toddlers to paint, stick, make craft projects, use play and salt dough, create with food, and cut & colour.

ceramic cafés
Ceramic cafés are definitely a place to visit with children. They can have great fun decorating some pottery, or you can get a momento plate/mug of your baby's hand or foot print. Great creative party venues too

All Fired Up Ceramic Café 01473 286 142
www.allfiredupceramics.co.uk
Check out these ceramic Christening plates which can be ordered mail order from anywhere in the UK. They send you the plate and appropriate paints for the feet, with Godparents and family writing their own messages - which are then glazed and fired (with any other hand painted designs added) and sent back to you.

CORNWALL
Kennack Pottery 01326 290 592
Kennack Sands, TR12 7LX

DEVON
Cardew Teapottery 01626 832 172
Newton Road, Bovey Tracey, TQ12 9DX

Clay Art 01752 665 565
57 Southside Street, The Barbican, Plymouth, PL1
www.clayart.co.uk

Devon Ceramics 01803 860 900
Station Road, Totnes, TQ9 5JR
www.china-blue.co.uk

Playdough
The texture of playdough is fascinating for toddlers of about 18mths. But if your shop bought playdough has hardened you can rustle up your own from our recipe below. Initially kids will need to be shown how to squeeze and squash it into recognisable shapes – and later you can provide implements for cutting. It's also a useful activity if you are in the kitchen cooking and they want to copy you.

Recipe
- 2 x teaspoons cream of tartar
- 1 x cup plain flour
- 1 x tablespoon oil
- 1 x cup water

Mix to form a smooth paste. Put in a saucepan and cook slowly, until the dough comes away from the side of the pan and forms a ball. When cool enough knead the dough for 3-4 minutes. When not in use keep in an airtight container in the fridge. Food colouring can be added to the water or the dough for colour variety.

Poole Pottery 01202 666200
The Quayfront, Poole, BH17 7PP
This pottery café has no studio fee and you can bring your baby to the "have a go" area for putting hand or footprints onto plates and mugs. Prices are fromo ££6.00 including posting the item when ready. Open 9am-3.30pm Mon-Sun.

GLOUCESTERSHIRE
Paint-a-Pot 01453 835 043
5 Cossack Square, Nailsworth, GL6 0DB
Enjoy coffee and cake whilst you select from a large range of ceramic shapes. Tues-Thurs 9.30-5pm and Sat/Sun 9.30am-6pm.

SOMERSET
Brush & Bisque-It 01749 880 045
The Mill House, Alhampton, Shepton Mallet, BA1
www.brushandbisque-it.com

Crock a Doodle Do 01225 442 700
78 Walcot Street, Bath

Glaze n Shine 01173 301 382
252 Soundwell Road, Kingswood, BS15 1PN

Inspiration 01454 313 011
4 Beaufort Mews, 7 Horse Street, Chipping Sodbury

toddler activities

WILTSHIRE
Master Plaster Casters　　01793 855 850
Studley Grange Craft Village, Wroughton
www.studleygrange.co.uk

Splash of Colour　　01722 322 250
72 Fisherton Street, Salisbury, SP2 7RB
Very popular ceramic café open daily, Mon-Fri 10am-5.30pm (Wed until 2pm) and Sat/Sun 11-3pm. Highly recommend booking during weekends and during school holidays. One off studio fee ££3.50 which includes the glazing and firing of all items.

circus schools

SOMERSET
Circus Bugz　　0117 947 7042
Office 8a, Kingswood Foundation, Britannia Road, Kingswood, Bristol, BS15 8DB
www.circusmaniacs.com
Circus Bugz is a special Introductory Circus Skills Training Programme designed for pre-school children.

clubs

Girl Guides Association　　020 7834 6242
www.guides.org.uk
Rainbows 5-7yrs, Brownies 8-12yrs. Parents interested need to put their child on a waiting list when they are 2-3yrs old. Call 0800 169 5901 for contact details of the local branch.

Scouts Association　　0845 300 1818
Bury Road, London, E4 7QW
Beaver Scouts 6-8yrs, Cubs 8-10yrs.

cooking

Sticky Mitts　　0870 240 6892
www.stickymitts.co.uk
Inspiring cookery courses you can do at home with your children.

SOMERSET
Kids in the Kitchen　　01225 832 105
220 Old Frome Road, Combe Down, Bath, BA2
5-14yrs

Monkton Combe School Enterprises　　01225 721116
Monkton Combe, Bath, BA2 7HG
Holiday workshops for children aged 6yrs+.

Quartier Vert　　0117 904 6679
85 Whiteladies Road, Clifton, BS8
www.quartiervert.co.uk
School holiday and weekend workshops for children aged 7yrs+ including just one hour look, learn and taste workshops which encourages children to taste and think about produce in season followed by hands-on cookery. Children get to take home what they have made.

dance

Most ballet classes are for children from $2^{1}/_{2}$ yrs-3yrs or 'out of nappies' and are great for posture, co-ordination and for graceful confidence. Some children will progress to professional ballet schools, but many more will experience dance as a pleasure and a cherished childhood memory. It will also encourage an appreciation of dance throughout adult life

Stagecoach　　01932 254 333
www.stagecoach.co.uk
Stagecoach, Britain's largest part-time theatre school, offers drama, dance and singing tuition at weekends to young performers from 4-16. Skills for life not just for the stage are on offer to all young people with an interest in the performing arts whatever their ability - there is no audition to join. There are over 500 Stagecoach schools throughout the UK. For further details about your nearest one and for information about holiday workshops please call freephone 0808 087 8243 for your nearest school (see inside front cover).

Royal Academy of Dance　　020 7326 8000
36 Battersea Square, London, SW11
www.rad.org.uk
The RAD is an internationally recognised body for teaching, training and setting an exam syllabus for classical dance. Teachers who qualify can apply for membership, and parents can send an sae or request an email of local teachers.

Imperial Society of　　020 7377 1577
Teachers of Dancing
www.istd.org.uk
Find out about modern, jazz or tap dancing in your area.

International Dance Teachers　　01273 685 652
www.idta.co.uk

CORNWALL
Saltash & Geraldine Lamb
Dance School　　01752 843 513
Bredon, Lower Port View, Saltash, PL12
www.geraldinelambdance.co.uk

The Purple Dance Studio　　01726 882 625
Parkengear Farm, Probus, Truro, TR2
www.FreeWebs.com/jenniemusgrove

Liz Nolan Dance School　　01736 752 833
21 Gwel Trencrom, Trelissick Fields, Hayle, TR27
Ballet from 3yrs+.

Jason Thomas Dance　　01872 262 358
32 Edward Street, Truro, TR1
www.jasonthomasdance.co.uk
Ballet classes from 21/2yrs in Truro, St Ives, Lanner, Ladock and Mount Hawke. Boys are particularly welcome.

toddler activities 147

DEVON
Dunsford School of Dancing 01392 811 322
2 Darnaford Cotts, Longdown, Exeter, EX6 7BB
www.dunsfordschoolofdancing.co.uk

Sally Gray School of Dance 01392 424 073
20 Moorland Way, Exwick, Exeter, EX4 2ET

Joanne Mardon Dance 01392 824 492
23 Eager Way, Exminster, Exeter, EX6 8TJ

Janet Moon Academy of Dancing 01803 521806
72 Falcon Park, Totnes Road, Paignton, TQ4 7PZ

DORSET
Blackwell Dance Academy 01202 723 640
3 Mount Road, Parkstone, Poole, BH14 0QW

Bridport School of Dancing **01308 427769**
9 Barrack Street, Bridport, DT6 3LJ
Join the Teddy Bear's club and enjoy an hour of Teletubbies, Birdie dance, Hokey Cokey, Nellie the Elephant, Can-Can, disco and lot's more to encourage movement to music and inspire confidence (from 2yrs+).

Julie Adams Stage School 01202 511 916
112 Haviland Road Boscombe Bournemouth BH7

The Elite Academy Of Dance 01202 891 956
12 Medway Road, Ferndown, Dorset, BH22 8UX

GLOUCESTERSHIRE
Hillary Saxby School of Dance 01242 251206
St Christoper's Church Hall, Salisbury Avenue, Warden Hill

Step n Style Dance Group 01452 613 294
42 Oakwood Drive, Hucclecote, Gloucester, GL3

**Steve Holmes
School of Dance** 01453 791 206
48 Devereaux Crescent, Ebley, Stroud, GL5 4PU

Wingfield School of Ballet 0117 9503916
The Pembles, Fishpool Hill, Brentry, S. Glos

SOMERSET, BRISTOL & BATH
Susan Hill School of Dancing 01761 432 607
8 Bristol Road, Radstock, Bath, BA3 3EE

Davies School of Dance 01934 521338
12 The Hedges, St Georges, Weston Super Mare, BS22 www.davies-school-of-dance.co.uk
Classes held in Clevedon, Portishead, Nailsea, Burnham and Worle.

The Elite Dance Company 0117 960 7998
184 Dunridge Lane, St George, Bristol, BS5 8SX

Nicky Jenks School of Dance 01823 660 931
45 Tonehill, Wellington

South West School of Dance 01225 834 534
The Fitness Factory, 3 The Tanyard, Leigh Road, Street, BA16 0HD

WILTSHIRE
Florian School of Dance 01794 388 932
3 Old Iron Foundry, King's Somborne, **SO20 6RP**
www.floriandance.com

Salisbury Dance Studios 01722 329 007
15 Wilton Road, Salisbury, SP2 7ED
www.salisburydancestudios.co.uk

Sullivan School of Dance 01793 872 682
9, Elm Grove, Nine Elms, Swindon, SN5 5PG

Tanwood School 01793 523 895
Dowling St, Swindon, SN1 5QZ
www.tanwood.co.uk

drama

If you already have a drama queen (or king) in the family, you might as well capitalise on any natural talents. These drama groups offer a small range of activities for the 3yrs+ which are fun, confidence-building, and increase co-ordination and concentration

NATIONAL
Stagecoach 01932 254 333
www.stagecoach.co.uk
Stagecoach, Britain's largest part-time theatre school, offers drama, dance and singing tuition at weekends to young performers from 4-16. Skills for life not just for the stage are on offer to all young people with an interest in the performing arts whatever their ability - there is no audition to join. There are over 500 Stagecoach schools throughout the UK. For further details about your nearest one and for information about holiday workshops please call freephone 0808 087 8243 for your nearest school (see ad on inside front cover).

Helen O'Grady Academy 01481 200 250
www.helenogrady.co.uk
Helen O'Grady's Drama Academy has over 37 branches across the UK for children aged 5yrs+. Check the website or call for class locations.

football

We love these mini-football groups. It seems such an obvious idea for using up all that explosive boy energy that you might think you could just go to the garden and kick a ball around. Well, there's more to these classes than you imagine. Firstly it's all inside, so there'll never be the disappointment of being rained off. Secondly, it's more about taking turns, working as a team, and practising what one 3yr old told us was "really tricky moves". Then there's the socialising aspects, which the pre-schoolers really appreciate - not least their dads.

toddler activities

Little Kickers   01235 833 854
www.littlekickers.co.uk
Little Kickers classes introduce pre-school children to football. The programme was developed by a group of FA qualified coaches and nursery schoolteachers. The programme is tailored to incorporate a number of early learning goals.

Socatots Bristol   07990 831 970
www.socatots.com
Socatots is the worlds first play-related football programme for children from 6mths-5yrs. Classes take place in Bath and are 40 mintues and are held during termtime and the holidays. There is a waiting list so call Robert for further details.

foreign language

Le Club Francais   01962 714036
www.leclubfrancais.com
Fun clubs for children from 3yrs+ to learn French.

El Club Espanol   01962 714 036
www.leclubespanol.com
Spanish fun clubs for children from 3yrs+. Classes throughout the UK so check their website for your local class.

La Jolie Ronde   01949 839 715
www.lajolieronde.co.uk
French for children 3-11yrs. Classes throughout the UK so check their website for your local class.

gyms : mini

DEVON
Baby Joey's & Gym Joey's   01392 253 353
Baby Joey's soft play (9-18mths), Gym Joey's 18ths - school age held at Clifton Hall Sports Centre, Belmont Road in Exeter.

DORSET
Tumble Tots (Poole)   01202 749 249
www.tumbletots.com
Lorraine Exley holds classes are held in Canford Heath, Ferndown, Poole, Southbourne, Wimborne, Winton.

GLOUCESTERSHIRE
Tumble Tots (Gloucester)   01453 886 212
www.tumbletots.com
Jackie Brown holds classes held in Longlevens, Charlton Kings, Hatherley, Abbeydale, Quedgeley and Cirencester. Call on the number above or 07974 107 779.

SOMERSET
Tumble Tots (Bath)   01225 811 579
www.tumbletots.com
Vikki Matcham holds classes held in Bath, Chippenham, Melksham and Trowbridge.

WILTSHIRE
Tumble Tots (Salisbury)   01264 394 370
www.tumbletots.com
Annette Headech holds classses in Salisbury, Andover and Thatcham.

indoor playcentres

Most centres operate a last admittance policy one hour prior to the stated closing times Perfect for rainy days or as party venues. Supervision not provided so you have to expect a few knocks. Best for girls to wear trousers as a slim-fitting skirt is a bit restrictive. Equipment includes ball pits, climbing ropes, slides and tunnels

CORNWALL
Brocklands Adventure Park   01288 321 920
West Street, Kilkhampton
www.brocklands.com
Bumper boats, slides, trampolines and ball pools. Open 10-5pm daily. Also does birthday parties.

Dweezils Adventure Centre   01326 375 847
Within Asda, Kernick Road, Penryn, TR10 9LY
Dweezils operate a creche/indoor playarea for children aged 2-5yrs in the Asda store. It is particularly good to use during termtime 10am-3pm as the weekends gets a little busier. They have specially trained nursery nurses and are ofsted registered. ££3.50 per hour.

DEVON
Fun Factory   01803 201606
59 Market Street, Torquay, TQ1 3AW

Deep Sea Adventure & Sharky's   08712 225 760
Play & Party Warehouse
Custom House Quay, Weymouth,
Indoor adventure playground and nautical history (shipwrecks) and Paint your own pottery at First 4 Art and laser shoot out from 6pm onwards.

DORSET
Gus Gorilla's Jungle Playground   01202 717 197
Poole Park, Poole, **BH15 2SF**

Serendipity Sam's   0845 450 7200
Reid Street, Christchurch, BH23 2BT
www.serendipitysams.co.uk
Indoor play venue with slides, ball pools etc in a safe and supervised evironment

Tower Park   01202 723 671
Poole, BH12 4NY

GLOUCESTERSHIRE
Fundays   01451 822 999
8 Willow Court, Bourton Industrial Park, Bourton-on-the-Water, Cheltenham, GL54 2HQ

Go Bananas   01453 769 120
Embley Wharf Mill, Stroud, GL5 4SR

Little Follies   01594 833 229
The Barn, Mile End Rd, Coleford, GL16 7QD

toddler activities

Manor Farm Estate   01367 253 821
Blakemore Park, Little London, Longhope, GL17

SOMERSET, BRISTOL & BATH
Alphabet Zoo   01179 663 366
Old Bingo Hall, Winterstoke Road, Bedminster, BS3

Castaways   01179 615 115
Bourne Chapel, Two Mile Hill Road, Kingswood, Bristol, BS15 1AJ

Explorers of the Lost World   01179 831 343
39 Brislington Hill, Brislington, BS4 5BE

Hullaballoo   01458 833 262
Silver Street, Glastonbury, BA6 8BS

Jungle Jungle   01935 433 833
4 Artillery Road, Lufton Trading Estate, Yeovil, BA22 8RP

Little Terrors   01373 453 670
4 Rawlings Mill, South Parade, Frome, BA11 1EJ

Panda-Monium   01761 419 091
The Warehouse, Pows Orchard, Midsomer Norton, BA3 2NY

Planet Kids   01179 538 538
Arena One, Brunel Way, Ashton Gate, Bristol, BS3

Playtime Magic   01823 257 722
Memorial Hall, Paul Street, Taunton, TA1 3PF

Rascals   01278 433 330
4 Fishermans Wharf, West Quay, Bridgewater, TA6

Rug Ratz   01935 476 989
Stourton Way, Yeovil, BA21 3AR
www.rug-ratz.co.uk

Sea Urchins Adventure Play   01278 78693
Pier Street, Burnham-on-Sea, TA8 1BT

The Elmgove Centre   0117 924 3377
Rumpus Room, Redland Road, Cotham, BS6 6AG
Soft play for under 7's. Mon-Fri 9.30am-1.30pm. Party hire available

WILTSHIRE
Bonkers   01793 855 566
Studley Grange Garden & Leisure Park, Hay Lane, Wroughton, SN4 9QT

Boomerang   01225 702 000
Merlin Way, Bowerhill, Melksham, SN12 6TJ
www.boomeranguk.com

Coral Cove   01380 739 944
Hopton Park, London Road, Devizes, SN10 2EY
www.coral-cove.co.uk
Soft play centre with slides and rope bridges. Separate toddler area and café. Open Mon-Thurs 9.30-6pm, Fri and Sat 9.30-7pm, Sun 10am-5pm. Price is ££3.30 for 3yrs+ and ££1 adults.

Jolly Roger Adventure   01793 522 044
Greenbridge Road, Swindon,
www.jollyrogerplay.com
Huge indoor play centre with large soft adventure play area, bouncy castles and ball pools

Jungle Jacks   01373 824 824
Headquarters Road, West Wilts Trading Estate, Westbury, BA13 4JR

leisure centres

All these leisure centres have swimming pools, including some extra warm learner pools which are perfect for babies and young children. They also offer a mixture of mini-gym groups, activity play zones and daytime creches to allow you to exercise in peace

CORNWALL
Camelford Sports Centre   01840 213 188
Dark Lane, Camelford, PL32 9UE

Carn Brae Leisure Centre   01209 714 766
Station Road, Redruth, TR15 3QS

Dragon Leisure Centre   01208 751 715
Lostwithiel Road, Bodmin, PL30 5AB

Helston Sport Centre   01326 563 320
Church Hill, Helston,

Hengar Leisure Centre   01208 850 382
St Tudy, Bodmin, PL30 3PL

Lux Park Leisure Centre   01579 342 544
Coldstyle Road, Liskeard, PL14 3HZ

Phoenix Leisure Centre   01566 772 551
Coronation Park, Launceston, PL15 9DQ

Polkyth Leisure Centre   01726 223 344
Carlyon Road, St Austell, PL25 4DB

Saltash Leisure Centre   01752 840 940
Callington Road, Saltash, PL12 6DL

Wadebridge Leisure Centre   01208 814 980
Bodieve Road, Wadebridge, PL27 6BU

DEVON
Exe Valley Leisure Centre   01884 254 221
Bolham Road, Tiverton, EX16 6SG

www.babydirectory.com

toddler activities

Exmouth Sports Centre 01395 266 381
1 Royal Avenue, Exeter, EX8 1EN

Honiton Sport Centre 01404 42325
School Lane, Honiton, EX14 1QW

Lords Meadow Leisure 01363 776 190
Commercial Road, Crediton, EX17 1ER

North Devon Leisure Centre 01271 373 361
Seven Brethren Bank, Barnstaple, EX31 2AP

Pyramids Leisure Centre 01392 253 553
Heavitree Road, Exeter, EX1 2LA

Quayside Leisure Centre 01548 857 100
Ropewalk Road, Kingsbridge, TQ7 1HH

Riverside Leisure Centre 01392 221 771
Cowick Street, Exeter, EX4 1AF

Riviera Centre 01803 299 992
Chestnut Avenue, Torquay, TA2 5LZ

South Dartmore Leisure Centre 01752 896 99
Leonards Road, Ivybridge, PL21 0SL

Torbay Leisure Centre 01803 522 240
Penwill Way, Paignton, TQ4 5JR

Torridge Sports Centre 01237 471 794
Churchill Way, Northam, Bideford, EX39 1SU

Totnes Pavillion 01803 862 992
Borough Park Road, Totnes, TQ9 5JG

DORSET

Blandford Leisure Centre 01258 455 566
Milldown Road, Blandford Forum, DT11 7DB

Ferndown Leisure Centre 01202 877 468
Cherry Grove, Ferndown, BH22 9EZ

Gillingham Leisure Centre 01747 822 026
Hardings Lane, Gillingham, SP8 4HX

Littledown Leisure Centre 01202 417 600
Chaseside, Bournemouth, BH7 7DX

Oakmead Sports Centre 01202 774 644
Duck Lane, Bournemouth, BH11 9JJ

Purbeck Leisure Centre 01929 556 454
Worgret Road, Wareham, BH20 4PH

Queen Elizabeth Centre 01202 888 208
Blandford Road, Wimborne, BH21 4DT

Rossmore Leisure Centre 01202 738 787
Herbert Avenue, Parkstone, Poole, BH12 6DT

Shaftesbury Leisure Centre 01747 854 637
Salisbury Road, Shaftesbury, SP7 8ER

Thomas Hardye Centre 01305 266 772
Coburg Road, Dorchester, DT1 2HT

Two Riversmeet Centre 01202 477 987
Stony Lane South, Christchurch, BH23 1HW

GLOUCESTERSHIRE

Bourton Leisure Centre 01451 824 024
Station Road, Bourton-on-the-water,

Bradley Stoke Leisure Centre 01454 867 050
Fiddlers Wood Lane, Bradley Stoke, BS32 9BS

Brockwood Sports Centre 01452 863 518
Mill Lane, Gloucester,

Cheltenham Leisure Centre 01242 528 764
Tommy Taylors Lane, Cheltenham

Chipping Campden Centre 01386 841 595
Cindermill Lane, Chipping Campden,

Cotswold Leisure Centre 01285 654 057
Tetbury Road, Cirencester,

Five Acres Leisure Centre 01594 835 388
Berry Hill, Coleford

Gloucester Leisure Centre 01452 396 666
Bruton Way, Gloucester

Heywood Leisure Centre 01594 824 008
Causeway Road, Cinderford,

Newent Leisure Centre 01531 821 519
Watery Lane, Newent

Patchway Sports Centre 01454 865 890
Hempton Lane, Almondsbury, BS12 4AJ

Stratford Park Leisure Centre 01453 766 771
Stratford Road, Stroud

Yate Leisure Centre 01454 865 800
Kennedy Way, Yate, BS37 4DG

Whitecross Leisure Centre 01594 842 383
Church Road, Lydney

SOMERSET

Aquasplash 01634 708000
Seaward Way, Minehead, TA24 6UT

Backwell Leisure Centre 01275 463726
Farleigh Road, Backwell, BS19 3PD

Blackbrook Pavilion 01823 333435
Blackbrook Way, Taunton

Castle Sports Centre 01823 322934
Wellington Road, Taunton,

Chilton Trinity Sports Centre 01278 429119
Chilton Street, Bridgewater, TA6 3JA

toddler activities

Churchill Sports Centre 01934 852303
Churchill Green, Churchill, BS25 5QL

Downend Leisure Centre 01454 865894
Garnett Place, Downend, BS16

Fitness Factory 01458 941941
3 The Tanyard, Leigh Road, Street, BA16 0HD

Glastonbury Leisure Centre 01458 830090
St Dunstan's School, Wells Road, Glastonbury, BA6

Goldenstones Leisure Centre 01935 474166
Brunswick Street, Yeovil, BA20 IQZ
25m pool and 12m learner pool, swimming classes for babies from 6mths

Gordano Sports Centre 01275 843942
Gordano School, Portishead, BS20 7QR

Horfield Sports Centre 0117 952 1650
Dorian Road, , Horfield, Bristol, BS7 0XW

Hutton Moor Leisure Centre 01934 635347
Hutton Moor Road, Weston Super Mare, BS22 8LY
www.pramsrus.co.uk
25 mtr pool and learner pool

King Alfred's Sports Centre 01278 786868
Burnham Road, Highbridge, TA9 3EE

Kingsdown Sports Centre 0117 942 6582
Portland Street, Kingsdown, BS2 8HL

Parish Wharf Leisure Centre 01275 848494
Harbour Road, Portishead, BS20 9DD

Robin Cousins Sports Centre 0117 982 3514
West Town Road, Avonmouth, Bristol, BS11 9GB

Scotch Horn Centre 01275 856965
Brockway, Nailsea, BS19 1BZ
Creche facilities - ring for details

Shepton Mallet Lesiure Centre 01749 346644
11 Charlton Road, Shepton Mallet, BA4 5PG

St Katherines Sport Centre 01275 373287
St Katherine's School, Pill,

Strode Sports Centre 01275 879242
Strode Way, Clevedon, BS21 6QG
25 mtr pool and learner pool

Swiss Valley Sports Centre 01275 877182
Clevedon School, Cleveon, BS21 6AH

Wellington Sports Centre 01823 663010
Corams Lane, Wellington,
Creche facilities - ring for details

Wells Sport Development Centre 01749 836222
The Blue School, Kennion Road, Wells, BA5 2NR

Whitchurch Sports Centre 01275 833911
Barnfield, , Whitchurch, Bristol, BS14 0XA

Wincanton Leisure Centre 01963 824 400
West Hill, Wincanton,

WILTSHIRE

White Horse Leisure Centre 01249 814 032
White Horse Way, Calne,

Olympiad Leisure Centre 01249 444 144
Monkton Park, Chippenham,

Springfield Sports Centre 01249 712 846
Beechfield Road, Corsham

Cricklade Leisure Centre 01793 750 011
Stones Lane, Cricklade,

Devizes Leisure Centre 01380 728 894
Southbroom Road, Devizes

Marlborough Leisure Centre 01672 513 161
Barton Dene, Marlborough,

Pewsey Sports Centre 01672 562 469
Wilcot Road, Pewsey

Five Rivers Leisure Centre 01722 339 966
Butts Hulse Road, Salisbury,

Dorcan Recreation Centre 01793 533 763
St Paul's Drive, Covingham, Swindon

Oasis Leisure Centre 01793 445 401
North Star Avenue, Swindon

Tidworth Leisure Centre 01980 847 140
Nadder Road, Tidworth,

Trowbridge Sports Centre 01225 764 342
Frome Road, Trowbridge

Warminster Sports Centre 01985 212 946
Woodcock Road, Warminster

Lime Kiln Leisure Centre 01793 852 197
Wootton Bassett

Ridgeway Leisure Centre 01793 813 280
Inverary Road, Wroughton

model agencies

ALBA 0871 717 7170
www.albamodel.info
The UK's only independent modelling advice service to the UK.
Lists genuine agencies which adhere to strict codes of practice.

Models South West 01643 862 676
Dovercourt House, High Street, Pollock, TA24 8PS
www.modelssouthwest.co.uk

toddler activities 153

music groups

Babies and children love music and singing songs and these groups and workshops are great for boosting physical, musical and emotional development, in addition to the CDs and tapes you might play at home.

British Suzuki Institute 020 7471 6780
www.britishsuzuki.org.uk
Look here to find individual musical tuition from 3yrs+.

Jazz-Mataz 01962 714 036
www.jazz-mataz.com
Fun music workshops for Under 5s to enjoy music, games and much more. Call for your local class details.

Kindermusik 01276 62407
www.kindermusik.co.uk
Kindermusik an established music and movement programme for children newborn to 7 yrs. It provides quality classes and home materials including CDs, books and instruments to continue the Kindermusik experience at home. Classes are held across Dorset, Somerset, Bath, and Wiltshire.

Youth Music 020 7902 1075
www.youthmusic.org.uk
Funding, information and advice for music projects for prenatal babies - 5yr olds.

CORNWALL

Caterpillar Music 01726 891 845
www.caterpillarmusic.com
Baby Music Sessions - Caterpillars (0-3yrs), Butterflies (18mths-4yrs) in Lostwithiel & St Austell.

Jo Jingles 01209 313 266
www.jojingles.co.uk
Baby and Toddler Music groups covering Camborne, Falmouth, Redruth, St Austell, Truro for ages 6mnths-7yrs.

Monkey Music 01208 732 12
www.monkeymusic.co.uk
Heigh Ho for 6mths-2yrs, Jiggety Jig 2-3yrs and Ding Dong 3yrs+. Classes in Bodmin, Liskeard, Newquay and Wadebridge. Classes also coming to Launceston & St Austell. Musical birthday parties can also be booked.

Sing & Sign 01209 614 783
www.singandsign.com
Sarah Curnow runs classes in Helston, Truro, St Newlyn East, Perranwell, Falmouth, Ladock and Pool.

DEVON

Sing and Sign 01404 548 829
www.singandsign.com
Classes are held in Honiton.

ATTENTION ALL PARENTS

Music, Singing, Movement for Pre-School Children aged 6 months - 5 years

* Fun music sessions with an educational slant
* Weekly themed & structured classes
* Children's Percussion Instruments
* Children's parties

Jo Jingles
THE MUSIC & MOVEMENT EXPERIENCE

Cornwall - Helston, Penzance, St Ives & Hayle
Naomi Chance - 01209 832910
Devon - Plymouth, Ivybridge & Buckfastleigh
Claire Jones - 01752 698651
Somerset & Wiltshire - Bath, Chippenham, Frome & Trowbridge
Sally Long - 01225 422638
Bristol & Surrounding Areas
Pamela MacLeod - 01454 610553
Dorset - Poole, Broadstone & Ringwood
Liz Wilson - 01202 739444

DORSET

Baby College 01202 657 677
www.babycollege.co.uk
0-3yrs activity and music groups in Poole and surrounding areas.

Boogie Bear 01935 817 378
www.boogiebear.co.uk
Music for the Under 5s in locations across Dorset.

Coda Music Centre 01425 276161
www.coda.org.uk
Chewton Farm Road, Highcliffe, Christchurch, BH23

Colourstrings Music 01305 262 806
www.colourstrings.co.uk
Termtime musci groups in Dorchester.

Dorset Rural Music School 01258 450 884
The Close, Blandford Forum, DT11 7HA
Music groups in Blandford Forum (Early Years 6mths - 3yrs and Music Workshops from 3yrs).

Jo Jingles 01202 739 444
www.jojingles.co.uk
Classes held in Poole, Broadstone and Ringwood.

Sing and Sign
www.singandsign.com
Classes held in:
• Bournemouth. 07880 720 047
• Dorchester, Blandford 01258 459 414
  and Motcombe (nr Shaftesbury).

www.babydirectory.com

toddler activities

GLOUCESTERSHIRE

Jo Jingles   01453 839 464
www.jojingles.co.uk
Baby and Toddler Music groups covering Cirencester, Stroud & Bishops Cleeve, Cheltenham.

Monkey Music   01242 890 200
www.monkeymusic.co.uk
Heigh Ho for 6mths-2yrs, Jiggety Jig 2-3yrs and Ding Dong 3yrs+. Classes in Gloucester, Bishops Cleeve, Hucclecote, Bourton on the Water & Cheltenham (Up Hatherley & Charlton Kings).

Sing and Sign   01275 830 553
www.singandsign.com
Classes held in Bristol, SW, NE and South Glos.

SOMERSET

Jo Jingles   01454 610 553
Classes held in North Bristol, Redland, Thornbury, Yate, Bradleystoks, Almondsbury and Chipping Sodbury.

Mother & Toddler Music Group   01275 818 705
Music groups by qualified nursery teacher for 2yrs and under (10am Wed) and 2-4yrs (11am Wed) in Portishead. Sessions last 40min. Please call for location details.

Sing and Sign
www.singandsign.com
Classes held in:

- Taunton and Bridgwater   01823 698 514
- Bath and Trowbridge   01225 783 737
- Frome and Midsomer Norton, Wells and Shepton Mallet.   01225 480 692
- Bristol, NW, SE and Portishead   0117 950 0017
- Bristol, SW, NE and South Glos.   01275 830 553

The Triangle Club   01749 671 131
www.tingrandle.co.uk
Music group for 3-5yr olds in Wells, every Thurs 2-2.45pm. Call for further details. Also written a book called Triangle Club - The Book of the Revolutionary Music Scheme.

WILTSHIRE

Caterpillar Music   01373 859 225
www.caterpillarmusic.com
Baby Music Sessions - Caterpillars (0-3yrs), Butterflies (18mths-4yrs) in Trowbridge, Warminster & Westbury.

Jo Jingles   01225 422 638
www.jojingles.co.uk
Classes held in Bath, Chippenham, Corsham, Keynsham, Melksham and Bradford-upon-Avon.

Music Bugs   01793 722 072
www.musicbugs.co.uk
Music Bugs provide fun and friendly music classes for bouncing babies, toddlers and pre-schoolers throughout Swindon and surrounding areas.

Tunes for Tots   07986 354 510
www.tunes4tots.blogspot.com
Music groups - Tiny Tots (5mths - walking) Toddling Tots (walking - 2yrs) Pre-school Tots (2 - 4yrs) in Bradford-on-Avon.

riding

The Pony Club   02476 698 300
www.pcuk.org
Founded in 1929 the Pony Club is the largest association for those interested in ponies and riding. There is no lower age limit for membership of the pony club and you can either join as a branch member (if you have regular access to your own pony), or as a centre member (using a riding club pony). Riding Centres affiliated to the Pony Club will be able to offer lessons, tests, own-a-pony days as well as information about pony shows. To find your nearest riding centre, you can visit the website and select your area from a drop-down list.

swimming classes

CORNWALL

Phil Goldman: 01637 850 046
private instruction
Private swimming instructor offering one to one classes from 3yrs + at the Bedruthan Steps Hotel, Maugan Porth, Nr Newquay, North Cornwall. He is an ASA Club Coach. Mobile No. 0788 682 2190.

St.Mellion International   01579 352 015
Hotel & Country Club
St Mellion, Nr Saltash, PL12 6SD
www.st-mellion.co.uk
Swimming Classes from 3 yrs, during term time. Sunday afternoons - Fun time - Wet'n'Wild session with inflatables & fountains. Call the Aero Reception on 01579 352 003.

Swim Academy for Babies   0870 240 1478
Aqualight swim academy for Babies - classes in Cornwall at various venues; The Garrack Hotel, Burthallen Lane, St Ives. The Swim Academy now attracts over 200 mothers, having started with just 8. Infants as young as 6 weeks are even mastering the art of diving.

DEVON

Aqua Joey's   01392 667 020
Northbrook Swimming Pool, Beacon Lane, Exeter
Aqua Joey's (Parent & child) - Mon 1.30pm & 2pm. Swimming classes for 3.5 yrs and above, 7 days a week, Mon-Fri from 4pm, Sat from 8.30am, Sun from 9am.

Aquarius Swim School   01271 329 750
www.aquariusswimschool.co.uk
The Aquarius Swim School runs its own tuition programme based on water safety, building confidence and basic water skills. Baby Swimming from birth takes place at the Pathfields Hydrotherapy Pool, Pathfields Special Needs School, Barnstaple - with parent in the water (max of 9 babies). From 18mths plus group sessions take place at West Buckland School, nr. Barnstaple (max of 8 children). Also offer private tuiton from 3yrs + (subject to pool availability).

toddler activities

The Original Sing and Sign
The phenomenon everyone is talking about!

Baby signing helps your baby to communicate BEFORE speech

Learn the fun way!

Traditional and original songs
Nursery rhymes
Puppet & Props
Instruments
Lots of fun!

(From 7-18months)

For details of our classes nationwide visit

www.singandsign.com

or call 01273-550587

RECOMMENDED BY EXPERTS

Or learn at home with our video/DVD

Splash Swim School   01392 660 716
www.splashswim.co.uk
The Splash Swim School offers both group and private swimming tuition, following the Little Dippers Curriculum. Classes are held at The Stable Club, Friends Provident, Winslade Park, Clyst St Mary, Exeter and The Ellen Tinkham School, Hollow Lane, Exeter and also as the Southgate Hotel, Southernhay, Exeter (member only). The classes are for 0-3yrs, 3 & 4yr olds and 5yrs + (max of 8 per group).

Swimworld Swimming Tuition   01803 845 881
Cherry Trees, 1 Broadsands Park Road, Paignton
Both group and private swimming tuition offered, taking place at the Paignton Holiday Park, Totnes Road, Paignton. Water Babes takes place on a Wednesday and is a class for babies plus parent (3mths +). The group sessions run throughout the week for 3yrs + (without parent in the water). Max of 5 children per class. Also offer one to one or one to two tuition.

The Lesley Evered Swim School   01364 723 83
www.swim-devon.co.uk
The Lesley Evered swim school aims to provide a happy and safe environment in which to teach pupils to swim and enjoy all aspects of water skills pertaining to swimming. Tuition if available from 3yrs plus with group and one to one classes available. Several pools are used for the classes - Ivybridge, Bittaford, Eddeswell Farm (Rattery) and the Totnes Leisure Centre. They use Duckling Grades 1-5 for the younger children.

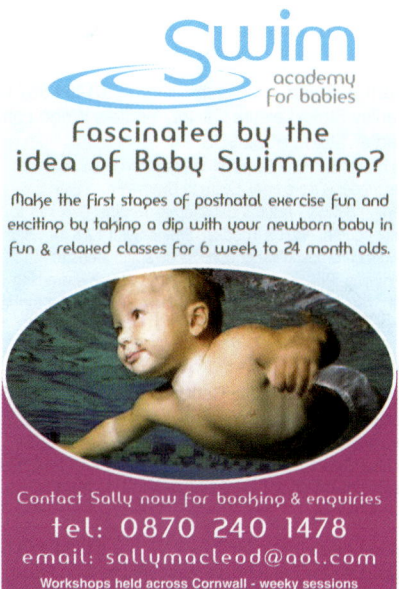

Swim academy for babies

Fascinated by the idea of Baby Swimming?

Make the first stages of postnatal exercise fun and exciting by taking a dip with your newborn baby in fun & relaxed classes for 6 week to 24 month olds.

Contact Sally now for booking & enquiries
tel: 0870 240 1478
email: sallymacleod@aol.com

Workshops held across Cornwall - weeky sessions in Falmouth, Helston & St.Ives

156 toddler activities

DORSET
Kingfisher School of Swimming   01202 383 761
Both private and group swimming tuition of children over 3yrs and also Mother & Baby water aerobics. Taking place at the Montacute School Pool, The Lodge Hill Centre, Canford Heath.

SOS School of Swimming   01202 699 451
www.sos-swim.co.uk
Swimming School but also a swimming shop stocking everything to do with swimming (costumes, nappies, floats, arm bands, towels etc). Baby classes (with adult) take place at the Splashdown Pool, Tower Park and Tuition (group & private) for 3yrs + takes place at Splashdown and also St Michael's School, Colehill, Wimborne and Talbot Combined School, Wallisdown. Classes are arranged on a termly basis (not one offs).

Swalings   08707 101 012
www.swimming-lessons.com
Infant Aquatics (2mths-3yrs) by Birthlight qualified teacher. 6 courses run per week in the Poole & Bournemouth area (various locations). Call or email for further information.

GLOUCESTERSHIRE
Aquatots   01684 296 296
www.aquatots.co.uk
Parent & Baby swimming classes for 4wks-18mths run in various locations in Gloucestershire - Bettridge School, Cheltenham - Paternoster School, Cirencester - Tewkesbury Cascades & Tewkesbury Park Hotel - Shrubberies School, Oldends Lane, Stonehouse, Stroud - Milestone School, Longford Lane, Gloucester. All teachers fully ASA qualified. Please call or visit the website for further details.

Learn to Swim   01454 867 050
Bradley Stoke Leisure Centre, Fiddlers Wood Lane, Bradley Stoke, BS32 9BS
Big Bathtime- Parent & Toddler session in small pool with toys (under 3's are free). Learn to Swim - From Birth to Starting School - Adult & Baby (up to 18mths) 6wk into to water course. Adult & Toddler(18mths-3yrs) 12 & 14 wk courses promoting water confidence & first steps to swimming. Pre-School (3-4.5yrs) Intro to basic swimming skills. Also offer one to one swimming tuition. Call for further information - 01454 867 072.

SOMERSET
Hutton Moor Leisure Centre   01934 635 347
Hutton Moor Road, Weston-Super-Mare, BS22 8LY
Parent & baby/toddler structured swimming sessions. 6-18mths Tues 10.30-11am, Wed 9.30-10am, Fri 11-11.30am. 18mths-3yrs Mon 11.30-12noon, Wed 10-11.30am, Fri 11.30-12noon.

Nikki Lopez   01934 515 522
Nikki Lopez teaches small groups of children (from 3yrs+) in various locations around Weston-super-Mare, following the ASA Award Scheme. (one to one tuition not available).

Swimfants   01935 863 169
Infant Aquatics in Yeovil - Please call for further information.

SwimStart   01454 228 102
www.swimstart.com
Swimming lessons and tuition available from pre-school age and also some baby swimming in and around the Bristol area. Call or visit the website for further information (mobile 0777 629 2813).

TeamBath Swim School   01225 383 690
www.teambath.com
Swimming classes take place in the 25m pool at Bath University, Claverton Down. Parent & Baby swimming from 6mths-2yrs and pre-school swimmin fror 2-4yrs. Call for further details.

Water Babies   0117 373 7959
www.waterbabies.co.uk
Water Babies is a national organisation with classes all over the UK. Their programme is specifically designed for babies from 0-24mths and all pools used are 30 degrees. The lessons last for ?Ω hr and the class sizes are small. Baby wet suits are also provided if necessary. The classes are all about introducing babies to water, gradually increasing water confidence, experience and understanding. They are also highly recommended for Special Needs children. The programme lasts for 1 yr and is split into terms. Classes take place in the following venues: Bristol Royal Infirmary, Marlborough St, Bristol - Freeways, Leigh Court Day Centre, Pill Rd, Abbots Leigh - Esporta, Hunts Ground Rd, Stoke Gifford - Claremont, Henleaze Park, Westbury-on-Trym - Marriott, College Green, Bristol - St Monicas Trust, Cote Lane, Westbury on Trym - The Campus, Highlands Lane, Weston Super Mare.

WILTSHIRE
The Swim Academy   01793 532 407
Parent & Toddler swimming sessions held at The Marriot Hotel, Swindon, for 2.5yrs + by ASA qualified coach (20yrs experience) or call the mobile 07718 137 702.

tennis - mini

The LTA (Lawn Tennis Association) launched mini-tennis for children aged 4yrs+ in 2000. The game consists of 3 colour-coded stages: red, orange and green (akin to traffic lights). At the first stage children play on small courts with low nets, small rackets (17") and large, foam balls. The balls bounce low and slower giving children a good chance of hitting it. There are over 770 clubs offering mini-tennis in the UK and they can be found on www.arielminitennis.co.uk.

Please say you saw the listings in
The South West Baby Directory

parties

Birthdays, for children, are synonymous with parties. And so, whether you like it or not, you will be throwing one for at least the first five years of your child's life. Fear not: here we offer enough tips, ideas and resources to make it a breeze, with listings of party entertainers, cake-makers and sources of party-bag fillers, bouncy castles and themed tableware. And if it all gets too much, you can always call in a party organiser, who will take care of the whole event

parties

First Birthdays
The first birthday party is a baptism by fire for most first-time parents. Most plan to hold it at home with family, a few friends, and not too many competing babies - as this is an excuse for grown-ups to shower your angel or urchin with adoration and gorgeous baby gifts (see pg 45). NB Presents should be targeted to delight mum rather than baby, who will invariably find the wrapping paper more interesting. The key to making the party flow is to provide lots of booze and food.

Second and Third Birthdays
A tea party at home with small tables and chairs (see party equipment) will ensure that the catering aspect of the party contains itself to one room and not your carpet. A ball pond or a few tunnels will provide plenty of excitement for 2yr olds – but remember to put away toys that you don't want to be played with (especially the favourites or new presents). Party games like "pass the parcel" don't really work at 2yrs – so you can leave that one for another year.

Things begin to get serious by the age of 3. The party needs orchestrating and guests corralling, to avoid tears and tantrums before your party fairy or Spiderman has got as far as cutting the cake. We highly recommend a musical party (see music groups on page 176).

You must plan to cater for parents as well – and make it clear whether siblings can come. We recommend that you just invite children from your child's age group otherwise you will find you have older children getting bored and running riot.

Fourth and Fifth Birthdays
If your child attends a nursery or playgroup, then you will find that this can become a whole class event - although it doesn't have to be!

Parents are not expected to stay and you can let them know what time to pick the children up afterwards. You also need space if you want to hold the party at home – so many opt for an indoor activity centre (see toddler activities), or a party venue that has a party programme pre-prepared. Themed parties with dressing up are very popular. You can also play traditional party games or try making things (see arts and crafts).

Party entertainers are in their element with 4-5yr olds. Magic, silly songs, puppets, balloon modelling, bubble machines, face painting, white rabbits, doves, snakes – all delight and entrance; and such is their popularity you need to book around 3-4 weeks ahead, particularly during festive seasons such as Christmas. Entertainers normally attend for around 2 hrs with a 45 minute session whilst you are getting the food ready, then another 45 minutes after the meal. What makes a good entertainer? Getting all the children to remain seated, fully engaged and responsive for the whole session – and they're worth every penny.

Tips from the experts
• Book your entertainer well ahead. If you haven't found a venue locally then many party organisers sometimes have a whole range at their fingertips for every postcode.

• Try and orientate parties around your child's natural mealtimes so that everyone has a good appetite. For 2-3yrs they recommend 11-1pm or 12-2pm rather than afternoons, and for 3-5yrs 12.30-2.30pm or 3.30-5.30pm.

• Don't forget to liaise with other parents if children's birthdays in the same class clash across one weekend.

• Make sure the sweet things aren't on the table before the savoury – and decide whether to put the cake in the party bag or serve it at the table. Ask parents to mention allergies before the day so you can cater accordingly.

• Party bags are one of the most popular parts to the party, but if you stick to your budget you'll be surprised how much you can find that delights the under 5s (see party supplies).

For children who find it difficult having lots of people around at the same time - don't feel compelled to invite anyone other than a best friend - or you could treat just the family with a trip to the cinema/theatre/zoo.

cakes

Nothing can beat a home-made cake topped with candy-striped candles and chocolate Smarties, but for parents who don't have the inclination or skill for home-baking, you could go with a supermarket version of Thomas the Tank Engine, or go to one of these highly recommended local bakeries for something more original (particularly good for those wanting carrot or gluten free cakes). Blow the expense, it's only once a year!

CORNWALL
Malcolm Barnecutt Bakery   01208 731 20
Carminnow Road Industrial Estate, Bodmin, PL31 1EP
www.mbarnecutt.com
Bakery with shops in Bodmin, Liskeard, Wadebridge, St Austell & Launceston - will do pretty much any sort of novely cake - Winne the Pooh, Clifford, Nemo, Scooby Doo, Woody, Postman Pat, Noddy, Pony cake, Groovy Chick etc.

parties

Cakes By Design   01736 793 260
Berwyn, Pen Porth Avenue, St Ives, TR26 1EU
www.cakes-bydesign.co.uk
Bespoke Celebration Cakes (look fantastic!) - Anything seems to be possible - Fimbles, animals, fisherman, Beefeater, Spiderman, tugboats, Christening Cakes etc. (mobile - 07947 185 302).

April's Cakes   01736 754 609
6 Chy Kensa Close, Hayle, TR27 4RR
www.aprilcakes.net
Will do any sort of cake for any occasion - Vehicles, dolls, Bob the Builder, Tweenies, football shirts, animals etc. (mobile 07813 767 071)

Simply Scrumptious   01326 564 424
c/o The Juniper Restaurant & Tearooms, Mounth Pleasant Road, Porthleven, Helston, TR13 9JS
www.simplyscrumptious.org
Specialist in Children's novelty birthday cakes - will do anything (within reason…Ö) - Harry Potter, Superman, Thomas the Tank Engine, Thunderbirds, Barbie, Trains, Aeroplanes, Boats etc. & photo cakes. (mobile - 07717 741 329.

DEVON
Tavistock Cake Craft   01822 614 256
69 West St, Tavistock, PL19 8AJ
Wide selection of childrens cakes available - dinosaur, cars, truck, mouse, bunny, cow, rugby ball, clown, train, duck, puppy…Ö.to name but a few!

Cake Box   01769 540 780
Narracott, Umberleigh, EX37 9AJ
www.devoncakebox.co.uk
Will do any sort of novelty children's cake (Thomas the Tank Engine - Tweenies etc).

Crafty Cakes   01392 210 243
104-105 Cowick Street, St Thomas, Exeter, EX4 1JE
www.craftycakes.com
Brilliant novelty birthday cakes - pretty much anything possible - have a look at the website for some ideas (Monsters Inc, Tweenies, Bob the Builder, dinosaur, racing car, speed boat, Bagpuss, farmer/tractor cake, etc

Sweet Creations   01752 691 669
7 Glanvilles Mill, Ivybridge, PL21 9PS
www.sweetcreations.co.uk
Specialist cake maker will do any sort of celebration cake, including novelty and christening cakes.

DORSET
Sheer Elegance Cakes   01202 740 404
The Studio, 9 Lincoln Road, Parkstone, Poole, BH12 2HT
www.sheerelegancecakes.co.uk
Specialist cake maker - will do anything from aeroplane, Minnie Mouse, owls, Winnie the Pooh, Bicycles, dogs, cranes, boats etc.

Patisserie Filigrana Ltd   01935 816 245
The Old House, South St, Sherborne, DT9 3LU
Makers of bespoke celebration and speciality cakes - will do anything…Ö

Anna Harley Maker of   01202 523 404
Bespoke Cakes
353 Charminster Road, Bournemouth, BH8 9QR
www.annaharley.co.uk
Any sort of novelty children's birthday cake from tigers to cars,dogs & tractors, Nemo, Thomas the Tank Engine.

Creative Cakes by Nicki   01202 672 838
9 Middle Road, Poole, BH15 3SH
www.creativecakesbynicki.co.uk
Quality cakes for any occasion by award winning cake maker - Birthday and Christening, incl. Novelty cakes. Nicki has over 18 yrs experience as a qualified pastry chef. Visit her website to see some amazing creations.

GLOUCESTERSHIRE
Cake Modern   07890 572 727
Gilberts, Gilberts Lane, Brookthorpe, Gloucester, GL4 0UB
www.cakemodern.com
Amazing range of cakes available - anything you can possibly imagine and more - sports themed, seashells, castles, ballerinas, horses, jungle, princess etc etc, Also do brilliant fairy cakes and biscuits in lots and lots of different designs and themes. Visit the website to get an idea!

Janette's Celebration Cakes   01453 886 766
35 Bluebell Rise, Chalford, Stroud, GL6 8NP
Bespoke celebration cakes - from Postman Pat, Noddy, Garfield, Taz, cricket cake, paint box, angels, ballerinas, Noah's Ark etc

Scrumptious Cakes   01594 563 033
White Cottage, The Tufts, Bream, Lydney, GL15 6HW
www.scrumptious-cakes.com
Home-made celebration cakes - all sorts of novelty children's party cakes available - Noddy, ponies, clowns, cats, Paddington Bear, Tiger, Bugs Bunny, Ninja, Spiderman, Tweenies, trains etc

A Piece of Cake   01242 694 389
4 Leyson Road, The Reddings, Cheltenham, GL51 6RU
Individually designed cakes for all occasions - teddy bears, character cakes, tractors, ballerinas, ponies, princesses, cars etc

SOMERSET, BRISTOL & BATH
Art in Icing   01935 841 660
11 Esmonde Drive, Ilchester, Yeovil, BA22 8JW
www.artinicing.co.uk
Fantastic contempory cake design - she will do almost anything or visit the website for some ideas.

www.babydirectory.com

160 parties

Sugar & Ice 01643 706 442
25 Friday Street, Minehead, TA24 5UB
www.sugarandice.co.uk
Great selection of children's novelty cakes possible - castle, car, train, truck, fire engine, hot air balloon, Postman Pat etc, visit the website to see more.

Cakes by Nessie 01225 859 881
7 Catherine Way, Bath, BA1 7NY
www.cakesbynessie.co.uk
Hugely experienced bespoke cake maker - will do virtually any sort of formal or novelty cake for any occasion.

Artistry in Sugar 01373 812 330
Woodcot, Rashwood Lane, Mells, Frome, BA11
www.o-cakes.co.uk
Quality, bespoke cakes made by hugely experience cake maker Sue O'Callaghan. Special birthday and Christening cakes. Area covered - Somerset & Wiltshire as a whole + South Gloucestershire & North Dorset.

WILTSHIRE
Ruth's Cakes of Marlborough 01672 512 933
Flat 4, Stoneking Court, George Lane, Marlborough, SN8 4PQ
Happy to do any sort of bespoke celebration cake.

Nikki Montefiore 07870 621 432
15 Wheeler Close, Pewsey, SN9 5HZ

Laurie Temple & The Party Wizard Company

Comedy magic, juggling, puppets, guitar & song, mini-disco, balloons, prizes, storytelling and games.

"Laurie is a regular favourite with all our nurseries" - A. Cook, Director Happy Child Nurseries Ltd.

"Highly Recommended" Time Out

Tel: 07951 596 240
www.thepartywizard.co.uk

---

www.nmontefiore.co.uk
Brilliant selection of handmade novelty cakes - anything from footballs, cars, tractors, balloons, unicorn, doll, spaceship, trains, chocolate house, mermaid, fairy castle etc.

Beverley's Creative Cakes 01725 513 758
53 The Borough, Downton, Salisbury, SP5 3LX
Will do 'anything that comes through the door…Ö.' - tractors, cars, castles etc etc

The Iced Lily 01793 488 732
29 Commercial Road, Swindon, SN1 5NS
www.icedlily.co.uk
Will do any sort of cake for any occasion - from Princess Castles - Winnie the Pooh.

party entertainers

Twizzle Parties & Events 020 8789 3232
www.twizzle.co.uk
Organisers of children's parties from 2yrs+, offering a range of different activities and themes for small children.

CORNWALL
Alan's Amazing Balloons 01841 540 429
Member of the magic circle and well regarded for his children's magic shows. Also does wonderful balloon animals.

Butterfingers the lady giant 07074 256 967
Based in Launceston.

Harry Kazzam 01726 723 07
Children's magic and fun games, balloons and mini-discos.

Jollity the Giant 01872 560 392
Based in Truro.

Punch & Judy Shows 01637 860 370
Based in Newquay.

DEVON
Alan Austin 01803 311 077
Magic shows, balloon animals and fun children's games. Based in Torquay.

Crackles the clown 07876 471 187
Clowns, magic, balloon modelling, goody bags and the organisation of bouncy castle hire.

Jungle Jim 01803 812 478
Wild and a bit wacky, comedy puppet shows and ventriloquism. Based in Newton Abbot.

DORSET
Ivo the Clown 01202 473 752
Ivo does a lot of children's parties in the Christchurch area - and is "very good with little ones".

Little People's Parties 01202 268 020
Fancy dress parties, party food and bags all arranged for a great, no hassle children's party.

parties

Princess Parties Based in Verwood.	01202 821 224
Puppetunes Childrens Parties Based in Bournemouth.	01202 248 659

GLOUCESTERSHIRE

Fillipo The Magical Clown Based in Gloucester.	01452 331380
Kid's Craft Parties Craft parties avilable at home. Based in Cheltenham.	07973 301 924
Laurie Temple: party wizard www.thepartywizard.co.uk Highly recommended for young children's birthday parties. Also can organise a lot of the party for you.	07951 596 240
Robert Ford: punch & judy Based in Tetbury.	01666 880 099

SOMERSET, BRISTOL & BATH

Hocus Pocus Based in Yeovil.	01935 706 701
Humble Pie Puppet Pantomime Based in Bath.	01761 435656
Kidstime Children's Parties Including face painting and mini-discos. Based in Bristol.	0117 904 5907
Mr Tricky Nicky Based in Bristol.	0117 914 1198
Mr Brown's Pig Puppets www.puppetsonline.co.uk Based in Bristol.	0117 963 4929
Magical Mandy Based in Bath.	01225 429876
Patchy Peter & Snowy Patchy Peter and snowy (his talking dog) create happy parties for all ages. Magic, balloon modelling, ventriolquism, puppets and a live white rabbit. Highly recommended.	01442 261 767
Tallulah Swirls www.tallulahswirls.co.uk Beautiful hand-crafted puppet shows based in Bristol, but will travel to Bath, Somerset, Gloucester and beyond! Lots of audience participation, singing and laughing followed by a chance for everyone to see how the show operates.	01173 774 543
Uncle Henry's Magic Puppets Based in Taunton.	01823 270 347
Wizard Prang Based in Glastonbury.	01458 834 192
Wizzo the wizard www.wizzothewizard.com Silly magic and games for children of all ages. Balloon modelling and prizes.	01179 508 312

Happy Parties for all ages
★
Balloons
★
Live Rabbit
★
Magic
★
Puppets
★
Ventriloquism

Patchy Peter & Snowy (his talking dog)

★ ★ ★

Peter Cass The magical comedian

01442 261767   patchypeter@aol.com

WILTSHIRE

Fairy Parties Based in Devizes.	01380 848 278
Kooky the Clown Based in Devizes.	01380 813 658
Smartie Pants Parties Based in Swindon.	01793 723 993
Ticklish Allsorts Based in Salisbury.	01722 744 949
Uncle John Children's Magic Based in Swindon.	01793 764 431

party equipment

CORNWALL

Fun2Bounce 01326 311 829
18 Penhale Road, Golden Bank, Falmouth, TR11 5UZ
www.fun2bounce.co.uk
Themed bouncy castles of all shapes and sizes, assault courses, party bages, bubble machine and space hopper racing - lots of fun party things. Covering West Cornwall (from St Austell to Penzance and up to Bodmin) Call for more details (mobile 07836 714 359).

parties

North Cornwall Bouncy   07779 475 837
Castle & Slide Hire
Church Square, Bodmin, PL31 2DP
www.bouncyfuncastles.co.uk
All sorts of themed bouncy castles and inflatables - slide, play pens, ball ponds. Face painting.

Big on Bouncing   01637 876 686
20 Pembroke Rd, Newquay, TR7 3HW
www.bigonbouncing.com
Lots of different bouncy castles available for hire. Also do balloons and balloon modelling, face painting and party packs.

DEVON
Funtime Leisure   01884 253 621
16 Barle Court, Tiverton, EX16 6UZ
Several different sizes of bouncy castle for hire as well as an inflatable slide. Free local delivery.

Bliss Bouncy Castles   01392 424 042
21 Fortescue Road, St Thomas, Exeter, EX2 8JZ
www.blissbouncycastles.co.uk
All sorts of inflatables for hire - themed bouncy castles - dinosaur, dalmation, circus, jungle etc, plus giant slides and ball pools. Free local delivery and collection.

Fun-Tasia Inflatables   01752 704 350
255 Blandford Road, Plymouth, PL3 6HT
www.fun-tasia.co.uk
Inflatables for hire - castles, assault course, fantasy run, circus time, jungle run, bungee run, also trampolines. Fully insured, member of BIHA. Delivery free around the Plymouth area, charge for other areas. Call for further information (website 07973 682 114)

DORSET
Little Monkeys Bouncy Castles   0800 298 5412
30 Shottford Road, Oakdale, Poole, BH15 3DU
Bouncy castles, soft play equipment (ball pond, soft slides, foam rockers) for hire. Delivery included in price. No cancellation fee applies.

Maiden Castles   01305 266 300
3 Maiden Castle Farm Cottages, Dorchester, DT2 9PR
Maiden Castles have several castles and slides available for hire, all in bright colours. They cover Weymouth, Dorchester, Portland, Bridport and Blandford. Mobile - 07855 457 522.

Castlefun   01202 535 1QT
77 Gresham Road, Charminster, Bournmouth, BH9 1QT
www.castlefun.co.uk
Covering the Bournemouth area plus a radius of about 10miles outside. They have a wide range of themed inflatables - castles, slides & games.

Castlemania   01202 693 909
4 Sharlands Close, Broadstone, BH18 8NB
www.castlemania.co.uk
Loads of themed inflatables to chose from - from Slides

(Monsters Incl, Spiderman, Dudley the Dinosaur etc) to Castles (Pirate, mermaid, Loony Tunes, Pokemon, Jungle Book, Harry Potter, Thomas the Tank). Giant games, bungee run and mini marquees. Covers Poole, Bournemouth, Blandford, Ringwood, Wareham & Verwood.

GLOUCESTERSHIRE
Dean Bouncy Castles   01594 826 112
42 Flaxley Street, Cinderford, GL14 2DH
www.deanbouncycastles.co.uk
Member of the BIHA - Large range of castles and slides in stock. Call for more details.

Cotswolds Bouncy Castles   01242 231 899
35 Albemarle Gate, Pittville, Cheltenham, GL50 4PH
www.corporateinflatables.com
All sorts of inflatables for hire - bungee run, obstacle courses, themed castles (jungle and dalmation), sumo, gladiator, slides etc. Mobile 07973 719 891.

Eazi-Up   01594 838 550
Plot 7, Forest of Dean Business Estate, Stepbridge Road, Coleford, GL16 8PJ
www.eazi-up.co.uk
Wide range of inflatables for hire - games, castles (themed), play areas, soccer, pool inflatables, slide pools, ball ponds etc. Call or visit the website for further information.

SOMERSET
Activity Bouncers   01823 451 157
Edgeborough Farm Cottage, Staplegrove, Taunton, TA2 6SP
Bouncy castles for hire in various themes plus a toddler roundabout. Don't deliver - collection only.

MacBounce   0800 093 3068
www.macbounce.co.uk
Large selection of bouncy castles or all sorts of colours, shapes and sizes, also Softplay, ball ponds, slides and an assault course. Member of BIHA.

Somerset Bouncy Castles   01935 840 003
Dunroamin, Back Lane, Ilchester, BA22 8LZ
www.somersetbouncycastles.co.uk
Big selection of inflatable castles (Clown, Winnie the Pooh, Scooby Doo etc), slides, assault course and games for indoor and outdoor use. Delivery, set-up and collection free within 10miles of Ilchester. Fancy Dress and all sorts of party bags available too. Visit the website or call for further information.

WILTSHIRE
Sky's the Limit Entertainment   01793 527 754
123 Ridge Nether Moor, Swindon, SN3 6NE
Highly recommended Wiltshire based bouncy castle hire company with 15yrs experience.

Please mention you saw the listings in the
South West Baby Directory

parties

Bouncing off the Walls   01793 771 320
46 Vasterme Close, Purton, Swindon, SN5 4EZ
www.bouncingoffthewalls.co.uk
Bouncy castles, soft play, giant games, snakes & ladders, ball pools, party tents, sports packs, and party bags, and kids karaoke.

1st Choice Bouncy Hire   01793 535 082
110 Tydeman Street, Swindon, SN2 8AU
www.1stchoicebouncyhire.co.uk
Specialise in garden sized inflatables - bouncy castles, ball pools and gladiator challenge. Member of BIHA. All covered by public liability insurance. Mobile 07798 843 359.

VB Leisure   01225 708 865
17 Lime Avenue, Melksham, SN12 6UY
www.vbleisure.co.uk
Huge variety of inflatables for hire, they are a member of the BIHA (British Inflatable Hirers Association) - Bouncy castles in all sorts of different shapes and sizes, ball ponds, bouncy slides, bouncy boxing, assault course and gladiator challenge. Many of the inflatables are covered to protect from sun and rain. Also do party invites. Delivered and collected locally - Westbury, Devizes, Calne, Chippenham, Box, Corsham, Melksham, Bradford on Avon and Trowbridge.

party shops

CORNWALL
The Party Box   01326 372 509
69 The Terrace, Penryn, TR10 8EH

Juggling Shop   01579 348 471
Station Road, Liskeard, PL14 4BX

Huff n Puff Balloons   01736 369 624
13, Barton Close, Penzance, TR18 3JA
Huff n Puff can provide any type of helium balloon and will deliver across southern Cornwall.

DEVON
Bonky Whale   01392 664 422
153 Cowick Street, Exeter, EX4 1AS

Balloons & Blossoms   01803 325 555
139 Reddenhill Road, Babbacombe, Torquay
Personalised helium balloons - for any age or even with the birthday child's name (give them a few weeks notice). Will also deliver locally.

Streamers   01548 854 742
37b Fore Street, Kingsbridge, TQ7 1PG
Small range of themed tableware as well as helium balloons and gifts for goody bags (ie bubbles, pop-up bugs, blowers).

Cohen's   01752 667 401
34 Western Approach, Plymouth, PL1 1TQ

DORSET
Lets Party   01202 723 227
327 Ashley Road, Poole, BH14 0AP
Helium balloons (both laytex and foil), tableware in themed ranges such as Old Macdonald, under the sea, pirates, princesses and a good selection of goody bag gifts - parachute men, bubbles, crayons, chalks etc.

Party in Style   01202 764 821
54 Poole Road, Westbourne, Bournemouth, BH4
Helium balloons as well as party bags and boxes with little toys and sweets. Tableware range includes Harry Potter, Barbie or Clowns as well as the rull range of plain colours. Party streamers, Happy Birthday banners and party poppers also available.

Peeks Party Store   01202 489 361
Avon Trading Park, Reid Street, Christchurch, BH23
At Peeks Party Store you can buy pre-packed party bags - themed to the style of your birthday at a price point of either ££1 or ££2 - alternatively they sell boxes and separate gifts for you to select your own. They offer a large range of tableware including the Bob the Builder favourites. Helium balloons also available in a range of styles/colours.

GLOUCESTERSHIRE
Giant Party Shop   01453 750 075
16 Merrywalks Shopping Centre, Stroud, GL5 1RR
www.giantpartyshop.com
Great range of children's fancy dress costumes (from ££9.99 to ££22.99) as well as helium balloons, tableware, goody bag gifts etc They also have a great website with everything on display including wigs and accessories (ie witches hat and hair for Halloween). Branches in Bath, Swindon and Stroud.

Balloons Spectacular   01453 824 229
45 Canberra, Stonehouse, GL10 2PR

Ultimate Party Shop   01242 524 433
86 High Street, Cheltenham, GL50 1EG

Party Animal   01608 652 631
7 High Street, Moreton-in-Marsh, GL56 0AH

Party Bizniz   01452 310 069
47 Westgate Street, Gloucester, GL1 2NW

SOMERSET
Giant Party Shop   01225 336 632
49 Moorland Road, Bath, BA2 3PJ
www.giantpartyshop.com
Great range of children's fancy dress costumes (from ££9.99 to ££22.99) as well as helium balloons, tableware, goody bag gifts etc They also have a great website with everything on display including wigs and accessories (ie witches hat and hair for Halloween). Branches in Bath, Swindon and Stroud.

Please visit us at www.babydirectory.com

parties

Glow Wild   01179 593 526
126 Hallen Road, Henbury, Bristol, BS10 7RB

Flingers Party Shop   01179 312 206
73-75 Gloucester Road, Patchway, Bristol, BS34

Kidzstuff - Party Shop   01643 707 409
39 The Avenue, Minehead, TA24 5AY
www.party-balloon.co.uk
Party shop with balloon service and themed party boxes - pirate, farm, teddy, under the sea, surprise and lots more.

WILTSHIRE
Giant Party Shop   01793 695 858
183 Victoria Road, Old Town, Swindon, SN1 3DF
www.giantpartyshop.com
Great range of children's fancy dress costumes (from £9.99 to £22.99) as well as helium balloons, tableware, goody bag gifts etc They also have a great website with everything on display including wigs and accessories (ie witches hat and hair for Halloween). Branches in Bath, Swindon, Chippenham and Stroud.

Giant Party Shop   01249 660 111
13 The Brigde, Chippenham, SN15 1HA

Party Seasons   01722 416 013
3 Market Walk, Salisbury, SP1 1BT
Well established and highly recommended local party shop stocking full range of tableware, balloons, jokes, magic tricks, children's fancy dress.

Party Box   01793 853 976
13 Apsley House Arcade, 50 High Street, Wootton Bassett, Swindon, SN4 7AQ
Delightful party shop stocking all the essentials such as helium balloons, tableware, goody bags and toys.

Smiles Party World   01793 433 900
38-39 Market Hall, Market Street, Swindon, SN1

party supplies (online)

Great Little Parties   01908 266 080
www.greatlittleparties.co.uk
Great Little Parties is a specialist supplier of children's party products. Everything you see on the website is in stock including: themed invitations, party bags and presents (eg stickers, bubbles) and specific ranges for boys and girls, as well as balloons, games and even candles for the cake. They also stock wrapping paper, a great selection of Party cooking books for making your own fairy cakes - as well as thank you notes. Great website, well laid out, and quick/easy to use.

Monster Parties   07092 262 837
www.monsterparties.co.uk
Pre-filled party bags available to purchase online from 99p.

Party Directory 4 Kids   01252 851 601
www.partydirectory4kids.co.uk
A-Z kids party supplies by post. Over 700 great party products and ideas. We like the great selection of original party bag items such as notebooks, novelty pens, bubbles, bracelets - the list is endless; and prices much cheaper than highstreet. Also games, music, pinatas, sweets, hats, blowers and squawkers!

Parties in the Bag   01273 271 405
www.partiesinthebag.co.uk
Themed party bags from £1.50 for some really great toys - pre-packed and delivered in just 3 days.

Party Pieces   01635 201 844
www.partypieces.co.uk
Party Pieces has been providing children's party supplies by mail order (and now online) since 1987. Their new website offers a huge range of party ideas; from dressing up with lion or tiger hoods, party games including a pre-wrapped Parce the Parcel.

Party supplies on-line
Over 50 pre-filled party bags
Christening, Baby Shower, Themed tableware, balloons, candles, games & much more..
Order on-line or telephone 07092 262 837

days out

165

Youngsters in the South West are brought up to the wild outdoors, with westerly sea breezes and green luscious farmland. But for those who prefer their nature tamed, there are farms, natures reserves, zoos, castles and theme parks. Information and inspiration for fun days out can be found in this section.

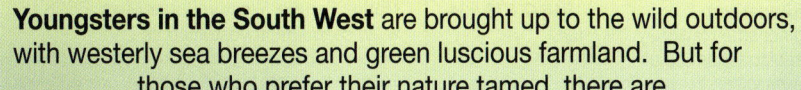

eden project

166 days out

aquariums

Blue Reef Aquarium　　　01637 878 134
Towan Promenade, Newquay, TR7 1DU
www.bluereefaquarium.co.uk
See local marine species from the Cornish coast as well as hundreds of tropical species in the gigantic ocean tanks complete with underwater tunnel. They also have a fresh water turtles, alligator snapping turtles, mud turtles, fly-river turtles and mata mata turtles. Open daily from 10am, last admission 5pm.

Cornish Seal Sanctuary　　　01326 221 361
Gweek, Nr Helston, TR12 6UG
www.sealsanctuary.co.uk
This Seal Sanctuary is set in the picturesque Helford estuary. The Sanctuary is a busy rescue centre, and also has resident Grey Seals, Common Seals, Californian and Patagonian Sea Lions, Goats, Ponies and Otters.

National Maritime Museum　　　01326 313 388
Discovery Quay Falmouth TR11 3QY
www.nmmc.co.uk
Housed in an award winning building on the Falmouth harbour-side, the National Maritime Museum takes you into the world of small boats and Cornish maritime history. Many of the attractions are a little advanced for the under 5s but visit the Tidal Zone area where you can go underwater and look out into the harbour through two large windows. You might catch a glimpse of a cormorant diving or crabs, shrimps and much more.

DEVON

National Marine Aquarium　　　01752 600 301
Rope Walk, Coxside, Plymouth, PL4 0LF
www.national-aquarium.co.uk
This was the first aquarium in the UK to be set up solely for the purpose of education, conservation and research. It tackles issues such as over-fishing, pollution and other man-made problems. Open 10am-5pm.

DORSET

The Bournemouth Aquarium　　　01202 311 993
Pier Approach, West Beach, Bournemouth, BH2 5AA
www.oceanarium.co.uk
The Oceanarium is a fully interactive experience with touch screen games, feeding demonstrations and talks, walk-through underwater tunnels and exhibits to help you discover more about the underwater world. The exhibits include the Amazon, Great Barrier Reef, Africa, the Ganges, Hawaii. Open 10am to 6pm – last admission 5pm.

Weymouth Sealife Park　　　01305 788 255
Lodmoor, Weymouth, DT4 7SX
www.sealifeeurope.com/uk/weymouth
Excellent aquarium offering great exhibitions of marine life. The under 5s love the otters, seals and penguins and more to look forward to in 2006 with the new ocean tunnel where you can see sharks and turtles.

SOMERSET, BRISTOL & BATH

SeaQuarium　　　01934 641 603
Marine Parade, Weston Super Mare, BS23 1BE
www.seaquariumweston.co.uk
Discover the fascinating secrets hidden beneath the Severn Estuary and the sea beyond. There are over 30 different displays as well as a café and gift shop. Open daily from 10am-4pm.

beaches

These beaches are award-winning beaches, which are clean, well managed and have good water quality for swimming and paddling. Let us know if you have other recommendations.

CORNWALL

Bude: Amongst the many beaches of bude we liked Summerleaze beach, which has fine white sands. The beach is encompassed by grassy dunes, is perfect for picnics and offers a tranquil haven away from the crowds. It also has a natural sea-fed swimming pool which provides safe swimming area away from the Atlantic waves. Less than a 5 minutes away is Bude with a good selection of shops, restaurants and recreational activities, including a modern indoor heated swimming pool!

Newquay, Porth Beach: Newquay is renowned for its vibrant surfing scene, and Porth beach is no exception. But the wide beach is also ideal for families, with lots of room to build giant sandcastles. There is a pub, cafe and mini-market directly facing the beach and although low cliffs surround the location, access for prams is good.

Padstow, Trevone Bay: is a sandy and naturally curved beach sheltered by cliffs. Although a popular place for intrepid surfers, the activities do not in anyway interfere with family activities. There is a car park nearby along with toilets and disabled facilities. Good beaches nearby are Treyarnon and Harlyn Bays.

Padstow, Constantine Bay: This is a long, wide, sandy beach looking up towards low headlands and is backed by dunes. To the far end is it still one of Britain's foremost surfing beaches, with the surfing pros riding some of the largest waves in the area (ie not for the inexperienced). Discovering the many rock pools, body surfing, the sand dunes and enjoying the white sand are all popular activities for children.

St Austell, Porthpean: This little cove is sheltered, with a rocky pool at its southern end. The beach slopes gently into the sea and is ideal for families with easy access for pushchairs, plus the toilet and refreshment facilities means you can come without a pre-prepared picnic.

St Ives, Porthmeor: St Ives is a great location for a family day out, both for it's sandy beach as well as a centre for the arts, with the Tate St. Ives art gallery close by.

days out 167

DEVON

Dawlish, Coryton Cove: is a secluded sandy beach within walking distance of Dawlish, a small seaside town famous for its Black Swans. There is a good beach café and huts are also available to hire. There are plenty of rock pools to explore and you might even spot the odd dolphin.

Ilfracombe, Tunnels Beaches: four tunnels provide access to a beautiful area of beach. A large tidal swimming pool is still in use and is hugely popular with children who can enjoy their inflatables and snorkelling in safety.

Salcombe: Nestled between two sheltering headlands, the beach at Salcombe is very popular with families. However, it becomes totally submerged at high tide – so you need to watch the tide timetable. There is a shop and café and limited parking.

Torbay, Broadsands: out of the many Torbay beaches you could visit this is a beautiful red-coloured sandy beach in a wonderful rural setting. It has a gently slopping gradient and easy access make it a popular choice for families with children or those wishing to distance themselves from amusement arcades. Cafe, restaurant, shops, and toilets are all available close by.

Woolacombe: This beach has two miles of golden sand backed by sandy hills and the Woolacombe Downs. There are ample facilities available including beach huts, deckchair hire and lifeguards are regularly on duty.

DORSET

Bournemouth, Boscombe beach: this is a long stretch of sandy beach along the seafront of Bournemouth. Gently sloping it provides the ideal destination for safe paddling and there is a free kids' beach club in the summer. The nearby Boscombe Gardens provide an oasis of tranquillity and a land train links to all the seafront attractions.

Lulworth Cove: and surrounding bays form part of 'The Jurassic Coast' and it is an excellent place to search for fossils along wonderful coastal paths. If you are a beginner check out the small museum, which introduces the area and provides some simple tips for finding fossils.

Lyme Regis: this bay although not sandy has recently been become a World Heritage Site partly because of its famous geology and fossil finds. Many families take advantage of coastal walks with the children being carried in backpacks.

Sandbanks: this popular family friendly beach gradually slopes away, ensuring it is safe for little ones. It has fine golden sand and excellent array of facilities with local cafés and restaurants nearby. There is also a swimmers only zone and on duty lifeguards make swimming at this beach a safe option. And just a short ferry trip away (past Brownsea Island) are the wonderful golden sands of Studland bay – also worth a visit (with good café/restaurant/toilets).

Swanage: gently sloping sands with a promenade backed by colorful gardens. The bay is sheltered and the sea is safe for paddling with all the amenities/cafés and restaurants close at hand. You can also go on short boat trips to fish for mackerel or take the steam train to Corfe Castle.

Weymouth Bay: is a sandy beach overlooked by a magnificent Georgian seafront. Very sheltered with a gradual sloping seabed and clean swimming water. It has lots of seasonal festivals, summer firework displays, Punch and Judy shows and that perfect combination of deckchairs and ice cream. A stone's throw from the beach is the historic harbour overlooked by restaurants, cafes and craft shops.

SOMERSET, BRISTOL & BATH

Burnham-on-Sea to Brean: is a seven-mile stretch of sand with an enormous tidal range. There are extensive flats, perfect for walking and beach sports and popular with sea anglers, who have to fish three hours a day either side of the high tide. The sands are backed by dunes that are rich in wildlife and include a local nature reserve with a way-marked trail. Car parking is allowed on sections of the beach and there are public conveniences, cafes and other leisure amenities around.

Weston-super-Mare: With miles of golden sand, Weston-super-Mare is a quintessential British seaside resort. It is an ideal location for families looking for fun-packed entertainment. Attractions include historic pier, miniature railway, sea-life centre, amusement arcades, land train and the famous Weston Donkeys. The Victorian style promenade is wide and flat and there is always a good selection of seafront events held throughout the year..

castles

CORNWALL

Launceston Castle　　　　　　　　　　01566 772 365
Launceston, PL15 7DR
The castle at Launceston dominates the surrounding landscape as it is perched on top of a large, natural mound.

St Michael's Mount　　　　　　　　　　01736 710 507
www.stmichaelsmount.co.uk
St Michael's Mount is an 11th century stone Benedictine priory and a royal fortress dating from 1194 located on an island and is accessed by a causeway or ferry boats at high tide. The site is owned by The National Trust and is open Sunday to Friday 26th March to October 10:30-5:30pm. Open when tides and weather are favourable, Nov-Mar.

Pendennis Castle　　　　　　　　　　01326 316 594
Falmouth, Cornwall TR11 4LP
This is a three-storey round tower and gatehouse, surrounded by a large Elizabethan fort. The site is owned by English Heritage and is open daily, Jul-Aug 10am-6pm, Apr-Jun and Sept 10am-5pm, Oct-Mar 10am-4pm.

St Mawes Castle　　　　　　　　　　01326 270526
St Mawes, TR2 3AA
This is a stone artillery fortress, founded by Henry VIII in 1540. Built in a clover leaf plan, it has a perfectly preserved four storey round tower, with three single storey batteries attached. The site is owned by English Heritage and is open daily to the same times as Pendennis Castle above.

168 days out

Tintagel Castle   01840 770 328
Tintagel, PL34 0DB
This is a spectacular 12th century stone enclosure fortress, founded by the Earl of Cornwall. It is also home to many legends including Merlin the Magician and King Arthur. There is quite a steep climb from the car park so not suitable for pushchairs.

DEVON

Compton Castle   01803 842 382
Marldon, Paignton, Devon TQ3 1TA
Compton Castle is an H-shaped stone fortified manor house, with square corner towers. It has a charming flowering walled garden and the kitchen offers a unique insight into medieval domestic life.

Dartmouth Castle   01803 833588
Dartmouth, TQ6 0JN
This is a well preserved 14th century stone coastal fortress, which juts out into the narrow entrance of the Dart Estuary. You can take a boat trip from the quayside at Dartmouth, which lands you just a short walk from the castle entrance.

Powderham Castle
www.powderham.co.uk
Powderham Castle is the historic home of the Earl of Devon. The Castle is still lived in by the Courtenay family and is one of England's most popular stately homes. The castle lies in a beautiful setting in an ancient 4,000 acre deer park alongside the River Exe. New for 2006 is Courtenay Fort, an adventure play castle for the under 12's. It has monkey bars, suspension bridge, V net, climbing wall and much more to keep children entertained. Open daily except Sat 10am-5.30pm between Easter- end Oct.

DORSET

Corfe Castle   01929 481 294
The Square, Corfe Castle, BH20 5EZ
This is a National Trust castle perched up on a natural ridge just outside Corfe town. You can also consider incorporating the Swanage steam railway into your expedition. The castle has impressive (and rather windy) views across the south coast and is great fun to scamper around.

Lulworth Castle   0845 4501054
Lulworth, BH20 5QS
An early 17th-century hunting lodge, the castle later became a country house and is set in beautiful parkland. Open daily 10.30am-4pm or later in summer.

SOMERSET, BATH & BRISTOL

Dunster Castle   01643 821 314
Dunster, nr Minehead, TA24 6SL
www.nationaltrust.org.uk
Dunster is a National Trust castle with beautiful turrets and towers. It was remodelled in the 19th century, but was an important fortress for over 1,000 years. It sits in a dramatic hilltop location with sweeping views over Exmoor and the Bristol Channel. The gardens are terraced with sub-tropical plants.

WILTSHIRE

Old Wardour Castle   01747 870 487
Tisbury, Nr Salisbury, SP3 6RR
This is one of England's most romantic castles, in a secluded lakeside setting. It is an unusual six-sided castle, unique in medieval English architecture. Wonderful for picnics. Open daily 10am-4pm.

houses, parks and gardens

CORNWALL

Trevarno Estate Gardens   01326 574 274
Crowntown, Nr Helston, TR13 0RU
www.trevarno.co.uk
Wonderful 35 acre gardens with many interesting rare trees and shrubs giving interest throughout the year. Also worth visiting to see their craft workship where they make an organic range of natural skincare products (including camomile baby soaps, creams and salves). There's a bee centre with honey making exhibition, a toy museum, large adventure play area, lake and boathouse. Open daily 10.30-5pm.

Eden Project   01726 811 911
Bodelva, St Austell, PL24 2SG
www.edenproject.com
Two vast greenhouses (biomes) nestle in the base of this abandoned clay pit, each one creating micro-climates from around the world. We loved the lush, moist air of the tropical forest complete with butterflies. Children under 5 free. Open 10am-6pm summer season (Mar 29-Oct 29) - doors open at 9.30am last entrance 4.30pm - or 3pm in winter.

DEVON

Rosemoor Gardens   01805 624 067
Great Torrington, EX38 8PH
www.rhs.org.uk
Wonderful rose gardens, winter gardens and a new mediterranean garden set in this infamous wooded valley.

DORSET

Mapperton Gardens   01308 862 645
Beaminster, DT8 3NR
www.mapperton.com
Italian terraced garens, grottoes to explore and lots of secret paths. Open daily 11am-5pm Mar-Oct.

GLOUCESTERSHIRE

Sudeley Castle   01242 602 308
Winchcombe, GL54 5JD
www.sudeleycastle.co.uk

SOMERSET, BATH & BRISTOL

Roman Baths   01225 477 785
Abbey Church Yard, Bath, BA1 1LZ
www.romanbaths.co.uk
Open daily 9.30am-5.30pm.

days out 169

Hestercombe Gardens 01823 413 923
Cheddon Fitzpaine, Taunton, TA2 8LG
www.hestercombegardens.com
Open daily 10am-6pm.

WILTSHIRE
Bowood House 01249 812 102
Derry Hill, Calne, SN11 9PQ
www.bowood.org

Stourhead Gardens 01747 841 152
Stourton, Warminster, BA12 6QD
www.nationaltrust.org.uk
Wonderful 18th century gardens landscaped by Capability Brown. Paths lead you around a large lake, with lots of grottoes to explore. Open daily 9am-7pm.

farms

CORNWALL
Colliford Lake Park 01208 821 469
Bolventor, Bodmin Moor, St Neot, Liskeard
www.collifordlakepark.com
Colliford Lake Park is a farm based attraction with 8 acres of woodland, 30 acres of farm stock with sheep, goats, red deer and other animals. They also have 20 acres of parkland set aside for Family Entertainments, including a protected wetlands area.

Dairyland Farm World 01872 510 246
Newquay, TR8 5AA
www.dairylandfarmworld.com
Meet lots of animals including lambs, kids, rabbits, donkeys, piglets and Lawrence the Llama. Daily events include bottle-feeding, pat-a-pet, pony rides and have-a-go milking with Clarabelle the cybercow.

Trethorne Leisure Farm 01566 86324
Kennards House, Launceston, PL15 8QE
www.trethorneleisure.co.uk
A large family owned farm with indoor and outdoor activities throughout the day like bottle-feeding lambs and touch the animals areas.

DEVON
North Devon Farm Park 01271 830 255
Landkey, Barnstaple, EX32 0NN
www.farmpark.co.uk
This farm has 60 acres of beautiful river walks, ponds, lakes (all spring-fed -never dry out) with abundant wild-life. The site is one of the oldest farms in North Devon you can play and feed all the farm animals.

Pennywell Farm 01364 642 023
Buckfastleigh, TQ11 0LT
www.pennywellfarm.co.uk
Farm animals including Wallabies and Rheas.

TREVARNO
'one of Cornwall's secrets'

35 Acre Garden · Italian Garden · Many rare Shrubs & Trees · National Museum of Gardening · Soap & Skincare Workshops · Soap Museum · Vintage Toy Museum (Small additional charge) · Estate Walk · Lake & Boathouse · Restoration Projects · Plant Sales · New Adventure Play Area · Children's Trails · Fountain Garden Conservatory serving refreshments & Shop

Trevarno Manor Helston Cornwall TR13 0RU
Telephone: 01326 574274 Facsimile: 01326 574282
Email: enquiry@trevarno.co.uk www.trevarno.co.uk

Prickly Ball Farm 01626 362 319
Denbury Road, East Ogwell, Newton Abbot, TQ12
www.pricklyballfarm.co.uk
Prickly Ball farm is a busy 'hands on' hedgehog hospital and wildlife garden centre where you can meet, touch, and learn about hedgehogs and other farm animals.

Sorley Tunnel Farm 01548 854 078
Loddiswell Road, Kingsbridge, TQ7 4BP
www.sorleytunnel.com
Working organic eco-friendly dairy farm; superb new indoor play area; farm animals; pony rides; restaurant; shop selling local produce and crafts and picturesque walks.

The Big Sheep 01237 477916
Abbotsham, Bideford, EX39 5AP
www.thebigsheep.co.uk
Sheep racing and miniature sheepdog trials with dogs, ducks and children are among the highlights of this large farm attraction. Also features unique horse whispering shows.

DORSET
Abbotsbury Children's Farm 01305 871 817
New Barn Road, Abbotsbury, DT3 4JG
www.abbotsbury-tourism.co.uk
The ancient Tithe Barn site is home to a host of friendly farm animals. Many can be stroked and fed at regular times throughout the day. Toy tractor racing all day and pony ride sessions twice a day (for which a small extra charge is made).

days out

Abbotsbury Swannery   01305 871 817
New Barn Road, Abbotsbury, DT3 4JG
www.abbotsbury-tourism.co.uk
This is home to a colony of friendly mute swans. Sheltered by the famous Chesil Beach, this ancient and special site provides protection for hundreds of nesting swans and their broods. From the end of May onwards you can wander safely around the nests, observing at close quarters the antics of fluffy cygnets.

Farmer Palmer's Farm Park   01202 622 022
Organford, Poole, BH16 6EU
www.farmerpalmer.co.uk
Go to meet the farm animals or play in their barns.

Putlake Adventure Farm   01929 422 917
Langton Matravers, Swanage
Situated on the Jurassic coastline meet farm animals, feed lambs and kids, play in the ball barn or on ride-on toys. Picnic area and tearoom.

GLOUCESTERSHIRE

Barn Owl Centre   01452 865 999
The Tithe Barn, Brockworth Court, Gloucester
www.barnowl.co.uk

Bibury Trout Farm   01285 740 215
Bibury, Cirencester, GL7
www.bibury.com

The Baby Show

The UK's biggest day out for mums, dads, babies and toddlers

- Huge savings on 1000s of nursery essentials
- Expert advice on pregnancy and early parenting
- Fun for the little ones

For a full list of companies, dates and venue visit
www.thebabyshow.co.uk/bd

Cattle Country Adventure Park   01453 10 510
Berkeley, GL13 9EW
www.cattlecountry.co.uk
Farm Park has exotic cattle including a herd of American Bison, Gloucester Old Spot pigs, pets corner, gift shop and refreshments. Large adventure playgrounds including indoor area with big slides and an outdoor paddling pool.

Cotswold Farm Park   01451 850 307
Guiting Power, GL54 UG
www.cotswoldfarmpark.co.uk
There are lots of activities for the youngsters; rabbits and guinea pigs to cuddle, lambs and calves to bottle feed, tractor and trailer rides, battery powered tractors, seasonal farming demonstrations, including lambing, shearing and milking, together with great children's play areas both indoors and out.

National Birds of Prey Centre   0870 990 1992
Newent, GL18 1JJ
www.nbpc.co.uk

Prinknash Bird and Deer Park   01452 812 727
Cranham, Gloucester, GL4 8EX
www.prinknash-bird-and-deerpark.com

Slimbridge Wetlands Centre   01453 891 900
Slimbridge, GL2 7BT
www.wwt.org.uk

SOMERSET, BATH & BRISTOL

Avon Valley Country Park   01179 864 929
Keynsham, postcode?
www.avonvlleycountrypark.co.uk

Horseworld   01275 540 173
Staunton Lane, Whitchurch, Nr Bristol
www.horseworld.org.uk
Horseworld is home to horses (obviously), donkeys and farm animals. You can groom, take pony rides, go on tractor tours and play in the indoor or outdoor adventure playgrounds. Cafe/restaurant.

Noah's Ark Zoo Farm   01275 852 606
Failand Road Wraxall Bristol BS48 1PG
www.noahsarkzoofarm.co.uk
The "hands-on" zoo farm, with over 80 different types of animal. You can feed many animals including baby lambs, goats, deer, llamas, camels, and a wide variety of birds.

WILTSHIRE

Bush Farm Bison Centre   01747 830 263
West Knoyle, Mere, BA12 6AE
www.bisonfarm.co.uk
Bush Farm consists of 100 acres of grass fields and 30 acres of old oak woods. Visitors take a circular tour round the farm and see herds of bison, wapiti and red deer.

days out 171

Butterfly World   01793 852 400
Studley Grange, Wroughton, Swindon
www.studleygrange.co.uk

Cholderton Rare Breeds Farm Park   01980 629 438
Amesbury Road, Cholderton, Nr Salisbury, SP4
www.rabbitworld.co.uk
Farm park offers an opportunity to see rare farm animals in a scenic setting of paddocks and gardens. You'll meet pigs, ponies, cows and goats, sheep and poultry. One of Britain's largest collection of breeds of rabbit, pets' park, ponds. Water gardens, toddlers' play area, adventure playground. Pig racing, tractor/trailer rides in peak season.

Farmer Giles Farmstead   01722 716 338
Teffont, Salisbury, SP3 5QY
www.farmergiles.co.uk
Family leisure farm with large selection of animals, set in acres of glorious rolling Wiltshire down-land. Feed lambs and get to know a host of other farm animals and pets.

theme parks

Adventure Wonderland   01202 483 444
Merritown Lane, Hurn, Christchurch, BH23 6BA
www.adventurewonderland.co.uk
Adventure Wonderland is an all inclusive day out which combines the timeless fun and games of the Alice in Wonderland story with the thrilling outdoor Adventure rides of the Main Park and the undercover Lost Aztec World of Wild Thing.

Alton Towers   0870 520 4060
Alton, ST10 4DB
www.altontowers.com
For white-knuckle water rides head to this theme park and model farm. Using the Parent-Q-Share pass you can help minimise waiting in long queues with young children. Price £21, 4-11yrs.

Chessington World of Adventures   0870 444 7777
Leatherhead Road, Surrey, KT9 2NE
www.chessington.co.uk
You pay a one-off fee to enter Chessington which allows you to go on as many rides as many times as you like. For little ones (free for under 4s) there are roundabouts, carousels, Toytown, Professor Burp's Bubble Works and a small circus with trapeze artists and clowns. There is also a zoo which you can see on a monorail and a creepy crawly cave of spiders and insects. Open March-Nov, 10am-5.15pm.

Legoland   0870 504 0404
Winkfield Road, Windsor, Berkshire
www.legoland.co.uk
This year they have installed the miniature Millennium Eye and Buckingham Palace – young ones will be amazed to see what they can build with the basic lego brick. Go outside school holidays to avoid the queues which can be colossal.

trains

The great thing about these train trips is everything happens rather slowly and it's fun to see the children's faces when the train heads off in great puffs of steam. They almost always have a Santa specials at Christmas and 'Thomas the Tank Engine' visits annually

Avon Valley Railway   0117 9327 296
Bitton, Bristol, BS30 6HD
www.avonvalleyrailway.co.uk

Bodmin & Wenford Railway   01208 73666
General Station, Bodmin, Cornwall, PL31 1AQ
www.bodminandwenfordrailway.co.uk

Dean Forest Railwy   01594 845 840
Forest Road, Lydney, GL15 4ET
www.deanforestrailway.co.uk

**Gloucestershire and
Warwickshire Railway**   01242 621 405
Toddington, Gloucestershire, GL54 5DT
www.gwsr.com

Lappa Valley Railway   01872 510 317
St Newlyn East, Newquay, Cornwall, TR8 5HZ
www.lappavalley.co.uk

Perrygrove Railway   01594 834 991
Coleford, Gloucestershire, GL16 8QB
www.perrygrove.co.uk

Swanage Railway   01929 425 800
Swanage, Dorset
Dorset's premier steam railway with wonderful views of Corfe Castle.

Swindon & Cricklade Railway   01793 771 615
Tadpole Lane, Blunsden, Swindon, Wilts, SN25
www.swindon-cricklade-railway.org

zoos & nature reserves

CORNWALL

Newquay Zoo   01637 873 342
Trenance Gardens Newquay Cornwall TR7 2TW
www.newquayzoo.org.uk

Porfell Animal Land   01503 220 211
Trecangate, **Nr. Lanreath, Liskeard**, PL14 4RE
www.porfellanimalland.co.uk
At Animal Land you will meet wallabies, marmosets, iguana, lemurs, meerkats, porcupines and of course 'Bert' the capybara as well as all your favourite farmyard animals and pets.

days out

DEVON

Combe Martin 01271 882 486
Wildlife and Dinosaur Park
Combe Martin, North Devon, EX34 0NG
www.dinosaur-park.com

Paignton Zoo 01803 697 500
Totnes Road, Paignton, TQ4 7EU
www.paigntonzoo.org.uk

DORSET

Dinosaur Museum 01305 269 880
Icen Way, Dorchester, DT1 1EW
www.thedinosaurmuseum.com

Monkey World 01929 462 537
Nr Wareham, BH20 6HH
www.monkeyworld.org

GLOUCESTERSHIRE

Birdlands Park & Garden 01451 820 480
Rissington Road, Bourton-on-the-Water
www.birdlands.co.uk

Cotswold Wildlife Park 01993 823 006
Bradwell Grove, Burford, Oxfordshire, OX18 4JW
www.cotswoldwildlifepark.co.uk

SOMERSET, BATH & BRISTOL

Bristol Zoo Gardens 0117 974 7399
Clifton, Bristol, BS8 3HA
www.bristolzoo.org.uk

Noah's Ark Zoo Farm 01275 852 606
Failand Road, Wraxall, Bristol
www.noahsarkzoofarm.co.uk

The Wildlife Park 01460 30111
Cricket St Thomas, Chard, TA20 4DD
www.cstwp.co.uk
The Wildlife Park has over 600 animals and birds from around the world and is home to more than 70 different species, many at risk from extinction. The walk-through lemur wood is sanctuary for three different species of lemurs - a unique setting amongst the largest of its kind in the world. Amur leopards, pets corner, safari train, 1,000 acres in scenic and peaceful countryside.

WILTSHIRE

Longleat Safari Park 01985 844 400
Warminster, Wiltshire
www.longleat.co.uk

Please say you saw these listings in
The South West Baby Directory

travel

Some parents swear that travel abroad and babies do not mix. They may well be right. Or they may be missing out. Here we offer ideas for both the adventurous and the stay-at-homes, featuring family-orientated travel companies and websites, camping and ski companies and homeswap agencies, as well as child-friendly hotels and holiday centres in the UK. Bon voyage!

174 travel

hotels and holidays

The following hotels offer special facilities for children and babies, ranging from crèches and child-listening to playgrounds and pools

Avon
The Bath Spa Hotel   01225 444 424
Sydney Road, Bath
www.bathspa-hotel.co.uk

Channel Islands
Stocks Island Hotel   01481 832 001
Manor Valley, Sark
www.stockshotel.com

Fowey Hotel   01726 833 866
Hanson Drive, Fowey
www.luxuryfamilyhotels.com
One of the group of four excellent country-house hotels aimed at families, with all-day crèches, babysitting, etc, to allow parents a luxury break (see ad pg 142).

Bedruthan Steps Hotel   01637 860 555
Mawgan Porth
www.bedruthan.com

Sands Family Resort   01637 872 864
Watergate Road, Porth
www.sandsresorts.co.uk

Tredethy House Country Hotel   01208 841 262
Helland Bridge, Bodmin
www.tredethyhouse.co.uk

Watergate Bay Hotel   01637 860 543
Watergate Bay, Newquay
www.watergate.co.uk

Wringford Down Hotel   01752 822 287
Cawsand
www.cornwallholidays.co.uk

Cumbria
Cumbria Allerdale Court Hotel   01900 823 654
Market Place, Cockermouth
www.allerdalecourthotel.co.uk

Armathwaite Hall Hotel   0176 877 6551
Nr. Keswick
www.armathwaite-hall.com

Castle Inn Hotel   01768 776 401
Bassenthwaite, Keswick
www.corushotels.com/castleinn

Hilton Keswick Lodore   01768 777 285
Borrowdale Road, Keswick

Devon
Langstone Cliff Hotel   01626 868 000
Mount Pleasant Road, Dawlish Warren, Dawlish
www.langstone-hotel.co.uk
19 acres of woodland, children's suppers, indoor and outdoor pools, tennis, therapy rooms, go-karts.

The Bulstone Hotel   01297 680 446
Higher Bulstone, Branscombe, Sidmouth
www.childfriendlyhotels.com

Thurlestone Hotel   01548 560 382
Thurlestone
www.thurlestone.co.uk

Dorset
The Knoll House   01929 450 450
Studland Bay
www.knollhouse.co.uk
Gardens, pools, tennis, golf, health spa, playroom, children's restaurant, adventure playground.

Moonfleet Manor   01305 786 948
Moonfleet, Nr Weymouth
www.luxuryfamilyhotels.com
Play area, crèche, extensive leisure facilities including indoor pool (see ad pg 142).

Fairfields Hotel   01929 450 224
Swanage Road, Studland Bay
Small super-child-friendly hotel with a garden full of toys and great early suppers.

Sandbanks Hotel   01202 707 377
15 Banks Road, Sandbanks, Poole
Child-orientated hotel with direct access to the gorgeous sandy beach.

Essex
Swallow Churchgate Hotel   01279 420 246
Churchgate Street Village, Old Harlow
Comfortable hotel with indoor pool. Convenient for Stansted airport.

Gloucestershire
Calcot Manor   01666 890 391
Tetbury
www.calcotmanor.co.uk
Lovely Cotswold manor house with spa and pool. Additional beds and cots provided; play zone in a converted barn, children's videos, baby listening.

Hampshire
Watersplash Hotel   01590 622 344
The Rise, Brockenhurst

www.babydirectory.com

travel

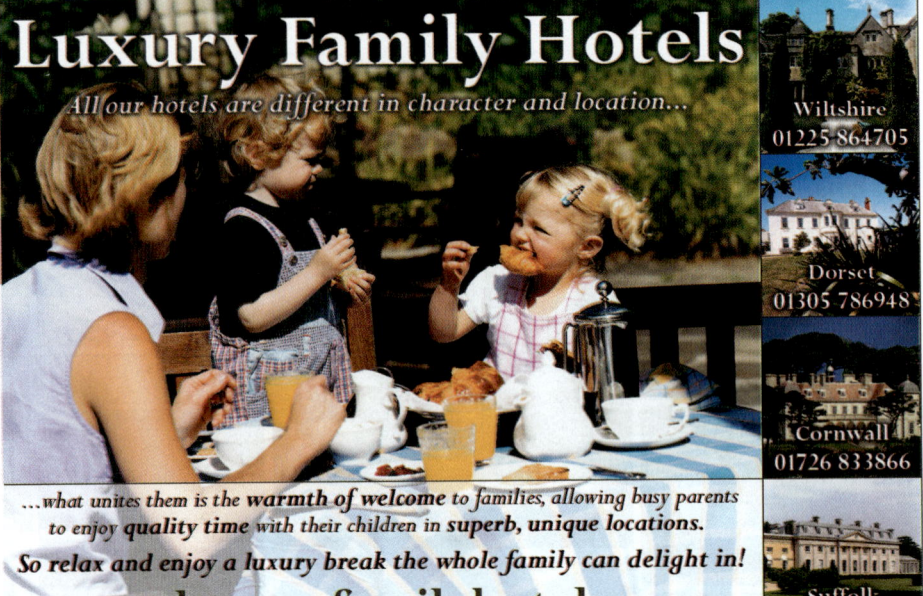

Luxury Family Hotels
All our hotels are different in character and location...

Wiltshire 01225 864705
Dorset 01305 786948
Cornwall 01726 833866
Suffolk 01284 735350

*...what unites them is the **warmth of welcome** to families, allowing busy parents to enjoy **quality time** with their children in **superb, unique locations**. So relax and enjoy a luxury break the whole family can delight in!*

www.luxuryfamilyhotels.com

Hertfordshire
The Grove   01923 807 807
Chandler's Cross
Fabulous designer hotel in stately home and grounds, with state-of-the-art spa, golf course, and Anouska's crèche and play area, which will occupy your children all day if required.

Inverness
Polmaily House Hotel   01456 450 343
Drumnadrochit, Loch Ness

Isle of Wight
The Clarendon Hotel and Wight Mouse Inn   01983 730 431
Newport Road, Chale
Family-friendly hotel/inn on the picturesque south coast.

Priory Bay Hotel   01983 613 146
Eddington Road, St. Helens
www.priorybay.co.uk
Beautifully decorated, friendly country house hotel with private beach, outdoor pool, pretty grounds and tennis courts.

Lancashire
St Ives Hotel   01253 720 011
7 South Promenade, St Anne's on Sea
Family-owned hotel overlooking the beach, pier and promenade.

Leicestershire
Field Head Hotel   01530 245 454
Markfield Lane, Markfield

Northumberland
Granary Hotel   01665 710 872
Links Road, Amble

Ryecroft Hotel   01668 281 459
Ryecroft Way, Wooler

Perthshire
Gleneagles Hotel   0800 328 4010
Auchterarder
Playground, crèche.

Shropshire
Redfern Hotel   01299 270 395
Cleobury Mortimer

Suffolk
Ickworth Hotel   **01284 735 350**
Nr Bury St Edmonds
www.luxuryfamilyhotels.com
East wing of Ickworth House, within 1,800 acre National Trust estate. Indoor pool and nursery with spa and both adult and children areas (see ad above).

travel **177**

Warwickshire
Lea Marston Hotel 01675 470 468
Haunch Lane, Lea Marston

Wiltshire
Woolley Grange Hotel 01225 864 705
Woolley Green, Bradford on Avon
www.luxuryfamilyhotels.com
Play area, crèche, outdoor pool, bicycles (see ad left).

overseas travel

Holidays which the kids want do not necessarily match the holiday that their parents need. It all comes down to the type of childcare you want and can afford - from taking your own nanny, relying on childcare provided by a tour operator (crèche or kids' clubs) or simply baby listening. Babies do require their own passport to travel overseas. The companies we have selected below can offer advice (and special offers) throughout the year

Quo Vadis? Family Travel 01279 639 600
www.quovadistravel.co.uk
Luxury family holiday experts - independent advice on the best holidays available, tailored solutions and hassle-free booking service.

Travelling with Children 01684 594 831
www.travellingwithchildren.co.uk
The one-stop shop for all your family holiday and day-to-day travel needs.

camping

Canvas Holidays 08709 022 022
www.canvas.co.uk
An independent family camping holiday company providing self-drive camping and mobile home holidays in France and the rest of Europe.

Eurocamp 0870 366 7558
www.eurocamp.co.uk
Eurocamp is the market-leader in self-catering holidays to Europe. Holidays cater for families (including babies) on 167 superbly equipped holiday parcs in 9 European countries.

Keycamp Holidays 0870 700 0123
www.keycamp.co.uk
Fully equipped tents with 4 bedrooms or a luxury mobile home with shower and toilet. Camping sites are across France, Spain, Italy, Luxembourg, Austria, Switzerland and Holland.

homeswaps

National Childbirth Trust 0870 444 8707
The NCT Homeswaps register has been active for over 25 years, but welcomes non-NCT members. Mainly UK properties, with London homes being the most popular.

Home Base Holidays 020 8886 8752
www.homebase-hols.com
International home holiday swaps.

Homelink International 01344 842 642
www.homelink.org.uk
With over 12,000 members in 50 countries.

family villages and resorts

CenterParcs 0990 200 200
www.centerparcs.com
20 holiday villages throughout Europe, including Longleat Forest in Wiltshire, Sherwood Forest in Notts, Oasis Whinfell in Cumbria and Elvedon Forest in Suffolk (see below).

Club Med 020 7581 1161
Kennedy House, 115 Hammersmith Road, W14
www.clubmed.com
All-inclusive holiday villages located all over the world. A number of them offer childcare facilities for babies and young children during the day with good family discount packages.

Sunsail 023 9222 2300
The Port House, Port Solent, PO6 4TH
www.sunsail.com
Family resorts in Antigua, Turkey and Greece. Many parents have recommended the Sunsail winter holiday in Antigua (but lament that taking a toddler on such a long-haul flight almost ruined it). Childcare additional.

CENTREPARCS

If you are looking to have a long-weekend or short mid-week family break then you should consider the CentreParcs formula. Celebrity mum Kim Wilde swears by her half-term breaks in Wiltshire and so we went to discover what goes on at Elvedon Forest in Suffolk.

We were amazed at the silence of the wooded park, and at the abundant wildlife in the adventure play areas. It was almost like Teletubby land with rabbits just grazing as we sipped our cappuccinos.

Everything we did had a gentle introductory version for the very youngest guests, such as special mother and baby swimming times in the sub tropical swimming pool. Bicycles had trailers or baby seats, and without the worry of cars on the road, we made picnics and explored at leisure.

For recharging mum's batteries we headed for the spa with our three-hour ticket - whilst our bambini were being taken care of at the nursery with fully-qualified nannies. Foot spas, massage, hot tubs, steam rooms and endless beauty treatments...need we say more.

Although we didn't find the villas the height of glamour, they provided all the right equipment - and best of all the children had a blast.

travel

family ski companies

Chilly Powder   020 7289 6958
www.chillypowder.com
The Chilly Powder chalet is situated in Morzine on the French/Swiss border. Their in-house nanny can look after babies (2mths+), with bottle-warming, sterilizer and baby-listening service also available. A crèche in Morzine (1-4yrs) provides all-day entertainment for toddlers and from 4yrs+ ski school is provided by the Ecole de Ski.

Meriski   01285 648 518
www.meriski.co.uk
If you have your heart set on Méribel, then Meriski provides either in-chalet nannies or crèche facilities (maximum of 8 places) from 9am-5pm Mon-Sat. Cots and highchairs are provided in the chalets, as well as kids' meals cooked separately by your chef. From 3yrs+ children can ski with Les Petits Loups, a ski school run by Ecole de Ski Français, accompanied by an English-speaking nanny.

Ski Beat   01243 780 405
Ski Beat offers holidays with childcare in 4 French resorts (La Plagne, Les Arcs, La Tania and Val d'Isère). Crèches, nannies and afternoon care. Care is provided between 8.45am-5pm and includes lunch and facilities for sleeping as well as toys, games and art & craft materials. If you are taking a whole chalet you may want to hire a private chalet nanny.

Ski Esprit   01252 618 300
Holidays in France, Italy and Austria. Their Classic Childcare option caters for children from 4mths-3yrs and the Spritelets Ski School from 3yrs-5yrs (max 6 in a class). A Snow Club in the afternoon keeps the non-skiing 3-5yr olds well entertained. The nannies are all English-speaking. Care is available 6 days per week from 8.30am-5pm.

Ski Famille   01223 363 777
www.skifamille.com
Ski Famille doesn't charge extra for childcare. They provide fully qualified nannies to your chalet where playrooms are equipped with toys, games and arts/craft materials. When the weather allows they encourage children to play outside. For older children they ensure they are at ski school on time and pick them up afterwards. Childcare is available between 9am-4.30pm except on Saturday or Wednesday. They have children's ski clothes for hire, sell nappies at cost and provide baby bottles, sterilizers, highchairs, cots and bedding.

Ski Scott Dunn   020 8767 0202
Ski Scott Dunn provides private nannies, children's clubs and the famous Scott Dunn Ski Schools to get even the youngest snowbears off to a good start. Chalets are well equipped with cots, highchairs, even Pampers, to enable you to travel lightly. Children are also not expected to share their parents' bedroom (for no additional cost).

"It is the personal touch which is so important and has always distinguished a Meriski holiday."

Understanding the needs of you and your family is our speciality and the main reason why so many of our guests return year after year. Our alpine team in Méribel are constantly on hand to help – from making you a cup of tea to running you to the shops with our complimentary minibus shuttle service. Meriski even has its own dedicated crèche in Méribel for children of all ages.

Here's looking forward to welcoming you to another great season in Méribel.

MERISKI
The Méribel Specialists

Call us now to reserve your brochure: 01285 648518
or visit: www.meriski.co.uk

good advice

And finally… our indispensable list of contacts and helplines, to help you navigate your way swiftly to the people, places and advice you need.

good advice

adoption

To adopt you need to be approved by the British authorities [at least 6mths]. The first step is to contact your local authority where a social worker will conduct a Home Study to assess your suitability to adopt. To adopt from overseas the government has to formalise the paperwork [6-9mths] and send the papers to the British Embassy in your chosen country

Adoption UK   0870 770 0450
www.adoptionuk.org.uk

After Adoption   0161 839 4930
www.afteradoption.org.uk

BAAF   020 7593 2000
www.baaf.org.uk
British Association for Adoption and Fostering. Information and advice for prospective parents; list of UK children looking for families [normally 5yrs+].

OASIS   0870 241 7069
www.adoptionoverseas.org.uk

Intercountry Adoption Centre   020 8449 2562
www.icacentre.org.uk
Advice and information and workshops for parents wanting to adopt from overseas.

For information on Childminders, Pre-Schools, Nurseries, Parent & Toddler Groups and other Services for Children including Children with Special Needs

**FREEPHONE
0800 056 36 66**

www.devon.gov.uk/disc

Devon County Council

councils

Your local council is an excellent source of information. Ask for the Children's Information Service department for enquiries about play centres, parks etc, the Early Years department for childcare and early education. Some produce little booklets about what's on offer for children in the borough.

CORNWALL
Cornwall Family Information Service   0800 587 8191
Main source for all Ofsted registered childcare and other family services and support organisations throughout the county, as well as holiday activities from 0-19yrs. They also work closely with employers and the childcare voucher scheme. You can get one-to-one advice either via their freephone number or at their drop-in shop at 61 Lemon Street, Truro.

DEVON
Devon & Torbay CIS   01392 385 535
www.devon.gov.uk/disc
Providing up-to-date information on all aspects of childcare in the Devon and Torbay areas (see ad pg 53).

Plymouth CIS   0800 783 4259

DORSET
Bournemouth CIS   01202 456 222
Dorset CIS   01305 228 451
Poole   01202 261 999

GLOUCESTERSHIRE
Gloucestershire CIS   0800 5420 202
South Gloucestershire CIS   01454 868 666
www.southglos.gov.uk/ed/cis
Offering FREE, up-to-date, impartial advice and guidance on registered childminders, nurseries, playgroups, out of school clubs and holiday play schemes, creches and lots more .

SOMERSET, BRISTOL & BATH
Bath & NE Somerset CIS   0800 073 1214
www.bathnes.gov.uk/fis

Bristol CIS   0845 129 7217
www.cisbristol.co.uk

North Somerset CIS   01275 888 778
www.childcarelink.gov.uk

Somerset CIS   0845 600 7171

WILTSHIRE
Swindon CIS   01793 541 786
Wiltshire CIS   08457 585 072

good advice 181

fatherhood

Families Need Fathers   020 7613 5060
134 Curtain Road, London, EC2A 3AR
www.fnf.org.uk

www.fathersdirect.com
The UK's national information centre for fatherhood.

naming ceremonies

If you want a secular naming ceremony, as opposed to a christening, then you have many options available to you. If you choose to focus the event on naming the child and making a public declaration of the commitment of parents and godparents then the following organisations will be able to guide you with a selection of formats (formal or informal)

Baby Naming Ceremonies   020 7079 3580
1 Gower Street, London, WC1E 6HD
www.humanism.org.uk

For a personal, unique and beautiful welcome for your child, the BHA, which has years of experience in preparing non-religious ceremonies, can help. Your child's naming ceremony can be an unforgettable public declaration of your commitment as parents and guide parents. The ceremonies are designed to be inclusive, so that families and friends can relate to what is said - whether or not they have religious beliefs.

money matters

In an area fraught with industry speak we asked Josephine Blythe, who is a mother of two and a partner of St. James's Place Partnership, to outline some of the things that we all should think about when it comes to finance.

"Having a baby can be the most exciting time in any woman's life and there is no doubt that it can also be the most worrying time for many reasons, not least of which is the financial impact it may have on your household.

Firstly there is the issue of loss of the mother's income while she is on maternity leave and how this may impact the monthly household budget.

There may be **maternity benefits** paid by an employer to claim, or you may be entitled to some maternity benefits from the state. And, once your child is born you are entitled to **Child Benefit**.

There is also the **Child Trust Fund** initiative whereby the Government will make a contribution of £250 for any child born after 31st August 2002. The website **www.childtrustfund.gov.uk** has a good amount of information and a list of CTF funds.

The Baby Show

The UK's biggest event dedicated to new parents and parents-to-be

- Pregnancy and parenting advice from midwives
- Celebrity experts take to the stage
- Information on all the latest products

For a full list of companies, dates and venue visit
www.thebabyshow.co.uk/bd

Once you have dependents you have to think more seriously about what would happen if the income of the household were to stop if the major breadwinner were to die prematurely or become too ill to work. A careful review of your **life assurance**, critical illness cover and income protection policies is vital. As is writing a formal **Will**, to make certain that money passes into the right hands on your death.

You may be keen to build up capital for your child's future for, perhaps, school fee planning, stakeholder pensions or there may be gifts of money from grandparents which you want to invest. There are a raft of different products available offering very tax-efficient ways of investing.

And what about if you have finished work to bring up your child, what do you do with the pension scheme left behind at your employer and equally, how are you going to provide for your own old age if you no longer earn an income?

Whatever your goals and aspirations for your new family, it will be your financial position which will allow those goals to be fulfilled. As a mother, I strongly urge all parents to have a thorough and regular review of their financial affairs.

josephine.blythe@sjpp.co.uk

good advice

helplines

Action for ME Pregnancy Network www.afme.org.uk	01749 670 799
Action for Sick Children www.actionforsickchildren.org	020 8542 4848
Action on Pre-Eclampsia www.apec.org.uk	020 8427 4217
Anaphylaxis Campaign www.anaphylaxis.org.uk	01252 542 029
Anti-Bullying Campaign	020 7378 1446
Assoc for Improvements in Maternity Services www.aims.org.uk	020 8390 9534
Association for Postnatal Illness www.apni.org	020 7386 0868
Baby Milk Action www.babymilkaction.org	01223 464 420
Bedwetting Education Advisory Line www.bedwetting.co.uk	0800 085 8189
Birth Crisis Network	01865 300 266
Birth Defects Foundation	08700 707 020
British Allergy Foundation www.allergyfoundation.com	020 8303 8583
British Association for Early Childhood Education www.early-education.org.uk	020 7539 5400
British Dyslexia Association www.bda-dyslexia.org.uk	0118 966 8271
British Epilepsy Association www.epilepsy.org.uk	0113 210 8800
British Institute for Brain Injured Children www.bibic.org.uk	01278 684 060
British Institute for Learning Disabilities www.bild.org.uk	01562 723 010
British Stammering Association www.stammering.org	020 8983 1003
Caesarian Support Network	01624 661 269
Cerebral Palsy Helpline (SCOPE) www.scope.org.uk	0808 800 3333
Child Bereavement Trust www.childbereavement.org.uk	01494 446 648
Child Death Helpline	0800 282 986
ChildLine www.childline.org.uk	0800 1111
Children's Information Service www.childcarelink.gov.uk	0800 960 296
Cleft Lip And Palate Association (CLAPA) www.clapa.com	020 7431 0033
Coeliac UK www.coeliac.co.uk	01494 437 278
Contact-A-Family www.cafamily.org.uk	020 7383 3555
Cot Death Society www.cotdeathsociety.org.uk	0845 601 0234
Council for Disabled Children www.ncb.org.uk	020 7843 6000
Cruse Bereavement Care www.crusebereavementcare.org.uk	0870 167 1677
Cystic Fibrosis Trust www.cftrust.org.uk	020 8464 7211
Daycare Trust www.daycaretrust.org.uk	020 7840 3350
Diabetes UK (ex-British Diabetes Association) www.diabetes.org.uk	020 7323 1531
Disability Alliance www.disabilityalliance.org	020 7247 8763
Down's Heart Group www.childrens-heart-fed.org.uk/downs.htm	01525 220 379
Down's Syndrome Association www.dsa.uk.com	020 8682 4001
Dyspraxia Foundation www.dyspraxiafoundation.org.uk	01462 454 986
Enuresis Resource & Information Centre (ERIC) www.eric.org.uk	0117 960 3060

good advice

Foundation for the Study of Infant Deaths — 020 7233 2090
www.sids.org.uk/fsid

Fragile X Society — 01371 875 100
www.fragilex.org.uk

Group B Strep Support — 01444 416 176
www.gbss.org.uk

Herpes Viruses Association — 0845 123 2305
www.herpes.org.uk

Home Education Advisory Service — 01707 371 854
www.heas.co.uk

Home-Start UK — 020 7388 6075
www.home-start.co.uk

Hyperactive Children's Support Group — 01903 725 182
www.hacsg.org.uk

Kidscape — 020 7730 3300
www.kidscape.org.uk

Meet A Mum Association (MAMA) — 01761 433 598
www.mama.co.uk

Meningitis Research — 08088 003 344
www.meningitis.org

Meningitis Trust — 0845 600 0800
www.meningitis-trust.org.uk

Miscarriage Association — 01924 200 799
www.miscarriageassociation.org.uk

Multiple Births Foundation — 020 8383 3519
www.multiplebirths.org.uk

National Advice Centre for Children with Reading Difficulties — 0845 604 0414

National Asthma Campaign — 020 7226 2260
www.asthma.org.uk

National Autistic Society — 020 7833 2299
www.nas.org.uk

National Childbirth Trust — 0870 444 8707
www.nctpregnancyandbabycare.com

National Council for One-Parent Families — 0800 185 026
www.oneparentfamilies.org.uk

National Deaf Children's Society — 020 7250 0123
www.ndcs.org.uk

National Eczema Society — 020 7388 4097
www.eczema.org

National Endometriosis Society — 020 7222 2781
www.endo.org.uk

National NEWPIN — 020 7358 5900
www.newpin.org.uk

NSPCC Child Protection — 0800 800 500
www.nspcc.org.uk

Parentline Plus — 0808 800 2222
www.parentlineplus.org.uk

Parents At Work — 020 7628 2128
www.parentsatwork.org.uk

Parents for Inclusion — 020 7735 7735
www.parentsforinclusion.org

Relate: National Marriage Guidance — 020 8367 7712
www.relate.org.uk

RNIB — 020 7391 2245
www.rnib.org.uk

SCOPE — 020 7619 7100
www.scope.org.uk/

Serene (incorporating Cry-sis) — 020 7404 5011

Stillbirth And Neonatal Death Society (SANDS) — 020 7436 7940
www.uk-sands.org

TAMBA — 0870 770 3305
www.tamba.org.uk

The SHE Trust (Simply Holistic Endometriosis) — 01522 519 992
www.shetrust.org.uk

Women's Domestic Violence Helpline — 0161 839 8574
www.wdvh.org.uk

Women's Health — 020 7251 6580
www.womenshealthlondon.org.uk

Gingerbread — 0800 018 4318
www.gingerbread.org.uk
Leading support group for single parents.

Single Parent Travel Club — 0870 241 621
www.sptc.org.uk

index

a
3d scans	3
abacus nursery	**138**
abbotsbury swannery	170
abc poppins	**55**
accessories	19
active birth centre	3
acupuncture	10
adoption	180
adventure wonderland	171
alphabet childcare	**54**
alton towers	171
ameda lactaline	**20**
ante-natal 3d scans	3
ante-natal classes	3
a-one au-pairs & nannies	**52**
aphrodite swimwear	32
aquariums	166
aromatherapy	10
art & crafts	145
au pair agencies	52
autosafe	20

b
babies r us	35
babitens	**8**
baby bjorn	20
baby goods	35
baby premier	3
babylist	19
babymoon	**8**
babysitters	52
babyworld	**19**
babyworld	**37**
ballet	146
bambino	**36**
barn owl centre	170
bath & ne somerset cis	**54**
beaches	166
beastfeeding	4
belaf	**52**
belly casting	3
big sheep, the	169
bill amberg	21
birth announcements	19
birthlight	15
birthworks	**8**
bitsnstuff	**19 & 29**
blooming marvellous	**25**
blue reef aquarium	166
body paintsers	3
bohemia aupairs	**52**
bonne nuit	19
born	**34**
bottles	20
bouncy castles	161
bowood house	169
bravado designs	**32**
breast pumps	20
bristol cis	**54**
bristol zoo	172
brownies	146

c
caboodle	50
cakes	158
cameracraft	**43**
camping	176
car safety	20
carriers & slings	20
castings	21
castle court school	**93**
castles	167
cattle country adventure park	170
cells 4 life	**8**
centerparcs	177
ceramic cafés	145
cheltenham college 114 junior school	
cheltenham nannies	**55**
chessington	171
chilcare	51
choice antenatal	3
christening gifts	21
christening gowns	22
christening stuff	**22**
circus schools	146
clothing shops: fashion	22-26
clothing: online/mail order	26
clothing: outdoor	26
club med	177
combe martin	172
complementary health	10
compton castle	168
cookery	146
corfe castle	168
cornwall family information services	**54**
cots & cribs	27
cotswold farm park	170
cotswold wildlife park	172
councils	180
cranial osteopathy	14
crave maternity	**31**
cricket st thomas	172
cubs	146

d
dance	146
dartmouth castle	168
david lloyd leisure	11
david mcgirr photography	**43**
days out	165
devon & torbay cis	**54**
dinosaur museum	172
doulas	54
drama	147
dressing up	27
dunster castle	168

e
easy2name	33
eden nannies	**55**
eden project	168
education	59
embody	3
entertainers	160
esporta	11
european nursery furniture	**27**
everlasting castings	3
exercise	11
exmouth nursery supplies	**38**

f
farms	169
fatherhood	181
fig	30
first aid	11
first years	20
food: organic	27
football	147
foreign languages	148

g
garden toys	28
genevieve brown au pairs	**52**
gifts	28
good advice	179
graco	50
great little parties	**164**
grobag	**30**
groe baby	**26**
groovy mummy	19
gyms – mini	148

h
hairdressers	29
halfords	20
handbag bar at akino	50
hanford school	**98**
happyhands	**19 & 21**

index

having a baby co	3	
health	9	
healthvisitors.com	**58**	
helplines	182-183	
hestercombe gardens	169	
hippins	**29**	
hippychick	**19 &**	
	21 & 30	
holidays	173	
holmes place	11	
home births	4	
homeopathy	12	
homeswaps	176	
horseworld	170	
hospitals: nhs	4	
hospitals: private	5	
hotels (uk)	174	
houses, parks & gardens	168	
huggababy	21	
hurwoods nursery		
world	**39**	
hypnotherapy	12	

i

images photography	**43**
immunisation	12
indoor playcentres	148
infertility	12
isabella oliver	**31**

j

jazz mataz	**154**
jeyarani birth	3
jo jingles	**153**
jojo maman bebe	**23**

k

kaboodle	**23**
kernow natural light	
photography	**43**
kiddi caru day	
nurseries	**61**
kittysash	**19**
knoll house, the	**175**

l

la leche league	4
lansinoh	4
le club francais	**148**
leapfrog day	
nurseries	**124**
legoland	171
leisure centres	150
lice	13
linen	29

lionwitchwardrobe	35
little acorns (devon)	**36**
little angels	
photography	**43**
little people	**38**
longleat safari park	172
lotions & potions	30
lulworth castle	168

m

magazines	30
mama tens	8
mapperton gardens	168
massage	13
maternity bras	32
maternity nurses	54
maternity wear	32
mayfair maternity	54
medela	20
melba maternity	32
messy monsters	145
midwives independent	55
midwives	7
midwivesonline	**6**
model agencies	152
money matters	181
monkey music	**154**
monkey world	172
monster parties	**164**
mothercare	35
mucky pups	145
mums essentials	4
murals	33
music groups	153
my day diary	29

n

name tapes	33
name-it labels	**33**
naming ceremonies	181
nanny agencies	55
nanny tax	**57**
nappies, cloth	34
national maritime	
museum	166
nct	3
newquay zoo	171
next maternity	32
nhs	3
nippers hairdressers	**29**
nits	**13**
noah's ark zoo	172
nomad	50
noonoo design	
company	**29**
north somerset cis	**54**
nuk	20

nursery furniture	34
nursery goods	35
nurseryworld	**36**
nurturer	**11**
nurturer	**13**
nurwoods nursery	
world	**39**
nutrition	13

o

obtens	**8**
old wardour castle	168
osteopathy	14
overseas travel	176

p

paignton zoo	**172**
parties	157-164
party shops	163
party supplies (online)	164
pennywell farm	169
personal presents	29
peter pan	**36**
photography	43
playdough recipe	145
plymouth cis	**54**
porfell animal land	171
portland hospital	7
powderham castle	168
pregnancy & birth	1
preschool express	145
preview ultrasound	3
prickly ball farm	169
putlake adventure farm	170

r

rachel's babies	**54**
ragtags	**38**
reflexology	15
riding	154
rocking horses	43
roman baths	168
rosemoor gardens	168

s

salisbury cathedral	
school	**140**
samsonite	50
sarah north	
photography	**43**
schmidt natural	
clothing	**26**
scooters nursery	
stores	**38**
seaquarium	166

index

sex choice	8
sheila's nannies	**55**
sherborne preparatory school	**97**
shoe shops	43
shoes	43
shopping	17
sing & sign	**153-155**
skiing	177
sleeping bags	29
south gloucestershire cis	**54**
splashdown waterbirth services	**8**
st anthony's leweston nursery	**97**
st john's ambulance	11
st michael's mount	167
stagecoach	**147**
stem cells	**7**
stork gifts	**29**
stork post	**19**
stourhead gardens	169
sudeley castle	168
sue learner	**4 & 55**
sunsail	177
swim academy for babies	**154**
swimming	154
swimwear	45

t

taxing nannies	**57**
teddies nurseries	**142**
tennis – mini	156
tens hire	8
that's my baby	**39**
theme parks	171
tinies childcare	**55**
tintagel castle	168
toddler activities	145
toy shops	45
toys: early development	49
toys: online	49
trains	171
travel & changing bags	50
travel cots	50
travel	176
trevarno estate gardens	**168**
tumbletots	**149**

u

unicef	4

v

venus maternity wear	**32**

w

walls of the wild	**33**
waterbirth pool hire	8
weymouth sealife park	166
whittlestone	20
wilkinet	21
win green company	50
wrightson & platt	21

y

yarrells prep school	**91**
yoga	15
yogabugs	15
young england	27

z

zita west	**13**
zoos & nature reserves	171
zpm	19

happyhands™

The ulltimate birth announcement or thank you cards

"Ingenious idea" *Pregnancy & Birth*
"Simply Irresistible" *Prima Baby*

Your own baby's foot prints on personalised cards

An easy to use inkless footprint kit is provided

Call us on **020 8671 2020**
www.happyhands.ws

Scribble pad

feedback

READERS

If you think there is a service or product we should know about and include in the next edition, drop us a line, or an e-mail: **editor@babydirectory.com**

☐ This is a new product, service or facility.

☐ Oops! You've missed this.

☐ Change of address, new branch, etc.

☐ Please send me a media pack.

Name of product, service or location ....

Address ....

....

Postcode .... Tel No ....

E-mail address .... www ....

Contact name and tel no (if different from above)

....

We would very much appreciate your comments about errors or omissions, please let us know.
You will receive a free copy of next year's book for your efforts.

Page ....

Feedback...

....

....

Your own name, address, 'phone number, e-mail address (all optional)

....

....

Many thanks for taking the time to fill in this form

Please send completed form(s) to:

The Baby Directory, 7 Brockwell Park Row, London SW2 2YH
Tel: 020 8678 9000   Fax: 020 8671 1919   E-mail: editor@babydirectory.com

188 order form

To order by telephone call: **020 8678 9000**
or order via our secure website at **www.babydirectory.com**
or send this order form with your cheque to:
The Baby Directory, 7 Brockwell Park Row, London SW2 2YH

Title	Price	Qty	Postage	Total
The London Baby Directory (All London postcodes)	£8.99		£1.50	
The East Baby Directory (Essex, Cambridgeshire, Suffolk & Norfolk)	£5.99		£1.00	
The Central Baby Directory (Oxfordshire, Berks, Bucks, Northants, Beds & Herts)	£5.99		£1.00	
The South East Baby Directory (Surrey & S. Middlesex, Hampshire, Sussex & Kent)	£5.99		£1.00	
The South West Baby Directory (Somerset, Dorset, Wiltshire, Gloucestershire, Devon & Cornwall)	£5.99		£1.00	
			Total Order Value	

Please print clearly
Name ....
Address ....
....
.... Postcode ....
Tel .... E-mail address ....

METHOD OF PAYMENT (please tick appropriate box)
Cheque/Postal Order ☐   Credit Card ☐
Please make cheques payable to **The Baby Directory Limited**
Card Number ☐☐☐☐ ☐☐☐☐ ☐☐☐☐ ☐☐☐☐
Issue No ☐☐   Expiry Date ☐☐☐☐   Valid from ☐☐☐☐   Security code ☐☐☐

Signature ....
How did you hear about the Directory?............................... Leaflet Code ☐☐
If you would like to receive our monthly e-newsletter please tick here ☐

index **189**

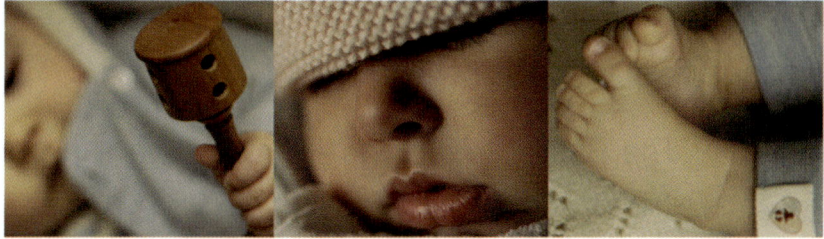

Helping parents choose the best baby equipment

Babylist helps you choose everything you need for your new baby.

We give you independent, unbiased advice on all baby equipment and nursery items helping you make the right decisions for you and your new baby.

All the best-known brands are here on display in our London showroom. Once you've chosen (everything is at Recommended Retail Price) we'll deliver everything direct to your door.

Please call 020 7371 5145 for further information.

www.babylist.com

what's been written...

The Baby Directory is an invaluable reference guide for mothers-to-be
The Times

Forget about wading through the local paper for mother and baby contacts - The Baby Directory has done it for you
Pregnancy & Birth

Indispensable and essential
Practical Parenting

A mine of useful information
The NCT